A Feminist Companion to Paul

A Feminist Companion to

Paul

edited by
Amy-Jill Levine
with Marianne Blickenstaff

THE
PILGRIM
PRESS
Cleveland

Published in the USA and Canada (only) by
The Pilgrim Press
700 Prospect Avenue East, Cleveland, Ohio 44115-1100, USA
www.thepilgrimpress.com

© T&T Clark International, 2004

Typeset in Great Britain by Fakenham Photosetting Ltd, Fakenham, Norfolk NR21 8NN
Printed in Great Britain by Bath Press

ISBN 0-8298-1608-9

CONTENTS

PREFACE

A Feminist Companion to Paul is the sixth volume in a new series with excellent precedent. These volumes on the texts and history of Christian origins adopt the model established by Athalya Brenner, editor of the enormously successful Feminist Companion to the Bible. This sister series to FCB, originally published by Sheffield Academic Press, marks an important new dimension in the areas of feminist hermeneutics and theology, and its contents underline the extent to which feminist critique is established as a core discipline of biblical, historical and theological research.

The new series, like FCB, contains contributions by new as well as established scholars; it presents both previously published work (primarily from sources either out of print or difficult to find) and new essays. In some cases, scholars have been invited to revisit their earlier work to examine the extent to which their arguments and approaches have changed; in others, they have sought to apply their earlier insights to new texts.

We wish to thank Marianne Blickenstaff for her numerous organizational contributions as well as her discerning insights. We also wish to thank the Carpenter Program in Religion, Gender, and Sexuality at Vanderbilt Divinity School for financial and technical support.

It is our hope that this series will quickly establish itself as a standard work of reference for scholars, students and others interested in the New Testament and Christian origins.

Amy-Jill Levine, Vanderbilt Divinity School
Philip R. Davies for T&T Clark International

Acknowledgments

The publishers are grateful to the following for permission to reproduce copyright material:

- *Representations* for 'Paul and the Genealogy of Gender', by Daniel Boyarin, from *Representations* 41;
- Princeton Theological Seminary for 'Our Mother St Paul: Toward the Recovery of a Neglected Theme', by Beverly Roberts Gaventa, from *Princeton Seminary Bulletin* 17;
- E.J. Brill for 'Gesetzesfreies Heidenchristentum – und die Frauen?' by Luise Schottroff, from *Von der Wurzel Getragen: Christlich-feministische Exegese in Auseinandersetzung mit Antijudaismus*; and
- HarperSanFrancisco for 'Paul on the Relation between Men and Women', by Richard B. Hays, from *The Moral Vision of the New Testament*.

AB	Anchor Bible
ABD	David Noel Freedman (ed.), *The Anchor Bible Dictionary* (New York: Doubleday, 1992)
AGJU	Arbeiten zur Geschichte des antiken Judentums und des Urchristentums
AGsJU	Arbeiten zur Geschichte des späteren Judentums und des Urchristentums
AnBib	Analecta biblica
ANRW	Hildegard Temporini and Wolfgang Haase (eds), *Aufstieg und Niedergang der römischen Welt: Geschichte und Kultur Roms im Spiegel der neuren Forschung* (Berlin: W. de Gruyter, 1972–)
ASNU	Acta seminarii neotestamentici upsaliensis
BAGD	Walter Bauer, William F. Arndt, F. William Gingrich, and Frederick W. Danker, *A Greek–English Lexicon of the New Testament and Other Early Christian Literature* (Chicago: University of Chicago Press, 2nd edn, 1958)
BBB	Bönner biblische Beiträge
BETL	Bibliotheca ephemeridum theologicarum lovaniensum
BHT	Beiträge zur historischen Theologie
Bib	*Biblica*
BibInt	*Biblical Interpretation*
BIS	Biblical Interpretation Series
BJS	Brown Judaic Studies
BN	*Biblische Notizen*
BR	*Bible Review*
BTB	*Biblical Theology Bulletin*
BZ	*Biblische Zeitschrift*
BZNW	Beihefte zur *ZNW*
CBQ	*Catholic Biblical Quarterly*
CBQMS	*Catholic Biblical Quarterly*, Monograph Series
CSEL	Corpus scriptorum ecclesiasticorum latinorum
CurTM	*Currents in Theology and Mission*
EBib	Etudes bibliques
EDNT	Horst Balz and Gerhard Schneider (eds), *Exegetical Dictionary of the New Testament* (3 vols; Grand Rapids, MI: Eerdmans, 1990–).
EKKNT	Evangelisch-Katholischer Kommentar zum Neuen Testament
EncJud	*Encyclopaedia Judaica* (16 vols; Jerusalem: Keter, 1971)
ENPK	H.J. Frede (ed.), *Ein neuer Paulustext und Kommentar* (Freiburg im Breisgau: Herder, 1974).
ETL	*Ephemerides theologicae lovanienses*

FC	Fathers of the Church
FFNT	Foundations and Facets: New Testament
GNS	Good News Studies
GRBS	*Greek, Roman, and Byzantine Studies*
HDR	Harvard Dissertations in Religion
HeyJ	*Heythrop Journal*
HNT	Handbuch zum Neuen Testament
HR	*History of Religions*
HTKNT	Herders theologischer Kommentar zum Neuen Testament
HTR	*Harvard Theological Review*
HTS	Harvard Theological Studies
IBC	Interpretation Bible Commentary
ICC	International Critical Commentary
Int	*Interpretation*
JAAR	*Journal of the American Academy of Religion*
JAC	*Jahrbuch für Antike und Christentum*
JBL	*Journal of Biblical Literature*
JECS	*Journal of Early Christian Studies*
JFSR	*Journal of Feminist Studies in Religion*
JJS	*Journal of Jewish Studies*
JNES	*Journal of Near Eastern Studies*
JR	*Journal of Religion*
JSNT	*Journal for the Study of the New Testament*
JSNTSup	Journal for the Study of the New Testament, Supplement Series
JSOT	*Journal for the Study of the Old Testament*
JSOTSup	Journal for the Study of the Old Testament, Supplement Series
JTS	*Journal of Theological Studies*
LCC	Library of Christian Classics
LCL	Loeb Classical Library
LD	Lectio divina
LSJ	H.G. Liddell, Robert Scott and H. Stuart Jones, *Greek–English Lexicon* (Oxford: Clarendon Press, 9th edn, 1968)
LXX	Septuagint
MeyerK	H.A.W. Meyer (ed.), Kritisch-exegetischer Kommentar über das Neue Testament
NAB	New American Bible
NCB	New Century Bible
NEB	New English Bible
NHS	Nag Hammadi Studies
NIB	*New International Bible*
NICNT	New International Commentary on the New Testament
NIGTC	The New International Greek Testament Commentary
NJB	*New Jerusalem Bible*
NovT	*Novum Testamentum*
NPNF	Nicene and Post-Nicene Fathers
NRSV	New Revised Standard Version
NTA	*New Testament Abstracts*

NTS	*New Testament Studies*
OBT	Overtures to Biblical Theology
RNT	Regensburger Neues Testament
RSV	Revised Standard Version
SANT	Studien zum Alten und Neuen Testament
SBL	Society of Biblical Literature
SBLDS	SBL Dissertation Series
SBLEJL	SBL Early Judaism and its Literature
SBLMS	SBL Monograph Series
SBLSP	SBL Seminar Papers
SE	*Studia Evangelica*
SNTSMS	Society for New Testament Studies Monograph Series
SR	*Studies in Religion/Sciences religieuses*
ST	*Studia Theologica*
Str-B	Hermann L. Strack and Paul Billerbeck, *Kommentar zum Neuen Testament aus Talmud und Midrasch* (7 vols; Munich: Beck, 1922–61)
SVF	Stoicorum Veterum Fragmenta
TD	*Theology Digest*
TDNT	Gerhard Kittel and Gerhard Friedrich (eds), *Theological Dictionary of the New Testament* (trans. Geoffrey W. Bromiley; 10 vols; Grand Rapids: Eerdmans, 1964–)
TextsSR	Texts and Studies in Religion
THKNT	Theologischer Handkommentar zum Neuen Testament
TPI	Trinity Press International Commentary Series
TToday	*Theology Today*
UBSGNT	United Bible Societies' *Greek New Testament* (London; New York: United Bible Societies, 3rd edn, 1971)
VC	*Vigiliae christianae*
VT	*Vetus Testamentum*
WBC	Word Biblical Commentary
WUNT	Wissenschaftliche Untersuchungen zum Neuen Testament
ZNW	*Zeitschrift für die neutestamentliche Wissenschaft*

LIST OF CONTRIBUTORS

Daniel Boyarin, University of California at Berkeley, Berkeley, CA, USA
Kathleen E. Corley, University of Wisconsin, Oshkosh, WI, USA
Beverly Roberts Gaventa, Princeton Theological Seminary, Princeton, NJ, USA
Faith Kirkham Hawkins, Candler School of Theology, Emory University, Atlanta, GA, USA
Richard B. Hays, Divinity School, Duke University, Durham, NC, USA
Margaret Y. MacDonald, St Francis Xavier University, Antigonish, Nova Scotia, Canada
Luzia Sutter Rehmann, Basel, Switzerland
Luise Schottroff, Universität Gesamthochschule, Kassel, Germany
Diana Swancutt, Yale Divinity School, New Haven, CT, USA
Sara B.C. Winter, Eugene Lang College, New School for Social Research, New York, NY, USA

Introduction

AMY-JILL LEVINE

Paul's statements concerning gender and sexuality are frequently adduced to support the claim that 'Paul was not a systematic theologian'. On the one hand is Paul the proto-feminist who welcomed women as deacons and apostles (Romans 16), dismantled gender-based distinctions (Gal. 3.28), supported women's prophecy (1 Corinthians 11), and promoted connubial mutuality (1 Corinthians 7)? On the other is Paul the repressed misogynist who insisted that women remain silent in churches (1 Cor. 14:33b–36), cover their heads in worship (1 Corinthians 11) and regard themselves as subordinate to men? This Paul not only condemns homosexuality but promulgates sarcophobia with his endorsement of celibacy and his less-than-enthusiastic concession, 'it is better to marry than to burn with passion'. Consequently, efforts to locate consistency even in the securely authentic epistles (Romans, Galatians, 1 and 2 Corinthians, Philemon, and 1 Thessalonians) are doomed.[1]

Yet as Daniel Boyarin suggests in the opening essay of this volume, on the questions of gender and sexuality, Paul may be more consistent than conventional wisdom teaches. Feminist studies appear to be moving toward a consensus that recognizes Paul as a product of his own time: he is androcentric and patriarchal and he does value the spirit over the flesh, but he also supports women's leadership, agrees that in baptismal ecstasy divisions of ethnos (Jew and Greek), status (slave and free) and gender/sex (male and female) collapse, and endorses marital relations for those lacking the gift of celibacy. The hermeneutical problem may be less Paul's own inconsistency than the result of interpreters' choices.

Subjectivity will never be eliminated from historical investigation: the questions posed, passages highlighted, intertexts imported, applications made, and audiences addressed are all products of the researcher's considerations. This subjectivity does not indicate a failure of process (to have presuppositions is not the same thing as to be wrong). Instead, within feminist analysis it is, or at least should be, a goad to rigorous investigation rather than a warrant to kick against the pricks, a warning against solipsism in argument, and a signal that interpretation has political import. For Paul, questions feminist (and non-feminist) readers bring to the texts are substantial: how is Paul to be understood in light of women's historical marginalization in church and society, or the ordination of gay bishops, or today's culture wars over family values?

Thus, we do not come to Paul's texts as innocents. Paul's letters have always influenced Christian thought, and so have had effects not simply in church contexts, but

---

1 Scholars debate the Pauline authorship of six other epistles written in Paul's name; see the articles on 2 Thessalonians, Colossians and Ephesians, and the Pastoral Epistles (1 and 2 Timothy and Titus) in volume 7 in this series, Amy-Jill Levine (ed.), *A Feminist Companion to the Deutero-Pauline Epistles* (London: T. & T. Clark, 2003).

in settings where community ethos and public discourse are derived from biblical teaching. Our cultures, and so we, are heirs to Paul's legacy. Within biblical studies narrowly construed, the tradition-history of the epistles impacts exegesis. Given this situation, most feminists (and feminists are not alone here) find it insufficient to restrict analysis to first-century history. To respond to Paul is also to respond to all those who have been and continue to be influenced by him.

While such history needs to inform today's readers, we also need to guard against both simplistically regarding all cultures as uniform and projecting our experiences back (we historians do sometimes think we are looking through windows into the past when we are actually looking into mirrors). To be complicit in either move is to colonize history. My point is not that naïve readers (or the non-academic reader) should lack a voice in interpretation; to the contrary, academic readers should be attuned to what the laity are saying, for often they see nuances our professional eyes miss. I am arguing, however, that (feminist) academics, gifted with historical infor-mation and linguistic skills, can bridge the gap between laity and professional, church and academy, and so provide informed guidance to all readers. We have the skills to determine not only what Paul taught, but also the social contexts (class-based, regional, political, cultural, personal …) in which he taught and the effects carrying out his teachings had not only for Paul's original audiences, but for readers subsequently.

Responsible academic argument requires all the tools of traditional exegesis: histo-riography, linguistics, manuscript analysis, cultural studies, ideological critique, etc. Readers must determine the contexts for each epistle: Jewish or pagan, Cynic or Stoic, novel or philosophy, epitaph or hymn, private home or market place, dominical logion or pastoral polemic, or a combination of all. We also need to recognize the provisionality of our conclusions, for the extant primary sources are incomplete and biased toward the upper classes, and Paul's own writings offer only half the story. We can with some confidence reconstruct the situations Paul addresses, although the possibility must remain open that Paul's responses are based on false or incomplete premises and may not respond to the questions asked (anyone who has read student responses to essay questions will likely resonate with this situation). Moreover, we may be missing cultural messages that Paul and his readers shared.

Acknowledgment of personal experience, attention to constructions of the marginal or 'other' (usually pursuant to categories of gender and sexuality), and recognition of the political nature of exegesis are typical of feminist interpretation, but I hesitate to offer a formal description of what makes a work 'feminist'. To impose a definition would narrow interpretive options and so suppress some feminist voices. At times scholars self-identify as feminist; at times the label is applied by others; at times works have been debated as to their feminist content or even classified as 'bad feminism'. For some interpreters, especially those within conser-vative cultural or ecclesial contexts, the identification of their work as 'feminist' is a signal of damnation, of mushy-mindedness, of man-hating, etc. Like the term 'Christian', 'feminist' will have a range of connotations, both positive and negative. Those invited to contribute new articles to this volume were asked to define 'feminism' however they chose.

The Feminist Companion to the New Testament and Early Christian Literature began by requesting articles from scholars with explicit feminist interest (e.g. they contributed to such classics as *Searching the Scriptures*;[2] they gave explicitly feminist talks at Society of Biblical Literature or Catholic Biblical Association meetings; they published explicitly feminist books and articles). Some of those invited contributed new articles, some reconsidered earlier pieces in light of new information or method, and some recommended the reprinting of articles (in this case, we sought articles not easily accessible and not likely to be summarized by the contributions to the volumes). Among those who declined to contribute, the most common response was a commitment to other projects that precluded producing yet another article. Clearly, feminist writers, or writers who can offer a feminist perspective, are much in demand.

Taking a very broad approach to 'feminism', the Companion sought out not simply contributors who might be located within 'liberal' or 'non-traditional' camps; we also solicited materials from conservative and Evangelical writers. We were also deliberate in inviting scholars from outside Western Europe, the USA, and Canada; whereas the response rate from this set of invitations was less than ideal, nevertheless yet another group of names, and viewpoints, emerged. To facilitate this global perspective, Vanderbilt Divinity School and the Carpenter Program in Religion, Gender, and Sexuality provided funds to offset the expenses of translation.

All initial invitations requested suggestions for other contributors, especially on the junior level (the process might be considered feminist networking). With this second round, the Companion series not only gained a chorus of new voices; it served to add another precious line to numerous renewal and tenure dossiers.

We also invited senior scholars not known for feminist publications, or even feminist inclinations, to engage feminist scholarship on the topics of their research. If they do not agree with the various feminist approaches to their text or topic, then they should say so, for feminists can then on the basis of such criticism sharpen our own views. If feminist study informs their interpretations, better yet. And if their future work adopts a feminist perspective, then these companions (Latin: 'with bread') will truly witness a multiplication of loaves bordering on both the miraculous, and the necessary.

Finally, the Feminist Companion series presents classical non-feminist works. Feminism emerged partially from the recognition of gaps in scholarship, such as the lack of attention to gender construction or the presumption of universal norms where experience reveals variation; thus, feminist critics must remain informed of what other studies on the topics of their investigations conclude. In some cases, the non-feminist work might strike readers as 'feminist' (again, definitions will vary); in others, such works will remind readers of issues that require additional attention. Moreover, if the authors of the non-feminist contributions then read the entire Companion volume in which their essays are included (or, ideally, assign the volume to their classes), so much the better. The ten essays in this collection display the range of topic, method, intertext, and insight that could together provide any class a solid introduction to Paul's thought.

Daniel Boyarin superbly conjoins feminist philosophical examination and historical-critical biblical interpretation to interrogate Paul's contribution to the

---

2 Elisabeth Schüssler Fiorenza (ed.), *Searching the Scriptures: A Feminist Introduction and Commentary* (2 vols.; New York: Crossroad, 1993, 1994).

Western discourse of gender. Ranging from Judith Butler and Simone de Beauvoir to Clement of Alexandria, Tertullian, Philo and Plato, and moving through Genesis 1 and 2, 1 Corinthians 7, 10, and 11, 2 Corinthians 4–5, Galatians 3 and 5, the *Acts of Paul and Thecla*, the *Gospel of Thomas*, and the *Martyrdom of Perpetua*, Boyarin traces the relationship between sex and gender, body and soul, men and women, celibacy and the married life. Although granting that Gal. 3.28 offers a vision wherein gender roles are erased and that 1 Corinthians inscribes gender bifurcation, Boyarin finds the presentations compatible. He does not, however, accept the traditional harmonizations: juxtaposing a tendentiously construed dualistic rabbinism with a positivistic understanding of Christianity as universalistic or concluding that Paul capitulated, despite his better judgment, to pagan gender ideology. Neither, as noted above, does he excuse Paul from an interest in consistency. Instead, he sees the epistles' universalizing and particularizing positions as resulting from Paul's debt to the myths of a 'primal androgyne' and Adam's rib.

According to Boyarin, 'Paul was motivated by a Hellenistic desire for the One, beyond difference and hierarchy.' The desire for the One or, in theological terms, the 'Spirit', requires that the flesh—the site of dualism whether anatomical (penis/vagina), inscribed (circumcised/non-circumcised), or even ascribed (e.g. honor/shame)—be overcome. The problem is that the androgynous One exists outside corporeality's matrix (or, momentarily, only in the ecstatic baptismal experience Gal. 3.28 defines). Consequently, the means of transcending gender (with the attendant categories of masculine disembodied universality and feminine disavowed corporeality) continue to be elusive. Whereas Paul in this view did think that Jews and Greeks could forgo their ethnic identities, and that slaves would cease being slaves, he did not find the erasure of the roles of husband and wife to be realistic. As Boyarin puts it, 'Wives are/were slaves, and their liberation would have meant an end to marriage.'

Not only Paul but also his heirs remain in this cultural and epistemological trap. For early Christianity, women's autonomy and attendant move toward the androgynous ideal required the sacrifice of the body. Conversely, rabbinic Judaism's rejection of dualism and consequent valorization of the body trapped women in the maternal role or, as Boyarin phrases it, 'the temperate and patronizing slavery of wifehood'. Paul and Judith Butler, clearly, have much to discuss.

The pervasive construction of gender and desire that marked first-century Roman thought also occupies **Diana Swancutt**'s impeccably detailed 'Sexy Stoics'. Looking not to myths prompted by Genesis 1–3 but to the *topos* of the Stoic sage, Swancutt offers an alternative to the prevailing understanding of Rom. 1.18–2.16. In her assessment, Paul's auditors would recognize Paul's foil, the hypocritical judge of Rom. 2.1, not as a self-satisfied Jew (the usual reading) but as a Stoic sage who taught 'natural' living while himself engaging in 'unnatural' behaviors such as transvestitism, pederasty, or effeminizing sexual passivity.

Once the rival teacher is correctly identified, the rationale for Paul's interest in 'natural' intercourse emerges. Stoics were known for insisting that they alone modeled consistency and embodied the cardinal virtues. Swancutt summarizes, 'it was Stoics' unique access to reason or "law" of nature that made them a living law and perfect rulers over those weaker than they'. As could be expected, satirists, moralists, and members of other philosophical schools begged to differ. Specifically, they denounced Stoics who touted 'natural' living while engaging in 'unnatural' sexual practices. To subvert the gender hierarchy or traverse the gender continuum wherein men/males were, *inter alia*, on top, active, and hairy, while passive, smooth, women/females were on the bottom was not only to corrupt one's students, it was to threaten the social fabric of family (*oikos*) and state (*polis*). Thus Swancutt's focus on the Stoics confirms Boyarin's generalized delineation of gender roles.

While Paul is often regarded as providing a program both distinct from and better than his Jewish and pagan contemporaries, Swancutt's study firmly contextualizes his teachings in light of conventional tropes and Roman values (the process also allows her to issue major challenges to earlier works on Romans 1.18ff., such as those by Bernadette Brooten[3] and Richard Hays[4]). To separate a particular Pauline instruction from this larger whole is thus to do both Paul and his readers a disservice, and the same point holds for removing Paul from the teachings of what he would consider sacred texts. In like manner, to read Pauline instructions only from the perspective of our own constructs (e.g. definitions of sexuality, homosexuality, gender roles, desire) risks imposing our views without allowing the historical text, in its context, its own voice. Finally, to see Paul as entirely unique when it comes to matters of sexuality and gender risks confirming for today's reader negative views of non-Christians and inculcating Christian triumphalism.

Luzia Sutter Rehmannn, like Boyarin and Swancutt, both places Paul within his own cultural context and draws from her analysis contemporary implications. Artfully adducing genre criticism, the study of metaphor, the Exodus narrative, the works of Josephus and Philo, lexical investigation, Roman imperial history, and the liberationist desires of all creation, she provides a rich setting for understanding Rom. 8.22–23. Refusing to dismiss Paul's imagery as simply a staple of Jewish apocalyptic, Rehmann gives birth to a new and inspirational understanding of how 'the whole creation has been groaning in travail' while men and women 'groan inwardly as we long for adoption as children, the redemption of our bodies'.

Within the first few paragraphs, Rehmann succinctly lays out the miscarriages of prior work on the couplet. As she defines it, the dominant view proposes that Paul both advocates a patient waiting and sees '*suffering as a condition of humanity*' (italics hers). Redemption is thus only a metaphysical option. But this reading brings with it a denigration of the physical and so promotes dualism; worse: by jettisoning liberation from material reality, it cannot provide comfort or relief to people suffering now. For Rehmann, Paul is not talking about 'Christian patience'; he is, instead, drawing upon apocalyptic—a genre she defines as 'resistance literature'—to promote active resistance. Paul's point is not to suffer silently, but to protest, to demand. The 'waiting' is not passive; it is, like giving birth, active and intense, a fighting for new life. The labor of birth is not associated with death or terror (cf. Isa. 13.8; Jer. 4.31), but with hope.

Rehmannn does not end with articulating this liberative potential. She also warns that the birthing imagery can discredit women who have never been mothers even as

3 Bernadette J. Brooten, *Love between Women: Early Christian Responses to Female Homoeroticism* (Chicago: University of Chicago Press, 1996).

4 Richard B. Hays, *The Moral Vision of the New Testament: A Contemporary Introduction to New Testament Ethics* (San Francisco: HarperSanFrancisco, 1996).

Paul's arrogation of birthing language to himself (Rom. 9.2) can denigrate female experience. Given Paul's express preference in the Corinthian correspondence for celibacy and his own appropriation of maternal language (explored in the next essay by Beverly Roberts Gaventa), Rehmannn's point is acute. And yet, her conclusion is sanguine: where 'the experiences of women occupy a central place' is where we may find 'resistance and cooperation' and the 'birth of a new world'.

Beverly Roberts Gaventa's analysis of the birth imagery, addressed by Rehmann as well as other Pauline birthing and maternal references, is a lucid model of exegetical procedure. Rather than simply aggregating the seven references, Gaventa offers several justifications for combining them, including appeals to the imagery's comparative complexity (what she calls 'squaring the metaphor') and a refusal to collapse the references into the category of paternal imagery. Paul's maternal images in fact concern ongoing relationships whereas his paternal images focus on the seminal stages of congregational development. This justification precludes the tendency to lump all 'woman-identified' images together and so risk either imposing a pattern on discrete texts or interpreting all references through a singular and (as Rehmannn also points out) often skewed lens.

Next, investigating the methods by which this collection can be illuminated, Gaventa finds three approaches essential. The first two—noting comparisons in earlier and contemporaneous Jewish literature (e.g. biblical material, Qumran texts) and delineating aspects of Paul's own (Roman) cultural context—together avoid the exegetical traps of divorcing Judaism from Hellenism and over-emphasizing particular social codes (such as the honor–shame mechanism). Third, Gaventa looks to the cognitive character of metaphor. This control prevents the crass readings that find metaphors to be merely decoration or illustration instead of prompts to reflection. As she states, following Max Black,[5] 'Metaphors ask us to change our minds', and we choose either to resist or to accept their challenge. Thus metaphors can carry theology. Extending (dilating?) this point, Gaventa underscores the relationship between metaphor and intimacy. Accepting the metaphor, we create a cord between ourselves and its progenitor as well as a boundary between ourselves and those who reject the imagery. Finally, metaphors do more than prompt intimacy. Specific metaphors of kinship promote biological and social expectations.

Gaventa's speculum reveals several new insights into 'Our Mother St Paul'. Perhaps a pregnant response to Boyarin's comments on androgyny and autonomy, Gaventa's notice that Paul's maternal images fit securely into neither 'egalitarian' nor 'hierarchical' categories—rather, they subvert both—forces readers to find new categories by which to understand Paul, the church's leadership, and our own (insecure) biological and social roles.

From feminine images of birth and maternal care Paul—and so Paul's readers—turn to the androcentric language of adoption in antiquity. The Inclusive Language Lectionary Committee of the National Council of Churches avoids the exclusionary implications of Paul's term (Rom. 8.15, 23; 9.4; cf. Gal. 4.5; Eph. 1.5) for adoption, υιοθεσία (literally, 'adoption as sons'), by translating 'adoption as the children [of God]'; thereby it imports an egalitarian theological vision. Conversely, numerous conservative commentators argue that Paul's emphasis is on the particular privilege

---

5 Max Black, *Models and Metaphors* (Ithaca, NY: Cornell University Press, 1962).

of the son (and not the daughter). Yet neither inclusive nor restricted translation rests upon any detailed study of such questions as why the ancient texts use different language to describe the adoptions of boys and girls and whether or not both boys and girls were adopted for the same reasons. **Kathleen E. Corley** redresses these absences and so, finally, provides the context for understanding Paul's language.

Corley's analysis of Jewish and Gentile (Greek and Roman) texts demonstrates that adoption (however defined) served a major role in determining inheritance, and, in these cases, the gender-specific translation 'adoption as sons' is warranted. Within the Roman system, which Corley finds to be the epistles' most likely background, laws of inheritance treated women and men differently: the amount women could inherit was limited, a woman married *cum manus* had no rights to her father's property, and the woman's brothers had priority in testamentary succession. Corley's exhaustive study not only of laws concerning adoption but also of papyrus adoption contracts and alienation documents reveals a consistent use of gender-specific language. However, within both wills and petitions concerning inheritance, both women and men are designated as heirs by the masculine noun κληρονόμος.

Even given the gender-specific connotations of Paul's adoption metaphor, women could and probably did see themselves included in the 'sonship' conferred on believers in the Christ. The result of this reading is, finally, not dissimilar to the *Inclusive Language Lectionary*'s approach: in both cases, women are included. Yet the gender-specific terminology requires a second step, that is, the masculinization of the woman or, more benignly, the not-uncommon move of women's identifying with the male subject. Readers today have a choice: we can for historical and textual reasons keep the androcentric language but nevertheless find woman's place within it or, for pastoral reasons, we can adapt the translation to an ahistorical (but theologically apposite) gender-inclusivity. The former approach implies that a woman 'must have maleness conferred on her before she can be made a son'; the latter blurs Paul's hierarchically constructed gender roles and so imposes our own values on the text even as it erases the site of women's struggle for inclusion. Adopting either strategy, as in any adoption, produces gain and loss, inheritance and alienation.

That the first-century family is not equivalent to the family today is best indicated by antiquity's pervasive system of slavery. This matter is a feminist one, for reasons ranging from its implications for social justice to its focus on the marginal to the first century's cultural connections between women and slaves. And, as with matters of gender and sexuality, Paul has been appropriated by proponents of various perspectives (sermons and tracts from the *antebellum* United States starkly illustrate Paul's utility for both slaveholder and abolitionist). Whereas today the thesis that Paul's letter to Philemon promotes resistance to slavery is increasingly popular, the alternative—that Paul supported slavery in general and the slavery of Onesimus in particular—remains entrenched in both scholarly and popular interpretations. Some interpreters see Paul as embedded in his own culture, where slavery was an accepted, 'natural' (so Aristotle) fact of life. Others regard the letter to Philemon as a sign of Paul's practical nature. With Christians distrusted by the wider culture, and himself in prison, to transgress the status quo would be suicidal. To advise the release of slaves would have signaled to Paul's captors, and to the society at large, that the Christian movement sought to undermine *oikos* and *polis*. Other interpreters see Paul as operating less in a utilitarian than in an apocalyptic context: since the world-as-we-know-it was soon to end, for Onesimus to 'remain in the state in which he was called' (1 Cor. 7.20) would be no exceptional burden (whether Onesimus would have agreed remains unanswered). **Sara B.C. Winter**'s understanding of Philemon breaks through several of these dichotomous readings; she firmly situates Paul in his own cultural context even as she draws out the implications of his letter for contemporary application.

First, Winter argues that Paul is neither condoning slavery nor seeking the manumission of Onesimus: there would be no need to ask simply for clemency, for in her view Onesimus was not a fugitive. Providing both philological and historical support, Winter recognizes that Onesimus was sent by his owner to aid Paul in prison, and the letter is Paul's request that Onesimus remain with him to continue the work of the church. Carefully explaining the relationship between Colossians and Philemon—the former relying on the latter for its authority—she then demonstrates how the Colossian household code 'serves to isolate Paul's plea for Onesimus as a special case, not a commitment to social equality'.

Second, her attention to address recovers 'Apphia the sister' whom Paul greets along with 'Philemon, our beloved fellow worker', 'Archippus our fellow soldier', and 'the church in your [sing.] house'. Both the order and the grammar remove Apphia from her usual assignment of 'wife of the owner of the house-church' or 'wife of Onesimus's master' (mentioned because she would have been in charge of the household and so, as one scholar put it, 'had to give her opinion when the question of taking back a runaway slave was raised'). Determining that Archippus is the most likely candidate for both householder and slave-owner, Winter proposes that Apphia and Philemon were not heads of a house-church; they were a missionary couple. Apphia stands on her own, not as wife, but as 'the sister'. Her absence, along with that of Philemon, from the other pairs mentioned in Colossians then becomes explicable: they are traveling evangelists rather than Colossian residents.

Third, Paul himself models what might be considered a partially feminist approach: he makes his case from a position of humility rather than of dominance, of explication rather than demand. Such an approach may well have been counter-intuitive for Paul; humility is not one of his strong points. Paul speaks of both his personal need and his theologically informed view of humanity; as Winter summarizes: 'a baptized person cannot be the slave of another baptized person'. Paul's request is formulated in the dualistic language of apocalyptic, for he finds that 'brother' and 'slave' are mutually exclusive roles.

Richard B. Hays's 'Paul on the Relation between Men and Women', along with his essays on divorce and homosexuality in *The Moral Vision of the New Testament*, perhaps best articulates what might be called a Protestant 'conservative' or 'traditional' view and, as such, should be engaged by feminist and non-feminist alike. Attuned to the concerns of lay as well as clerical and academic readers, Hays notes that whereas Paul's sexual ethics do not correspond to today's conceptions of 'healthy sexuality' (determining if these notions are themselves healthy is another matter), neither should Paul's statements be seen as polemicizing against sex. Further, because Paul is not writing a treatise but responding to particular concerns, responsible interpretation requires determining not only the 'what' but also the 'why' of Paul's ethic. Finally, Hays appropriately insists on the next step: assessing which Pauline teachings should have bearing on today's ethics, why, and how.

Hays locates Paul's argument in 1 Corinthians not only in the context of Hellenism's correlation of piety with celibacy but also in relation to early Christian traditions concerning life in the 'new creation', such as Gal. 3.28's apparent erasure of sexual difference. Concluding that Paul argues against 'an idealistic hyperspirituality that forswears sexual union even within existing marriages', Hays finds Paul stating that married couples '*must*' [emphasis his] continue to engage in sexual intercourse (so 1 Cor. 7.3–4). (Hays does understand the verb 'to have' as 'a common euphemism for sexual intercourse'; Gaventa's observations on the implications of metaphor would here be instructive.) For Hays, Paul's ethical stance is comprehensible only in the context of his 'dialectical eschatology': men and women are equal in Christ, but sexual distinctions do persist, and Paul's teachings must be assessed in relation to the question of community formation.

Paul's prescribing of 'mutual submission' is, as Hays acknowledges, disjunctive with today's notion of 'the sexual autonomy of each individual'. Additionally, since most marriages in antiquity were arranged and since we lack the surety that the wife (or the husband for that matter) had any desire to engage in intercourse, Paul's injunction might have forced unwilling partners into the other's bed. Hays correctly observes that Paul does not speak of sexual union as an expression of love (although he suggests it may be implied); nor does Paul, perhaps given his eschatological orientation, speak of procreation as the purpose of intercourse. For Paul, marital intercourse should continue because it is part of an 'obligation' shared by the spouses and because it serves as a prophylactic against temptation. In a society where women legally as well as culturally were subordinate to men and where slavery was the norm, the model of the 'self-sacrificed love' that Hays—and Paul—endorse might serve further to enslave and marginalize. But in cases where personal interests override community needs (a situation that traverses all class, racial, ethnic, etc., boundaries), such insistence on mutuality might take on fresh meaning.

Margaret Y. MacDonald also investigates both the cultural values that shaped Paul's advice to the Corinthians and the possible effect of that advice on virgins, widows, and wives in the church. By complementing anthropological reconstructions of Mediterranean values with descriptions of other first-century sectarian groups (especially the Therapeutae), comparing the rhetoric of 1 Corinthians 7 to other Pauline texts (especially 1 Corinthians 11, Gal. 3.28, and the Pastorals), looking to non-canonical Christian texts as well as to pagan authors from Philo to Galen to Epictetus to the *Gospel of the Egyptians*, MacDonald avoids the potential skewing of data a singular method or comparison can yield.

Paul is not, in MacDonald's view, contrasting chaste holiness with marital worldliness. Nor is he simply repeating the Cynic view, expressed by Epictetus, that marriage promotes anxiety. Nor yet again has he fully capitulated to Roman social and political pressures. Rather, 1 Corinthians expresses his concern that not all who seek to live celibately have the spiritual resources necessary. Not only marriage, but also compulsory celibacy, can lead to anxiety. Paul does not so much oppose celibacy and marriage, although his eschatologically influenced preference is certainly for the freedom celibacy grants, as he opposes either celibacy and marriage on the one hand, and immorality on the other.

MacDonald turns from the usual focus on male asceticism—men are the presumed proponents of this position, given their subject role in the slogan 'it is well for a man not to touch a woman'—to women's practice. Analysis of the appearance of παρθένος ('virgin') reveals a particular interest in women's chastity masked by English versions that translate the term variously as 'virgin', 'betrothed', and 'unmarried'. Concerning the chapter's puzzling use of both 'unmarried woman' (γυνή ἄγαμος) and παρθένος (virgin), MacDonald argues against the thesis that Paul addresses different groups of women (such as older widows supporting younger members) and in favor of a focused audience: any woman seeking holiness through chastity. Such women may have been willing to remain veiled while prophesying, but they had another, permanent means of demonstrating their spirit-enthused eschatological freedom. Comporting with the dominical logion of the *Gospel of the Egyptians* (see also Gal. 3.28), which proclaims the unification of male and female, the women manifested their new state to the world through their celibacy. But such action could lead both to destabilization and loss of honor. Roman wives were expected to follow their husband's wishes, not only religiously, but also conjugally. Paul's advice that the Christian wife should remain with her non-Christian husband consequently sanctions what MacDonald calls 'a type of marital infidelity'. Although, in some cases, women's chastity could be socially commendable, the Roman system strongly endorsed both marriage and child-production; to participate in such 'family values' could be economically advantageous; to refuse could mark one as an enemy of the state.

Similar social and pastoral concerns mark Paul's teachings in 1 Corinthians 8 concerning the eating of meat offered to idols, and the connections reinforce the point that feminist analysis is not restricted to passages in which the topics of women, gender, or sexuality explicitly appear. As **Faith Kirkham Hawkins** observes, Paul's remarks on specific groups, from slaves to pagans to those who do not find food to be a stumbling block, also hold ramifications for his treatment of other groups. The argument follows from the recognition both that markers of particularity assume varied forms (race, ethnicity, religious affiliation, class, sexual orientation, health, gender...) and that these markers function as indications of difference if not deviance from the 'perceived, idealized, and privileged' norm (in the West, the white, Christian, not-poor, male heterosexual). Because groups classified in contradistinction from the norm are interrelated interpretive categories, the experiences of one group will have implications for understanding the experiences of the others.

The topic of differentiation permeates 1 Corinthians and reflects the struggles of the nascent community over such central matters as ethics, worship, leadership, eschatology, and relationship with the wider society. Debates over food offered to idols are symptomatic of the divisions: one group claimed 'knowledge' and did not find food a stumbling block; the other, the 'weak', struggled with the association of meat with 'idols' and so with the paganism they rejected. Through careful assessment of Paul's language and the structure of his argument, Kirkham Hawkins reveals a pastoral argument: Paul responds to these differences within the congregation not by seeking to erase them but by locating the 'weak' and 'those with knowledge' within the larger whole, the 'body of Christ'. The ethical consequence is the sharply worded recognition that 'wounding a conscience', 'causing a brother to fall', and even 'destroying a brother for whom Christ died' (8.11) are equivalent. Consequently, Paul emphasizes what all members share, from their newfound monotheism and love of God to its consequences in distinguishing the members from their pagan context. His use of the *topos* of the community as building implies that the unity he seeks is the prior state of the group, not something new, and kinship language further reinforces this emphasis. Indeed, as Kirkham Hawkins notes, Paul may not subscribe (or may subscribe less than is sometimes thought) to the 'logic of identity' with its instantiation of oppositional difference. It is a scholarly construct, she argues, not the result of Paul's rhetoric, that sees in 1 Corinthians 8 a hierarchical opposition between 'the Weak' and 'the Strong'. Paul rather speaks of 'Weak' and 'you who have knowledge'. His shifting of true knowledge from the claim of some Corinthians to the purview only of God similarly refuses to prioritize opposition, as does his blunt point that neither eating nor abstaining will bring one closer to God.

Among the several implications for feminist analysis Kirkham Hawkins draws from her study, perhaps most the striking concerns 'ways of knowing'.[6] As she states, 'The links that Paul makes in 1 Corinthians 8 among "knowledge", "custom" (that is, previous experience), and "conscience" are links that feminist epistemology also emphasizes.' Notable as well is her recognition of the role of biblical theology—done from a feminist perspective—as a means of decreasing factionalism or breaking down hierarchical divisions. Thus, on subjects ranging from identity politics to group dynamics to pastoral intervention to the divine perspective, Kirkham Hawkins shows that Paul, in various senses of the expression, 'Makes a Difference'. More, she shows how feminist criticism does as well.

This volume concludes with **Luise Schottroff**'s perceptive study not only of Pauline theology but also of its interpreters. Drawing upon feminist discussion of anti-Judaism, sin, and Christology, Schottroff documents how the 'law free' rubric ascribed to Paul is anti-Jewish in offering a reified stereotype, misogynistic in its obsession with circumcision, and imperialistic in its determination that it possesses the only mechanism for eliminating sin. Schottroff goes as far as to posit what might be seen as the return of the repressed in scholarship on this topic; she claims that 'the Christian depiction of Pharisaism as a fraternity of men and of synagogue worship is tantamount to Judaism becoming a surrogate for particular Christian desires'.

Schottroff's study takes on a special poignancy given her explicitly noted social location: 'I am a German Christian writing after Auschwitz.' Further, she recognizes that some may find her thesis—that Gentile Christian women, such as the unnamed test case in 1 Cor. 7.15, should be regarded as part of the large group of Jewish proselytes; they worshiped Israel's God and followed the 'Jewish' way of life—an apologetic seeking to exculpate the New Testament for its anti-Judaism. But Schottroff does not find the 'Second Testament' to be 'anti-Jewish', for she sees even the Gospel of John as reflecting an internal Jewish debate. Otherwise put, she regards the 'Second Testament' as a 'Jewish book', and this presupposition is her starting point for a new understanding of Paul. Comparing Paul's various statements in Galatians and Romans on 'sin' with commentary from 2 Esdras, Schottroff highlights sin as the '*false practice of living* that destroys the life God wills' and, in an echo of Rehmann, as promoting 'structures of domination'. The means to break such systemic evil is to live, as

---

6 I am reminded of Mary F. Belenky, Blythe Clinchy, Nancy Goldberger, and Jill Tarule, *Women's Ways of Knowing: The Development of Self, Voice, and Mind* (New York: Basic Books, 10th anniversary edn, 1997).

Schottroff puts it, 'in accordance with Torah' rather than to adopt a 'law free' lifestyle. Her goal then is to think together, and so live together, with Jews, as well as with Muslims and peoples of other faiths.

Schottroff is certainly correct that anti-Judaism and sexism are a common pair and that feminists should seek the eradication of both. Her historical observations concerning the New Testament as a 'Jewish book' or the gentile Christians in the Pauline congregations as 'Jews' of a sort will not convince all readers (at least, they do not convince me), but her conclusions about the need to work together certainly should. Perhaps the next step in this program would extend the working together today to a studying together of the texts of antiquity. It would be salutary for Jewish readers to know of Schottroff's own perspectives on the Gospels and Epistles, even as it would be for those who hold her more sanguine views of the Christian texts to see how other historians reach their conclusions. Ultimately, it may not be history but theology that resolves the biblically situated problems with sexism and anti-Judaism.

The ten essays in this volume address not only the biblical texts in their original context, but also their ongoing effects, and the possibilities—both positive and negative—they can offer the future. As we assess them, we learn more about the benefits and drawbacks of particular approaches, what arguments we accept and what we reject, what we had never been able to see, and what we see afresh. Paul's writings will continue to be debated, and they will continue to have theological, social, and political import. In all these areas, and more, the essays in this volume advance the discussion.

Paul and the Genealogy of Gender*

Daniel Boyarin

Recently feminist theory has provided us with extraordinary subtle analyses of the ways that the mind/body split is inextricably bound up with the Western discourse of gender. The work of Judith Butler is of particular importance. She argues that the critique of dualism is in fact at the heart of the founding text of modern feminist theory, Simone de Beauvoir's *The Second Sex*:

> Although Beauvoir is often understood to be calling for the right of women, in effect, to become existential subjects and, hence, for inclusion within the terms of an abstract universality, her position also implies a fundamental critique of the very disembodiment of the abstract masculine epistemological subject. The subject is abstract to the extent that it disavows its socially marked embodiment and, further, projects that disavowed and disparaged embodiment on to the feminine sphere, effectively renaming the body as female. This association of the body with the female works along magical relations of reciprocity whereby the female sex becomes restricted to its body, and the male body, fully disavowed, becomes, paradoxically, the incorporeal instrument of an ostensibly radical freedom. Beauvoir's analysis implicitly poses the question: Through what act of negation and disavowal does the masculine pose as a disembodied universality and the feminine get constructed as a disavowed corporeality?[1]

I wish to trace one of the historical trajectories along which this act of negation, disavowal, and construction takes place. In her book *The Man of Reason: 'Male' and 'Female' in Western Philosophy*, Genevieve Lloyd has described the historical process within philosophy wherein the universal mind came to be identified as male, while the gendered body became female.[2] In my current work, I am trying to do two things: to

* Originally published in *Representations* 41 (1993), pp. 1–33. Reprinted by permission. Author's note: This paper was written while I was enjoying the stimulating intellectual fellowship of the Shalom Hartman Institute for Advanced Jewish Studies. I wish to thank Jeremy Cohen, Sidra DeKoven Ezrahi, Menahem Lorberbaum, and especially Elizabeth Castelli and Richard Hays for reading a draft of this paper and making important interventions. On 5 April 1992 a version of the paper was presented to the Center for Hermeneutical Studies of the Graduate Theological Union in Berkeley, where I had the privilege of receiving very serious and important formal responses from Karen King, Steven Knapp, and Antoinette Wire, as well as the informal responses and criticisms of an extraordinarily learned audience, and especially David Winston, who saved me from some errors in the interpretation of Philo. This version of the paper represents several substantial revisions made in response to that discussion. The full text of the paper in its former version as well as the responses and discussions has been published as: Daniel Boyarin and Christopher Ocker (eds.), *Galatians and Gender Trouble: Primal Androgyny and the First-Century Origins of a Feminist Dilemma* (Berkeley: Center for Hermeneutical Studies, 1995). Of course, only I am responsible for the results, particularly as I have not always taken the advice of my interlocutors.

1 Judith Butler, *Gender Trouble: Feminism and the Subversion of Identity* (London: Routledge, 1990), p. 12.

2 Genevieve Lloyd, *The Man of Reason: 'Male' and 'Female' in Western Philosophy* (Minneapolis: University of Minnesota Press, 1984), pp. 7, 26.

further specify the cultural mechanisms which rendered this gender ontology dominant in our formation, and to show how 'the Jew' has been constructed analogously to 'Woman' within the culture, and by a very similar historical vector.[3] Here, I will concentrate on the question of gender through a close and contextualized reading of the crucial Pauline texts.

Paul's 'Backsliding' Feminism

My reading of Paul is the following. Paul was motivated by a Hellenistic desire for the One, which among other things produced an ideal of a universal human essence, beyond difference and hierarchy. This universal humanity, however, was predicated (and still is) on the dualism of the flesh and the spirit, such that while the body is particular, marked through practice as Jew or Greek, and through anatomy as male or female, the spirit is universal. The strongest expression of this Pauline cultural criticism is Galatians and especially 3.28–29, a passage to be read in some detail below. 1 Corinthians, on the other hand, has been read and used within much Christian practice as a powerful defense of a cultural conservatism. Making 1 Corinthians the hermeneutical key to Paul has had fateful cultural consequences, although to be sure such a reading has also been the *product* of the very ideologies that it eventually underpinned. The task of my reading here, among other things, is to articulate a coherent reading of Paul as a social and cultural critic, one that takes Galatians very seriously but also makes sense of 1 Corinthians.

I am, of course, not the first critic to attempt this task. In her justly famous feminist reconstruction of Christian origins, *In Memory of Her*, Elisabeth Schüssler Fiorenza reproduces an 'apocryphal' female epistle of Phoebe written by one of Schüssler Fiorenza's students. This document contains the following lines:

> The second story is one I would like to discuss with Paul who lately seems so concerned with putting women back in 'their proper places'. He is so taken up with giving a good impression to the pagans that he is reverting to his rabbinic prejudices I think. As if the proper place of woman was in the home bearing children—'woman is the glory of man' indeed! Surely with his background he would know where Genesis puts woman: 'in the image of God he created them; male and female he created them'. What a strange man he is. In his letter to us he so firmly emphasized the equality of woman and man in marriage; in the same letter he raged on and on about hairstyles in the assembly ... And, even more pointed, are these words from his letter to our Galatian neighbours: 'For as many of you as were baptized into Christ have put on Christ. There is neither Jew nor Greek, there is neither slave nor free, there is neither male nor female, for you are all one in Christ Jesus'. I do fear that some people hear, not these words of Paul which so clearly reflect the attitude and teaching of Jesus our Wisdom but hear instead his return to the past before he received the freedom of the Spirit. I shudder to think that some time in the future a leader of one of the churches will say, 'Gentiles, slaves and women cannot become part of the ministry of the Word because Jesus did not entrust the apostolic charge to them'. When I said that to Paul, he laughed uproariously and exclaimed, 'Phoebe you are a person with the strangest

---

3 In drawing this analogy, I should make it clear that I am not reducing the problem of gender domination to an epiphenomenon of difference; nor would I so reduce anti-Semitism. The analogies seem, nevertheless, illuminating as partial accounts of both and, moreover, help explain the historically very well attested association of Jewishness with femaleness as a *topos* of European culture.

notions! If any of my letters do survive, only someone bewitched will fail to see the difference between my preaching of the Good News and my ramblings about cultural problems and situations. People from another age will easily disregard the cultural trappings and get to the heart of the message'. If only the distinction were as clear to the rest of us as it is to Paul![4]

Schüssler Fiorenza, of course, quotes this discourse approvingly. This student writing, according to her, 'can highlight the educational and imaginative value of retelling and rewriting biblical androcentric texts from a feminist critical perspective'. What we have here, in fact, is a fairly typical move of certain Christian feminists. One aspect of Pauline discourse, indeed constituted by only one (crucial) verse in Galatians, is rendered the essential moment of his message about gender, while the rest is relegated to an incompletely exorcized, demonized Jewish past. I submit here two propositions: the first is that such a reading of Paul will simply not stand up critically and, indeed, trivializes him beyond retrieval. Paul's so-called 'ramblings' about cultural problems and situations are, indeed, at the heart of his ministry, as Schüssler Fiorenza herself indicates.[5] The second is that no feminist critical perspective will be progressive if it is dependent on false and prejudicial depictions of Judaism or, for that matter, so-called paganism.[6]

If I have cited Schüssler Fiorenza here, this is not because she is in any way an egregious offender in these respects; if anything, she has made special efforts not to fall into such traps.[7] For that reason, however, this lapse is all the more symptomatic. If her student has failed to produce an acceptable solution, she certainly has exposed the problem. For there is a major issue for Pauline studies. On the issue of gender, as on several other matters of equal significance, Paul seems to have produced a discourse that is so contradictory as to be almost incoherent. In Galatians Paul seems, indeed, to be wiping out social differences and hierarchies between the genders in addition to those that obtain between ethnic groups and socioeconomic classes, while in Corinthians he seems to be reifying and reemphasizing precisely those gendered hierarchical differences. Schüssler Fiorenza's student's answer to this dilemma comprehends, in fact, two standard approaches to such problems in Pauline studies. One is that there is conflict within Paul between an unreconstructed Jewish past and

4 Elisabeth Schüssler Fiorenza, *In Memory of Her: A Feminist Theological Reconstruction of Christian Origins* (New York: Crossroad, 1983), pp. 63–64.

5 Schüssler Fiorenza, *In Memory of Her*, p. 226.

6 I wish to spotlight the eloquent remarks of Adele Reinhartz, 'From Narrative to History: The Resurrection of Mary and Martha', in Amy-Jill Levine (ed.), *'Women Like This': New Perspectives on Jewish Women in the Greco-Roman World* (Atlanta: Scholars Press, 1991), pp. 161–85 (183): 'While I am concerned about the roles of women within the Jewish community and can offer a critique of their ambiguous portrayal in Judaism's foundational documents, I deplore superficial and apologetically motivated attempts to demonstrate the superiority of Christianity to Judaism on the basis of the respective roles they accord women.'

7 See the brief discussion of her work from this perspective by Reinhartz, 'From Narrative to History', pp. 166–67. However, I must admit that I find bizarre Schüssler Fiorenza's comment on Jewish manumission of slaves: 'The slave gained complete freedom except for the requirement to attend the synagogue' (*In Memory of Her*, p. 214), as if 'Christian freedom' did not carry with it also a series of religious obligations. Is the requirement to participate in the eucharist somehow more free than the requirement to attend synagogue? I feel an echo of a very ancient polemic (and dispute) here.

his Christian present, and the other is that Paul was given to caving in under external 'pagan' pressures on even fundamental and critical points in his ideology.[8] In a third approach to this and other similar problems, Paul is granted absolution, as it were, from the sin of inconsistency by being absolved of any desire for consistency to start with. According to this version, Paul was not a systematic thinker, and all of his pronouncements are oriented toward the local problems with which each of his epistles is dealing.[9] Thus, while writing to the Galatians Paul emphasized the social equality of the sexes in the new Christian reality, but when writing to the Corinthians, for whom such notions of equality had apparently become spiritually and socially dangerous, he backtracked or backslid and reinstated gender difference and hierarchies.

In my view, none of these ways of understanding Paul is adequate, and I wish to propose here a different way of reading him, one that is generated, no less than the reading produced by Schüssler Fiorenza's student, by feminist reading practices, politics, and theory. Let me begin by restating the problem. First of all, there is the question of apparent contradiction between Galatians and Corinthians. This contradiction obtains on two levels. First, in the baptismal formula in Gal. 3.28, the phrase 'There is no male or female' is included, while in the Corinthians version, it is dropped (1 Cor. 12.12–13). Second, much of the advice on marriage and general discussion of gender in Corinthians seems to imply that there very much was and ought to be a male and female in the Christian communities and households, certainly insofar as marriage is to continue. Finally, even within Corinthians itself, there seems to be much tension between 'egalitarian' notions of the status of the sexes and rigidly hierarchical ones. I am going to propose a partially new resolution of these contradictions within the context of an overall interpretation of Paul's thought, because these expressions and tensions function within the entire system. I will argue in the end that Paul is caught here on the horns of a dilemma not of his own making, as it were, and one on which we are impaled into post-modernity and (embryonic) post-patriarchy—the myth of the primal androgyne.

The construction I wish to build here is constituted on the following notion. The famous 'myth of the primal androgyne'—together with the myth of Adam's rib—provides the ideological base of gender in our culture until this day. According to this myth, the first human being was an androgyne who was later split into the two sexes. However, and this is the catch, in the Hellenistic world and late antiquity the primal androgyne was almost always imagined as disembodied, so that the androgyne was

---

8 There seems to be a little recognition that these two explanations are at least partially contradictory, or at any rate render each other otiose. If it was the 'pagans' who pressured Paul to insist on male–female hierarchy, then what is the function of 'rabbinic prejudices' here other than to provide a gratuitous slap at Judaism? Incidentally, at the time of Paul, the rabbinic movement did not yet exist, so 'rabbinic prejudices' is in any case an anachronism. In fact, as we shall see below, it is also an inaccurate (although widespread) description of the relationship between Pauline '*halakha*' and that of contemporary Judaism(s), but I anticipate myself.

9 A prominent and extreme representative of this school of Pauline interpretation is the Finnish scholar Heikki Räisänen, 'Galatians 2.16 and Paul's Break with Judaism', *NTS* 31 (1985), pp. 543–53; and *idem*, 'Legalism and Salvation by the Law: Paul's Portrayal of the Jewish Religion as a Historical and Theological Problem', in Sigfred Pedersen (ed.), *Pauline Literature and Theology* (Teologiske Studier, 7; Århus, Finland: Århus Universitet, 1980), pp. 63–84.

really no-body, and dual-sex was no-sex.[10] This myth, I suggest, encodes the dualist ideology whereby a spiritual androgyny is contrasted with the corporeal (and social) division into sexes.

The Spirit and the Flesh

The linchpin of my reading of Paul is that he is mobilized by as thoroughgoing a dualism as that of Philo. This, to be sure, is a very controversial claim to make about Paul, so I had better begin here by defending it and establishing the terms in which I make it. Moreover, the morphology of this dualism has to be carefully delineated, *because it does not imply a rejection of the body*, and this non-rejection of the body is the key to the solution of the problem I am considering here. Let me begin, then, to outline my general approach to Paul.[11]

For a variety of partly unspecifiable reasons, various branches of Judaism (along with most of the surrounding culture) became increasingly platonized in late antiquity. By platonization I mean here the adoption of a dualist philosophy in which the phenomenal world was understood to be the representation in matter of a spiritual or ideal entity that corresponded to it. This has the further consequence that a hierarchical opposition is set up in which the invisible, inner reality is taken as more valuable or higher than the visible outer form of reality. In the anthropology of such a culture, the human person is constituted by an outer physical shell, which is nonessential, and by an inner spiritual soul, which represents his/her true and higher essence. 'In this life itself, what constitutes our self in each of us is nothing other than the soul' (Philo, *Laws* 12.959.a.7–8). For Philo, 'the soul may be seen as entombed in the body'.[12] This was a commonly held conception through much of the Hellenistic cultural world.

---

10 The spherical humans described by Aristophanes in Plato's *Symposium*, while obviously related genetically to the myth of the primal androgyne, encode quite a different set of meanings. First of all, they are physical, and second of all they are not all androgynes by any means. Aristophanes' myth comes rather to provide an etiology for sexualities than to be an 'articulation of the notion that human perfection is only accessible apart from sexual difference', as Elizabeth Castelli would have it in an article otherwise wholly admirable: ' "I Will Make Mary Male": Pieties of the Body and Gender Transformation of Christian Women in Late Antiquity', in Julia Epstein and Kristina Staub (eds.), *Body Guards: The Cultural Politics of Gender Ambiguity* (London: Routledge, 1991), pp. 29–50 (31). A very important discussion of the Aristophanes text may be found in Thomas Laqueur, *Making Sex: Body and Gender from the Greeks to Freud* (Cambridge, MA: Harvard University Press, 1990), pp. 52–53 and p. 260 n. 82. As I mention below, Philo, who strongly endorses the myth of the primal androgyne in his writing, is thoroughly contemptuous of Aristophanes' story.

11 An elaboration of this thesis can be found in Daniel Boyarin, *A Radical Jew: Paul and the Politics of Gender Identity* (Berkeley: University of California Press, 1994). My general argument is that Paul was primarily motivated by what is essentially a social vision of human unity or sameness, one that would eradicate all difference and thus hierarchy. The dualism of the body and the spirit that I am about to address was primarily assumed by him and utilized as the vehicle for the moral and political transformation that he envisioned. I read Paul as a Jewish cultural critic.

12 David Winston, 'Philo and the Contemplative Life', in Arthur Green (ed.), *Jewish Spirituality from the Bible through the Religious Ages* (World Spirituality: An Encyclopedic History of the Religious Quest, 13; New York: Crossroad, 1988), pp. 198–231 (212).

Paul also uses similar platonizing dualist imagery although, significantly enough, without negative imagery of the body.[13] The clearest example of this in his writing is in 2 Cor. 5.1–4:

> For we know that if the earthly tent we live in is destroyed, we have a building from God, a house not made with hands, eternal in the heavens. Here indeed we groan, and long to put on our heavenly dwelling, so that by putting it on we may not be found naked. For while we are still in this tent, we sigh with anxiety; not that we would be unclothed, but that we would be further clothed, so that what is mortal may be swallowed up by life.

Now it is beyond any doubt that Paul here is referring to a resurrection in the body, however at the same time the resurrected body is not the same kind of body as the one 'we dwell in' now. Paul does consider some kind of body necessary in order that the human being not be naked, and he polemicizes here against those who deny resurrection in the flesh. He is not, then, to be understood as holding a radical flesh/spirit dualism that despises the fleshly. Nevertheless, the image of the human being that Paul maintains is of a soul dwelling in or clothed by a body, and, however valuable the garment, it is less essential than that which it clothes. It is 'the earthly tent that we live in'; it is not *we*. The body, while necessary and positively valued by Paul, is, as in Philo, not the human being but only his or her house or garment.[14] The verse just preceding this passage establishes its platonistic context beautifully: 'While we look not at the things which are seen (τὰ βλεπόμενα), but at the things which are not seen: for the things which are seen are temporal (πρόσχαιρα); but the things which are not seen are eternal (αἰώνια)' (2 Cor. 4.18). What could possibly be more Platonic in spirit than this double hierarchy—on the one hand the privileging of the invisible over the visible; on the other hand, the privileging of the eternal over the temporal? The continuation of the passage dramatizes this point even more:

> We know that while we are home in the body we are away from the Lord . . . and we would rather be away from the body and at home with the Lord.

Rudolf Karl Bultmann recognized that these verses 'are very close to Hellenistic-Gnostic dualism, but not identical because of the "indirect polemic against a Gnosticism which teaches that the naked self soars aloft free of any body" '.[15] I could not agree more.

In the hermeneutics of such a culture, language itself is understood as being such an outer, physical shell as well, and meaning is construed as the invisible, ideal, and spiritual reality that lies behind or trapped within the body of the language. When

---

13 Philo also, however, can refer to the body as 'a sacred dwelling place or shrine fashioned for the reasonable soul' (*Op. Mund.* 137), a much less misomatist but just as dualist image. See also Daniel Boyarin, ' "Behold Israel according to the Flesh"; On Anthropology and Sexuality in Late Antique Judaism', *Yale Journal of Criticism* 5 (1992), pp. 25–55, n. 6.

14 Another elegant argument for this interpretation of Paul's anthropology is provided by Phil. 1.19–26, for which see Robert H. Gundry, *Sôma in Biblical Theology: With Emphasis on Pauline Anthropology* (Grand Rapids, MI: Academie Books, 1987), p. 37. ' "To depart" is to die bodily death. "To be with Christ" is to be absent from the body (cf. 2 Cor. 5.7–9).'

15 Quoted in Gundry, *Sôma in Biblical Theology*, p. 48 n. 1.

this philosophy is combined with certain modes of interpretation current in the ancient East, such as dream reading in which one thing is taken for another similar thing, then allegory is born—allegory in the most strict sense of the interpretation of the concrete elements of a narrative as signs of a changeless, wholly immaterial ontological being.[16] Language is thus a representation in two senses—in its 'content' it represents the higher world; in its form it represents the structure of world as outer form and inner actuality.[17] The human being is also a representation of world in exactly the same way; in his/her dual structure is reproduced the very dual structure of being. It is for this reason that the literal can be referred to by Paul as the interpretation which is 'according to the flesh' (κατὰ σάρκα), while the figurative is referred to by him as 'according to the spirit' (κατὰ πνεῦμα).[18] Literal interpretation and its consequences; observances in the flesh, for example, circumcision; commitment to the history of Israel; and insistence on procreation are all linked together in Paul's thinking, as are their corresponding binaries: allegorical interpretation *per se* and in the facts of circumcision as baptism, of Israel as a signifier of the faithful Christians and of spiritual propagation. As Karen King has put it, 'Here allegory is not just an interpretive tool to lay *Tanakh* (Hebrew Bible) bare to Paul's whims but a constitutive part of his world view.'[19]

Given this general understanding of the context of Pauline thought and expression, I can begin to set out my interpretation of the differences and apparent contradictions between Galatians and Corinthians on gender. To put it briefly and somewhat

16 David Dawson, *Allegorical Readers and Cultural Revision in Ancient Alexandria* (Berkeley: University of California Press, 1992), is an excellent discussion of this history.

17 Cf. Sallust who writes, 'The universe itself can be called a myth, revealing material things and keeping concealed souls and intellects', quoted by A.J.M. Wedderburn, *Baptism and Resurrection: Studies in Pauline Theology against its Graeco-Roman Background* (WUNT, 44; Tübingen: J.C.B. Mohr [P. Siebeck], 1987), p. 127.

18 It has become current in Pauline studies to understand the key terms κατὰ σάρκα (according to the flesh) and κατὰ πνεῦμα (according to the spirit) as axiological/sociological terms—the former meaning, in one typical formulation, 'human life organized without reference to God and his purposes', and the latter the opposite. Perhaps the key passage is 'the Christ which is according to the flesh' (ὁ Χριστὸς τὸ κατὰ σάρκα), Rom. 9.5. I submit that it is impossible to gloss this expression as 'the Christ who lives without reference to God' or 'the Christ who seeks justification by works'. The passage must be understood as the Christ in his human, fleshly aspect, Christ before Easter. This Christological duality is matched by a homologous hermeneutical duality as well, which works perfectly, because that interpretation which is literal, 'according to the flesh'—the outer meaning of the language—is precisely the mode of interpretation that on the plane of content privileges physical observations, physical kinship, and the *paradosis* of the 'historical Jesus', ὁ Χριστὸς τὸ κατὰ σάρκα. Circumcision, of course, is in the flesh par excellence. Because the ways of both Jews and the Jerusalem Christians emphasize precisely these values, they can be identified by Paul as 'according to the flesh', not because they are self-righteous, without reference to God or against the will of God. Life or interpretation κατὰ σάρκα only become pejoratively marked terms when they have the negative social effects in Paul's eyes of interrupting the new creation of the universal Israel of God. Fuller demonstration of this point is made in Boyarin, *A Radical Jew*.

19 From her response at the Center for Hermeneutical Studies. I wish to be clear on this. I am not claiming that Paul was a philosopher; I am claiming that such fundamental dualist conceptions of the world, language, and humanity were commonplace for virtually all in that culture. The closest analogy is the way that conscious and unconscious, drives and repression have become the commonplace ways of describing the human psyche even for those in our culture who have no other knowledge of Freud and no commitment to his system other than these *topoi*.

crudely: Galatians is, on my reading, a theology of the spirit and Corinthians a theology of the body.[20] In Galatians Paul's major concern is to defend his doctrine of justification by faith as a means of including the Gentiles in the Israel of God, and he violently rejects anything that threatens that notion and that inclusion: 'for you are all children of God through faith in Christ Jesus. For as many of you as were baptized into Christ have put on Christ: "There is neither Jew nor Greek; there is neither slave nor freeman; there is no male and female. For you are all one in Christ Jesus". If, however, you belong to Christ, then you are Abraham's offspring, heirs according to the promise' (Gal. 3.26–29).

In Deut. 14.1 we find the Jews referred to as the 'children of God'. But Paul is most troubled by the notion that one particular people could ever be referred to as the children of God to the exclusion of other peoples, which is apparently exactly what the opponents were propounding to the Galatians. To disprove that claim, Paul cites the baptismal formula that the Galatians themselves recited or heard recited at the time of their baptism.[21] He moreover interprets the text. In the baptism there was a new birth, which is understood as substituting an allegorical genealogy for a literal one. In Christ, that is in baptism, all the differences that mark off one body from another as Jew or Greek (circumcision considered a 'natural' mark of the Jew!), male or female, slave or free are effaced, for in the Spirit such marks do not exist. Accordingly, if one belongs to Christ, then one participates in the allegorical meaning of the promise to the 'seed', an allegorical meaning of genealogy that was already hinted at in the biblical text itself, when it said that in 'Abraham all nations would be blessed', and even more when it interpreted his name as 'Father to many nations'. The individual body itself is replaced by its allegorical reference, the body of Christ of which all the baptized are part.[22] This is what the 'putting on' of Christ means.

In order to keep a focus on Paul's dualism, *which does not radically devalue the body, but nevertheless presupposes a hierarchy of spirit and body*, we do best by considering the nature of Christ, which was so central in Paul's thought. Christ inscribes a dualism of spirit and body as well as valorizing body, at least insofar as God became flesh. For Paul, in this sense, the historical Jesus, while subordinate to the risen Christ, certainly is not deprived of value, and likewise the individual human body is not deprived of value vis-à-vis the soul.

On the present reading, the fundamental insight of Paul's apocalypse was the realization that the dual nature of Jesus provided a hermeneutic key to the resolution of the enormous tension that he experienced between the universalism of the Torah's content and the particular ethnicity of its form. Paul understood both the dual nature

20 Cf. Jerome H. Neyrey, 'Of all Paul's letters, 1 Corinthians is thoroughly and intensely concerned with the physical body' (*Paul, in Other Words: A Cultural Reading of his Letters* [Louisville, KY: Westminster/John Knox Press, 1990], p. 114). 'Word-statistics show a sudden rise in the frequency of *sôma* in 1 and 2 Corinthians and Romans. The denigration of the body at Corinth provides the reason' (Gundry, *Sôma in Biblical Theology*, p. 50). See below for other symptoms of the 'corporeality' of Corinthians.

21 Wayne A. Meeks, 'The Image of the Androgyne: Some Uses of a Symbol in Earliest Christianity', *HR* 13.1 (1974), pp. 165–208.

22 The parallel citation of the formula in 1 Cor. 12.13 makes this even more explicit: for in one spirit we were all baptized into one body.

of Christ's person as well as the crucifixion in the light of the familiar Platonic dichotomy of the outer and the inner, the material and the spiritual, or in Paul's own terminology the flesh and the spirit. Jesus was explicitly of a dual ontology, having an outer aspect of the flesh and an inner aspect of the spirit, or in more properly hermeneutic terms: there was a Christ according to the flesh (Rom. 9.5; which corresponds to the literal, historical Jesus) and a Christ according to the spirit (the allegorical, risen Christ). By a simple analogy, the dual nature of Jesus the Jew became the sign of a dual signification of all the Jews, of Israel. The particularity of Israel came to be read as the signifier of which the universal was its signified. This is how a Christology becomes cultural politics:

> Concerning His son who was born of the seed of David according to the flesh, and declared to be the son of God in power, according to the spirit of Holiness, by the resurrection from the dead (Rom. 1.3–4).

Jesus is the son of David according to the flesh but the son of God according to the spirit. Even less ambiguous, it seems to me, is 2 Cor. 5.16: 'Wherefore from now we know no man according to the flesh, and if we did know Christ according to the flesh, we will no longer know him', in a context discussing the death and resurrection of Christ.

The dual person of Christ in the world is a perfect homology then to the dual nature of language and the necessity for allegorical interpretation to fulfill the spiritual meaning of concrete expression. Corporeal difference yields to spiritual universalism.[23] This structure is manifested beautifully in 1 Cor. 10.1–11, where the manna and water given the Jews in the wilderness is called 'spiritual' (10.3), and the rock that followed the Jews in the wilderness is interpreted as Christ (10.4). And thus '*our* ancestors were all under the cloud' (10.1), that is Paul's and the Corinthians' ancestors were all under the cloud, interpreted as baptism! As Hans Conzelmann remarks, ' "our ancestors": Paul is speaking as a Jew, but includes also Gentile-Christian readers. The church is the true Israel.'[24] Just as there is a Jesus according to the flesh and a Jesus according to the spirit, so also there is an Israel according to the flesh (1 Cor. 10.18), which clearly entails an Israel according to the spirit. Israel according to the flesh corresponds to the literal, concrete history talked about in the Torah and to the literal concrete, embodied practices of the Torah, which indeed mark that Israel off from the other nations of the world. On the other hand, Israel according to the spirit corresponds to the allegorical meaning of the historical narrative and the commandments, which do not mark Israel off from among the nations.

Paul's allegorical reading of the rite of circumcision is an almost perfect emblem of his hermeneutics of otherness. By interpreting circumcision as referring to a spiritual and not corporeal reality, Paul made it possible for Judaism to become a world religion. It is not that the rite was difficult for adult Gentiles to perform; that would hardly have stopped devotees in the ancient world; it was

---

23 See David Boyarin, 'Allegoresis against Difference: The Metalinguistic Origins of the Universal Subject', forthcoming in *Paragraph*.

24 Hans Conzelmann, *1 Corinthians: A Commentary on the First Epistle to the Corinthians* (trans. James W. Leitch; Hermeneia; Philadelphia: Fortress Press, 1975), p. 165.

rather it symbolized the genetic, the genealogical moment of Judaism as the religion of a particular tribe of people. This is so in the very fact of the physicality of the rite—its grounding in the practice of the tribe and in the way it marks the male members of that tribe—but even more so, by being a marker on the organ of generation, it represents the genealogical claim for concrete historical memory as constitutive of Israel. The fact that the Hebrew word for 'flesh,' בשׂר, has widespread metaphorical usage as 'penis' and as 'kinship' has made a mighty contribution to this hermeneutic as well. By substituting a spiritual interpretation for a physical ritual, Paul at one stroke was saying that the genealogical Israel, 'according to the flesh', is not the ultimate Israel; there is an 'Israel in the spirit'. The practices of the particular Jewish people are not what the Bible speaks of; rather what is spoken of is faith, the allegorical and universal meaning of those practices. I argue, therefore, that the major motivating force behind Paul's ministry was a profound vision of a humanity undivided by ethnos, class, and sex. If Paul took 'no Jew or Greek' as seriously as all of Galatians attests that he clearly did, how could he possibly—unless he is a hypocrite or incoherent—not have taken 'no male and female' with equal seriousness?

But in 1 Corinthians, Paul is fighting against pneumatics who seem both radically anti-body and radically antinomian.[25] He thinks the whole Christian mission is in danger, having fallen into the peril that he anticipated at the end of Galatians of allowing the spirit to provide opportunity for the flesh, because the realities of the flesh and its demands have not been attended to. He produces, therefore, a theology of the body that balances and completes, but does not contradict, the theology of the spirit of Galatians. It is no wonder, then, that this is the text which is richest in '*halakhic*' prescriptions, and no wonder, as well, that it is this text which inscribes hierarchy between men and women in the marriage relationship.[26] In the life of the spirit, in Paul as in Philo, there may be no male and female, but in the life of the body there certainly is. Next is the fact that in Corinthians there is an explicit and frequent appeal to both Jewish tradition and that of apostolic, Jewish Christianity. Paul several times in this letter refers to his passing on of tradition (παράδοσις), which he had received, and all but one of his citations of traditions attributed explicitly to Jesus appear in this letter as well.[27] All this is in direct contrast (not contradiction) to Galatians, in which Paul emphasizes that he is not authorized by tradition, by the teaching of Jesus in the flesh, that he is an apostle not from men but from God, authorized by his visionary experience of the spirit. It is no accident that the Pauline text which most thematizes the body is the one that also most manifests such fleshly

---

25 There is nothing particularly new in this formulation *per se*. What is new in my interpretations is that the differences between Galatians and Corinthians, while contextualized by different discursive, 'political' contexts, nevertheless form a consistent pattern and social theory on Paul's part.

26 'A letter remarkable for its parenthetical character is First Corinthians' (Peter T. Tomson, *Paul and the Jewish Law: Halakha in the Letters of the Apostle to the Gentiles* [Compendia Rerum Iudaicarum ad Novum Testamentum, 3.1; Minneapolis: Fortress Press, 1990], pp. 57 and 69).

27 Tomson, *Paul and the Jewish Law*, pp. 72–73; Antoinette Clark Wire, *The Corinthian Women Prophets: A Reconstruction through Paul's Rhetoric* (Minneapolis: Fortress Press, 1990), p. 272, goes even further and argues that the one other apparent citation of Jesus in Gal. 5.14 is to be interpreted differently, strengthening this point further.

concerns as rules and regulations, tradition, literal interpretations, and authority. I suggest that we best read Paul as a middle way between the insistence on literality and corporeality, perhaps even the monism of the Jerusalem church, on the one hand, and the radical dualism of gnostics (and gnostic-like tendencies in the early church) on the other.[28] Paul's is a dualism that makes room for the body, however much the spirit is more highly valued. In this light I will reread Paul on gender.

'There Is No Male and Female'

Crucial to an understanding of Paul on gender is a proper appreciation of the history of the phrase 'There is no male or female' in Gal. 3.28: 'For you are all children of God through faith in Christ Jesus. For as many of you as were baptized into Christ have put on Christ: "There is neither Jew nor Greek; there is neither slave nor freeman; there is no male and female. For you are all one in Christ Jesus."' It has been recognized, at least since the publication of Wayne Meeks's landmark 'The Image of the Androgyne', that Paul is here citing Gen. 1.27: 'And God created the earth-creature in His image; in the image of God, He created him; male and female He created them.'[29] One of the proofs that the verse is being alluded to in the Pauline formula is the latter's language. Note that he shifts from nouns—*Jew, Greek, slave, freeman*—to adjectives, using ἄρσεν, 'male', and θῆλυ, 'female', instead of the expected ἀνήρ, 'man', and γυνή, 'woman'. Second, the use of καί, 'and', in place of the οὐδέ, 'or', used in the other phrases gives this away. The 'ungrammaticality' marks this as a site of intertextuality, sociolinguistic heterogeneity, dialogue in the Bakhtinian sense of the word.[30]

Meeks and, more recently, Dennis Ronald MacDonald have demonstrated that in his baptismal formula is encapsulated a very early Christian mythic formation and its liturgical expression in the pre-Pauline church.[31] What was the meaning of this 'original' baptism? According to Meeks, this was a 'performative' ritual utterance in which 'a factual claim is being made, about an "objective" change in reality which fundamentally modifies the social roles'.[32] Whatever the 'original meanings',

---

28 Dawson, *Allegorical Readers*, p. 17, reads 'the emergence and domestication of radical *gnosis* in its countless forms' as the 'common feature in these struggles that recur throughout the [Western] history of interpretation'. Karen King has emphasized to me that the term *gnostic* itself is a highly problematized one in current research, and has suggested simply abandoning it in this context. I think, however, that as long as we define our terms and use the term to refer to specific spiritual, ideological tendencies it still serves a useful purpose.

29 Meeks, 'Image of the Androgyne', p. 185.

30 By 'ungrammaticality' here I mean the stylistic infelicity of the formal difference between the different clauses of the Pauline formula, that stylistic infelicity which marks formally the site of a citation and thus points to the intertext. This provides the strongest argument for Meeks's view that Gal. 3.28 has a proto-gnostic background (to use J. Louis Martyn's terminology) and not an apocalyptic one. Martyn claims: 'Nothing in the text or context of Gal. 3.28 indicates that the thought is that of *re*-unification' ('Apocalyptic Antinomies in Paul's Letter to the Galatians', *NTS* 31 [1985], pp. 410–24 [423, n. 16]); but precisely this argument that Paul is citing Gen. 1.27 and alluding to the 'myth of the primal androgyne' does constitute an indication of reunification.

31 Dennis Ronald MacDonald, *There Is No Male and Female: The Fate of a Dominical Saying in Paul and Gnosticism* (HDR, 20; Philadelphia: Fortress Press, 1987); and *idem*, 'Corinthian Veils and Gnostic Androgynes', in Karen L. King (ed.), *Images of the Feminine in Gnosticism* (Philadelphia: Fortress Press, 1988), pp. 276–92.

32 Meeks, 'Image of the Androgyne', p. 182.

however, I think that the entire context of the passage in Galatians leads rather to the conclusion that what is being referred to is an ecstatic experience, in which not social roles are modified but ontological categories in the pneumatic moment of initiation. Paul's whole claim at this moment is based on an appeal to the Galatians' *memory* of their ecstatic experience at baptism.[33] This interpretation would tend, of course, to make Pauline baptism more similar to the initiatory rites of the Mysteries, in which, as Meeks himself argues, 'the exchange of sexual roles, by ritual transvestism for example, was an important symbol for the disruption of ordinary life's categories in the experience of initiation. This disruption, however, did not ordinarily reach beyond the boundaries of the initiatory experience—except, of course, in the case of devotees who went on to become cult functionaries.'[34] Following the researches of MacDonald we can further assume that the expression 'no male and female' originally referred indeed to a complete erasure of sexual difference in some forms of earliest Christianity and is cited by Paul here from such contexts.[35] In such groups, the declaration that there is no male or female may very well have had radical social implications in a total breakdown of hierarchy and either celibacy or libertinism.

Philo and the Primal Androgyne

In order to establish the background for this interpretation of Paul, I would like first briefly to consider the writings of another crucially important first-century Jew, Philo of Alexandria. I should make it clear that I am *not* claiming that Philo is the background for Paul, but only that he provides a background for my *reading* of Paul; that is, certain themes which are explicit in Philo seem to me to be useful for understanding inexplicit moments in Paul's texts.[36]

The myth of a primal androgyne was very widespread in late antiquity, particularly among platonists in the Jewish (and then Christian) traditions.[37] One of the motivations of this myth is the fact that the first and second chapters of Genesis contain two different accounts of the creation of humanity. In the first story God creates male and female simultaneously: 'Male and female created he them', while in the second the familiar

33 Thus, I completely disagree with Schüssler Fiorenza, who claims that 'the immediate context in Galatians speaks neither about baptism nor about social relationships' (*In Memory of Her*, p. 208). From the very beginning of the chapter until its end, that is all that is being spoken of.

34 Meeks, 'Image of the Androgyne', p. 170. Below I will argue further that Pauline baptism functioned in this way, providing a momentary experience of breaking of categories in the experience of 'the spirit'.

35 See MacDonald, *No Male and Female*. I am, of course, aware that MacDonald's reconstructions are not universally accepted.

36 It is important to emphasize how crucial the thinking of these two men has been in founding the culture of the West. For Paul this is obvious to all; however, Philo, because of his decisive influence on much patristic thought, was also of enormous importance. See J.E. Bruns, 'Philo Christianus: The Debris of a Legend', *HTR* 66 (1973), pp. 141–45; David Winston (trans.), *Philo of Alexandria: The Contemplative Life, the Giants, and Selections* (New York: Paulist Press, 1981), pp. xi–xii and pp. 313–14; and Kerstin Aspegren, *The Male Woman: A Feminine Ideal in the Early Church* (ed. René Kieffer; Stockholm: Almqvist & Wiksell, 1990), pp. 81–82.

37 Meeks, 'Image of the Androgyne'; and Henri Crouzel, *Origen: The Life and Thought of the First Great Theologians* (trans. A.S. Worrall; San Francisco: Harper & Row, 1989), p. 94.

account of Eve's secondary creation is related. In the interpretation of Philo, the first Adam is an entirely spiritual being, of whose noncorporeal existence it can be said that he is male and female, while the second chapter first introduces a carnal Adam, who is male and then from whom the female is constructed. Bodily gender—structurally dependent, of course, on their being two—is thus twice displaced from the origins of 'man':

> It is not good that *any* man should be alone. For there are *two* races of men the one made after the (Divine) Image, and the one molded out of the earth ... With the second man a helper is associated. To begin with, the helper is a created one, for it says, 'Let us make a helper for him'; and in the next place, is subsequent to him who is to be helped, for He had formed the mind before and is about to form its helper (*Leg. All.* 2.4).

Philo here regards the two stories as referring to two entirely different creative acts on the part of God and accordingly to the production of two different races of 'Man'.[38] Thus both myths are included in his discourse: a primal androgyne of no-sex and primal male/secondary female. Since the two texts, that is the one in Genesis 1 and the one in Genesis 2, refer to two entirely different species, he can claim that only the first one is called 'in the image of God'; that is, only the singular unbodied Adam-creature is referred to as being in God's likeness, and his male-and-femaleness must be understood spiritually. The designation of *this* creature as male-and-female means really neither male nor female. We find this explicitly in another passage of Philo:

> After this he says that 'God formed man by taking clay from the earth, and breathed into his face the breath of life' (Gen. 2.7). By this also he shows very clearly that there is a vast difference between the man thus formed and the man that came into existence earlier after the image of God: for the man so formed is an object of sense-perception, partaking already of such or such quality, consisting of body and soul, man or woman, by nature mortal; *while he that was after the Image was an idea or type or seal, an object of thought, incorporeal, neither male nor female*, by nature incorruptible (emphasis added).[39]

Philo's interpretation is not an individual idiosyncrasy. As Thomas Tobin has shown, he is referring to a tradition known to him from before.[40] The fundamental point that seems to be established is that for the Hellenistic Jews, the oneness of pure spirit is ontologically privileged in the constitution of humanity. This Platonic Jewish anthropology is elegantly summed up with respect to Philo by Steven Fraade, who writes, 'Philo inherits from Plato a radically dualistic conception of the universe. In this

---

38 Philo contradicts himself on this point in several places. I am not interested here in sorting out Philo's different interpretations and their sources. Moreover, this has been very well done already in Thomas H. Tobin, SJ, *The Creation of Man: Philo and the History of Interpretation* (CBQMS, 14; Washington: Catholic Biblical Association of America, 1983). My interest here is rather in how the reading given here enters into a certain politics of the gendered body. For further discussion of this passage in Philo and his followers, see Tobin, *Creation of Man*, pp. 108–19; and Jeremy Cohen, *'Be Fertile and Increase, Fill the Earth and Master It': The Ancient and Medieval Career of a Biblical Text* (Ithaca, NY: Cornell University Press, 1989), pp. 74–76 and 228.

39 Philo, *Op. Mund.* 134.

40 Tobin, *Creation of Man*, p. 32.

view, the material world of sense perception is an imperfect reflection of the intelligible order which emanates from God. The human soul finds its fulfillment through separation from the world of material desires, a world that lacks true reality, and through a participation in the life of the spirit and divine intellect; the soul finally reunites *the true self* with its divine source and thereby achieves immortality' (emphasis added).[41] Since, as we have seen, that primal state is one of spiritual androgyny, in which male-and-female means neither male nor female, this fulfillment would naturally be a return to that state of noncorporeal androgyny. This notion had, moreover, social consequences as well in the image of perfected human life that Philo presents.

In his *On the Contemplative Life*, Philo describes a Jewish sect living in his time on the shores of Lake Mareotis near Alexandria. It is clear from the tone of his entire depiction of this sect and its practice that he considers it an ideal religious community. The fellowship consisted of celibate men and women who lived in individual cells and spent their lives in prayer and contemplative study of allegorical interpretations of Scripture (such as the ones that Philo produced). Once a year (or once in seven weeks), the community came together for a remarkable ritual celebration. Following a simple meal and a discourse, all of the members begin to sing hymns together. Initially, however, the men and the women remain separate from each other in two choruses. The extraordinary element is that as the celebration becomes more ecstatic, the men and the women join to form one chorus, 'the treble of the women blending with the bass of the men'.[42] I suggest that this model of an ecstatic joining of the male and the female in a mystical ritual recreates in social practice the image of the purely spiritual masculo-feminine first human of which Philo speaks in his commentary—indeed, that this ritual of the Therapeutae is a return to the originary Adam.[43] This point is valid whether or not the community of Therapeutae ever really existed. In either case the description is testimony to the translation of anthropology into social practice in Philo's writing. If they did exist, moreover, we have further strong evidence that Philo is representative of larger religious traditions and groups. Although, obviously, the singing and dancing are performed by the body, the state of ecstasy (as its etymology implies) involves a symbolical and psychological condition of being disembodied and thus similar to the primal androgyne. The crux of my argument is that a distinction between androgyny as a mythic notion and one that has social consequences is a false distinction. The myth of the primal androgyne, with all of its inflections, always has social meaning

---

41 Steven D. Fraade, 'Ascetical Aspects of Ancient Judaism', in Arthur Green (ed.), *Jewish Spirituality* (2 vols.; New York: Crossroad, 1986), I, pp. 253–88.

42 Ross Kraemer, 'Monastic Jewish Women in Greco-Roman Egypt: Philo on the Therapeutrides', *Signs: A Journal of Women in Culture and Society* 14.1 (1989), pp. 342–70, is the most recent and fullest description of the Therapeutae.

43 Cf. Meeks, 'Image of the Androgyne', p. 179; and MacDonald, 'Corinthian Veils', p. 289. This hypothesis also explains the otherwise seemingly unmotivated reference in Philo's text to the *Symposium* of Plato and especially to Aristophanes' story of double-creatures (not necessarily androgynes by any means) at the origins of humanity. Philo is counterposing to this 'abhorrent' image of physically double bodies an ideal one of spiritually dual humans. Philo's reversal was double-reversed by the rabbis, who restored the myth as one of physical androgyne, as I argue in 'Behold Israel'.

and social significance, for Paul no less than for Philo, for rabbis and for Corinthian Christians.

Now what is crucial here as background for a reading of Paul on gender are the following two points. First of all, the society and religious culture depicted by Philo *does* permit parity between men and women, and religious, cultural creativity for women as for men. Second, this autonomy and creativity in the spiritual sphere is predicated on renunciation of both sexuality and maternity.[44] Spiritual androgyny is attained only by abjuring the body and its difference. I think two factors have joined in the formation of this structure—which will be repeated over and over in the history of Western religion, including at least one instance within Early Modern Judaism. On the materialist level, there is the real-world difference between a woman who is bound to the material conditions of marriage and childbearing/rearing and a woman who is free of such restraints. Even more to the point, however, is the symbolic side of the issue. Just as in some contemporary feminist philosophy the category 'woman' is produced in the heterosexual relationship, so in Philo as well a female who escapes or avoids such relationships escapes from being a woman.[45] This division in Philo is reproduced in his interpretations of the status of female figures in the Bible as well, who fall into two categories: women and virgins![46] Those biblical figures defined as 'virgins' by Philo are not women and thus do not partake of the

---

44 Antoinette Wire has made the valid point that Philo describes the Therapeutae as 'aged virgins', which, given his usage discussed below, might very well mean formerly sexually active women. In a sense, then, these women had 'had their cake and eaten it too'. The symbolic incompatibility, however, between sexuality and spirituality is nevertheless reinforced, and, as we shall see, in many groups the renunciation had been total and permanent. Furthermore, it is important to note that the women of the culture may not have experienced this 'renunciation' as a sacrifice but as a liberation, and I am making an open judgment here which draws on my own contemporary values, which is valid to the extent that I am involved here in a critique and analysis of contemporary culture using the ancient materials as one tool of analysis. In any case, however, it is clear that an autonomy which is predicated on the forced choice of celibacy (in order to achieve autonomy) is a highly compromised autonomy, however it may have been experienced. It is not to be ignored, of course, that men as well in these systems are ideally expected to embrace celibacy. Male autonomy and creativity are *not*, however, predicated on such renunciation, except in one sphere. Thus noncelibate men have many avenues of self-expression and freedom together with sexuality and paternity, while women can only choose between an all-encompassing maternity or none at all. There are, to be sure, in both Judaism and Christianity, some hints at ruptures in this rule. See Daniel Boyarin, *Carnal Israel: Reading Sex in Talmudic Culture* (New Historicism, 25; Berkeley: University of California Press, 1993), pp. 167–96; and Verna E.F. Harrison, 'Male and Female Cappadocian Theology', *JTS* 41 (October 1990), pp. 441–71.

45 See also discussion of Tertullian *On the Veiling of Virgins* in Mary Rose D'Angelo, 'Veils, Virgins, and the Tongues of Men and Angels: Women's Heads in Early Christianity', in Howard Eilberg-Schwartz and Wendy Doniger O'Flaherty (eds.), *Off with her Head! The Denial of Women's Identity in Myth, Religion, and Culture* (Berkeley: University of California Press, 1995), pp. 131–64, where precisely the issue between Tertullian and his opponents is whether virgins are women or not!

46 Dorothy Sly, *Philo's Perception of Women* (BJS, 209; Atlanta: Scholars Press, 1990), pp. 71–90. See, for example, the characteristically Philonic usage, 'When a man comes in contact with a woman, he marks [makes her marked; notice the semiotic terminology] the virgin as a woman. But when souls become divinely inspired, from being women they become virgins' (Philo, *Quaest. in Exod.* 2.3). Now obviously Philo's usage is influenced by general Greek diction in which παρθένος is often contrasted to γυνή, as for instance in Xenophon, *Anabasis* 3.2.25: γ. καὶ παρθέοι, cited in

base status that he accords women. Any parity between 'male and female' subsists only in the realm of spiritual and ecstatic experience or in the symbolic spiritual myth of the primal androgyne. What about Paul?

Paul never intended for a moment to promulgate a truly 'gnostic' doctrine of escape from the body and rejection of it with all of the social consequences which that would entail. This is proven by Gal. 5.13–17—'For you were called to freedom, brothers, only do not use your freedom as an opportunity for the flesh', that is, do not misuse your Christian freedom to allow yourself hedonistic pleasure. Nor did he ever imagine a social eradication of the hierarchical deployment of male and female bodies for married people.[47] While it was possible for him to conceive of a total erasure of the difference between Jew and Greek on the level of the body—all he had to do was to eliminate circumcision, and Jews were just like Greeks; female Jews and Greeks having always been bodily alike—he, like anyone else of his time, could not imagine that male and female bodies would be in any condition other than dominant and dominated when they were in sexual relationship with each other, that is when they were living 'according to the flesh'. It is sexuality, therefore, that produces gender, for Paul as for Philo and, we shall see, within crucially paradigmatic texts of the Christian cultural tradition.[48]

There is thus no contradiction between Galatians and Corinthians on the question

---

LSJ. This Greek usage alone is significant, because it already encodes the idea that virgins are not women. In Hebrew, the word אמה), which also means both 'woman' and 'wife', can never be contrasted with בתולה, 'virgin', and indeed אמה בתולה), 'a virgin woman', is a common expression. Finally, even in Greek, one can speak of a γυνὴ παρθένος, 'virgin woman', as in Hesiod, *Theogeny* 514. The structural opposition between virgin and woman in Philo is thus very significant and revealing even if he is only exploiting and developing a sort of quirk of Greek, *a fortiori* if, as I hold, he is doing more than that. The passage from *Joseph and Aseneth*, cited by MacDonald, 'Corinthian Veils', p. 289, also supports this reading, for Aseneth is told, 'Because today you are a pure virgin and your head is like that of a young man.' When she is no longer a virgin, only then does she become a woman.

47 Steven Knapp has made the excellent point that the social entailments of a statement like 'There is no male and female' could not 'leak from one social space to another' as it were, nor do Paul's formulations have only the consequences that he intended them to have. 'On the other hand, there is some reason to think that marriage in what Boyarin calls "the Christian West" has evolved into a more egalitarian institution than marriage in at least some other cultures; if so, how would one go about excluding the possibility that this tendency was encouraged by the Pauline ideal of spiritual androgyny?' (response at the Center for Hermeneutical Studies presentation). The answer is that I am not trying to exclude such a possibility at all. I am here speaking of Paul's intent, not as a hermeneutical or historical control on his text, but as a construct in its own right and a way to understand what seem otherwise to be contradictory moments in his discourse. Of course, this 'leaking' goes both ways, for ultimately if a certain vision of gender equality that we share owes its origins to perhaps unintended consequences of Paul's discourse, it is perhaps equally the case that the general male–female hierarchy of even celibate Christian communities owes its origin to his discourse on marriage!

48 Note that in Colossians, a text which if not Pauline is certainly from circles close to him, the *Haustafel* follows hard by 'There is no Greek and Jew, circumcised and uncircumcised, barbarian, Scythian, slave, free man, but Christ is all in all' (Col. 3.10ff.). Schüssler Fiorenza acutely remarks that 'Paul has taken great care to give a double command covering each case of active sexual interaction between husband and wife. However, it would be reaching too far to conclude from this that women and men shared an equality of role and a mutuality of relationship or equality of responsibility, freedom, and accountability in marriage. Paul stresses this interdependence only for *sexual* conjugal relationship and not for all marriage relationships' (*In Memory of Her*, p. 224).

of gender. As I have suggested, Paul's preaching always intended a moderate pneumaticism—but not more—a spirit–flesh hierarchy in which spirit was, of course higher than flesh but the flesh—that is, sexual *morality*, propriety and ethics—is not thereby canceled (as the end of Galatians makes entirely clear). Assuming that Paul's original teaching of the Corinthians was similar to the doctrine of the first four chapters of Galatians, it is easy to see where they could have gotten their ideas: no male or female indeed! Gal. 5.25–6.10 shows how clearly Paul anticipated this danger, which seems to have been realized in Corinth.[49] If Paul was not troubled in Galatians by the implications (misreadings from his point of view) of the quoted ancient formula, it was because the 'error' in the understanding of Christianity that concerned him there was in the direction of too much physicality; so the pneumatic, gnostic implications of 'There is no male and female' were not a stumbling block. In 1 Corinthians, however, where his problem is Christians who have gone too far (from Paul's ideological standpoint) in the pneumatic direction and where he must emphasize, therefore, the theology and ethics of the body, 'no male and female' would be exactly antithetical to the message that he wishes to promote. And so it is dropped, because the way that Paul perceived it is open to serious misunderstanding as being applicable to life 'according to the flesh', and not only 'according to the spirit'.[50] There is thus no contradiction in Paul's thought at all. He held out the possibility of a momentary ecstatic androgyny but only that; on the corporeal level of human society, sex/gender difference was maintained. Paul on gender, it seems to me, represents then neither the more misogynistic trend of such thoroughly Hellenized Jews like Philo nor a breakthrough in the politics of gender as some Christian feminists would have it. His picture of the relations of married people seems most like that of Palestinian Judaism in general, a moderate, 'benevolent' domination of women by men, or rather wives by husbands, one that neither permits cruelty to women nor entirely suppresses the subjectivity of women.[51]

---

49 One consequence of my interpretation is that we need not assume 'outside' influences for explaining Corinthian Christianity.

50 Cf. also Wire, *Women Prophets*, pp. 137–38.

51 For a fairly thoroughly account of this 'benevolent' gender hierarchy, see my *Carnal Israel*. Note that in that form of Judaism, for all its genuine discrimination against women, it is not enshrined as law that wives must be obedient to their husbands' rule. The verse, which in certain Christian circles is usually cited as requiring wifely obedience, Gen. 3.16, 'And your desire shall be toward him, but he will rule over you', is interpreted in Talmudic law as that husbands must be particularly attentive to their wives' unspoken need for sex. Philo the misogynist does read this verse as encoding female submissiveness, but even he explicitly remarks that this servitude is not to be imposed through violence; Judith Romney Wegner, 'Philo's Portrayal of Women—Hebraic or Hellenic?', in Levine (ed.), *'Women Like This'*, pp. 41–66. None of this remark should be taken, however, as a covering-over or apology for the pervasive disenfranchisement of women in that culture and particularly their near total confinement to the roles of wife and mother. If individual men were somewhat restrained in this culture from cruel physical domination of individual women, the culture as a whole certainly was psychologically cruel in restriction of possibilities for female freedom. Once more, as in the case of celibacy, women may not have experienced this as cruel. From our perspective, nevertheless, it is. I am not prepared, however, to dismiss their experience as 'false consciousness'. As Karen King has remarked, 'The difference between men's imaginings of women and women's lives is such that we can affirm that women have found spiritual fulfillment and salvation in the practice of Judaism and Christianity despite what the texts would lead us to think' (response at Center for Hermeneutical Studies).

Paul's Ethic of the Body

What then is Paul's ethic of the body, his picture of the relations between married men and women, and how does it compare with the detailed rules for married life promulgated by the rabbinic Judaism of the second and following centuries? Careful study of 1 Corinthians 7 supports the conclusion drawn by Peter J. Tomson that Paul's ethic ('*halakha*') of sexuality and marriage and 'Paul's conception of women were not much different from his (Jewish) contemporaries'. Thus the famous pronouncement of vv. 3–5: 'Let the husband give the wife what is due to her, and let the wife likewise also give her husband his due' is identical to the provision of the Mishna that provides the same penalties to the husband who refuses sex to his wife as to the wife who refuses sex to her husband.[52] Rabbinic literature preserves,

---

52 Tomson, *Paul and the Jewish Law*, p. 107. Since this is the passage to which Schüssler Fiorenza's student refers as where 'he so firmly emphasized the equality of woman and man in marriage', then his apparent contradiction can hardly be seen as 'reverting to rabbinic prejudices'. Moreover, such provision for mutual consideration of husband and wife for each other's needs is hardly incompatible with gender hierarchy. As I have argued with regard to rabbinic Judaism and suggest here with regard to Paul as well, the attitude of husband to wife was expected to be one of benevolent dictatorship, which precluded any cruelty or lack of consideration. What is remarkable about the Corinthians passage is rather its rhetoric, the fact that Paul addresses men and women equally, whereas the implicit subject of the Mishna is always a man who both owes obligations to his wife and to whom she is obligated. This is an important distinction; however, we should not make too much of it, for we do not know what rhetorical form a pharisaic/rabbinic address to the populace, whether oral or epistolary, would have taken. Paul's rhetorical stance is usually every bit as androcentric as that of the rabbis: 'It is well for a person not to touch a woman'—not 'It is well for persons not to have carnal knowledge of other persons.' Conzelmann's argument that the reason he used this form is 'due to the formulation of their question' represents wishful thinking (Conzelmann, *Corinthians*, p. 115). Much more convincing is Wire's interpretation: 'The immorality he exposes is male. The solution he calls for is marriage, and here, for the first time in the letter, he refers to women as an explicit group. Paul is now telling the offending men to marry. This cannot happen without the cooperation of others and the others cannot be male' (Wire, *Women Prophets*, p. 78). This would certainly explain well the shift from androcentric to 'egalitarian' rhetoric in 7.2–3. See also her remark that with regard to the virgin, 'Paul does not repeat the same words to the woman but continues to the man, "But if you marry, you do not sin, and if the virgin marries, she does not sin" (7.28). In this way Paul manages to incorporate the rhetoric of equality, although the woman is only talked about, not addressed' (Wire, *Women Prophets*, p. 87). Karen King has contributed some very wise remarks which I think worth quoting extensively: 'My own work has shown that quite often a pattern can be discerned in men's writings about women: that is, the way that men view their own bodies and sexuality is structurally analogous to how they view women. In a sense, men often use women (or the category of woman) to think with. Control of one's own sexuality and the use and control of women seem to be two sides of the same problem. For Philo, a man's relationship to himself is one of control pure and simple: the control of the body by the mind. This control constitutes good order and the best interests of the self. Analogously, women are to be under men's control. They are not rejected, but it is understood that the good of society and man's spiritual progress can only be achieved by the subordination of women, for their own good. Women out of control again and again constitute Philo's primary metaphor for spiritual and social disaster... For Paul, however, the relation to the self is less one of control and more one of reciprocity. He does not abandon the body, but expects to see it transformed. Sexuality, body, and spirit are more fully integrated in his conceptuality of self than with Philo. Yet as you note, there still exists a clear hierarchical relation between spirit and body. Celibacy models this relation most clearly. It is also the inscription on the body of his ideal of unity expressed in Gal. 3.28. The model for relations between men and women is similarly one of reciprocity, not equality, as is shown in

moreover, strong polemics against men who out of desire for holiness cease sleeping with their wives.[53] There is, however, one element in Paul's thought on sexuality that divides him sharply from the later rabbinic tradition and connects him rather with certain other trends in first-century Judaism, and that is the question of celibacy, which, I argue, is crucial to solving the problem that I am concerned about in this chapter.

Tomson has provided us with a suggestive analysis of the cultural context of Paul's discourse on celibacy in 1 Corinthians 7.[54] The apostle prefers celibacy personally, practically, and religiously, but he is quite unwilling to consider the married state forbidden, condemned, or even disparaged by God. Moreover, since, as stated in his ethic of the obligations of married people to each other, he is close if not identical to Jewish traditions of his day, those who are presently married must fulfill those obligations. Finally, insofar as Paul himself, and Jesus whom he follows here, seem to reflect a particular (attested) ancient Jewish tradition against divorce, those who are married ought not to divorce, and neither can they separate from their partners to whom they are obligated.[55] We can thus explain all of the details of 1 Corinthians 7 on the basis of the assumption that Paul maintains a two-tiered system of thought regarding sexuality: celibacy as the higher state, but marriage as a fully honorable condition for the believing Christian as well.[56] This is by and large identical to actually attested forms of Palestinian Judaism and not very far from Philo either. Even Paul, whose hostility toward the body was so much less extreme, manifests quite a cold and ambivalent feeling about married sex, regarding it primarily as a defense against lust and fornication. As Peter Brown has written:

---

1 Corinthians 7 and 11' (response at Center for Hermeneutical Studies). I would only wish to emphasize, following Wire and the logic of King's own statement, that this reciprocity of male and female is hierarchical precisely in the way that spirit and flesh are for Paul, thus further confirming King's approach.

53 See Daniel Boyarin, 'Internal Opposition in Talmudic Literature: The Case of the Married Monk', *Representations* 36 (1991), pp. 87–113, for extended discussion and critique of rabbinic culture on this issue.

54 Tomson, *Paul and the Jewish Law*, pp. 105–108.

55 See Tomson, *Paul and the Jewish Law*, p. 111, for demonstration that there was such a trend of thought in one form of Palestinian Judaism, and that the prohibition was derived from Gen. 1.27!— just as Jesus had done. In addition to this, for Paul at any rate there is the general apocalyptic sense that everything should remain just as it is until the imminent Parousia. For this interpretation, see Vincent L. Wimbush, *Paul the Worldly Ascetic: Response to the World and Self-Understanding According to 1 Corinthians 7* (Macon, GA: Mercer University Press, 1987).

56 This interpretation carries with it the consequence that certain Orthodox Fathers of the church best represent the 'authentic' Pauline tradition—for instance, Clement of Alexandria, whose positive view of marriage is well known, but also such figures as Gregory Nazianzen, who writes, 'I will join you in wedlock. I will dress the bride. We do not dishonor marriage, because we give a higher honor to virginity' (quoted in David Carlton Ford, 'Misogynist or Advocate?: St John Chrysostom and his Views on Women' [PhD diss., Drew University, 1989], p. 25). I am also quite convinced by Ford's description of the later John Chrysostom's ideology of sexuality that his mature view was not very different from that of the rabbis (Ford, 'Misogynist or Advocate?', p. 49 and *passim*), but once again it is important to note that with all that, Chrysostom, himself, was celibate, and as Ford notes, 'he continued all his life to consider a life of virginity in dedication to God as an even higher calling' (p. 73). Others of the Cappadocian Fathers, including Gregory of Nyssa, seem also to reflect such positions. See Harrison, 'Male and Female'.

What was notably lacking, in Paul's letter, was the warm faith shown by contemporary pagans and Jews that the sexual urge, although disorderly, was capable of socialization and of ordered, even warm, expression with marriage. The dangers of *porneia*, of potential immorality brought about by sexual frustration, were allowed to hold the center of the stage. By this essentially negative, even alarmist, strategy, Paul left a fatal legacy to future ages. An argument against abandoning sexual intercourse within marriage and in favor of allowing the younger generation to continue to have children slid imperceptibly into an attitude that viewed marriage itself as not more than a defense against desire. In the future, a sense of the presence of 'Satan', in the form of a constant and ill-defined risk of lust, lay like a heavy shadow in the corner of every Christian church.[57]

Where I disagree with Brown is when he says, 'At the time, however, fornication and its avoidance did not preoccupy Paul greatly. He was concerned to emphasize, rather, the continuing validity of all social bonds. The structure of the household as a whole was at stake. This included the institution of domestic slavery. On this, Paul was adamant: slaves, like wives, must remain in their place.'[58] On my reading, the situation is exactly opposite. Paul called for freedom and the breaking down of all social bonds. Realizing, however, the unrealizability of that goal—for slaves because of the social unrest and suppression of Christianity that would result, for wives because of πορνεία—Paul settled for something else, something less than his vision called for, and thus the continuation of the domestic slavery of marriage for those not called to the celibate life. Rabbinic Judaism ultimately went in another direction entirely, increasingly rejecting not only the preferability of celibacy but ultimately even its permissibility. With the rejection, the one avenue of escape into autonomy for women was closed but a much richer and warmer appreciation of sexuality developed.[59]

This interpretation of Paul is coherent with the interpretation of his anthropology in general offered above. If celibacy corresponds to 'the spirit' and marriage to 'the flesh', then the axiological relationship between these two states fits perfectly, for, as I have argued above, the flesh, while lower than the spirit in Paul's thought, is by no means rejected or despised by him. The analogy with celibacy versus marriage is exact. Marriage is a lower state than celibacy—he who marries a virgin does well, and he who does not marry does better (v. 38)—but not by any means forbidden or despised.[60] However, and this is the crux, any possibility of an eradication of male and female and the corresponding social hierarchy is only possible on the level of the spirit, either in ecstasy at baptism or perhaps permanently for the celibate. In other words, I surmise that although Paul does not *cite* the myth of the primal androgyne, his gender discourse seems just as likely to be an outgrowth of that ideological

---

57 Peter Brown, *The Body and Society: Men, Women, and Sexual Renunciation in Early Christianity* (Lectures on the History of Religion; NS, 13; New York: Columbia University Press, 1988), p. 55.
58 Brown, *Body and Society*, p. 55.
59 Boyarin, *Carnal Israel*, is entirely devoted to this rejection and its cultural consequences, both promising and disturbing.
60 See Wire, *Women Prophets*, p. 88, for an excellent discussion of the interpretive problems of this verse, but the point being made here is not affected. Any way you cut it, the ratio between celibacy and marriage here is the same.

structure as is that of Philo—no male and female in the spirit, but in the flesh, yes indeed.[61]

'The Man Is the Head of the Woman'

The crucial text for strengthening this interpretation, or at least for rendering it plausible, is arguably 1 Cor. 11.1–16—'in the same letter he raged on and on about hairstyles in the assembly'.[62] In this passage, on my reading, Paul makes practically explicit the ratio between the politics of the spirit and the politics of the body. The crucial verses are 3, 7–9, and 11–12:

> [3] I would have you know, however, that every man's head is Christ, but a woman's head is the man, and Christ's head is God ... [7] For a man must not veil his head, since he is the image and reflection of God, [8] but a woman is the reflection of man. For man did not originate from woman, but woman from man. [9] Neither was man created for woman's sake, but woman for man's ... [11] Of course, in the Lord there is neither woman without man nor man without woman. [12] For just as woman originated from man, so, too, man exists through woman. But everything comes from God.

These verses have been much discussed from many points of view. It is far beyond the scope of the present paper to analyse either the theological or hermeneutic issues involved in the text, but, however we interpret them, it is clear that Paul explicitly thematizes two (partially opposed) forms of conceptualizing gender, one in which there is an explicit hierarchy and one in which there is none.[63] Paul himself marks this difference (the gap between the hierarchy of vv. 7–9 and the 'there is neither woman without man nor man without woman' of v. 11) as the situation of 'in the Lord' (ἐν κυρίῳ). I do not think it is going too far—nor is it unprecedented in

---

61 1 Cor. 6.16–17 is instructive here as well: 'Don't you know the one who is joined to the prostitute is one body with her, since it says, "the two will become one flesh", whereas one joined to the Lord is one spirit with him!' Now it would seem that the antithesis to one joined to the prostitute would be one joined to his lawful wife, as the cited verse from Genesis 2 would suggest as well. The fact that Paul refers rather to the spiritual joining with Christ leads strongly in the direction I am putting forth, that is of an ideal spiritual state in which sexuality is destroyed, in Paul as in Philo. In that state, I am suggesting, 'there is no male and female'. See also Wire, *Women Prophets*, pp. 77–78, and especially, 'Paul's words would be most congenial to women who have used their freedom to live separately from men, although the next chapter shows that he has no intention of ruling out sexual union for those in union with Christ. But his use of the Genesis quotation, "the two will become one flesh", to build the stark antithesis of two kinds of union appeals to those whose union with Christ replaces sexual union.'

62 I find that Wire's interpretation of this section (*Women Prophets*, pp. 116–20) is the only weak part of her argument. I think, moreover, that the reconstruction offered here strengthens her overall reading considerably.

63 Once again, let me make clear that even the explicit hierarchy which these verses reify does not necessarily authorize a tyranny of men over women, certainly not a vicious one. Κεφαλή may or may not mean 'ruler', but there can be no doubt that structurally there *is* here a hierarchical series of God > Christ > man > woman, whatever the value placed on that hierarchy. I thus find myself here, as in other respects, in complete agreement with Troels Engberg-Pedersen, '1 Corinthians 11.16 and the Character of Pauline Exhortation', *JBL* 110 (1992), pp. 679–89 (681, n. 9). See also Joseph Fitzmyer, 'Another Look at ΚΕΦΑΛΗ in 1 Corinthians 11.3', *NTS* 35 (1989), pp. 503–11, for a strong argument that this term *does* mean 'one having authority' in Jewish *koine*.

Pauline interpretation—to connect this 'in the Lord' with the 'in Christ' of Gal. 3.28 and read them both as a representation of an androgyny that exists on the level of the spirit, however much hierarchy subsists and needs to subsist in the flesh, in the life of society even in Christian communities.[64] These two levels might well correspond, indeed, to the two myths of the origins of the sexes as found in Genesis 1 and 2. The no-male-or-female that is 'in the Lord' or 'in Christ' would represent the androgyne of ch. 1, understood, as in Philo, as neither male nor female, while 'since he is the image and reflection of God, but a woman from man', which Paul cites here, would be a reference to the story as found in ch. 2.[65] 'In the Lord' might even be seen then as an allusion to 'in the image of God', and the latter human ch. 2 would be 'in the flesh' in contrast. This perhaps speculative interpretation is dramatically strengthened if Josef Kürzinger's suggestion is accepted that v. 11 means 'In the Lord woman is not different from man nor man from woman'.[66] Ultimately, as Karen King suggests, the two myths of gender 'are quite compatible in that both imagine the ideal to be a unitary self, whether male or androgynous, whose nature is grounded in an ontology of transcendence and an epistemology of origins'.[67]

Now, on the one hand, these verses demonstrate that Paul had not changed his mind or backslid from Galatians; they also explain, given the context of the Corinthian correspondence, why he chose to omit 'There is no male and female' in the Corinthian version of the baptism.[68] I suggest, therefore, that for Paul just as much as for the Corinthians, a state of androgyny, a cancellation of gender and sexuality, would have been the ideal. The difference between them lies in the appli-

64 Cf. Conzelmann, *Corinthians*, p. 185, n. 41: 'We must presume that these tendencies are bound up with enthusiasm: the Spirit makes all alike. Female charismatics can begin by drawing conclusions from this for their appearance. Paul would then be reminding them that the equality is equality "in Christ" and that consequently women remain women. Their personality does not disappear, as in enthusiasm'; and again, 'One must not read v. 11 in the first instance in isolation, without the expression ἐν κυρίῳ, "in the Lord". It maintains the central Pauline idea that the cancellation of distinctions has its specific place, that they are canceled "in the Lord", not "in us" ' (p. 190)—or, as I would put it, 'in the spirit', not 'in the flesh'. See also Madeleine Boucher, 'Some Unexplored Parallels to 1 Cor. 11.11–12 and Gal. 3.28: The New Testament on the Role of Women', *CBQ* 31 (1969), pp. 50–58, on these two verses. We find 'in the Lord' as the opposite of 'in the flesh', in Phlm. 16, and synonymous parallelism with 'in Christ' in Phlm. 20. And note also that in 2 Cor. 11.17–18 we find κατὰ κύριον in apparent opposition to κατὰ σάρκα. Note that Wire's reading of the passage does not take sufficient account of the crucial 'in the Lord' (*Women Prophets*, p. 128). On the other hand, in her response to this paper when it was presented at the Center for Hermeneutical Studies, she raised the substantial objection to my interpretation that v. 12 seems certainly to be speaking of birth!

65 This interpretation was suggested to me by Karen King. Antoinette Wire has proposed an entirely different reconstruction of the relation of the baptismal formula to Genesis, suggesting that it does not represent a return at all but a new creation which negates the original one. She accordingly disagrees with the Meeks–MacDonald interpretation. My construction of Paul is not crucially dependent on either one of these historical reconstructions being 'correct', although admittedly it is much neater following MacDonald.

66 Josef Kürzinger, 'Frau und Mann nach 1 Kor. 11.11f', *BZ* 22 (1978), pp. 270–75. I learned of this important paper from the citation in Schüssler Fiorenza, *In Memory of Her*, p. 229.

67 From her response at the Center for Hermeneutical Studies.

68 Contrast Hans Dieter Betz, *Galatians: A Commentary on Paul's Letter to the Church in Galatia* (Hermeneia; Philadelphia: Fortress Press, 1979), p. 200.

cation of the principle.[69] The Corinthians believe that they have already achieved a state of perfection which permits the acting out of the cancellation of gender difference, whereas Paul is skeptical of their achievements (cf. 4.8). This does not, however, imply that for Paul the ideal androgyny has no social consequences.

There are in fact three (not mutually exclusive) options for a social enactment of the myth of the primal androgyne: some gnostics (and perhaps the Corinthians) seem to have held that having once attained the spirit humans transcended gender entirely and for ever, whether celibacy or libertinage.[70] Philo, on the other hand, restricts such transcending redemption from gender to celibates and then only to special ritualized moments of ecstasy. Paul's strictures against women with short hair and the speaking out of woman prophets (14.37–38)—if the latter is genuinely Pauline— seem to suggest a third option: for all (not only celibates) there is no male and female, but only momentarily in the ritualized ecstasy of baptism. It is only then, in this life, that people attain the status of life in the spirit, in Christ or in the Lord in which there is no male and female. I am thus inclined to agree with Tertullian's view that the notion of Paul giving celibate women the power to teach, preach, and baptize—that is, functional, social equivalence to men—seems hard to credit.[71] On the other hand, it may not be gainsaid that he had women associates in his ministry, nor that he implied that virgins could achieve spiritual states unavailable to the married (7.32–35). All three of these possibilities are equally dependent, however, on a notion that gender difference only exists at one ontological level, the outer or physical, the corporeal, but that at the level of true existence, the spiritual, there is no gender, that is no dualism. Much of the immediate post-Pauline tradition seems to have adopted a version of the first option—namely that celibate women *could*

69 Compare MacDonald, 'Corinthian Veils', p. 286, and esp. p. 290, who sees a much more fundamental difference between Paul and the Corinthians than I do. Note that my interpretation of 'in the Lord' is diametrically opposed to his (p. 291). As in many cases in ch. 7 as well, as Wire points out, Paul grants a point in principle and disagrees in practice. Note, moreover, that the cases are exactly parallel.

70 For the latter, see Meeks, 'Image of the Androgyne', pp. 191, 199; and Wire's characteristically shrewd remarks: 'On the contrary, [the Corinthians] may claim in their prayer and prophecy to mediate between God and humanity so that through the spirit the perishable does inherit imperishability and the primal dissociation is breached' (*Women Prophets*, p. 23). This breaching of the dissociation between spirit and flesh, raising of flesh to the status of spirit, would be that which transcends gender as well and explains much of the Corinthians' behavior, including paradoxically both their tendencies toward celibacy and libertinage as well as the Corinthian women's apparent adoption of male styles of headdress (Meeks, 'Image of the Androgyne', p. 202; MacDonald, 'Corinthian Veils'). It is important to point out that, although less prominently, celibate men were also apparently sometimes imagined as androgynous. Verna Harrison has been doing very important work on this issue. It is tempting to speculate that Origen's self-castration fits into this paradigm, as well; a speculation that can take place, incidentally, whether or not it actually happened. See on this point also the important and stimulating remarks in Brown, *Body and Society*, p. 169. This pull to celibacy (and androgyny) for men is also a function of being freed from the constraints of the 'world and the flesh', correspondingly weaker insofar as those constraints were much less burdensome for men than for women to start with. Note that the priests of Agdistis used to emasculate themselves (Meeks, 'Image of the Androgyne', p. 169). Schüssler Fiorenza's reference to this cult in apparent support of her claim that Gal. 3.28 'does not express ... "gnosticizing" devaluation of procreative capacities' seems somewhat inapposite in this light (*In Memory of Her*, p. 213).

71 Tertullian, *De baptismo* 17.4–5.

attain a permanent state of the erasure of gender, a development which has had profound effects on the later discourse of gender in European culture.

Thecla and Perpetua: or, How Women Can Become Men

The 'myth of the primal androgyne'—that is, an anthropology whereby souls are ungendered and only the fallen body is divided into sexes—is thus a dominant structuring metaphor of gender for the early church and for the Christian West as a whole. There are many different versions of the application of this myth. In some versions of early Christianity, all Christians *must* remain celibate, and in that spiritual existence a total eradication of gender difference becomes imaginable.[72] In some communities such celibate men and women lived together in the same dwellings, arousing the suspicion/calumny of their pagan neighbors and the ire of more establishment Christian leaders. In other communities, more in tune with the Pauline and deutero-Pauline message, there was a two-tiered society: the celibate in which some form of gender parity obtained and the married for which the hierarchical *Haustafeln* were the definitive ethic. This could be accompanied by more or less approbation of the married state, more or less privilege for virginity/celibacy over marriage. In every case, however, virginity was privileged to greater or lesser extent over the sexual life, and, more to the point of the present argument, it was only in virginity, that is only in a social acting out of a disembodied spiritual existence, that gender parity ever existed.[73] Female humans could escape being 'women' by opting out of sexual intercourse. Just as in Philo, virgins were not women but androgynes, a representation, in the appearance of flesh, of the purely spiritual non-gendered, pre-social essence of human being.[74] For all these forms of Christianity, as for Hellenistic Judaism, this dualism is the base of the anthropology: equality in the spirit, hierarchy in the flesh. As a second-century follower of Paul, Clement of Alexandria, expressed it, 'As then there is sameness (with men and women) with respect to the soul, she will attain to the same virtue; but as there is difference with respect to the peculiar construction of the body, she is destined for child-bearing and house-keeping.'[75] As this quotation suggests and Christian practice enacts, this version of primal androgyny provided two elements in the gender politics of the early church. On the one hand it provided an image or

---

72 The classic study of this phenomenon is still Arthur Vööbus, *Celibacy: A Requirement for Admission to Baptism in the Early Church* (Stockholm: Estonian Theological Society in Exile, 1951); and see the excellent chapter in Brown, *Body and Society*, pp. 83–103.

73 Elizabeth Clark, 'Ascetic Renunciation and Feminine Advancement: A Paradox of Late Ancient Christianity', in *eadem* (ed.), *Ascetic Piety and Women's Faith: Essays in Late Ancient Christianity* (Studies in Women and Religion, 3; Lewiston, NY: Mellen Press, 1986), pp. 175–208.

74 See the important passage in the *Acts of Andrew*, cited by Aspegren, *Male Woman*, p. 126, in which the apocryphal apostle begs Maximilla to remain steadfast in her decision to cease having sexual intercourse with her husband in the following terms, 'I beg you, then, O wise man (ὁ φρόνιμος ἀνήρ), that your noble mind continue steadfast; I beg you, O invisible mind, that you may be preserved yourself.' Here it is absolutely and explicitly clear that through celibacy the female ceases to be a woman. The passage could practically appear in Philo.

75 Clement of Alexandria, in Alexander Roberts and James Donaldson (eds.), *The Fathers of the Second Century* (Grand Rapids: Eerdmans, 1989), p. 20.

vision of a spiritual equality for all women—which did not, however, have social consequences for the married;[76] on the other hand, it provided for a real autonomy and social parity for celibate women, for those who rejected 'the peculiar construction of the body', together with its pleasures and satisfactions.[77] As Clement avers in another place, 'For souls themselves by themselves are equal. Souls are neither male nor female when they no longer marry nor are given in marriage.'[78]

Much of the paradigmatic literature of early Christianity involves this representation of gender and its possibilities. Elizabeth Castelli has described the situation with regard to one of the earliest and most explicit texts of this type, the *Gospel of Thomas*:

> The double insistence attributed to Jesus in the *Gospel of Thomas* saying—that Mary should remain among the disciples at the same time as she must be made male—points to the paradoxical ideological conditions that helped to shape the lives of early Christian women. At once they are to have access to holiness, while they also can do so only through the manipulation of conventional gender categories.[79]

As I have suggested above, however, these were not only the paradoxical ideological conditions of Christianity but similar indeed to paradoxes of contemporary Judaism as well. The Therapeutrae also have access to the same spirituality as their male counterparts—for all of them, however, at the expense of conventional gender categories.[80] One of the most striking representations of such manipulation of gender is the story of the martyr Perpetua, brilliantly analyzed by Castelli.[81] This story enacts both sorts of gender erasure. On the social level, the marks of Perpetua's gendered status are indicated by her leaving of her family, renunciation of her husband (who is not even mentioned), and eventual giving up of her baby, together with a miraculous drying up of the milk in her breasts, that is a sort of symbolic restoration of virginity. The crux of the story, however, and of Castelli's argument, is that in

76 See, however, n. 47 above.

77 Interestingly enough, there is a unique historical case that suggests that this structure remained dormant even in Judaism as a marginal structural possibility. I refer to the one case of a postbiblical Jewish woman who functioned as an independent religious authority on the same level as men, the famous nineteenth-century 'Maid of Ludmir', and precisely the same mechanism operates: autonomy and religious leadership for a woman as an equal to men but only because she is celibate and therefore *not a woman*. Indeed, as soon as she engaged in marriage, at the age of 40, at the urging of male religious authorities—and a celibate marriage at that—her religious power disappeared, *because she had revealed that she really was a woman, and not man in a woman's body*, nor an asexual androgyne. See Ada Rapoport-Alpert, 'On Women in Hasidism', in A. Rapoport-Alpert and Steven J. Zipperstein (eds.), *Jewish History: Essays in Honour of Chimen Abramsky* (London: P. Halban, 1988), pp. 495–525.

78 Clement, *Strom.* 6.12.100, quoted in MacDonald, 'Corinthian Veils', p. 284.

79 Castelli, ' "I Will Make Mary Male" ', p. 33. Incidentally, Simon Peter's declaration in this text that women do not deserve life should be contrasted to the explicit statement in the Talmud that women must pray just as men do, 'because do not women require life (just like men)?'; *Kidd.* 34b.

80 This also suggests that it is not so obvious that the only direction of such gender blending or bending was from female to male, even for a misogynist like Philo, *a fortiori* for less misogynist Jews and Christians, even though it is not to be denied, of course, that the usual image was of a female becoming male.

81 Castelli, ' "I Will Make Mary Male" '. This story, as well as that of Thecla, has, of course, been discussed by myriad critics and commentators.

Perpetua's dream in which she becomes a man and defeats her opponent in the gladiatorial ring, her victory is, in fact paradoxically, a representation of her death as a martyr, while defeat for her would have meant giving in to her father, renouncing her Christianity, and continuing to live.[82] Life in the spirit represents death in the body and the converse, and the erasure of conventional gender is thus also an event in the spirit. This is, then, a drastic version of Paul's eradication of gender in Christ.

The best representation of an androgynous status for Christian celibate women in late antiquity is, however, the story of Thecla, also treated by Castelli. This apocryphal female companion to Paul refuses to marry, cuts her hair short like that of a man, dresses in a man's clothing, and accompanies Paul on his apostolic missions. Castelli notes with regard to this and similar stories:

> It is striking that in all of these narratives, the women who perform these outward gestures of stretching dominant cultural expectations related to gender are also embracing a form of piety (sexual renunciation and virginity) which resists dominant cultural expectations vis-à-vis social roles.[83]

If my reading of Philo and Paul and of the general situation is compelling, however, this connection is not so much striking as absolutely necessary. Insofar as the myth of the primal, spiritual androgyne is the vital force for all of these representations, androgynous status is always dependent on a notion of a universal spiritual self that is above the differences of the body, and its attainment entails *necessarily* one or another (or more than one as in the case of Perpetua) of the practices of renouncing the body: either ecstasy or virginity or physical death.[84] We thus see that from Philo and Paul through late antiquity gender parity is founded on a dualist metaphysics and anthropology in which freedom and equality are for pre-gendered, pre-social, disembodied souls and predicated on a devaluing and disavowing of the body, usually, but not necessarily, combined with a representation of the body itself as female.[85] On my reading, then, Christian imaginings of gender bending/blending do not really comprehend a 'destabilization of gender identity'. Rather, insofar as they are completely immured in the dualism of the flesh and the spirit, they represent no change whatever in the status of gender.[86] All of these texts are mythic or ritual enactments of the 'myth of the primal androgyne', and, as such, simply reinstate the metaphysics of substance, the split between Universal Mind and Disavowed Body.

82 Castelli, ' "I Will Make Mary Male" ', p. 42.
83 Castelli, ' "I Will Make Mary Male" ', p. 44.
84 In this light, the fact that the *Gospel of Thomas* most likely originates in the most rigidly celibate of all early 'Orthodox' churches, the Syrian church, takes on particular significance. See Meeks, 'Image of the Androgyne', p. 194. See also C.C. Richardson, *The Gospel of Thomas: Gnostic or Encratite?* (Rome: [publisher unknown], 1973).
85 According to Stevan Davies, *The Revolt of the Widows: The Social World of the Apocryphal Acts* (Carbondale, IL: Southern Illinois University Press, 1980), these texts were produced by women very similar in social status to the 'virgins' of Philo, older women who were either unmarried or who had left their husbands. Even Dennis Ronald MacDonald, 'The Role of Women in the Production of the Apocryphal Acts of the Apostles', *Iliff Review of Theology* 40 (1984), pp. 21–38, who disagrees with Davies, still agrees that the oral sources of these texts were produced among celibate women.
86 See also MacDonald, 'Corinthian Veils', p. 285.

It is striking how closely they match Butler's description of Beauvoir's critique of the 'very disembodiment of the abstract masculine epistemological subject':

> That subject is abstract to the extent that it disavows its socially marked embodiment and, further, projects that disavowed and disparaged embodiment on to the feminine sphere, effectively renaming the body as female. This association of the body with the female works along magical relations of reciprocity whereby the female sex becomes restricted to its body, and the male body, fully disavowed, becomes, paradoxically, the incorporeal instrument of an ostensibly radical freedom.

This trap is, I claim, based in the material conditions of heterosexual marriage, if not—even more depressingly—in the material conditions of heterosexuality itself, and to the extent that Paul was unwilling to disallow or disparage marriage, as some of his more radical followers were to do, precisely to that extent something like the pronouncements of 1 Corinthians 11 and the *Haustafeln* were almost a necessary superstructure. Rather than 'resting on the assumed natural differences between the sexes institutionalized in patriarchal marriage', as Schüssler Fiorenza puts it, I would suggest that patriarchal marriage—that is, at least until now, marriage—*produces* such naturalized gender differences.[87] To be sure, Christian women had possibilities for living lives of much greater autonomy and creativity than their rabbinic Jewish sisters, but always on the stringent condition and heavy price of sexual renunciation.[88] Let me make myself absolutely clear: I am not allying myself with Christian conservatives who argue that Paul's pronouncement in Gal. 3.28 did not have social meaning. Paul's entire gospel is a stirring call to human freedom and universal autonomy. I think that, within the limitations of *Realpolitik*, he would have wanted all slaves freed, and he certainly passionately desired the erasure of the boundary between Greek and Jew.[89] In arguing that 'no male and female' did not and could not mean a fundamental change in the status of wives, I am not arguing that he was inconsistent (nor that I am being inconsistent myself) in the name of the preservation of male privilege, but rather I am suggesting that *wives are/were slaves*, and their liberation would have meant an end to marriage.[90] Jews and Greeks need ultimately to cease being Jews and Greeks; slaves need to cease ultimately to be slaves; and the equivalent is that husbands and wives need ultimately to cease being husbands and wives—but Paul feels that the last is unrealistic for most people, even Christians:

87 Schüssler Fiorenza, *In Memory of Her*, p. 207.

88 Once more, I emphasize that neither they nor the Jewish women may have experienced their lives the way we predict owing to our own cultural prejudices.

89 Schüssler Fiorenza, *In Memory of Her*, p. 210. Incidentally, Schüssler Fiorenza errs when she writes there that in rabbinic Judaism, 'even the full proselyte could not achieve the status of the male Israelite'. This does not affect, however, her larger claim that the constitution of the Christian community through baptism was intended to be something entirely different from the solidarities of physical kinship that characterized Judaism. This fundamental change in the notion of kinship did not produce, however, only and always welcome socio-cultural effects, as Jews and Native Americans (among others) know only too well. In my forthcoming book on Paul, from which this chapter is taken, I explore further just these political consequences.

90 This should not be taken as a totalizing statement denying wives (either in Christianity or in rabbinic Judaism) all freedom and subjectivity, indeed, it is not inconsistent with the notion that married women could have positions of at least partial leadership in the Pauline churches (cf. Schüssler Fiorenza, *In Memory of Her*, pp. 232–33).

because of immorality, let each man have his own wife and let each woman have her own husband (7.2).[91] When Paul says, 'the form of this world is passing away' (7.31), it seems to me that he is doing two things. On the one hand, he is emphasizing why it is not necessary to engage in radical, immediate social change, in order to achieve the genuine radical reformation of society that he calls for, and, second, he is explaining why having children and families is no longer important. Procreation has no significance for Paul at all. From Paul on through late antiquity, the call to

---

91 In this sense, then, Paul essentially agrees with the Corinthians as to the way to gender equality (cf. Wire, *Women Prophets*, p. 65 and esp. p. 90), but Paul sees what he takes to be negative social and moral effects of the wrong people attempting to achieve such status. We need not necessarily accept as 'historically' accurate Paul's evaluation of the situation. Wire has argued that Paul's position involved a great deal of oppression of the Corinthian women: 'Apparently Paul sets out to persuade women to give up what they have gained through sexual abstinence in order that the community and Christ himself may be saved from immorality' (p. 79). I think that Wire's rereading of 1 Corinthians 6 and 7 is of great significance for our *evaluation* of Paul here, although for reasons I shall immediately lay out, not for our *interpretation*. By a very careful and close reading Wire has arrived at the following conclusions vis-à-vis this section of his text: Paul is primarily concerned with male immorality, and his injunctions to marry fall on women to provide legitimate sexual outlets for men, so that they will not fall into πορνεία. This includes those Corinthian women who have already achieved a high degree of spiritual fulfillment, who are now commanded to renounce this achievement for the sake of providing sexual service to men not called to the celibate life. Paul's discourse is, on this reading, considerably more compromised ethically than I have allowed above in that its hierarchical imbalance falls on all women, including those successfully called to the celibate life. The consequence of Wire's brilliant reconstruction is that 'Paul's agreement with the Corinthians concerning gender equality on principle is strictly a rhetorical ploy if he is, as you say, ruled by the "negative social and moral effects of the wrong people attempting to achieve such status"' (response at the Center for Hermeneutical Studies). It is here, however, that I wish to introduce a nuance, which, if it be apologetic, at least is not compromised by being apology for my own religious tradition, although there may be another factor working here: as a male Jew, all too aware of the gap between my own aspirations toward feminism and the shortcomings of my practice, I may be drawn to forgiving perceived—or constructed—analogous failures on the part of a forefather of sorts. Nevertheless, even given all the details of Wire's construction of the Corinthian women prophets and Paul's repressive reaction to them, I think we do not need to conclude that his agreement with them in principle is 'strictly a rhetorical ploy' but rather I think a genuine and failed vision. Whether or not the baptismal formula in Gal. 3.28 is, as I suppose, a reflection of the primal androgyne interpretation of Gen. 1.28, or whether it reflects a radical rewriting of Genesis in the new creation of Christ as Wire proposes, I think that it genuinely holds out the vision of social equality for all human beings. Paul, however, simply cannot think himself to an adequate social arrangement with equality for the sexes other than chastity, which for one reason or another he considers to be an unworkable solution at the present time. And yes, I agree, it may very well be that it is unworkable because of *male* sexual need in his view, and women may be the servants, for him, of that need; nevertheless I think that he as well as the Corinthians, as opposed to rabbinic Judaism, envisions an end to gender hierarchy. In any case, if, on the one hand, Wire points to the devastating history of male oppression of women in the name of Paul, one can also cite at least a nascent discourse and real history of chastity as female autonomy also carried out in his name in what is, after all, the *Acts of Paul and Thecla*, for notable example. Similarly—with regard to the parallel issue of slavery—Philemon has been used (maybe misused) as a text in the service of slavery. It is just as true, however, that Gal. 3.28 has been mobilized in anti-slavery discourses. The failure of consistency here does not involve Paul's aspirations but his achievements. Others who come after may indeed be able to put into practice that which in Paul is fraught with contradiction. I think that the ultimate elimination of slavery in all of the Christian world is an eloquent case in point, although it took nearly two thousand years for Paul's vision to be realized here.

celibacy is a call to freedom (7.32–34). Virgins are not 'women'. Rabbinic Judaism, which rejected such dualism and thus celibacy entirely, strongly valorized the body and sexuality but cut off nearly all options for women's lives other than maternity, trapping all women in the temperate and patronizing slavery of wifehood. This should not be read, however, as in any sense a condemnation of Christianity, nor, for that matter, of rabbinic Judaism, for, I suspect, all it means is that people in late antiquity had not thought their way out of a dilemma that catches us on its horns even now—in *very* late antiquity.

Sexy Stoics and the Rereading of Romans 1.18–2.16*

Diana Swancutt

In his nineteenth *Letter of the Parasites*, the Greek rhetorician Alciphron (150–200? CE) parodied philosophers who attended a friend's birthday party.[1] Even though professional entertainers and Athens's most important citizens came to the bash, the sages were its real stars. Including a Peripatetic, an Epicurean, a Pythagorean, a Cynic, and a Stoic named Eteocles, these 'wise men' looked so ridiculous and behaved so foolishly that even the hired clowns felt upstaged. For Alciphron, the sages' appearance and actions were notable because each philosopher possessed the characteristic foibles of his school. For example, 'our friend Eteocles the Stoic' Alciphron snidely portrayed as 'the dirty man (ῥυπαρός) with an unkempt head, the codger with a brow more wrinkled than his leather purse'.[2] He depicted their antics in similarly biting detail:

> ... the philosophers, as the dinner progressed and the loving cup swept constantly 'round, exhibited, each in turn, his own brand of tricks. Because of old age and a full stomach, Eteocles the Stoic stretched out and snored; and the Pythagorean, breaking his silence, hummed some of the *Golden Verses* to a musical tune. The excellent Themistagoras, since as a Peripatetic he defined happiness in terms of external goods as well as soul and body, demanded more cakes and an abundant variety of fine cuisine. Zenocrates the Epicurean embraced the harp girl, giving her languishing looks from half-closed eyes, and saying this was the 'tranquility of the flesh' and the 'consolation of pleasure'. The Cynic ... with Cynic indifference, relieved himself, loosening his robe and letting it drag on the floor; then he was ready to screw Doris, the singing girl, in full view of everyone, saying that nature is the prime cause of reproduction.[3]

Alciphron's caricatures are typical of criticisms comic poets, satirists, biographers, and moralists unleashed on philosophers from classical Greece through the waning years of the Roman Empire. Deploying familiar stereotypes (τόποι) like the seedy Stoic, hedonistic Epicurean, and urinating Cynic, they parodied philosophers' habits and pilloried them for their hypocrisies. In Lucian's (120–190 CE) *Vitarum auctio*, for example, Hermes sells individual philosophies to bidders (representing both the comedy's characters and its audience) who determine their worth based on the

---

* For their insights, questions, and criticisms of earlier drafts of this paper, I thank Harold Attridge, David Bartlett, Bart Ehrman, Peter Hawkins, Wayne Meeks, Robert Wilson, and, most especially, Dale Martin.

1 The dating of the otherwise unknown Alciphron depends on the assumption that he knew the work of Lucian, Menander, and other writers of New Comedy.

2 On dirtiness as a dig at Stoics, see F.D. Caizzi, 'The Porch and the Garden: Early Hellenistic Images of the Philosophical Life', in A.W. Bulloch, *et al.* (eds), *Images and Ideologies: Self Definition in the Hellenistic World* (Berkeley: University of California Press, 1993), pp. 303–29. Seneca's arguments against Cynic-inspired dirtiness are in his *Ep. Mor.* 5.1–3.

3 *Ep. Par.* 19[3.55].1–9; see Caizzi, 'The Porch', pp. 303–304.

consistency—or the absence of it—among sages' appearance, behavior, and beliefs. The moralist Dio Chrysostom (40–120 CE) also complained that 'people cannot help mocking and insulting someone in a cloak but no tunic, with flowing hair and beard … even though they know that the clothes he wears are customary with the so-called philosophers and display a way-of-life'.[4] Hence, comedies, satires, and outsiders' critiques are excellent sources of the common knowledge by which Greeks and Romans identified philosophers and evaluated their ideas, appearance, and actions.

In this essay, I use these sources to craft a τόπος of the Stoic sage and to determine thereby both the grounds upon which Stoics were commonly criticized and the ideas and actions first-century Greeks and Romans associated with them. I find that Stoics were well known as hypocrites who engaged in effeminizing sex while claiming to extirpate the passions, live naturally, and rule themselves and others perfectly. I then demonstrate that Rom. 1.18–2.16 is best read as a sustained censure of a hypocritical judge (2.1) modeled on the τόπος of the hypocritical, sexy Stoic. The rhetorical payoff of this identification is twofold. Stoicism is removed as the prime rival to the gospel, and by revealing the hypocrisy of Stoic claims to virtue, Paul proves the Stoic 'common law' of nature insufficient on its own to produce 'glory, honor, and immortality'. He therefore subjects it to the law of God.[5] This rereading of Romans 1–2 solves several interpretational dilemmas, including the function of 1.18–32, particularly 1.26–27, in the argument and the roles of φύσις and νόμος in 2.12–16. It also challenges the dominant interpretation of Romans as Paul's wrestling with Jews who try to make Gentile believers follow the law.

Who's Judging Whom? The Identity of the Judge as a Problem of Interpretation

Rom. 1.18–2.16 is the first argument of a letter Paul wrote in the mid-50s to a Gentile Roman audience,[6] and it immediately follows the letter's thesis (1.16–17) that the gospel (εὐαγγέλιον) will save the faithful, whether Jew or Greek, because through faithfulness a just God enabled just people to live. Indeed, because it inaugurates the first proof of the thesis, the importance of 1.18–2.16 for understanding the epistle's larger argument cannot be overstated. That proof, a speech of censure (ὁ ἐλεγκτικός), extends from 1.18 through 4.25, and through an elaborate comparison

---

4 *Or.* 72. See Caizzi, 'The Porch', p. 304.

5 For compatibilities between Paul's worldview and that of the Stoics, see T. Engberg-Pedersen's excellent monograph, *Paul and the Stoics* (Louisville, KY: Westminster/John Knox Press, 2000). The argument of this chapter, which was written before the publication of *Paul and the Stoics*, neither assumes or requires a structural compatibility between Stoicism and Pauline thought. Rather, it argues that Paul knows and employs common ideas about Stoicism in order to challenge the cultural dominance of Stoic thought and to usurp its power in order to elevate the status of the gospel. This argument is detailed fully in my forthcoming monograph, *Pax Christi: Empire, Identity and Protrepsis in Paul's Letter to the Romans.*

6 The *rhetoric* of Romans targets Gentiles (cf. 1.5–6, 13; 11.13–32, and 15.7–12, 15–16). On this subject, see especially Stanley Stowers, *A Rereading of Romans: Justice, Jews, and Gentiles* (New Haven & London: Yale University Press, 1994), pp. 21–33. Most scholars believe that the ethnic makeup of the Roman Christian community was mixed, composed of Gentiles and Jews. See the introductions to the subject and the bibliographies of J.D.G. Dunn, *Romans 1–8* (WBC, 38A; Dallas, TX: Word, 1988), pp. i, xliv–liv, and J. Fitzmyer, *Romans* (AB, 33; New York: Doubleday, 1993), pp. 68–84.

(συνκρίσις) of different ways-of-life it demonstrates that only the gospel of God's justice leads to human justice (δικαιοσύνη) and salvation (3.21–26).[7] The leading subsection of this *elenchus*, Rom. 1.18–2.16, is a coherent censure contending that God declares certain unjust judges (2.1) worthy of death but gives them a second chance at life through the gospel. Important because it is structurally parallel to 1.18–2.16, the second subsection of the speech is a censure and exhortation of a hypocritical Jewish teacher (2.17–4.25).[8]

The first argument (1.18–32) within 1.18–2.16 condemns past idolatry and its consequences. The judgment (κρίμα) begins with a terrifying description of the descent of God's wrath upon ungodly and unjust men who refused to honor God as creator. Because in some earlier era these fools failed to intuit God's greatness from nature, three things occurred: they worshiped the creation rather than God; God 'handed them over' to dishonor their bodies by indulging in unnatural sex (vv. 26–27); and God again 'handed them over' to impoverish their minds by doing foolish and unjust things. Otherwise put, God was not pleased with them. According to God's just verdict (δικαίωμα), issued in v. 32, idolaters who did or approved these things deserved to die.

The second argument launched in 2.1–16 compares this just judgment with the prejudiced verdicts of a hypocritical judge. In 2.1–5 Paul condemns the judge (ὁ κρίνων) for denouncing practitioners of the vices listed in 1.18–32 while doing them himself. Like them, he deserves God's verdict of death (κρίμα, cf. 1.32, 2.2). Yet, God patiently reserves his 'righteous-judgment' (δικαιοκρισία) so that the judge might have a μετανοία, or change of mind. The rest of this section warns the hypocritical judge of the character of God's justice: because God is a merciful, impartial judge (2.6, 11), the hypocritical judge can find eternal life if he pursues the truth, but if out of selfish ambition he continues his injustices (2.8), he will reap divine wrath (2.12–13, 16). The charged language of a courtroom, echoing throughout, enables the indictment of the 'hypocritical judge' by a superior Arbiter and the consequent deterioration of the judge's status as an opponent of Paul's gospel.

The critical question is, who was the defendant?

Most scholars give two answers. Like patristic authors, they generally think 1.18–32 targeted Gentiles.[9] After all, Romans 1 closely resembles Jewish narratives like the Wisdom of Solomon and *Jubilees*, in which Gentile idolatry led to rampant immorality.[10] But because the rhetorical audience shifts from 'they' to 'you' at 2.1,

7 For the *ho elegktikos* see the discussion of protreptic below.

8 I accept Stowers's thesis that Paul discusses the law and its relationship to *dikaiosyne* and *pistis* with a Jewish teacher from 2.17 to 4.22 (*Rereading,* pp. 194–250). Almost all scholars agree that the censure of the Jew extends through 3.8; some, through 3.21. For our purposes, it is only important that we agree that Paul debated with the Jew from 2.17 through at least 3.8.

9 Cf. Irenaeus, *Adv. Haer.* 33.1; Chrysostom, *Hom. Rom.* 3; Pelagius, *Com. Rom.* 66; Augustine, *Exp. Quar. Prop. Ep. Rom.* 3; Ambrosiaster, *Com. Ep. Paul.* 81.47, 49; Gennadius of Constantinople, *Ep. Rom.* (*NTA* 15) 358. W. Sanday and A. Headlam give a typical explanation of the function of 1.18–32: the Gentiles are chastised, so that the judgmental Jew can be declared guilty at 2.1 (*The Epistle to the Romans* [ICC; Edinburgh: T. & T. Clark, 1980], pp. 49–52).

10 On Romans 1 as a 'decline of civilizations' narrative blaming pagan idolatry on some ancient figure (e.g. Cain, Enosh), see Stowers, *Rereading,* pp. 91–100, and Dale B. Martin, 'Heterosexism and the Interpretation of Rom. 1:18–32', *Bib Int* 3.3 (1995), pp. 332–355, esp. 335. They disagree with the then-common consensus that decline narratives depicting idolatry were particularly Jewish in character.

scholars usually interpret 2.1–16 as a censure of a self-satisfied, law-abiding Jew who condemned Gentiles while himself doing wrong.[11] The implication is that Jews hearing 1.18–32 as invective against Gentile πορνεία would 'find [themselves] addressed by the same word of judgment ... [so that] the conventional attack on Gentile idolatry turns out to be also a description of the human condition'.[12] A related result is that the emphasis on Jewish hypocrisy found in 2.17–24 is pushed forward to 1.18, the beginning of Paul's argument.

Unfortunately, these moves downplay the role of Gentile wrongdoing in Paul's discussion and foster a misleading gospel-versus-Judaism dynamic. Stowers, recognizing these problems, counters that the hypocritical judge of 2.1 must be a Gentile.[13] First, the hortatory use of 'decline of civilization' narratives was not a Jewish purview; Greek, Roman, and other authors of protreptic speeches employed stories that blamed Greek vice on primitive acts of greed or idolatry. According to third-century BCE Cynics, the Scythian Prince Anacharsis described Greece as immoral in order to convince King Croesus to live virtuously[14]; the first-century CE Stoic Seneca admonished students with the story that greed ruined early human harmony and led to ὕβρις and false wisdom.[15] Second, the judge (ὦ ἄνθρωπε πᾶς ὁ κρίνων) was not a generic human, as the standard reading argues: rather, ancients generally employed the vocative ὦ ἄνθρωπε to mean 'sir', that is, a direct address to an interlocutor. In Athenaeus, for example, a certain Theognetus says, 'you'll be the death of me, *sir* ... you have stuffed yourself sick with the puny dogmas of the Painted Porch!'[16] Consequently, ὦ ἄνθρωπε πᾶς ὁ κρίνων means 'you sir, every judge', not 'O man, whoever you are, when you judge another' (RSV).[17] Third, 2.1–2 accuses the hypocritical judge of doing the very wrongs (τὰ τοιαῦτα) as the Gentiles censured in 1.18–32, not wrongdoing generally, as scholars argue; in Greek prose, τὰ τοιαῦτα normally refers to things listed previously in a narrative. In Rom. 1.32–2:3, 'those who practice τὰ τοιαῦτα' occurs three times, once at the end of 1.18–32 (v. 32) and twice at the beginning of 2.1–16 (vv. 2, 3). The repetition across the two subsections

---

11 Fitzmyer, *Romans*, p. 297. For a list of scholarly opinions, see D. Zeller, *Juden und Heiden in der Mission bei Paulus* (Stuttgart: Katholisches Bibelwerk, 1976), p. 149 and n. 36.

12 Richard Hays, *The Moral Vision of the New Testament: A Contemporary Introduction to New Testament Ethics* (San Francisco: HarperSanFrancisco, 1996), pp. 404–405 n. 21.

13 Stowers, *Rereading,* pp. 97–104 and, on 2.1–16 as a continuation of the argument in 1.18–32, see pp. 12, 100–109. As Stowers shows, only in the sixth century was 2.1 understood as a break in the argument begun at 1.18. Both the earlier *kephalaia majora* and *Codex Alexandrinus* mark 1.18–2.12 as one unit. Jouette Bassler argues on literary grounds that 2.1–11 is an integral part of 1.18–2.11, Paul's demonstration of God's divine impartiality ('Divine Impartiality in Paul's Letter to the Romans', *NovT* 26 [1984], pp. 43–58; *Divine Impartiality: Paul and a Theological Axiom* [SBLDS 59; Chico, CA: Scholars Press, 1982], esp. pp. 131–34).

14 On Anacharsis, see F.H.Y. Reuters, 'De Anacharsidis epistulis' (Inaugural dissertation; University of Bonn, 1957) and *Die Briefe des Anacharsis* (Schriften und Quellen der Alten Welt, 14; Berlin: Akademie Verlag, 1963).

15 See the Ninth Letter of Anacharsis and Seneca, *Ep. Mor.* 90.

16 *Deip.* 3.104.

17 There is slippage between the adjectival (2.1a, 2.3) and substantival (2.1b) uses of the participle ὁ κρίνων in 2.1–3. As I describe below, patristic interpreters understood the addressee to be either a specific person whose occupation included judgment (a ruler, prince, judge, philosopher, ecclesiastical authority) or persons who judged badly.

of the proof underscores the fact that the hypocritical judge is condemned for judging *and doing* the acts listed in Romans 1.

There are three problems with attributing these things to a Jew. First, in Rom. 2.17–24 Paul charged a Jewish teacher of Gentiles with hypocrisy for boasting about the Jewish law while committing faults such as stealing and adultery. *None* of the Jew's misdeeds repeat vices attributed to Gentiles in Romans 1. If the vices listed in 1.18–32 definitively condemned a hypocritical *Jewish* judge (the rhetoric of 2.1–12 presumes that they were potent enough to do so), the explicit judgment of Jewish hypocrisy in 2.17–24 is superfluous. Making a Jew the subject of 2.1–16 also requires ignoring the clear rhetorical shift to a Jewish teacher in 2.17. There, as in 2.1, the address changes from 'they' to 'you', and the shift is explicitly indicated by δὲ σύ.[18]

Finally, most scholars agree that male same-sex intercourse is the most potent rhetorical barb in Romans 1. Of all the vices listed, it is first in order as well as priority, described most explicitly and at greatest length, and, as 'unnatural sex', is most clearly contrasted with the 'natural world' that should have led Gentiles to worship God. The problem is this: first-century Jews were not vulnerable to the charge of having male same-sex intercourse; indeed, contemporary Jewish writers—including Paul—treated it as a uniquely Gentile sin.[19] Josephus (*Ant.* 4.290) and Philo (*Spec. Leg.* 1.324–35) took pains to emphasize that Jewish men did not engage in gender-bending activities such as same-sex intercourse[20]; further, no contemporary non-Jewish writers censured Jews for this practice. Thus, *Romans 1.18–32 is unconvincing as a censure of Jews.*

In sum, the Gentile use of decline narratives, the meaning of ὦ ἄνθρωπε as 'sir' rather than 'human', the specific function of τὰ τοιαῦτα in 1.32–2.3, Paul's subsequent judgment of a Jewish teacher for different vices than those listed in Romans 1, and the assumption that male same-sex intercourse was a Gentile activity, all indicate that ancients should have identified the hypocritical judge as a non-Jew. In fact, they did. Early patristic interpreters identified the judge either generally, as everyday hypocrites and evil men who judged poorly or by human laws,[21] or specifi-

18 The rhetorical marker δὲ σύ was commonly used to indicate a change of speaker or addressee. See Rom. 14.4, 10; and *Vit. auct.* 1, 14.

19 As Martin says, for Jews sexual immorality, 'as the sin of the Gentiles *par excellence*, [wa]s a polluted and polluting consequence of Gentile rebellion' ('Heterosexism', p. 336). Cf. 1 Thess. 4.5, Gal. 2.15, and 1 Cor. 5.1 for the view that Gentiles were, by definition, lustful sinners.

20 Josephus assumes this *topos* in his description of Zealots (some of his 'bad guys') as insatiable louts who dressed effeminately, 'imitated the passions of women' (i.e., played the woman/passive in sex), and, while parading as women, 'with mincing steps' attacked and murdered Roman soldiers (*War* 4. 561–63). For Josephus's imperial clients, the Zealots fit perfectly their stereotype of the overly passionate barbarian, the 'other' who lacked the *andreia* (manliness, courage) of the good soldier and the self-control of noble, educated Romans. For his Herodian audience in Rome, Josephus evoked not only this, but another, 'other', a group of utterly polluted, no-longer-Jews who turned their backs on the law, a people who thereby placed themselves, in the eyes of law-abiding Jews, outside the ethno-religious bounds of Judaism. Josephus's description of gender transgression works as a denunciation because Jews assumed that Jewish men did not dress like women or have (passive) same-sex intercourse.

21 See Ambrosiaster, *Com. Ep. Paul.* (CSEL 81.63); Constantius, *Frag. ap. Paul.* (ENPK 17). Irenaeus (*Adv. Haer.* 4.33.15), Theophilus of Antioch (*Ad Aut.* 1.14), and Origen (*Com. Ep. Rom.* 1.174, 182, 184, 186) read 2.1–8 as condemning Gentile detractors or heretics.

cally, as Greek and Roman rulers, judges, and philosophic leaders.[22] The 'Jewish reading' of 2.1 only took off after Augustine interpreted the judgment as including, along with Gentiles, those Jews 'who wanted to judge the Gentiles according to the law' (*On Rom. 7–8* 5).

The Topos of the Hypocritical Stoic

In the mid-first century CE, the Gentile judge can be identified more specifically as a Stoic sage.[23] The first piece of evidence is rhetorical. As Stowers and David Aune argue, Romans conforms to the standards of protreptic, a well-known speech form used by philosophers and other teachers to espouse or underscore the superiority of their ways of life.[24] This speech form often casts the orator as a teacher who debates rival teachers by means of censure (ἔλεγχος) and exhortation (προτροπή). Rom. 1.18–2.16 mimics this pattern nicely: Paul censures a rival teacher who touts the superiority of his way of life. Paul certainly employed censure and exhortation in his dialogue with the Jewish teacher (2.17–4.25); ancients familiar with protreptic would expect the letter's leading rebuke to target a teacher of philosophy.[25] In fact, several patristic authors—Origen, John Chrysostom, Ambrosiaster, Augustine, Pseudo-Constantius, and Prosper of Aquitaine—interpreted Romans 1 as addressing philosophers as fools and traitors to nature;[26] Origen even underscored the fact that the judgment of 2.1–5 addressed Gentile philosophers and others promoting heresies.[27]

---

22 Chrysostom, *Hom. Rom.* 5 (NPNF 1 11.360); Pelagius, *Com. Rom.* 69; Origen, *Com. Ep. Rom.* 1.170, 172, 174, 182, 184, 186.

23 I disagree with Stowers's conclusion that 2.1–16 applies to any Gentile boaster or *alazon* and, therefore, functions as a general apostrophe warning insiders of pretension. The same rhetorical effect could be achieved by censuring a more specific target, such as a Stoic philosopher, within a protreptic speech (*Rereading,* pp. 100–109; on the boaster as a type, see also O. Ribbeck, *ALAZON: Ein Beitrag zur antiken Ethologie* [Leipzig: Teubner, 1882]). For the suggestion that 2.1 might refer to a 'sophisticated Greek like Juvenal' or 'the Stoic who would agree that such vices as those listed in 1.29–31 were "unfitting" ', see Dunn, *Romans,* p. 79. He dismisses this conclusion because of the 'typically Jewish' character of Rom 1.18–32.

24 Stowers, *Rereading,* pp. 162–65. On popular awareness of protreptic in the first century, see D.E. Aune, 'Romans as a *Logos Protreptikos* in the Context of Ancient Religious and Philosophical Propaganda', in M. Hengel and U. Heckel (eds.), *Paulus und das antike Judentum* (Tübingen: J.C.B. Mohr [Paul Siebeck], 1991), pp. 91–124.

25 Protreptic speeches often censure and/or exhort several opponents in turn. E.g., *Vit. auct.* has the sale of a Pythagorean followed by that of a Cynic, Cyrenaic, Democritean, Heraclitean, Peripatetic, Stoic, and Sceptic; *Diog.* 2–4 censures Greeks, then Jews; Tatian's *Or. Graec.* 1–28 has a censure of Greeks followed by attacks on specific philosophers; and Justin Martyr's *Dial. Tryph.* 1–9, particularly 1.4–1.5, and 2.3–6.2, discusses philosophy generally, then Stoics, Peripatetics, Pythagoreans, and Platonists, before turning to Christianity.

26 Origen, *Com. Ep. Rom.* 1.142, 156, 158; Chrysostom, *Ep. Rom.* 3 (NPNF 1 11.354), 5 (1 11.360); Ambrosiaster, *Com. Ep. Paul.* (CSEL 81.43); Augustine, *Exp. Ep. Rom.* 3, *De Civ. Dei* 8.10; Pseudo-Constantius, *Frag. Paul. (Ein neuer Paulustest und Kommentar* 25); Prosper of Aquitaine, *Grace and Free Will* 12.4 (FC 7.380).

27 *Com. Ep. Rom.* 1.174, 182, 184, 186.

Why a Stoic? Stoics were the pre-eminent school of philosophy in the Hellenistic age and early empire, and Paul's Roman audience lived in the center of Stoicism.[28] Panaetius of Rhodes brought Stoicism to Rome in 146 BCE and, through the powerful friends of Scipio Africanus, helped disseminate it among influential Romans. By the mid-first century the Roman Stoa was established,[29] Stoic ideas had become common-places,[30] and Stoics contemporary with and subsequent to Paul (Seneca, Musonius Rufus, Epictetus, Marcus Aurelius) emphasized ethics. In the mid-50s CE, the Stoic Seneca even advised Nero Caesar in the good governance of the empire. Given Stoicism's influence on Roman government and morals, ancients may well have assumed that the judge was a Stoic teacher.

The stereotype of the hypocritical Stoic current in the first century greatly increases this likelihood. The most frequent characterization of Stoics by satirists and moralists was that they possessed a preposterous, but unshakable, belief in their own perfection. According to both Greek and Latin sources, Stoics asserted that the masses (αἱ ἰδιόται, οἱ πολλοί) were fools while they were models of consistency, the embodiment of the four cardinal virtues. Their consistent virtuosity meant that they alone were a living law or standard of conduct and, thus, they alone could be perfect rulers or judges.[31] Satirists and enemies scoffed at these perceptions, reveling in Stoics' imperfections while repeating the conventions. Addressing the Stoic self-identification as rulers, the Latin satirist Horace (65–8 BCE) quipped: 'the wise man is only surpassed by Jove, he is well off, respected, handsome, the free king above all kings. And above all being *right* in the head, he's always quite well … lest a cold

---

28 See M. Colish, *The Stoic Tradition from Antiquity to the Early Middle Ages* (Studies in the History of Christian Thought; Leiden: E.J. Brill, 1985); A.A. Long, *Hellenistic Philosophy: Stoics, Epicureans, and Skeptics* (Berkeley: University of California Press, 1986); M. Nussbaum, *The Therapy of Desire* (Princeton: Princeton University Press, 1994); J.M. Rist, *Stoic Philosophy* (Cambridge: Cambridge University Press, 1969); F.H. Sandbach, *The Stoics* (London: G. Duckworth, 2nd edn, 1994); R.W. Sharples, *Stoics, Epicureans and Skeptics: An Introduction to Hellenistic Philosophy* (London: Routledge, 1996).

29 Lucian alludes to this Stoic influence in *Vit. auct.* 20. There Hermes says of those seeking to buy the Stoic, 'at all events it looks as if the men who frequent the public square are waiting for him in great numbers'. See also A.J. Malherbe, *Moral Exhortation: A Greco-Roman Sourcebook* (Philadelphia: Westminster, 1986), p. 12; Stanley Stowers, *Letter Writing in Greco-Roman Antiquity* (Philadelphia: Westminster, 1986), p. 40; and Dale Martin, *The Corinthian Body* (New Haven: Yale University Press, 1995), pp. 9–12.

30 For examples and discussion, see Colish, *The Stoic Tradition*; G. Chesnut, 'The Ruler and the Logos in Neopythagorean, Middle Platonic, and Late Stoic Political Philosophy', in *Principat 16,2* (*ANRW*, 2.16/2; ed. W. Haase; Berlin: Walter de Gruyter, 1978); L. Gerson, '*Isa ta hamartemnata*: The Stoic Doctrine "All Errors are Equal" ', in D.V. Stump, *et al.*, *Hamartia: The Concept of Error in the Western Tradition: Essays in Honor of John M. Crossett* (TextsSR, 16; New York: Edwin Mellen Press, 1983); W. Haase (ed.), *Principat 36,3: Philosophie, Wissenschaften, Technik: Philosophie (Stoizismus)* (*ANRW*, 2.36/3; Berlin: Walter de Gruyter, 1989); R.E. Hock, ' "By the Gods, It's my One Desire to See an Actual Stoic": Epictetus' Relations with Students and Visitors in his Personal Network', *Semeia* 56 (1991), pp. 121–42; W. Klassen, 'The King as "Living Law", with Particular Reference to Musonius Rufus', *SR* 14.1 (1985), pp. 63–71; J.F. Phillips, 'Stoic "Common Notions" in Plotinus', *Dionysius* 11 (Dec. 1987), pp. 33–52; R.J. Rabel, 'Diseases of the Soul in Stoic Psychology', *GRBS* 22 (Winter 1981), pp. 385–93.

31 Chryssipus (Plutarch, *Mor.* 9.1035C), Cicero (*De Leg.* 1.6.18), Musonius Rufus, and Diogenes of Babylon said a Stoic should govern and judge since he alone was a living law. On the necessity of being a good judge, see also Epictetus, *Diss.* 3.7.21, esp. 30–33. On kingship, see *Diss.* 3.22.34.

keeps him in bed.'[32] Lucian likewise sniped, '[In the Stoic] I see virtue itself, the most perfect of philosophies ... he is the only wise man (σόφος), the only beautiful, just (δίκαιος), manly (ἀνδρεῖος) man—a king, rhetor, wealthy man, lawgiver, and everything else there is.'[33] Quoting Menander acidly, Plutarch added, 'If one has gotten virtue from the Stoa, one can ask, "if there's anything you wish: all will be yours".'[34]

Cicero (106–43 BCE) and Laertius attributed to the early Stoic Chryssipus the notions of perfection and unique ability to rule, judge, or execute other public duties (καθήκοντα[35]):

> ... according to them not only are wise men (σοφοι) free, they are also kings; kingship being irresponsible rule, which none but the wise can maintain. So Chrysippus in his treatise vindicates Zeno's use of terminology. For he holds that knowledge of good and evil is a necessary attribute of the ruler, and that no bad man is acquainted with this art. Similarly the wise and good alone are fit to be magistrates, judges (δικαστικούς), or orators, whereas among the bad there is not one so qualified. Furthermore the wise are infallible, not being liable to error.[36]

Plutarch cared less about the origin of the τόπος than about its usefulness for (repeatedly) charging Stoics with inconsistency:

> As many as do enter government, however, are contradicting their own doctrines still more sharply, for in holding administrative and judicial offices (δικάζουσι), in acting as councilors and legislators, in meting out punishments and rewards they imply that they are taking part in the government of genuine states and that those really are councilors and judges (δικαστόν) who are at any time so designated by lot ... so when they take part in government they are inconsistent too.[37]

> Well then, should the first object of our proceedings be the common and notorious notions which even they (Stoics) in easy-going admission of the absurdity themselves entitle paradoxes, their notions as to who alone are kings, and who alone are opulent and fair, and alone are citizens and judges (δικαστάς)...?[38]

---

32 *Ep.* 1.1.106–108. See also Plutarch, *Mor.* 13.2 1034.7D; Diogenes Laertius, *De Vit. Phil.* 7.92.

33 *Vit. auct.* 20, 23.

34 *Mor.* 13.2 1058. Of course, Plutarch thought this made Stoics into leeches, and he retorted that the only sources of income acceptable to them were gifts from kings and friends, and as a last resort, lecturing (1043).

35 On καθήκοντα cf. Laertius, *De Vit. Phil.* 7.108–10. Laertius describes *kathekonta* as those duties of the Stoic sage that are aligned with reason and, therefore, nature. These duties included 'honoring parents, brothers, country, and friends'. There was no clear delineation between public and private duties; the good householder was, because of his virtue, a good citizen and a participant in the πολιτεία.

36 Cicero, *De Fin.* 4.74; Laertius, *De Vit. Phil.* 7.122; cf. also *SVF* 1, fr. 222. The assumption is also present in the discourses of Dio Chrysostom (40–120 CE) on kingship, particularly in *First Disc.* 9 and *Third Disc.* 4–11 to Trajan. Formerly against Stoicism, particularly that of Musonius Rufus, Dio later embraced Stoic (as well as other schools of) thought, including the Stoic *topos* of the ideal king.

37 *Mor.* 13.2 1033.3.

38 *Mor.* 13.2 1060B.

Greek and Latin authors from the first century BCE to the third century CE not only roundly charged Stoics with hypocrisy for asserting that they were perfect and uniquely qualified to guide the affairs of the πολιτεία, they also criticized the basis of the commonplace, the Stoic tenet that the universe, or nature (φύσις), was the source of their ethics. According to Plutarch and Laertius, Stoics thought that divine *logos* (reason) infused nature, that they alone possessed that λόγος, and, thus, that they could best live according to nature (κατὰ φύσιν). Because their minds (νοῦς) were attuned to divine reason, they could rely on their νοῦς and their inner conviction (συνείδησις) to extirpate passions (πάθη, ἐπιθυμία) and live wisely.[39] As Laertius said, Stoic teachers taught that 'virtue is the goal toward which nature guides us' and that 'living virtuously is equivalent to living in accordance with [nature]'.[40] Simply put, it was Stoics' unique access to the common law or reason of nature that made them a living law and, thus, perfect rulers and judges.[41] Further, since their reasonable minds (λογικός νοῦς) gave Stoics endurance (ἀπαθεία) and self-control over passions (αὐταρχεία σωφροσύνε), it follows that overly passionate behavior was self-deception, an involuntary error (*plane*) of judgment.[42] Athenaeus assumed both ἀπαθεία and the importance of mind for right action when he applauded Celts for 'stoical endurance' and cited the Stoic Poseidonius as saying, 'other people can't control themselves because of the weakness of their minds'.[43] As for κατὰ φύσιν, many philosophers talked about living naturally; Aristotle's *Protrepticus,* written in the fourth century (384–332) BCE, may be the earliest famous exhortation for humans to live in harmony with nature. However, Seneca did say, 'our motto, as you know, is "Live According to Nature"'.[44] His statement assumed that people associated this phrase with Stoics. Persius (34–62 CE) and Plutarch confirm the assertion.[45] Speaking about non-Stoics, the satirist Persius said that 'the self-evident law of nature limits/the actions of incompetents and half-wits'.[46] Likewise, Plutarch remarked testily that, 'the common nature and the common reason of nature [must be] destiny and providence and Zeus, of this not

---

39　On *nous* in Stoic thought and Romans 7, see Stowers, *Rereading,* pp. 260–84; Epictetus, *Diss.* 1.20, 3.22.30–22. On Stoics as passionless wise men, cf. Laertius, *De Vit. Phil.* 7.117.

40　*De Vit. Phil.* 2.7.87.

41　Crystallized only later in Cicero as a νόμος φύσεως (*lex natura* in *De Rep.* 3.33), early Stoics discussed a common law (κοινοσ νομοσ) that existed by nature, was equivalent to *logos,* attributed to Zeus, and comprehended only by the sage. Although unlike early Stoics Cicero argued that proximate goods enabled men to become virtuous gradually, the functions of 'nature' and 'natural law' in Cicero and the early Stoics were compatible, enabling later Stoics to assert that those who acted according to nature, right reason/νοῦς, and their συνείδησις could live well and free themselves (ἀπαθεία) from troubling passions (πάθη). On Stoics as a living law, cf. Plutarch, *Fort. Alex.* 329 A–B (*SVF* 1.262); Laertius, *De Vit. Phil.* 2.7.87–89, 128; Pindar frg. 69 *On Law* (*SVF* 3.314, 1.537, lines 2, 24), and J.W. Martens, 'Romans 2.14–16: A Stoic Reading', *NTS* 40 (1994), pp. 55–67, esp. 64–66.

42　On both error and passion, cf. Laertius, *De Vit. Phil.* 7.110–15.

43　Athenaeus, *Deip.* 4.160E, 6.263.

44　*Ep. Mor.* 5.4: 'Nempe propositum nostrum est secundum naturam vivere.'

45　Cf. also Laertius, *De Vit. Phil.* 7.86–110; Athenaeus, *Deip.* 7.233C; Clement of Alexandria, *Strom.* 2–3.

46　*Sat.* 5.98–99.

even the Antipodes are unaware, for the Stoics keep harping on them everywhere'.[47] Hence, criticisms of Stoics' proprietary claim to live κατὰ φύσιν and to have minds attuned to nature evidence a general awareness of the commonplace.

This criticism leads to the seminal component of the τόπος. Although they did not usually level this charge at other philosophers, satirists and moralists frequently denounced Stoics who loudly espoused 'natural' living but effeminized their younger male sex-partners by shaving or sexual penetration or effeminized themselves by sexual passivity or transvestitism.[48] In the third and second centuries BCE, the poets Cercidas and Hermeias and the biographer Antigonus of Carystus called Stoics 'merchants of twaddle' and 'verbiage-fakers' for having sex with boys.[49] Athenaeus followed suit, charging Stoics with controverting nature through transvestitism and with requiring their boyfriends to shave their chins and butts in order to extend pederastic liaisons until their 'boys' reached the extraordinarily advanced age of 28. 'Your wise Zeno', he said, '[saw] the lives you would lead and your hypocritical profession ... that you give the name of effeminate (κίναιδος) to those who put on perfume or wore slightly dainty garments. You shouldn't then, when rigged up in that fashion ... take in your train lover-lads with shaven chins and posteriors.'[50]

Lucian and Plutarch repeat this commonplace to imply that Stoics inverted the appropriate (hierarchical) relationship between themselves and their students, making themselves passive recipients of their students' sexual advances and thereby corrupting their common pursuit of virtue. Lucian assumed the τόπος of the sexually passive sage in his attack on Stoics who charged their students fees for their (educational) services:

> Buyer: Then we are to say the same of the fees that you get for your wisdom from young men, and obviously none but the scholar will get paid for his virtue?
> Stoic: Your understanding of the matter is correct. You see, I do not take pay on my own account, but for the sake of the giver himself: for since there are two classes of men, the disbursive (ἔκχυτος) and the receptive (περιεκτικός), I train myself to be receptive and my pupil to be disbursive.

47 *Mor.* 13.2 1050. Plutarch's repeated denunciations of Stoics for not thinking consistently about nature or not living κατά φύσιν consistency all assume that Stoics were widely known for the tenet. Cf. *Mor.* 13.2 1060.4C–6E on nature, 1069.A–E on benefit, 1071.B and 1072.B–E on the goal (τελος) of philosophy, and 1073.A–D on love. I discuss ἔρως below. Cf. also Laertius, *De Vit. Phil.* 7.86–87, who says Zeno of Kition was the first to designate 'life in agreement with nature' as the *telos* of the philosophical life.

48 These barbs were generally used to poke fun, embarrass, or humiliate. See N. Rudd, *Themes in Roman Satire* (Oklahoma: University of Oklahoma, 1986), pp. 215–25. Among first- and second-century philosophers, Stoics were uniquely repudiated as hypocrites for effeminacy and sexual passivity (Martial, *Epigram.* 9.47, which targets individual philosophers of different schools [Democritus, Zeno, Plato, Pythagorus], is the exception). Stoics seemed to have inherited this dubious honor from Socrates and his ilk, who were regularly the butt of jokes in classical Athens. See A. Richlin, 'Not before Homosexuality: The Materiality of the *Cinaedus* and the Roman Law against Love between Men', *Journal of the History of Sexuality* 3.4 (1993), pp. 523–73, esp. 544.

49 Cercidas, *Meliamb.* 5.5–15, 6.14–15; Athenaeus, *Deip.* 13.563D–E (citing Hermeias) and 565D–F (citing Antigonus).

50 Athenaeus, *Deip.* 13.564F, 605D (*para physin*). See D. Halperin, *One Hundred Years of Homosexuality and Other Essays on Greek Love* (New York: Routledge, 1990), pp. 88, 181 n. 6.

Buyer: On the contrary, the young man ought to be receptive and you, who alone are rich, disbursive!
Stoic: You are joking, man. Look out that I don't shoot you with my indemonstrable syllogism.
Buyer: What have I to fear from that shaft?
Stoic: Perplexity and aphasia and a sprained intellect ...[51]

The inversion of power and sexual position between sage and student occurs earlier in two essays by Plutarch. The first passage, from *Stoicos Absurdiora Poetis Dicere*, alludes to the ugliness of the neophyte and contends that even though he tries to pass as a manly, just king, the Stoic is really a foolish, effeminate youth:

> ... the sage of the Stoics, though yesterday he was most ugly and vicious, today all of a sudden has been transformed into virtue ... the Stoic love consorts with the ugliest and most unshapely and turns away when by wisdom these are transformed into shapeliness and beauty ... Among the Stoics the one who is most vicious in the morning, if so it chance to be, is in the afternoon most virtuous. Having fallen asleep demented and stupid and unjust (ἄδικος) and licentious, and even, by heaven, a slave and a drudge and a pauper, he gets up the very same day changed into a blessed and opulent king, sober and just (δίκαιος) and steadfast and undeluded by fancies. He has not sprouted a beard or the tokens of puberty in a body young and soft. But in a soul that is feeble and soft and unmanly and unstable has got perfect disposition, knowledge, free from fancy, and an unalterable habitude and this not by any previous abatement of his depravity but by having changed instantaneously into what may almost be called a kind of hero or spirit or god.[52]

De Communibus Notitiis Adversus Stoicos uses the same language to claim that by extending sexual liaisons with students into adulthood, Stoic sages obliterated their claim to live naturally:

> Comrade: Yes, for love, they say, is a kind of chase after a stripling who is undeveloped but naturally apt for virtue.
> Diadumenus: Why then, my dear sir, are we now trying to do anything else but convict their system ...? For if passion is not at issue, no one is trying to keep the zeal of sages about youths from being called a 'chase' or a 'friend-making'; but one ought to call 'love' what all men and women understand and call by the name: 'All of them hotly desired to be couched by her side in the bride bed' ... Yet, while casting their theory of morals off upon troubles like [ἔρως], 'twisted, unsound, and all circuitous', they belittle and disparage the rest of us as if they alone uphold nature and common experience ...[53]

The subject of the passage is the inconsistency of the Stoic doctrine of *eros,* which most people assumed was desire for sex, but which according to Plutarch and Diogenes Laertius (2.7.130), Stoics defined as 'an impulse to make friends'. Of greatest interest to us is Plutarch's allusion to 'ugly, stupid' youths who matured into 'beautiful, wise' men while retaining their sex appeal to pederastic sages. Like

51 *Vit. auct.* 24.
52 Plutarch, *Mor.* 13.2 1057.2E–1058.B.
53 *Mor.* 13.2 1073.A–D.

Lucian and Athenaeus, therefore, Plutarch assumed that the Stoic *desideratum* to be perfect, to be a manly, wise ruler who lived according to nature, was a ruse.[54]

Among Roman satirists, Martial (40–103 CE) and Juvenal (60–130 CE) also scourged Stoics for looking manly and criticizing vice when they were *cinaedi*.[55] According to Juvenal's second satire (ca. 100–112), Rome lay in ruins because of the behavior of certain sages. Initially unidentified, these fools appeared masculine—with hirsute limbs (2.11), taciturn speech (2.14), and crew cuts (2.15)—and defended the city from license (2.39) in their roles as judges and lawmakers (2.51, 76).[56] Using the voice of the female character Laronia, Juvenal later unveiled the culprits as 'our Stoic brethren' (2.64) who swished about like women soliciting advances from manly men. Juvenal then depicts a particularly debauched Stoic judge named Creticus who wore a transparent toga to court (2.64–81) and visited people who dressed in drag (2.84–116), donned chartreuse outfits (2.97), and held mirrors, props always associated with women (2.99).[57] The satirist finally thanked Nature for rendering these 'androgynous monsters' sterile (2.138–39).

Κίναιδοι, *Gender Trouble, and the Un/Making of the Sage*

In the first century CE, denouncing Stoics as transvestites, sexual passives, or pederasts who effeminated their students was a typical way to strip authority from Stoic claims to live naturally and to be wise rulers. For ancients, who lacked a conception of sexual orientation[58] and who defined 'males' as hairy, naturally superior, sexual penetrators, these were intimately related acts of weakness that erased the sage's manliness (ἀνδρεία) precisely because they flowed from the same source, femininity.

Although this point is well known among scholars who study ancient constructs of gender and desire, New Testament scholars' general reticence to accept it suggests that unpacking is in order. In ancient Greece and Rome, two interactive frameworks governed conceptualizations of intercourse: the hierarchical ordering of the cosmos and the regulation of desire. In the cosmic hierarchy, people were ranked in a gender spectrum in which 'masculinity' and 'femininity' were its most and least preferable

---

54 The same complex occurs in Athenaeus, *Deip.* 605D, with the phrase *para physin*.

55 Cf. Martial, *Epigram.* 1.24, 1.96, 2.36, 6.56, 7.58, 12.42.

56 Richlin, 'Not before Homosexuality', p. 544. On the very old connection between manliness, *andreia,* and lawmaking, cf. Plato, *Rep.* 429c.

57 I am paraphrasing Richlin's colorful description, 'Not before Homosexuality', p. 545.

58 On the well-established distinction between ancient constructions of desire and 'homosexuality', a construct dependent on eighteenth-century psychological and physiological interpretations of the human body, see A. Carson, 'Putting Her in her Place: Women, Dirt, and Desire', in D. Halperin, J. Winkler, and F. Zeitlin (eds), *Before Sexuality: The Construction of Erotic Experience in the Ancient Greek World* (Princeton: Princeton University Press, 1990), pp. 135–69; K.E. Corley and K.J. Torjesen, 'Sexuality, Hierarchy, and Evangelism', *TSF Bulletin* March–April (1987), pp. 23–27; K.J. Dover, *Greek Homosexuality* (Cambridge, MA: Harvard University Press, 1989); D. Greenberg, *The Construction of Homosexuality* (Chicago: University of Chicago Press, 1988); Halperin, *One Hundred Years*; and T. Laqueur, *Making Sex: Body and Gender from the Greeks to Freud* (Cambridge, MA: Harvard University Press, 1990). For dissenting opinions, see most recently B. Brooten, *Love between Women: Early Christian Responses to Female Homoeroticism* (Chicago: University of Chicago Press, 1996); and Richlin, 'Not before Homosexuality'.

assignments. As ancient medical texts indicate, the spectrum's ends did not refer to two genetically and biologically differentiated sexes, 'male' and 'female'. Rather, the ancient human was constructed on a one body, multi-gendered model in which the perfect body was deemed 'male/man'. 'Females/women' and other gendered humans[59] were differently imperfect versions of the male body whose relative imperfections reflected their physical and emotional health.[60] Males/men consequently attracted the adjectives rational, physically and politically strong, spiritual, superior, active, dry, and penetrative, while females/women embodied the body's negative qualities: irrationality, physical and political weakness, fleshliness, inferiority, passivity, wetness, penetration. No less human, female 'weaknesses' nevertheless made them less than perfectly human (that is, perfectly 'masculine/male').

Females' anomalous state as imperfect males meant that they were not only weak, but also inherently dangerous to family and state. 'Intimate with formlessness and unbounded in their alliance with the wet, the wild, and raw nature', women were 'pollutable, polluted, and polluting in several ways at once'.[61]

> They are, as individuals, comparatively formless themselves, without firm control of personal boundaries. They are, as social entities, units of danger, moving across boundaries of family and οἶκος, in marriage, prostitution, or adultery. They are, as psychological entities, unstable compounds of deceit and desire, prone to leakage. In sum, the female body, the female psyche, the female social life, and the female moral life are penetrable, porous, mutable, and subject to defilement all the time ... [and i]t is in her erotic life that woman most vividly lacks completion. Sexually the female is a pore. This porous sexuality is a floodgate of social pollution, for it is the gate of entry to οἶκος and πόλις.

The Hellenistic cosmic hierarchy constructed gender as the inscribed interrelation of masculinity or femininity (superior/inferior), societal status (more/less powerful),[62] and sex role (penetrator/penetrated); embodying the negative polarities, females/women represented both the weaknesses of, and dangers to, the social structure. It should not be surprising then that a Greek or Roman woman was *by definition* the penetrated, the empty vessel (σκεῦος, see 1 Thess. 4.4) her husband

---

59 As I discuss below, these included androgynes, *cinaedi* (effeminates), and *tribades* (dominatrices). Philo of Alexandria imagined a sixth, the 'unnatural monsters' produced when women or men mated with animals, 'whence possibly the Hippocentaurs and Chimeras and the like, forms of life hitherto unknown and with no existence outside mythology, will come into being' (*Spec. Leg.* 3.43–45).

60 Aristotle, *GA* 728a18–20; 737a25–35; 775a15. Laqueur discusses medical texts from Aristotle to Soranus (2nd century CE) and demonstrates their conception of the one 'sex' body (*Making Sex,* p. 29). Herophilus, Hippocrates, and Galen conceived of women anatomically as men with internal genitalia (see A.E. Hanson, 'The Medical Writers' Woman', in Halperin, Winkler and Zeitlin (eds.), *Before Sexuality,* pp. 309–38, esp. 390–91). For Hippocrates and Galen, who thought male and female seed commingled after sex, this meant that a baby's gender depended on 'which type of seed predominated or the temperature of the uterine quadrant in which it lodged' (Hanson, p. 391). Hence, modern distinctions between biological sex and gender are anachronistic when applied to the ancient world.

61 Carson, 'Putting Her in her Place', pp. 158–59.

62 On the Roman sex/class system, see Richlin, 'Not before Homosexuality', pp. 532, 533 n. 24.

filled,[63] while the male/citizen (Gr. ἀνήρ/Lat. *vir*) was legally free and expected to penetrate inferior sex-partners (his wife, slaves, prostitutes, and occasionally actors or dancers).[64]

This cosmic schema had one huge danger: its gender continuum could be traversed;[65] since gender was not conceived as a stable characteristic independent of sexuality, but a spectrum of assigned, mutable, and binarized acts, *maleness was not a genetic, but an achieved, state*. Hence, the stability of the cosmic hierarchy was vulnerable at three points. By penetrating an unacceptable partner (a freeborn youth or another *vir* [*similes*]), a man could cause his sex-partner's effemination, thereby subverting his superior male nature and the divine order it represented. Alternatively, by adopting feminine practices (dress, hairstyles, cosmetics, receptive intercourse), a man could become more female, mutating into a *cinaedus* or androgyne. Finally, a woman could become androgynous by assuming masculine habits and/or acting as a *tribas*, a dominatrix who sought to penetrate boys, girls, men, or other women.[66]

---

63 Cf. Seneca, *Ep. Mor.* 95.21 *pati natae*: women are 'born to be penetrated'. While in Imperial Rome elite women gained certain freedoms, these freedoms did not result in a shift in perspective about woman's natural inferiority or her nature as a child-bearer. See S. Dixon, *The Roman Family* (Baltimore: Johns Hopkins University Press, 1992), pp. 76–77; Laqueur, *Making Sex,* p. 54 notes that Aristotle, who was immensely concerned about the sex of free men and women, recognized no sex among slaves.

64 For the *vir*, only the causes of *infamia*, such as *stuprum* and transgressions of the *lex Iulia de adulteriis coercendis*, were legally prohibited. The issue is not so much a legal one as one dealing with the customary and acceptable. On *infamia* and *stuprum*, see Richlin, 'Not before Homosexuality', pp. 554–66. By the early third century CE *per vim stuprum* (rape) of 'boy, woman, or anyone' could be punished legally (based on the *lex Iulia de vi publica*) with the execution of the perpetrator. But public and private punishments of *stuprum cum vi* and general aversion to intercourse with freeborn males were known in late Republican and Imperial Rome (Richlin, 'Not before Homosexuality', pp. 562–66 and 562 n. 93). The Augustan reforms (*Lex Papia Poppaea, Lex Iulia*) outlawing adultery with married women and fornication (*stuprum*) with unmarried women were widely known, but not necessarily widely esteemed, followed, or successful in producing more upper-class citizens (Dixon, *Roman Family,* pp. 78–82; Tacitus, *Ann.* 3.24).

65 John Winkler, *The Constraints of Desire: The Anthropology of Sex and Gender in Ancient Greece* (New York: Routledge, 1990), p. 50; see also Hanson, 'Medical Writers' Woman', p. 391; Stowers, *Rereading,* pp. 42–82; and Corley and Torjesen, 'Sexuality, Hierarchy, and Evangelism', pp. 23–27.

66 The *tribas* was culturally defined not as a lesbian but as a dominatrix who defied her appropriate gender role. This is the danger assumed in Martial, *Epigram.* 7.67, 70. There Philaenis is represented as becoming more male through her sexual exploits. Described as 'a *tribas* of the very *tribades*', she buggers boys and batters eleven girls a day, 'quite fierce with the erection of a husband'. Brooten, observing that this is invective and that ancient sources rarely depict female pederasty, argues that we should take the root meaning of *tribas* as a 'woman sexually oriented to other women' rather than as that applied to Philaenis, an 'insatiably phallic woman sexually aggressive toward other women, as well as toward boys and girls' (*Love between Women,* pp. 7–8). Brooten's conclusion has several problems. Since she believes that women with lifelong homoerotic orientations (i.e., lesbians) existed in antiquity (pp. 9–10, 185), she ignores the evidence that *tribades* were treated as pederasts of girls *and* boys (cf. Ovid, *Trist.* 2.365; Plutarch, *Vita Lyc.* 18.9; Shenute *De Vit. Mon.* 21, 26) and were said to exhibit other masculine behaviors such as athletics (Brooten, p. 46), grow penises (Laqueur, *Making Sex,* p. 53; Dover, *Greek Homosexuality,* pp. 60–68; Halperin, *One Hundred Years,* p. 166 n. 83), suffer from balding and other masculine diseases (Seneca, *Ep. Mor.* 95.20), aggressively pursue women and men (Seneca, *Ep. Mor.* 95.20), and occasionally require cliterodectomy to prevent them from penetrating women and men (Brooten, p. 25). Brooten also glosses over attribu-

Thus, while censure for gender violations might have had nothing to do with sex acts, boundary-blurring sex acts were condemned as gender violations.

Ancient moralists criticized pederasty on this basis. Although they usually described it as appropriately asymmetrical, marked by accepted sexual and sociopolitical power differentials between citizen-males and boys, critics sometimes denounced the penetrated boys and their penetrators.[67] When they derogated the boy (*puer*) as a *mollis* ('soft' or 'unmasculine'), their criticisms were not based on his having sex with another male (in fact, the boy was not yet a male/citizen, an ἀνήρ or *vir*). Rather, moralists worried that by assuming the feminine, receptive sex role habitually a freeborn *puer* would grow to like it too much and therefore fail to mature into a *vir*.[68] For example, Philo of Alexandria asserts (*Spec. Leg.* 3.37–41) that by adopting gender-bending behaviors, the boy could *become* an androgyne and so deserve death:

> Pederasty is now a matter of boasting not only to penetrators but also to the passives, who habituate themselves to endure the disease of effemination … and leave no ember of their male sex-nature to smoulder. Mark how conspicuously they braid and adorn the hair of their heads, and how they scrub and paint their faces with cosmetics and pigments and the like, and smother themselves with fragrant unguents (for of all such embellishments, used by all who deck themselves out to wear a comely appearance, fragrance is the most seductive); in fact their contrivance to transform, by scrupulous refinement, the male nature to the female does not raise a blush. These persons are rightly judged worthy of death by those who obey the law, which ordains that the androgyne who debased the currency of nature should perish unavenged, suffering not to live for a day or even an hour, as a disgrace to himself, his household, his homeland, and the whole of humanity.[69]

The pederast's major vice was his effemination of the future citizen-male: 'He sees no harm in becoming a tutor and instructor in the grievous vices of unmanliness

---

tions of excessive desire, such as Philaenis's dedication to gluttony (46) and supposed sadomasochism (Juvenal, *Sat.* 6.422). Finally, she explains away or rereads the overwhelming use of active (penetrative) verbs for *tribades* (and passive verbs for their love interests). *Tribades* were castigated as physically mannish and sexually aggressive toward women, girls, *boys, and men.* This censure does not work within a culture treating *tribades* as 'women-loving women'; it only works within a culture treating *tribades* as penetrators, regardless of their object choice. The reasons they were denounced are similar to the censures of the womanish κίναιδος/*cinaedus* (see below). Both are depicted as driven by desire toward gluttony and excessive intercourse. More, they were cast as 'others', neither 'men' nor 'women'. As Laqueur said, 'The actions of the mollis [sexually passive male] and the tribade [sexually active female] were … unnatural not because they violated natural heterosexuality but because they played out—literally embodied—radical, culturally unacceptable reversals of power and prestige' (*Making Sex,* p. 53). Hence, it makes perfect sense that Martial deemed Philaenis something like a third-gendered being.

67 Authors did display a general disgust for boy-prostitutes and for those who enslaved them. Cf. 1 Tim. 1.10, ἀνδροποδισταῖς.

68 See texts cited by Richlin, 'Not before Homosexuality', p. 537. Cf. also Plutarch, *Mor.* 751C, E, which refers to Plato's condemnation of the sex-role of the penetrated male as 'contrary to nature' ('they allow themselves to be covered and mounted like cattle'). As Martin puts it, '[Same-sex] penetration affronts nature due to its disruption of the male-female cosmic hierarchy … What is unspoken but clearly presupposed is that it is perfectly "natural" for women to be "covered and mounted like cattle".'

69 Cf. also *Vit. Cont.* 60–61; *Abr.* 135–36.

(ἀνανδρία) and effeminacy (μαλακία) by prolonging the bloom of youth and emasculating the flower of their prime, which should rightly be trained to strength and robustness' (3.37).[70] (As Philo's use of the language of instruction and as criticisms by Plutarch and Lucian show, pederasty was perceived as an aid or hindrance to the education and maturation of *pueri*.) Connoting weakness, cowardice, daintiness, sexual unrestraint, prostitution, and unmanliness, disparaging synonyms for the *puer* (e.g. μαλακός) support the case that men's fear of effemination, not same-sex intercourse *per se,* prompted the condemnation of the *puer*.[71]

As we have seen, writers cast these same aspersions on adults, calling them κίναιδοι (Lat. *cinaedi*) or ἀνδρόγυνοι. According to the lexicographer Pollux, *cinaedus* had a range of meanings similar to μαλακός, from generalized moral reproach to softness, sexual passivity, and prostitution. Generally treated as sexual deviants, *cinaedi* were overwhelmingly characterized by their effeminacy, the same characteristics attributed to androgynes (ἀνδρόγυνοι). Indeed, Pollux equated them (6.126–27), the second-century physiognomist Polemo described them identically,[72] and Quintilian told his pupils to avoid their mannerisms (mincing walk, shifty eyes, provocative glance, limp upturned hands, thin voice).[73] Hence, ancients conceived of both *cinaedi* and androgynes as having 'something of the shape of a man, but [being] feminine in all other respects'.[74] Given that androgynes were (from our point of view) sexually indeterminate from birth, the oft-seen equation of the *cinaedus* and androgyne is a telling indicator that criticisms of the *cinaedus* were based on the perception that they engaged in gender-bending activities.

Particularly among Stoics,[75] the *cinaedus* was portrayed as depilating his beard— *the* sign of adulthood—and otherwise crafting his body to remove his *vir*-ility. As Maud Gleason notes, 'Stoics liked to moralize about hair because it was a term in the symbolic language of masculinity that could be construed as not merely a conventional sign, but as a symbol established by Nature itself.'[76] Thus, Musonius Rufus, Seneca, and Epictetus railed against coiffing and depilating since the presence and

---

70 Pliny discusses natural substances (hyacinth root, ant eggs, lamb testicles) used to halt boy-prostitutes' maturation (21.170; 30.41; 30.132). Seneca also bemoans the state of the *puer* (*Ep. Mor.* 47.7).

71 Cf. Athenaeus, *Deip.* 12.540F, 528D; Aristophanes, *Eccles.* 1058; and other texts cited by Dale Martin, '*Arsenokoitês* and *Malakos*: Meanings and Consequences', in R.L. Brawley (ed.), *Biblical Ethics and Homosexuality: Listening to Scripture* (Louisville: Westminster John Knox, 1996), pp. 117–36. Other synonyms include *pathicus, pullus* ('chick'), *pusio, delicatus, tener* ('dainty'), *debilis* ('weak'), *effeminatus, discinctus* ('loose-belted'), *morbosus* ('sick'), μαλακός, μαλθακός, θηλυδρίας ('womanish'), ἐκτεθηλύσμενος, and γύννις ('she-man'). See Richlin, 'Not before Homosexuality', p. 531, and Hanson, 'Medical Writers' Woman', pp. 396–97. A slave, who was not a *vir* (citizenship was not at issue), could be called a *puer* all his life because of his sexual vulnerability.

72 M.W. Gleason, 'Semiotics of Gender: Physiognomy and Self-Fashioning in the Second Century CE', in Halperin, Winkler, and Zeitlin (eds.) *Before Sexuality*, p. 395. According to Polemo, *cinaedi* were fleshy of hip, fluid of gate, fainthearted, weak-kneed, and dry-eyed.

73 *Inst.* 11.3.76, 78–79, 69, 83, 126, 128–29. Cf. also Seneca, *Ep. Mor.* 52.12.

74 Gleason, 'Semiotics of Gender', p. 394, translating Suetonius, who is describing androgynes in *Peri Blasphemion* 61.

75 Gleason, 'Semiotics of Gender', pp. 399–402.

76 Gleason, 'Semiotics of Gender', p. 401.

roughness of hair announced from afar, 'I am a man. Approach me as such.'[77] Influenced by Stoic thought, Dio Chrysostom and Clement of Alexandria also aligned this behavior with debauchees who 'violated nature's laws' and engaged in 'unnatural acts'.[78] The critical point is that like the *puer*, the *cinaedus* was characterized by his attempt to approximate womankind so successfully that he was sometimes indistinguishable from an androgyne.[79] The '*cinaedus* was defined not in terms of the gender of his sex partners, but by his own gender deviance'.[80]

The regulation of desire, the second lens through which ancients conceptualized sexual intercourse, further complicates—and illuminates—the definition of gender. For Greeks and Romans, desire was a common reservoir of pleasure and danger. Although considered morally neutral, pleasure (ἡδονή) could be indulged too much, and since its threat was the weakness (μαλακία) and lack of self-control (ἀκρασία) inherent in women,[81] sexual indulgence rendered a man weak and womanish. Overly passionate behavior was gender trouble, leading easily to gender deviance. Consequently, philosophers fought hard to foster the manliness (toughness, asceticism, and rationality [λόγος]) they deemed critical to virtuous living, for 'life [was] war, and masculinity [had] to be achieved and constantly fought for'.[82] The winning strategy was a rigorous ethic of management called self-mastery (ἐνκράτεια),[83] and the goal was σοφρωσύνη, 'moderation' or 'self-restraint' in the use of sex (χρῆοις σοφρωσύνη).[84] Since sages asserted that they alone were truly moderate, they dismissed as fools those who insufficiently guarded themselves against erotic pleasures and preferred hotter pursuits such as pederasty, group trysts, and bestiality, to more mundane, procreative sex with women. As Dio Chrysostom said, the uncontrolled man abandoned as 'utterly feminine' the natural sexual use of women for reproduction and, inflamed, turned to adultery, prostitution, and assaults on boys.[85] The gendered linkage between lack of self-control and unmanliness explains why ancient authors, particularly philosophers, condemned pederasts and *cinaedi* for their lack of moderation.[86]

---

77 Musonius Rufus, fr. 21; *Diss.* 1.16.11, 3.1.26–27, 31; Seneca, *Ep. Mor.* 52.12, 95.21. Cf. also Atheneus' report about Diogenes, who censures a man with a plucked chin by saying. 'It cannot be, can it, that you fault nature because she made you a man instead of a woman?' (*Deip.* 13.565B–C).

78 Dio Chrysostom, *Or.* 33.52, 60; *Paid.* 3.15.1–2, 19.1.

79 Gleason, 'Semiotics of Gender', p. 398, highlights astrological alignments explaining how *cinaedi* might be born, rather than made.

80 Gleason, 'Semiotics of Gender', p. 411. See especially *Chaereas and Callirhoe* 1.4.9, the Pseudo-Aristotelian *Physiog.* 808a34, and Laertius, *De Vit. Phil.* 6.54, which denounce effeminates who coif themselves in preparation for their pursuit of women (Martin, '*Arsenokoitês* and *Malakos*', p. 126).

81 Aristotle, *Nic. Eth.* 7.1150b.

82 Stowers, *Rereading*, p. 45. Cf. also Epictetus, *Diss.* 3.24.31–37.

83 For the link between manliness and philosophy, cf. Lucian, *The Eunuch* 12, where practicing philosophy is compared to penetration of a woman. To be a sage, one had to *have* the right parts and *use* them correctly.

84 Moderation was also regularly represented as a quality particularly of those in the upper classes, with higher status and more responsibility in the *polis*.

85 *Or.* 7.133–36, 149, 151–52. Dio's emphasis on reproduction within marriage as the 'normal (κατὰ φύσιν) intercourse and union between male and female' comes in 133–36 and sets the tone for the denunciation of lustful pursuits that follows.

86 Halperin, *One Hundred Years*, p. 68.

The linked semiotics of gender and desire illuminate the logic guiding critics' denunciation of Stoics as pederasts and *cinaedi*. Among first- and second-century philosophers, the Roman Stoics were perhaps best known for striving to extirpate desire, and they advocated σωφροσύνη in the use of sex to maintain the manliness critical to living κατὰ φύσιν.[87] Musonius Rufus attempted to reduce the threat of excess desire to *sophrosyne* by proclaiming that procreative sex between husband and wife was the only 'natural' sex.[88] Epictetus likewise castigated Epicureans, saying that according to nature the sage's duties (καθήκοντα) were 'citizenship, marriage, begetting children, reverence to God ... to hold office, judge uprightly (κρινεῖν δίκαιως) ... [thus] no woman but your wife ought to look handsome to you, [and] no boy ...'.[89] Seneca condemned the *voluptas* he saw among Epicureans, twice coupling it with the traits of an effeminate.[90] Finally, several Stoics said that adultery was contrary to nature.[91] Thus, Roman Stoics intent on maintaining their manliness and virtuosity through the regulation or elimination of passion often circumscribed 'natural sex' to married, procreative intercourse and criticized non-Stoics as immoderate effeminates. The power of the charges that Stoics 'unnaturally' effeminized themselves or their (younger male) students is clear. To charge a Stoic who deemed himself the perfect man, king, and judge, with hypocrisy based on unmanly, unnatural sex was a particularly biting criticism, equivalent to saying Stoics were women rather than men, fools rather than wise men.

Rereading Romans 1.18–2.16 with Sex in Mind

When we compare the *topos* of the hypocritical Stoic to Rom. 1.18–2.16, the 'Gentile decline' narrative (1.18–32) resounds with Stoic commonplaces turned rhetorically to censure the hypocritical Stoic judge of 2.1. In 1.18–32, Paul elicits several common Stoic notions—ideas about the cosmos, attention to nature through a mind attuned to *logos*, moderate, manly sex, public duties (καθήκοντα), and perfect wisdom and judgment—in order to remind Paul's audience of Stoic judgments of non-Stoics, particularly other philosophers, for foolishness and overpassionate, effeminate sex. In 2.1–16, Paul then explicitly evokes the τόπος of the sexy Stoic, together with an allusion to the sage as 'living law', in order to turn these judgments back upon the Stoic. By revealing the utter inadequacy of his judgment and (self) rule, Paul thereby embarrasses the Stoic judge, undermines the efficacy and seeming supremacy of the Stoic way of life in Rome (2.1–11), and subjects the Stoic *summum bonum* of life 'in accord with nature' to the final judgment of Paul's God (2.12–16).

Paul's deployment of the τόπος follows immediately his declaration of God's verdict against the impiety and injustice of idolaters (1.18, cf. 1.32). The first proof, strong enough to leave the adjudged without a defense (ἀναπολογήτους, 1.20; 2.1), is that the created world teaches them what can be known of God (1.19–20). This point coheres nicely with the Stoic τόπος, which depicts the universe, or nature, as

---

87 See M. Nussbaum, 'The Stoics on the Extirpation of the Passions', *Apeiron* 20 (1987), pp. 129–77, and *idem, Therapy of Desire*.

88 R.B. Ward, 'Musonius and Paul on Marriage', *NTS* 36 (1990) pp. 281–89.

89 *Diss.* 3.7.26, 21. *Diss.* 2.4.10–11; Origen, *Contr. Cels.* 7.63; *SVF* 1.58.11–15; Fr. 244.

90 *Vit. Beat.* 7.3, 13.4; *De Ben.* 4.2, 13.

91 *Diss.* 2.4.10–11; Origen, *Contr. Cels.* 7.63; *SVF* 1.58.11–15; Fr. 244.

revealing divinity because the divine λόγος or rationality permeates it.[92] Although Stoics were known for identifying the universe *as* God, even the language of God as 'Creator' of nature (1.20) and of the impiety (ἀσέβεια) of those who did not worship God (1.18, 21) is consonant with Stoic thought. Laertius nicely described the Stoic understanding of God: 'The deity, they say, is a living being, immortal, rational, perfect, intelligent in happiness, allowing entry to nothing evil, taking providential care of the world and everything in it, but he is not of human shape. He is, however, the artificer of the universe and the father of all, both in general and in the particular part of him that is all-pervading.'[93]

> The language [in Romans] is scarcely characteristic of earliest Christian thought (καθοράω, 'perceive' and θειότης, 'divinity, divine nature', occur only here in the NT; *aidios*, 'eternal' elsewhere only in Jude 6; and *poiema*, 'what is made', only here and Eph. 2.10). It also for the most part plays an insignificant role in the OT. But it is familiar in Stoic thought: the closest parallel to the ἀόρατα/καθορᾶται wordplay comes in Pseudo-Aristotle, *de Mundo* 399b.14ff ... and for θειότης cf. particularly Plutarch, *Mor.* 398A; 665A ... Paul is trading upon, without necessarily committing himself to, the Greek (particularly Stoic) understanding of an invisible realm of reality, invisible to sense perception, which can be known only through the rational power of the mind.[94]

The role of mind (νοῦς) in recognizing the relationship of nature to the divine introduces the second allusion to the τόπος. Inaugurated by the ἀόρατα/καθορᾶται (invisible things/perceive) wordplay in v. 20, the language of (false) reasoning skyrockets in Rom. 1.21–23: knowing (γνόντες) God is juxtaposed to the befuddling (ἐματαιώθησαν, ἐμωράνθησαν, ἐσκοτίσθη) of those who are senseless (ἀσύνετος) in their reasonings (διαλογισμοῖς, καρδία).[95] As in the *topos*, the involuntary false thinking of senseless minds leads fools into other forms of falsehood (vv. 23, 25), which are also involuntary errors of judgment (see *plane*, v. 27). Typical of decline narratives, the foremost error is the idolatry of fools who mistake representations of nature for its Creator (1.23, 25).[96] Paul's reversal of the categories of the wise man

92 For the concept of *logos* as divine Wisdom in Romans, cf. Rom. 10.1–21, esp. 10.8. See also Hays, *Echoes of Scripture in the Letters of Paul* (New Haven: Yale University Press, 1989), pp. 34–83; M.J. Suggs, ' "The Word Is Near You": Romans 10.6–10 within the Purpose of the Letter', in W.R. Farmer, C.F.D. Moule, and R.R. Niebuhr (eds.), *Christian History and Interpretation: Studies Presented to John Knox* (Cambridge: Cambridge University Press, 1967), pp. 289–312. On Wisdom in Romans 12, see W. Wilson, *Love without Pretense: Romans 12.9–21 and Hellenistic-Jewish Wisdom Literature* (WUNT, 46; Tübingen: J.C.B. Mohr, 1991).

93 Laertius, *De Vit. Phil.* 7.147. Cf. also 7.134–36. Chryssipus identified the universe with God (Cicero, *De Nat. Deor.* 2.38), but this did not prevent Epictetus from talking about God as creating its constituent parts; see *Diss.* 1.14.10. Laertius emphasizes that Stoics saw themselves as both godlike and pious worshipers of the gods or God (2.7.119). Paul distinguished God from the universe in a way Stoics did not, but this distinction is not important for 1.18–32 to function as a censure of Stoics; Paul's opponent at 2.1, and thus, a Stoic interlocutor, only had to believe that people were judged for not recognizing God-in-nature and that God was worthy of worship.

94 Dunn, *Romans,* pp. 57–58.

95 S. Stowers, 'Paul on the Use and Abuse of Reason', in D.L. Balch, E.E. Ferguson, and W. Meeks (eds.), *Greeks, Romans, and Christians: Essays in Honor of Abraham J. Malherbe* (Minneapolis: Fortress, 1990), pp. 253–86. He analyses such terms in philosophical literature dealing with the function of reason in the pursuit of virtue.

96 Cf. Wisdom of Solomon 13–14, the Ninth Letter of Anacharsis, and Seneca, *Ep. Mor.* 90.

and fool (1.22, cf. 1.14) and allusions to the created world (vv. 20, 23)[97] underscore the irony of this mistake: those claiming to be sages (σοφοί) with access to the logic of nature were really fools.

The third allusion to the τόπος occurs in 1.24–27: the false reasoning about nature that led to idolatry now precipitates the involuntary exercise of passions in unnatural, immoderate sex (1.26–27).[98] In vv. 24–27, as in the τόπος, the vice of unnatural sex is a 'form of ignorance of those things whereof the corresponding virtues are the knowledge'.[99] The virtue or 'good' (cf. 2.8, 10) is intercourse in which couples enacted 'natural' sex roles: men were active penetrators of passive women. The sex roles, in other words, accorded with the work of nature's Creator. The language of vv. 26–27a indicates that the idolaters were guilty of reversing this norm: not only is the hierarchical gender pairing (woman–man) introduced,[100] the women are

97 Richard Hays highlights the importance of creation language for interpretation of Rom. 1.18–32 as a unit ('Relations Natural and Unnatural: A Response to John Boswell's Exegesis of Romans 1', *Journal of Christian Ethics* 14 [1986], pp. 184–215, esp. 191 and 212 n. 6). Hays adduces creation language (vv. 20, 25) and strong linguistic and thematic parallels between vv. 23–27 and Gen. 1.26–28 as evidence for hearing all of Genesis 1–3 as the warrant for the judgment leveled in Romans 1 (e.g. the Greek for image [εἰκών], likeness [ὁμοίωμα], birds [πετεινά], reptiles [ἕπτετα], male [ἄρρην], and female [θῆλυ] appears in both texts, and the order in Romans ['birds and tetrapods and reptiles'] replicates that of Gen. 1.26). For Hays, one important result is the (infelicitously stated) judgment that 'homosexual behavior' is 'a sacrament (so to speak) of the anti-religion of human beings who refuse to honor God as creator'. In other words, the actions depicted in vv. 26–27 are the primary sign of humanity's fall from a pristine natural state.

The linguistic connections indicate that Paul probably intended and his audience could have heard an allusion in Romans 1 to Gen. 1.26–28. However, neither the terms themselves nor a possible allusion determines *how* Paul intended the allusion to function or, more importantly, *how* his audience interpreted Rom. 1.18–32. Paul may have intended his idolatry language to allude to the creation as ground for recognizing God's superiority, nothing more, nothing less (cf. 1.5). Likewise, audience expectations of Rom. 1.18–32 are far easier to gauge based on general knowledge of the decline narratives following the pattern found in Romans 1 rather than on specific knowledge of one implicit scriptural allusion buried within that narrative. Even had Paul intended and ancients heard Gen. 1.26–28 (or another scripture alluding to Gen. 1.26–28) echoed in Romans 1, that doesn't determine its *impact* on them. Many other factors contributed to ancients' strategies of interpretation, including contemporaneous traditions of interpreting Gen. 1.26–28 and common definitions of 'woman', 'man', 'nature', and 'passion'. Like Romans 1, Wisdom of Solomon 13–14 (cf. 13.10–16; 14.12–31) uses creation language and a reference to non-procreative sex to prove that idolaters worshiped created things, rather than the creator. *Contra* Hays, however, ancients did not take these allusions to Gen. 1.26–28 or to 'bad sex' as reasons to interpret Wisdom 14 as an Edenic fall narrative, as Hays does of Romans. While 'the creation' is *inarguably* a pivotal basis for the proofs lodged against the idolaters in Romans 1, and the actions in 1.26–27 function as the prime examples of mindless idolatry, the narrative does *not* function as Hays claims. Ancients did not interpret Rom. 1.18–32 as an exegesis of Genesis 1–3 representing the 'natural complementarity between women and men' as we moderns understand it. Complementarity as Hays construes it is a concept born in nineteenth- and twentieth-century American discussions of women working outside the home. See A. Kessler-Harris, *Out to Work* (New York: Oxford University Press, 1982) and R. Rosenberg, *Beyond Separate Spheres* (New Haven: Yale University Press, 1982).

98 The involuntary character is underscored by Paul's repeated use of παρέδωκεν. God is the actor who 'hands over' the idolaters to their lusts (vv. 24, 26). The idolaters then act on their lusts, but the point is that false thinking *inevitably* brings these consequences, and God causes these results.

99 *De Vit. Phil.* 7.94. Laertius was discussing Stoics' understanding of vices generally.

100 On the Hellenistic cosmic gender hierarchy in 1 Corinthians 11, see Corley and Torjesen, 'Sexuality, Hierarchy, and Evangelism', and Martin, *Corinthian Body*, pp. 229–49.

portrayed as actively '*exchanging* (μετήλλαξαν) the natural use [of intercourse] for the unnatural', thereby embodying idolatry in their intercourse (μετήλλαξαν, v. 23), whereas the men merely 'gave up (ἀφέντες) the natural use of women'.[101] Given this allusion to sex-role reversal, the depiction of θηλείαι (women/females) and ἄρσενες (men/males) engaging in unnatural sex undoubtedly functioned as the critical proof of the mindlessness of their idolatry, of the ignorance underlying their failure to recognize that God was the Creator of nature. Significantly, the thrust of 1.24–27a parallels that of Epictetus's discourse on providence (πρόνοια): 'Assuredly from the very structure of all made objects we are accustomed to prove that the work is the product of a technician ... do not visible objects and vision and light reveal him? And the male (ἄρρην) and female (θῆλυ), and the zeal (προθυμία) they have for sex, and the faculty which makes use of the organs that have been constructed for this purpose, do not these things reveal their artificer?'[102] In vv. 24–27, as in Roman Stoicism, the exchange of natural for unnatural sex represented a mindless inversion of the cosmic hierarchy, arguably the most important work of the Artificer.

This point is further illuminated by the second allusion to the τόπος in vv. 24–27, the role of passion and desire in the inversion of the cosmic hierarchy. Like the τόπος, passion is portrayed as the result of false thinking. As Laertius put it, 'according to the Stoics, "falsehood results in distortion, which extends to the mind ... from this distortion arises many passions (πάθη), which are causes of instability. Passion is, according to Zeno, an irrational (ἄλογος) and unnatural (παρὰ φύσιν) movement in the soul or an impulse in excess."' Desire (ἐπιθυμία), one type of passion, is an 'irrational appetitive burning (ὄρεξις)', which exhibits itself, among other things, as love (ἔρως).[103] Verses 24–27 scream this language of passion, from 'the lusts (ἐπιθυμια, v. 24) of their hearts' (the synonym of a lustful mind 'irrationally and unnaturally moved'[104]) to 'passions of dishonor' (πάθη ἀτιμίας, v. 26), the 'unnatural use of sex' (μετηλλαξαν τὴν φυσικὴν χρῆσιν εἰς τὴν παρὰ φύσιν, vv. 26–27), and men's 'consumption in their burning' (ἐξεκαύθησαν ἐν τῇ ὀρέξει, v. 27) for each other.[105] Given the convergence of cosmic hierarchy and the governance of desire in the Stoic τόπος and in Roman Stoics' maintenance of 'natural' gender boundaries, we should expect that in vv. 24–27 immoderately

---

101 For a poignant example of the *assumed* unnatural results of women's gender-bending sexual activity, cf. Plutarch, *Mor.* 997 2B: 'just as with women who are insatiable in seeking pleasure, their lust tries everything, goes astray, and explores the gamut of profligacy until at last it ends in unspeakable practices (Empirius renders it, "into manly practices", εἰς τὰ ἀρρηνα); so too intemperance in eating passes beyond the necessary ends of nature and resorts to cruelty and lawlessness to give variety to appetite ...' See Brooten, *Love between Women,* pp. 245–46: 'The active verb (μετήλλαξαν) with a feminine subject is striking. The specific verbs for sexual intercourse are usually active when they refer to men and passive when they refer to women ...'

102 *Diss.* 1.6.8–9.

103 *De Vit. Phil.* 7.110, 113.

104 Καρδία (heart) and νοῦς (mind) were synonyms, as scholars have long recognized (see n. 42 above).

105 Often treated as a peculiarly Jewish formulation, even the language of impurity (ἀκαθαρσίαν, v. 24) that dishonors is consistent with this portrait: as Epictetus put it, 'In your sex-life preserve purity (καθαρευτέον) before marriage to the extent that you are able, and if you indulge, take only those privileges which are lawful' (*Encheiridion* 8).

indulged passion would invert natural gender relations. This is exactly what happens in v. 27, the rhetorical center of the decline narrative.

The rhetorical center is emphatically *not* vv. 26b–27a, as scholarly treatments suggest. Most readers focus on the gender of the women's sex objects in vv. 26b and, identifying them as fellow women, argue that vv. 26–27 condemn male and female homosexual behavior.[106] However, since Paul leaves unnamed the gender of the women's sex partners (that these partners were people, rather than animals or angels, is suggested by ἐν αὐτοῖς ['among themselves'] in 1.24), scholars can only make this claim by arguing that the adverb ὁμοίως ('likewise', 'in the same way', v. 27a) supplies the women's sex objects. Thus, in order to argue that Paul condemned women's sex with other women in 1.26b, and therefore all homosexual sex, they read 1.26–27 backwards, inferring from men's forsaking of 'the natural use of *women*' that women *likewise* exchanged sex with men for sex with other women.

However, the gender of their sex partners *cannot* be gleaned from ὁμοίως. Within the Pauline corpus, ὁμοίως suggests that conjugal duties due the husband are also due the wife (1 Cor. 7.3–4) and elsewhere links, without equating, two exchanges of status position (1 Cor. 7.22). In short, these uses of ὁμοίως do not imply that ὁμοίως connotes same-sex intercourse in Romans 1. In fact, the most cursory concordance search of New Testament texts indicates that ὁμοίως links actions without necessarily implying or determining the object, or indirect object, of the verb. In Mk 4.16, for example, ὁμοίως refers to two acts of sowing, but they occur in different places. In Lk. 3.11, it refers to sharing, once of a coat, but then of food. In Jn 6.11 and 21.13, it connects distribution of loaves with that of fish. Finally, in 1 Pet. 3.1, ὁμοίως connects a call to submission but demands different *types* of submission from slaves and wives; moreover, in 3.7 ὁμοίως links entirely different actions: husbands should be considerate *just as* wives are submissive.

These uses of ὁμοίως indicate that the important connection between Rom. 1.26 and 1.27 is the action, the 'exchange/forsaking of the natural use for what is contrary to nature'. What women exchanged 'the natural use' for is not clarified by ὁμοίως: Paul's audience could have assumed that the women of 1.26b had unnatural sex with other women, but given that ancients focused on the unnaturalness of sex-role reversal (active for passive), they could also have assumed their sex objects to be men, boys, or girls.[107] Thus, 1.26 lacks the critical data at the foundation of the

---

106 For exceptions, see Brooten, *Love between Women,* pp. 248–50. For a fuller analysis of this passage as a censure of male effeminacy and its ultimate threat, gender-shifting, see my article, ' "The Disease of Effemination": The Charge of Effeminacy and the Verdict of God', forthcoming in *Semeia Studies* (ed. Stephen Moore and Janice C. Anderson).

107 For patristic interpretations of this passage, see my essay, ' "The Disease of Effemination".' Thus, I disagree with Brooten (*Love between Women,* pp. 248–52), who concludes that Rom. 1.26 deals with female homosexual sex based on the arguments that Jews like Philo might treat sex with menstruants, non-procreative sex, pederasty, and bestiality as unnatural and that Paul did not mention menstruants, did not care about procreation, and dealt with human–human sexual contact in v. 26. Brooten does not discuss well Roman Stoic depictions of sex παρὰ φύσιν (p. 251 nn. 101, 103); further, first-century notions of unnatural sex cannot be circumscribed to the definitions of Philo or Paul. If we account for the standards of Musonius Rufus, Epictetus, and Seneca, the Romans could have treated as unnatural *any* unmarried, non-procreative sex (in this case, women pursuing another woman's husband and women penetrating boys, men, girls or women), as well as the forms of 'unnatural sex' Brooten lists and dismisses.

modern reading of 1.26–27, and in order to supply that information, fitting it into our modern subject–object paradigm of sexual intercourse, we must read the text backwards. In sum, the sex objects of the women in Rom. 1.26 are unstated, irretrievable, and unimportant to the larger argument in Romans.

What *is* important is the charge of effeminate intercourse in 1.27. After introducing the subject of gender reversal in vv. 26b–27a with the hierarchical gender polarity (woman–man) and gendered actions (women's active 'exchange' and men's 'giving up' of natural sex), the narrative moves quickly to highlight what was more important rhetorically, the actions of men 'who gave up the natural use of women' for intercourse παρὰ φύσιν (v. 27). Since the phrase 'the natural use of the woman' connoted the appropriately hierarchical penetration of a woman by a man,[108] the clause 'giving up the natural use of the woman, the men were inflamed in their burning for each other' (v. 27a–b) powerfully frames v. 27c–d as the inversion of the cosmic penetrator–penetrated gender paradigm by means of inordinately indulged passion.[109] The participial phrases of v. 27c–d confirm this framing by using the language of gender transgression to allude to the result of their behavior, effeminacy: 'by working unseemliness (τὴν ἀσχημοσύνην κατεργάζομαι) in men, men [the men who gave up the natural use of women] received in themselves the penalty fitting for their error'.[110] Gender transgression inheres in the phrase τὴν ἀσχημοσύνην κατερ-γάζομαι, but typical translations obscure its effect. The RSV and NRSV, reading 'men committing (κατεργαζόμενοι) shameless acts (τὴν ἀσχημοσύνην) with men and receiving in their own persons the due penalty for their error', translate the singular ἀσχημοσύν with the plural 'shameless acts' to emphasize repetition. Had Paul wished this effect, he could have used the plural ἀσχημοσύναι rather than the singular ἀσχημοσύνη.[111]

A review of the functions of ἀσχημοσύνη in ancient texts suggests a different reading of v. 27c–d. In addition to connoting shame, ἀσχημοσύνη meant 'deformity', 'unseemliness', and 'disgrace', and it described the unmanly weakness that accompanied excessive passion and prohibited the pursuit of virtue. In the Old Greek Scriptures, for example, its connection to sex is clear in its function as a euphemism for genital nakedness and intercourse (cf. Exod. 20.26; Lev. 18.6–20; Rev. 16.15). Philo interpreted Deut. 23.14, where ἀσχημοσύνη refers to excrement, as applying to the 'unruly desires' associated with food, drink, and sex that tested a man's self-control (*Leg. All.* 3.156–57): 'Let a shovel, that is, reason (λόγος), follow passion, preventing it from spreading abroad (3.154) … and bringing the shovel to bear you will cover your τὴν ἀσχημοσύνην.' Plutarch likewise used the synonymous adjective αἰσχρός to describe the effeminizing results of unnatural indulgence in food:

> Intemperance in eating passes beyond the necessary ends of nature and results in cruelty
> and lawlessness to give variety to appetite (ὄρεξις). For it is in their company that organs

108 See Brooten, *Love between Women*, pp. 245, 250.
109 Martin, 'Heterosexism', pp. 339–49.
110 I translate κατεργαζόμενοι as a circumstantial participle of means. The context indicates that ἀπολαμβάνοντες, 'receiving', expresses result.
111 For the singular as 'shameful act', see Josephus, *Ant.* 16.223. For the plural as shameless acts, see Philo, *Leg. All.* 2.66.

of sense are infected and won over and become licentious when they do not keep to natural standards ... From this our luxury and debauchery conceive a desire for shameful (*aischras*) caresses and effeminate titillations ... Just so intemperate intercourse follows a lawless meal, inharmonious music follows unseemly (*aischrois*) debauches, barbarous spectacles follow shameless (*anaischuntois*) songs and sounds ...[112]

Thus, the 'unseemliness' of ἀσχημοσύνη alluded to the threat of effemination that rendered a man impotent to act virtuously and therefore shamed him.

When ἀσχημοσύνη as the 'unseemliness/disgrace' of passion is paired in v. 27c with the verb κατεργάζομαι, which emphasizes the effect wrought by work,[113] the phrase 'men working unseemliness in men' connotes the cultivation of gender transgression that not only brought about the shame of social dishonor Paul had threatened since v. 24, but also resulted in deformity—the participants' effemination. As Epictetus described the consequences of indulging passions from grief to pleasure, 'the wages of fighting against God and disobedience (ἀπεθείας) will not be paid by "children's children", but by me myself in my own person'.[114] Early interpreters of Rom. 1.27d assumed that effeminacy was the wage or 'penalty of error' that men 'received in their own persons' for their mindless inattention to nature. Clement of Alexandria, John Chrysostom, and others assumed that 1.27 applied to sexual passives (κίναιδοι) who became sterile and exhibited other signs of bodily effemination as a result of being penetrated.[115] Hence, ancients interpreted vv. 26–27 as referring to the inversion of natural sex roles (penetrated for penetrator, feminine for masculine), the very inversion of the cosmic hierarchy that so threatened sages' pursuit of virtue and their reputations as wise men. From its emphasis on nature to its inversion of cosmic hierarchy through indulged passion, Rom. 1.24–27 is thoroughly consistent with Stoic denunciations of non-Stoic philosophers (particularly Epicureans) and others as 'the foolish masses' (v. 22) who ignore the reason, or law, of nature and who practice immoderate, unnatural sex.[116]

Rom. 1.18–32 ends with one more allusion to the τόπος of the Stoic sage: the idea that idolaters' totally enfeebled minds prohibited them from performing their natural duties as citizens (καθήκοντα). As Laertius said, the Stoic founder 'Zeno was the first to use the term καθῆκαν of conduct', which is 'an action in itself adapted to nature's arrangements'. By extrapolation:

Befitting acts (καθήκοντα) are all those which [natural] reason prevails upon us to do; and this is the case with honoring one's parents, brothers, and country, and intercourse with

---

112 *Mor.* 997 2B–C.

113 Κατεργάζομαι meant to produce, cultivate, or do something. Of its 22 occurrences in the New Testament, 19 are Pauline (the majority in Romans). Paul uses Κατεργάζομαι with each of the three connotations. Hence, 1.27c could be interpreted as emphasizing the act itself, 'men did/committed a shameless act ...'. However, the article, the use of ἀσχημεμοσύνη as a euphemism for the weakness associated with indulgence in passion, its linkage with Κατεργάζομαι, and the explicit language of result in the following participial phrase indicate that Κατεργάζομαι is better understood as connoting the effect wrought by work—what is produced or cultivated through an act. Cf. Rom. 2.9, where Κατεργάζομαι means 'produce', emphasizing actions with negative results.

114 *Diss.* 3.24.24. For the extended argument, see 3.24.22–39.

115 Brooten, *Love between Women*, pp. 303–57.

116 For the same suggestion, see Brooten, *Love between Women*, p. 254.

friends. Unfitting or contrary to duty (παρά τό καθῆκον) are all acts that reason deprecates, which are these very things (τὰ τοιαῦτα): to neglect one's parents, to be indifferent to one's brothers, not to agree with friends, to disregard the interests of one's country, and so forth.[117]

Evoking the Stoic idea of natural duties left undone (τὰ μὴ καθήκοντα, v. 28), Rom. 1.28–32 extends the theme of the unnatural results of ignorance from their destructive effects on idolaters' bodies (vv. 24–27) to their factionalizing effects on the body politic (vv. 29–31). This rhetorical move in v. 28 proceeds by several steps: charging the idolaters with ignorance for a fifth time ('failing to keep God in mind' [ἔχειν ἐν επιγνώσει], vv. 18–19, 21, 23, 25, 28); juxtaposing their poor judgment about God and their disqualified mind in a wordplay on mental fitness (ἐδοκίμασαν/ἀδόκιμον); describing them for a third time as 'handed over by God' (vv. 24, 26, 28) to the result of ignorance, an unfit mind (ἀδόκιμον νοῦν) that disabled acts of justice (ἀδικία, v. 29); and offering a vice list (vv. 29–31)[118] that emphasized the passions with interpersonal effects.[119] Since justice was a relational concept,[120] the prime placement of injustice (πάσῃ ἀδικίᾳ) in the vice list colors the remaining passions as relational errors. Precisely the kind of errors Laertius lists, these passions also underscore the contrast between idolaters' mindless injustice and the justice of the God (1.17) who now judged them (1.18, 32). Hence, the reference to idolaters' knowledge of God (ἐπιγνόντες) in v. 32 is an ironic inclusio of both vv. 28–32 and the whole decline narrative: the irony is that the mental confusion of the impious past and present was so complete,[121] and their distance from the Creator of the nature by which they supposedly determine right action so total, that they highly esteemed (συνευδοκοῦσιν) those guilty of the unnatural acts that God deemed worthy of death.[122] In *Ep. Mor.* 39.3–6, Seneca makes the same

117 *De Vit. Phil.* 7.107–109. See also 7.25.
118 Following Leitzmann, Dunn suggests that the vice list was particularly used among Stoics, but he quickly adds that Jewish and early Christian texts exhibit instances of this generally Greek nod at conventional morality (*Romans*, p. 67).
119 Cf. Laertius, *De Vit. Phil.* 7.110–15. Examples of other passions, according to the Stoics, included contentiousness, grief, pity, envy, jealousy, rivalry, anger, resentment, anguish, and distress.
120 Within Judaism, δικαιοσύνη translated *chesed* ('lovingkindness') and as such connoted the covenant relation between God and Israel and right action among Israelites and between Israelites and foreigners (Dunn, *Romans*, pp. 40–41). *Contra* Dunn and others, in Greco-Roman ideology it was not simply an ideal or ethical norm, one of the four cardinal virtues. δικαιοσύνη connoted right relations. Personified as *Dike*, Justice accused those who did wrong to others and avenged that wrongdoing (Hesiod, *Theog.* 902; *Op.* 256–264; Plato, *Laws* 715E, 827E, *Epin.* 988E; Ps-Demosthenes [Kern, *Orphicorum Fragmenta* 23] 25.11, cf. also Wis. 11.20). The term δικαίως was often used as a synonym for the *sophos*, 'wise man/sage'.
121 The two present-tense verbs, 'to do' and 'to approve', in an otherwise past-tense narrative are noteworthy.
122 Commentators widely agree that God's δικαίωμα ('just verdict', v. 32) that 'those who practice such things are worthy of death' appeals to a culturally accepted 'truth', placed in God's mouth, that people who are so wholly out of tune with acceptable conduct are refuse worthy of the worst punish-ments. Dunn hypothesizes that Paul alluded to the judgment of mortality given in Gen. 2.16–17 (*Romans*, p. 69); even though mortality is clearly in view, an allusion to Gen. 2.16–17 would be unexpected and would distract the audience from the point, that the idolaters are deemed wholly unable to judge rightly. Verse 32 reflects the widespread idea that God or the gods punish these

point by describing the man who had wholly succumbed to passion, and thus, wholly lost his mind:[123]

> The only excuse that we can allow for the incontinence (*inpotentiae*) and mad lust (*insanae libidini*) of [certain men prone to excess] is the fact that they suffer the evils which they have inflicted upon others. And they are rightly harassed by this madness, because desire must have unbounded space for its excursions, if it transgresses nature's mean ... for this reason they are most wretched, because they have reached such a pass that what was once superfluous to them has become indispensable. And so they are the slaves of their pleasures ... *Then the height of unhappiness is reached, when men are not only attracted, but even pleased, by shameful things*, and when there is no longer any room for a cure, now that those things which once were vices have become habits.

In Rom. 1.18–25, the impious fools who dishonored God, worshiping the creation, were precisely these insanely passionate men. Thus, from its emphasis on the importance of knowledge and judgment, unnatural sex, and failure to do one's natural public duties, to the idea that the universe revealed its Creator through a mind attuned to nature, Rom. 1.18–32 is consistent with criticisms ancients thought Stoics used to distance themselves from the uneducated and to degrade other schools of philosophy.

The coherence of the Stoic τόπος within Rom. 1.18–32 is what makes it so devastating as a criticism of the hypocritical Stoic sage in 2.1–16. The τόπος shows that even when criticized anonymously, the Stoic sage was widely recognized for thinking himself the perfect judge in the πολιτεία and the perfect instructor of young men in virtue. Of course, as the τόπος shows, the problem was that Stoics were as vulnerable as Epicureans to Stoic charges of effeminacy and indulging passions contrary to nature. Indeed, even as Roman Stoics touted strict gender differentiation and circumscribed natural intercourse to married, procreative sex, their founder Zeno was known to chase his students, laud the communal sharing of wives, and bid 'men and women to wear the same dress and keep no part of their bodies entirely covered'.[124]

Of all possible targets of Rom. 2.1, the 'hypocritical Stoic' was the most vulnerable to censure (ἀναπολόγητος) as being the opposite of the 'perfect judge' he claimed to be. He did *exactly* the same unnatural things (*ta toiauta*, 1.32; 2.1–2) as the fools upon whom he passed judgment (ἀναπολογήτους, 1.20; κρίνεις τὸν ἕτερον, 2.1). By effeminating maturing youths or being effeminated by them, he

---

people, who are unjust, for the passions that ruin their minds (see esp. 13.3–4, where rulers are empowered by God to inflict capital punishment for wrongdoing [Dunn, *Romans*, p. 764]). Even though Stoics actively taught that death was inconsequential and not to be feared *by sages* (see below), the idea of punishment *of fools* is present in Stoic thought (Stobaeus, 1.3.50, attributed to Epictetus the sentiment that God punished the unjust). Epictetus said that punishment, including 'destruction' of the faithful man, followed from disobeying God (*Diss.* 3.7.36); an unpleasant death awaited those who lived passionately (3.2.15); the greatest offences reaped the greatest punishments (3.24.41–43); and a shameful death was especially dreadful (2.1.13).

123 On foolishness as insanity, see also Epictetus, *Diss.* 2.15.13–15. For another parallel to 1.32, see *T. Ash.* 6.2.

124 On chasing boys, cf. Laertius, *De Vit. Phil.* 7.17, 21. On Zeno's advocacy of communal marriages and transvestitism, 7.33, 131. Zeno was esteemed as most temperate, 7.27.

demonstrated that he was a terrible teacher of virtue, and since he modeled his life on the teachings of his Stoic forebears, his mind must have been so thoroughly effeminated that he 'approved of' Stoics who acted unnaturally (v. 32). Hence, because of his mental weakness, he lacked the wisdom necessary to guide the affairs of the *politeia*, including the public duty (καθῆκαν) of judging people justly (1.28; 2.1).

Depicting himself as the Stoic's rival teacher, Paul highlighted the consequences of these judgments in Rom. 2.1–16.[125] First, Paul argued that the sage's weakness proved that his philosophy of living 'according to nature' could not bring adherents the benefits of virtuous living, honor, and immortality. Interrogating his Stoic opponent in diatribal style, Paul instructed the mindless judge that: his unnatural actions were proof that he was weak and, thus, certain to be condemned in God's final judgment (v. 3); he must recognize God's merciful kindness (χρηστότητος χρηστόν) and forbearance (ἀνοχῆ μακροθυμία) in not condemning him to death immediately (1.32; 2.4); and he must 'change' his mind (μετάνοια, v. 4) in order to live well and gain eternal life (2.7).[126] By deploying the idea fundamental to the Greek concept of nature, that idea that the strong naturally ruled the weak, Paul showed that God's superior power (δύναμις, 1.16, 20) and kingly benevolence (2.4) demonstrated his right to rule the weak Stoic.

Apropos of the *topos*, however, the Stoic judge remained impenitent because of his natural superiority (vv. 5, 8) and continued to believe that death did not concern him because 'glory and honor and immortality' were his sure reward (v. 7). As Epictetus said:

> As for me ... [trying to make my own moral purpose tranquil, unhampered, constrained, free] is what I wish to be engaged in when death finds me, so that I may be able to say to God, 'Have I in any respect transgressed your commands (ἐντολάς)? Have I in any respect misused the resources which you gave me? ... and now I am full of gratitude to you that you have deemed me worthy to take part in this festival with you and to see your works (ἔργα) and to understand your governance.'
> Why, what else [will you make of death] but make it your glory, or an opportunity for you to show in deed (ἔργα δι' αὐτοῦ) thereby what kind of person is a man who follows the will of nature.[127]

---

125 In 1 Cor. 4.1–13. Paul uses the same τόπος of the arrogant, hypocritical judge and ruler to argue that the Corinthians, who thought themselves 'filled', 'rich', 'kingly' judges should leave judgment-making to God and instead model their behavior on Paul, the opposite of those things.

126 For this sense of μετάνοια, which brings out the rhetorical play on mental incapacity that redounds in 1.18–2.16, see Marcus Aurelius 8.10, 'μετάνοια is a sort of self-reproach at some useful thing passed by; but the good must needs be a useful thing and ever to be cultivated by the truly good man; but the true good man would never regret having passed a pleasure by.' For the reversal of the commonplace that Stoics did not need to 'change their minds', see Lucian's *Herm.* 86. Convinced by Lycinus that the Stoic pursuit of virtue was not efficacious, Hermotimus proclaims his philosophical life a 'debauch' (83) and goes off to 'metamorphose' himself to purge himself from its insanity (see Rom. 12.2, where God is the metamorphosizer). On μετάνοια as 'repentance', see Ez. 33.11, 18.32; Ps-Aristeas 188; *y. Mak.* 2.6, 31d; *b. Yom.* 86b. Unlike the Stoics, Philo considered μετάνοια a virtue, the mark of a man of wisdom (*Virt.* 177; *Abr.* 26; *Somn.* 1.91; *Spec. Leg.* 1.103; *Quaest. in Gen.* 2.13).

127 *Diss.* 4.7.15–18; 3.7.7–11; 3.10.13–14. Stoics treated death as inconsequential to the sage (cf. 3.3.15, 3.18.2). Posidonius, Seneca, and Marcus Aurelius interpreted the myth of Hercules to mean that after passing through the fire that liberated their spirits/souls at death, sages who lived according to nature were raised to the level of gods and enjoyed immortality as their reward.

Since he lived κατά φύσιν, the Stoic thought he was just and did not need to 'change his mind'. In Paul's view, the Stoic's mental incapacity had rendered him impotent to recognize his own 'unnatural acts'. Thus, the Stoic was 'storing up for himself' divine wrath; if he continued his indulgence in self-interested (ἐξ ἐριθείας) and factious behavior (vv. 8, 10; 1.24–31), he would reap punishment at his death.[128]

For the Roman Christians, the irony of Paul's rhetoric is that they knew nature would have led a real wise man to recognize that the Creator of nature was the God of the gospel (1.16–17, 19–21). Only the God of Israel (1.1–6), of 'Jew first and also the Greek', was truly a just and impartial (2.11) Judge. The correlate of this claim is that only the God of Paul's gospel was free to choose the criteria by which right action was determined and just men (δίκαιοι) were granted the benefits of 'glory, honor, and immortality' (2.7; 1.17). This is the thrust of Rom. 2.2–11 and, as such, the first critical support of Paul's thesis (1.16–17). Against the Stoic who thought himself virtuous because of his exclusive ability to pursue wisdom naturally and his consequent superiority to the masses, Paul argued that God was Just because he was merciful to the undeserving. He was merciful because he postponed the immediate condemnation due the Stoic (and the Gentiles generally) for unnatural and unjust acts in order to give the Stoic (and by extension, the Gentiles) time to change his weak mind and to seek after the good that led to eternal life. Unlike the Stoic philosophy, which at best benefited the Stoic at the expense of the masses, the gospel about Paul's God and his merciful justice benefited all.

Rom. 2.12–16 reinforces this point by juxtaposing two elements of the Stoic *topos*, attention to nature as the yardstick of good conduct and Stoics as a living law. Recall that Stoics thought they were a 'living law' because the reason of nature, a divine standard or law, taught them to be perfect judges of the good.[129] Paul invokes this idea to place Gentiles, with Jews, under the obligation of the law while undercutting the efficacy of nature as a sufficient rule of conduct. He does this most clearly in 2.13–14 when he grants the hypocritical Stoic the point that Gentiles could in theory be just: 'When Gentiles who do not have the law do naturally what the law requires, they are a law to themselves ... they show that what the law requires is written on their hearts.' Taking the adverb 'naturally' to function here as it did in 1.26–27, to modify the main action in the sentence,[130] this statement seems to support the Stoic's belief that he was a living law taught by nature to do the good. However, Paul overturned this central tenet by evoking another commonplace shared by Stoics and their enemies: that only a few real wise men had ever lived.[131] In fact, Epictetus repeatedly said no one practiced Stoic ethics.[132]

---

128 This judgment is coherent with, and may echo, Wis. 6.1–21 (and see Wis. 1.1–15).

129 For nature as the divine law in Stoicism, see Klassen, 'The King as "Living Law"'. Cf. also Epictetus, *Diss.* 1.24.13, 3.24.42.

130 *Contra* Dunn's argument (*Romans,* p. 98) that we must read φύσει with the verb 'to do', grammatical and syntactical claims about whether the adverb φύσει should be linked with *echonta* ('those who possess the law') or with ποῖωσιν ('they do the law') are inconclusive. Therefore, a decision to read v. 14 as 'Gentiles who do not naturally have the law, do the law' or as 'Gentiles who do not have the law, do naturally what the law requires' is *necessarily* subjective. I read as our earliest extant audience, patristic authors, *overwhelmingly* did, as referring to some Gentiles' ability to do right naturally. See, e.g., Origen, *Com. Ep. Rom.* 1. 228, 230; Tertullian, *Ad. Marc.* 5. 13; Pelagius, *Com. Rom.* 73; Ambrosiaster, *Com. Ep. Paul.* 81.75.

131 Martens makes this argument, 'Romans 2.14–16', p. 66, esp nn. 45–46. E.g., Cicero, *De Off.* 3.16, *De Nat.*1.23, *De Leg.* 1.6.18; Plutarch, *Mor.* 9.1035C.

132 *Diss.* 3.7. See also Hock, ' "By the Gods, It's my One Desire to See an Actual Stoic" '.

Two consequences follow from this argument. First, God in his mercy was offering Gentiles a second chance to act rightly, which meant acting in accord with God's law which they, like Paul, thought encompassed nature;[133] but *at most*, only a few wise Gentiles were able to be law – to be δίκαιοι – by doing naturally what the Jewish law required. Thus, in 2.12–16 Paul accepts the τόπος that Gentile sages could be a living law naturally, but *argues* that very few Gentiles do so. According to vv. 15–16, '[the few wise Gentiles] show that what the law requires is written on their hearts, *although* their inner conviction (συνείδησις) testifies and their conflicting thoughts bring accusations or even make defenses among themselves on that day when according to my gospel, God judges the secrets of men by Christ Jesus'.[134] Because the συνείδησις was the 'knowledge within the self of past action performed by the subject, a conviction of past misdeeds; and as such it is portrayed as a pain, a disease, or an agent that punishes and inflicts pain', its testimony was almost always negative.[135] The conclusion of Rom. 2.1–16 is consequently that the Stoic philosophy of living according to nature was inefficacious for the majority of Gentiles. Unlike the gospel, which offered life to anyone who had faith in God's faithfulness and mercy (1.16–17), Stoicism promised everything to the few, and delivered nothing to the many.

Scholars have been blind to this reading largely because they understand Rom. 2.12 as contrasting Jews as hypocritical hearers of the law with Gentiles who actually do it. They translate: 'All who have sinned outside the law (ἀνόμως) perish outside the law, and all who have sinned under the law are judged through the law', and so conclude that Paul was disparaging the law and arguing that God would judge Gentiles on some other basis than the law, such as nature. However, again, for Roman Christians as for Hellenized Jews, nature would have been conjoined to the law as representing the will of God. More importantly, the normal meaning of ἀνόμως, the adverb translated 'outside the law' in 2.12, is 'wickedly' or 'lawlessly'. As Stowers has recognized, a better translation of 2.12 is 'for all who sin lawlessly will perish lawlessly, and all who sin under the law's ken will be evaluated (κριθή-σονται) through the law'.[136] (When Paul wanted to describe something 'outside' the law, he was perfectly able to use χωρὶς νόμου [3.21]. Further, in 3.4, Paul used κρίνεσθαι, 'to be judged', with the same sense it bears here, evaluation not condemnation. In 3.4, God's 'judgment' is assumed to have a positive outcome.) Read this way, 2.12 actually recaps the argument of 2.2–11: because he was merciful, God offered lawless Gentiles, even the Stoic who claimed exclusive access to natural wisdom, a second chance. In sum, in 2.1–16, Paul argued against the Gentile conception that nature was a sufficient rule of conduct in order to place Gentiles under the obligation of the law, while also eradicating the idea that natural reason alone enabled them to do the good works demanded by the law. This argument is nonsensical if, as most scholars think, Paul's goal was to undercut the Jewish law.

---

133 For the elision of nature into the law of God, see, e.g., Wis. 6.4; Ps-Aristeas 161; *4 Macc.* 1.16–17, 5.25; Philo, *Op. Mund.* 3, 143; *Leg. All.* 1.46, 93; *Mos.* 2.52; *Abr.* 16, 60.
134 I read the genitive absolute concessively here. For the excellent translation, see Dunn, *Romans*, p. 101.
135 Martin, *Corinthian Body,* p. 180. Cf. Seneca, *De Ira* 3.36.1 and *Ep. Mor.* 28.10.
136 Stowers, *Rereading,* pp. 134–38. See his discussion of ἀνόμως in 1 Corinthians 9.

Conclusions

Reading Rom. 1.18–2.16 in light of the τόπος of the hypocritical Stoic has important implications for our interpretation of the rest of Romans. First, like so many other protreptic speeches, Rom. 1.18–2.16 portrays the main speaker, Paul, as advocating his way-of-life as worthy of emulation by first censuring and debating rivals and then exhorting his audience to follow his way. In contrast to all scholarly analysis of Romans, therefore, I conclude that Paul's censure of the Stoic sage is the first of two rhetorical contests that ancients assumed he had to win before he could exhort the Roman believers to live according to the gospel (5.1ff.). Further, because the second debate with the Jewish teacher only begins at 2.17, and because crucial themes (self-control, nature, law, and mind) are introduced within the censure of the Stoic, we must read Romans afresh to see how discussions of these themes reflect Paul's comparison of *three* 'ways of life' (the gospel, Stoicism, the Judaism of Paul's rival), rather than *two* (the gospel, Judaism).

One place where this triangular comparison may come into play is the continuing role of law (νόμος). Already 2.11–16 emphasizes Jews' first place in God's salvation and establishes that Gentiles knew the good works required by the law but nature was not a sufficient guide for them in the practice of well-doing. As many scholars have recognized, the former emphasis seems defensive of Jews. Moreover, the latter rhetoric move could not have functioned to set up the obliteration of the law for Christian conduct (Paul takes pains throughout 6–8 to indicate its continued viability), only the removal of it as the measure for soteriological inclusion (2.15–16; as Paul tells the Jewish teacher in 3.21–28, God made the faithfulness of Christ the yardstick of salvation). Given that νόμος is best understood as a 'natural standard' of conduct in parts of Romans 7–8, the language of mercy, factionalism, and peaceableness throughout Romans may have functioned to silence 'strong' Gentiles who, like the Stoic, would derogate the law-loving and would emphasize 'nature' as the community's rule of conduct. Paul's consistent emphasis on the importance of the Scriptures as a testimony to Christ may indicate the means by which his rhetoric of peaceableness was supposed to function. νόμος, understood as the *Torah* that revealed Christ and his faithfulness, continued to be critical to Gentiles' pursuit of δικαιοσύνη (5.1–11; 10.5–17; 12.1–15.13).

This recognition is related to a third issue: how Paul's gospel was distinctive. Because 2.1–16 foregrounds God's mercy as the lens through which people should view God's justice and faithfulness to all, it follows that Roman believers would be expected to emulate God's mercy in their interactions within the Christian community. Emphasizing this theme is the primary function of the language of 'unnatural' factionalism and self-interest attributed to impious Gentiles (1.29–31) and the Stoic sage (2.8) as well as the call to peacableness that runs throughout 5.1–15.13;[137] differences in perspective (or mental reasonings, 14.1) about how to live as δίκαιοι (1.17) were not to rule interactions between community members. Gentiles who, like the Stoic, deemed themselves 'strong' and 'wise', perhaps because of their emphasis on natural reasoning, should have understood from Paul's rhetoric that they were to stop acting as if δικαιοσύνη was their exclusive purview.

---

137 Cf. esp. 5.1–11, reading the subjunctives; 11.18–24; 12.3–15.13.

Mercy toward those they deemed weak, rather than exclusive access to divine knowledge, was the defining quality of justice and faithfulness (12.3–8; 13.8–10; 14.1–15.6).

In sum, Paul and his Roman audience lived in an environment where philosophers pursued virtue vigorously and where gender ideology crafted the character, and others' characterizations, of that pursuit. First-century characterizations of the hypocritical Stoic indicate that Rom. 1.18–2.16 functioned as the first argument of a protreptic letter that touted the superiority of Paul's gospel to Stoicism and a rival form of Judaism, in the pursuit of δικαιοσύνη and eternal life. The overwhelming number of allusions to the τόπος of the hypocritical Stoic in 1.18–2.16—to conventions about nature, self-deception, the mind, and sex—functioned as a sustained censure of a Stoic sage and his claim that attending to nature resulted in rewards like eternal life. This censure posed the question, if wise men who touted living naturally acted contrary to nature, how could they teach others 'wisdom'? The answer: they could not. Rom. 1.18–2.16 deploys gender stereotypes about unnatural intercourse to shatter the Stoic's credibility and to eliminate the possibility that Roman believers would accept his philosophy of 'natural living' as efficacious. Reading the epistle with sex in mind functioned to convince the Romans that the gospel was the outworking of God's merciful justice and that mercy was the yardstick for both inclusion and right action within the Christian community.

These findings are highly relevant to feminists interested in using gender theory to pursue justice and practice mercy toward others. While peculiarly ancient in character, Paul's use of sexual rhetoric to censure Stoics highlights the central importance of gender to understanding sexual stereotypes and censures in the Scriptures. Rom. 1.26–27 addresses not homosexuality but the so-called 'natural' understanding of gendered behavior—that women should be passive/penetrated/ruled and men active/penetrators/rulers—and men's cultural fear of femininity, especially within themselves. The presence of this dynamic in Romans 1 should lead more feminist scholars to examine this text with care. (Unfortunately, Romans 1 has rarely been treated by feminist scholars, despite the clear—and clearly gendered—points of contact between 1 Corinthians 11 and Romans 1, such as allusions to nature, hierarchy, the male–female pairing, and the inversion of acceptable gendered behavior.[138]) It may also require feminists to wrestle with the fact that Paul embraced masculinist assumptions about 'feminine behavior'—indeed, reified them as the Creator's design—in order to humiliate his leading male opponents in Romans 1–2. Historically speaking, we can hardly then characterize Paul as a 'feminist.' Nevertheless, as Elisabeth Schüssler Fiorenza recognized long ago, naming the stereotypes and power-plays found in Romans 1 is a crucial step, both theologically and ethically, in challenging the disempowerment that results from them.

This essay also demonstrates the central importance of gender paradigms for understanding the larger theological, social and political formation of early

---

138 The two exceptions I know of are Brooten, *Love between Women*, and Corley and Torjesen, 'Sexuality, Hierarchy, and Evangelism'. The explanation for this fact may be the historical tendency of American feminist scholarship to avoid touchy subjects like homosexuality in order to fight more 'central' battles like that for women's rights.

Christianity. Because the cosmic hierarchy *itself* was constructed as the reification of the gender polarity between masculinity and femininity, between rule and subservience, gender dynamics must be treated as central, not peripheral, to the forging of believers' religious and sociopolitical identities vis-à-vis other groups and movements. In Romans, Paul used the most potent gender barb available—the stereotyped censure of sexual effeminacy in men—to lower the status of Stoicism as his prime rival in Rome and consequently to raise that of the gospel. The case is similar with other developments within early Christianity: everything from philosophy, religion, ethics, and politics to concepts of nature and God's final judgment are affected by gender. By implication, gender studies must increasingly be treated as fundamental to the study of the New Testament and emergent Christianity.

Finally, 'Sexy Stoics' underscores the tenacity of stereotyped ideas about Jewish 'ethnic' legalism and hypocrisy in Romans interpretation. Given the history of Romans as Western Christianity's supercessionist tractate par excellence, there is no more important social-justice issue for interpreters than to reveal and correct the ethnoreligious bias that has until recently determined both Christian and scholarly interpretations of this letter. Since the time of Augustine, the identification of Paul's leading opponent as a legalistic, hypocritical Jew has largely seemed self-evident (to Christians). But this gender analysis has revealed both that first-century Jews *could not* be the subjects of Rom. 2.1 (they were not vulnerable to the charge of male same-sex intercourse and effeminacy) and that Stoics, even when unnamed, were *widely stereotyped* for precisely the charges Paul leveled at the hypocritical judge. The consequence: *the prime censure of Paul's letter to the Romans did not target Jews but leading Stoic rivals in Rome.* While there are other implications of this finding, the most important for Christian feminists may well be the need to practice fully Paul's call to Gentiles to embrace 'others' in their communities, especially those who have been shunned by them, and to treat love of neighbor as the yardstick for just action. As Paul said, citing Lev. 19.18, 'Owe no one anything except to love one another; for the one who loves "the other" has fulfilled the law. All the commandments ... are summed up in this sentence: "You shall love your neighbor as yourself" ' (Rom. 13.8–10).

To Turn the Groaning into Labor: Romans 8.22–23*

Luzia Sutter Rehman

> Giving birth. But who gives it? And to whom is it given? Certainly, it doesn't feel like giving, which implies a flow, a gentle handing over, no coercion ... Maybe the phrase was made by someone viewing the result only ... Yet one more thing that needs to be re-named.[1]

The issue of androcentric language and translation has received much attention in the past years. The biblical texts as they are read by individuals or heard in the liturgy of the church, perpetuate the male bias and exclusiveness of our own culture and language. However, it has been pointed out that a feminist-critical analysis of biblical texts about women will not suffice.[2] The framework of androcentric perception and thought patterns must be critically considered as well.

Hence, a feminist reading of Paul consists of more than critical observation of how he speaks about women, and whether and how they are mentioned, so that an attempt can be made to venture a historical reconstruction of the Christian community of women and men.[3] For me, critical reflection of the framework implies both the framework of Paul, and that of prevalent interpretation, which often foists upon us a certain perception that itself has to be subjected to feminist critique.

In what follows, I wish to show how Rom. 8.18–25 may be critically analysed. Such critical reading is shaped, above all, by an *immersion* into the apocalyptic tradition as Paul uses it, as well as by *disassociation* from the androcentric blueprint of the interpretation of Paul. To recognize the apocalyptic-Jewish thinking of Paul means to take seriously his cultural and theological background.

According to mainstream opinion, here in the middle of the epistle the issue is 'groaning in suffering'.[4] Paul is appealing to Christian patience that has to bear *suffering as a condition of humanity*, patience that is itself born of the hope in freedom, glory, sonship, and redemption. All these benefits of salvation, like freedom from transitoriness, are metaphysical in character and can be claimed only in the future.

---

* Translated by Barbara and Martin Rumscheidt.

1 Margaret Atwood, 'Giving Birth', in *idem*, *Dancing Girls and Other Stories* (New York: Simon & Schuster, 1978), p. 225.

2 E.g. Elisabeth Schüssler Fiorenza, *In Memory of Her* (New York: Crossroad, 1983), p. 42.

3 Elizabeth Castelli, 'Romans', in Elisabeth Schüssler Fiorenza (ed.), *Searching the Scriptures* (2 vols.; New York: Crossroad, 1994), II, p. 298.

4 Examples of this are Ulrich Wilckens, *Der Brief an die Römer* (3 vols.; Neukirchen–Vluyn: Neukirchener Verlag, 1980), II, p. 49; Ernst Käsemann, *An die Römer* (Tübingen: J.C.B. Mohr, 1973), p. 227; C.H. Dodd, *The Epistle of Paul to the Romans* (London: Hodder & Stoughton, 1949), p. 134; C.E.B. Cranfield, *A Critical Exegetical Commentary on the Epistle to the Romans* (ICC; 2 vols.; Edinburgh: T. & T. Clark, 1975), I, pp. 412–19; W. Sanday and A.C. Headlam, *The Epistle to the Romans* (ICC; Edinburgh: T. & T. Clark, 5th edn, 1902), p. 205; F.F. Bruce, *The Letter of Paul to the Romans* (Grand Rapids: Eerdmans, 1985), p. 171.

Of course, these metaphysical benefits of salvation need to be examined from a feminist perspective; they are fraught with a cultural denigration of bodiliness that is millennia old and that identifies redemption with freedom from transitoriness. This dualism that consistently denigrates women and material reality was focused chiefly on the female body. But this vaunted 'Christian patience' needs also to be examined critically from the perspective of liberation theology. I doubt that patient waiting for better times brings relief in times of distress.

Moreover, I also doubt that this 'Christian patience' is what Paul has in mind and, for that reason, I want to take a second look. The apocalyptically colored verses of Rom. 8.18–25 intend to awaken or to affirm the motivation of those addressed to offer resistance. *Not* to sigh quietly and practice patience is precisely the point here; the issue is to cry aloud, to protest, to demand abundant life and justice. I derive this reading from taking seriously the metaphor of creation giving birth (8.22–23) as well as from the feminist understanding of giving birth as work for new life. This is an understanding that critiques the androcentric reduction of birthing to suffering, pain, and the production of sons. In doing so, a re-naming of giving birth can perhaps take place, connected to the work of a new generation, a new earth coming into being. This re-naming of women's work, of the powers of the body, would be a valorization of the body, of our personal and social body, of *the earth* as the being in which we exist and *the cosmos* to which we belong in a larger way.[5]

The Apocalyptic Perspective

We have to begin by immersing ourselves in the apocalyptic imagery of laboring— not as a metaphor for the end of the world, but as an image of hope of those who long for the onset of a new, more just and fulfilled time. In the framework of traditional exegesis, apocalyptic gets low grades. It is said that it paints the end of the world in dark colors, gets entangled in calculation and holds a pessimistic notion of humankind and the cosmos.[6] In addition, apocalyptic is often regarded as a late development in theology, a degenerate prophecy, or a wisdom only of epigones.

But such a negative interpretation of apocalyptic must be examined, since it is based in a perspectival blindness. It does not recognize *for whom the decline of the world (and its order)* signals a loss of privilege and power and *for whom the onset of a new time* represents a *necessity* and the beginning of a better life.[7] I read apocalyptic texts as the literature of resistance[8] written by people who with all their might

5 Ivone Gebara calls this revalorization an important dimension of resurrection. See her 'The Face of Transcendence', in Elisabeth Schüssler Fiorenza (ed.), *Searching the Scriptures* (2 vols.; New York: Crossroad, 1993), I, p. 184.

6 Werner Zager, *Begriff und Wertung der Apokalypse in der neutestamentlichen Forschung* (Frankfurt/Berlin/New York/Paris: Peter Lang, 1989); John Collins, 'Towards the Morphology of a Genre', *Semeia* 14 (1979), pp. 1–20.

7 Jürgen Ebach, 'Apokalypse—zum Ursprung einer Stimmung', in F.W. Marquardt et al. (eds), *Einwürfe* (2 vols.; Munich: Chr. Kaiser Verlag, 1985), II, pp. 5–61 (37–38).

8 See also Allan Boesak, *Comfort and Protest: Reflections on the Apocalypse of John of Patmos* (Philadelphia: Westminster Press, 1987); Pablo Richard, *Apokalypse: Das Buch von Widerstand und Hoffnung* (Lucerne: Exodus Verlag, 1998); Luzia Sutter Rehmann, 'Die Offenbarung des Johannes: Inspirationen aus Patmos', in Luise Schottroff and Marie-Theres Wacker (eds.), *Kompendium Feministische Bibelauslegung* (Gütersloh: Gütersloher Verlagshaus, 1998), pp. 725–41.

hope and wait for a transformation of existing conditions. But in reality, they do not wait, they reach out for redemption. Waiting usually connotes passivity, acceptance, keeping silent and adapting, but there is also a waiting that trembles with impatience. It is restless; all senses are focused on one event that is anticipated every new day.

That kind of reaching out in expectation of the event long yearned for is found in Rom. 8.19. In a metaphorical way, the head of creation is spoken of here; ἀποκαραδοκία alludes to the head of creation that is on the lookout. Creation extends its head, projecting it as far as it can (ἀπό), and its body is longing with intense expectation. It certainly does not mean that creation is passively waiting. On the contrary, creation is at work birthing a new world.

Deconstructing the Androcentric Perspective of Birthing

But before we engage this apocalyptic metaphor, we have to examine the reductionist understanding of birthing that we find in androcentric commentaries.[9] The androcentric perspective of numerous commentators on birthing perceives it only as a situation of suffering, as a sign of transitoriness and the decline of the old aeon, as a pinnacle of pain, and the like. According to this perspective, birthing has to do with *exertion and hard work*. Androcentric commentaries don't consider that women's bodies labor for a new life, their muscles perform hard work; every part of their bodies is called on to do great things if life is to be born. The pains are only one part of the birthing process and do not come close to describing comprehensively what women experience in the process. The experience of letting new life come out of oneself, of taking an active part in the work for a new life, is not or only marginally communicated and reflected on in patriarchal cultures. In any event, the perspective of those who give birth differs fundamentally from that of those who more or less passively wait for children being born to them.

In biblical and apocalyptic texts, birthing has to do with work, with fighting and wrestling for new life. This struggle transforms the one who gives birth. There is a togetherness of mother and child, of midwife and the one giving birth. Often the child's new life also signifies the start of a new life for the mother, a great transformation of her biological and social life, of her whole life situation.

Many pregnant women, near the end of their pregnancies, long for the release from their heavy bodies. After all these months of pregnancy, birthing seems less difficult than working, sleeping, and walking with the heavy body. And so, many women are oriented to the time of birthing in a great forward-leaning hope that delivery will bring release, redemption, and the start of new life.

To See the Picture: The Metaphor in Romans 8.22–23

For we know that the whole creation has been groaning in travail until now; and not only the creation, but we ourselves, who have the first-fruits of the Spirit, groan inwardly as we long for adoption as children, the redemption of our bodies (Rom. 8.22–23).

9 For a more extensive treatment see Luzia Sutter Rehmann, *Geh, frage die Gebärerin! Feministisch-befreiungstheologische Untersuchungen des Gebärmotivs in der Apokalyptik* (Gütersloh: Gütersloher Verlagshaus, 1995).

I wish now to look at this metaphor, adhering to the feminist premise that puts what is marginalized into the center. For this image of birthing is often already rendered invisible in the translation of the text itself[10] or it is dismissed as 'a common expression of Jewish apocalyptic'.[11] I propose to ask how Paul uses this motif, how it fits into his thinking and into the epistle as a whole. How does it give voice to women's experiences?

It is striking that not only creation groans (συστενάζειν) and gives birth, but 'we too', the women and men friends of Paul, groan (στενάζειν) because we long for the liberation[12] of our bodies. Paul does not position Christians here and creation there, the redeemed here and those who suffer there, a gender-neutral or male-oriented community here and a nature perceived as feminine there.[13] In applying the birthing image to the whole of creation as well as to the Christian community and himself, Paul does not isolate them from the event that has overtaken creation. They groan and birth together, and together they long for the beginning of new life. The labor pains of the Spirit make humans restless, whether or not they are part of the Christian community. Groaning binds them all together.

Paul speaks of creation being subjected against its will (8.20), and uses the words φθορᾶς (destruction, corruption) and ματαιότης (futility, vanity) in describing the condition that now weighs heavily on creation. He hears the groaning (στενάζειν) of creation. In its proper sense, this is a mythical metaphor. For creation has no head with which to be on the lookout, no mouth with which to groan. Paul depicts creation here as the mythical image of a living being; to be precise: that of a woman groaning.[14]

And yet, the metaphor is to be understood only within the apocalyptic hope for the onset of the new age. Paul sketches out an *apocalyptic analysis of time*. He takes up the experiences of suffering human beings, examines them and identifies the constraints of the present time and what caused them in order to develop plans for liberating action. The prevailing abusive conditions are often quite complex and the fears of people difficult to grasp. Here apocalyptic theology tries to name reality by means of mythical expressions and images, metaphors and citations, or collages from the prophets' writings. This is how fears get a face, how structural violence is exposed and in the midst of chaos a structure becomes visible.[15] From an apocalyptic analysis of time, there emerges clarity about the quality of the age. In announcing that the time of the ruling powers is drawing to a close, radical changes and transforming options come into view, new visions appear.

10 Cf. Dodd, *Romans*, p. 132.
11 Cranfield, *Romans*, pp. 412–19.
12 Ἀπολύτρόσις means to purchase the freedom of enslaved people.
13 Without addressing the metaphor of birthing, Elizabeth Castelli criticizes the Pauline dualism in Romans: ' ... the logic of Romans depends on an overarching hermeneutical and philosophical use of dualism ... A particularly explicit example of its presence may be found in chapter 8, where Paul characterizes life in the spirit, in opposition to life according to the flesh' (Castelli, 'Romans', p. 285). I agree with Elsa Tamez who says that Paul does, indeed, contrast spirit and flesh, but that he represents a completely different dualism than that of Plato. See Elsa Tamez, 'Der Brief an die Gemeinde in Rom.: Eine feministische Lektüre', in Schottroff and Wacker (eds), *Kompendium Feministische Bibelauslegung*, pp. 550–68 (568).
14 Often the image is understood as an expression of fallen creation. Even the fall of Gen. 3.15 is cited. Cf. Bruce, *Romans*, p. 169; Wilckens, *Der Brief an die Römer*, pp. 154–55.
15 For example, the Revelation of John is marked by rhythms that provide structure. It is, above all, the septimal rhythm that is used to portray new creation coming out of chaos.

The word ἀποκαλύπτειν means to uncover, to unmask, to unveil, to reveal. Apocalyptic theology brims over with images and color; it is evocative so that the unjust conditions are uncovered and new ways made apparent.[16] Paul begins his apocalyptic description by speaking of the suffering that weighs down 'the whole creation'. The whole creation groans. Why? Who has subjected it and led it into futility, far away from God?

To Hear the Groaning under Roman Domination

A significant theme in the epistle to the Romans is the universality of sin. In 1.18–3.20, Paul argues explicitly that sin pervades the life of every human being. In 5.12 he refers to sin entering and going through the world, manifesting its power in a vast number of ways. But Paul's speaking of sin refers to the daily reality of life in the Roman Empire, the *imperium romanum*.[17] His idea of sin is expressed in categories of domination and not those of guilt or action. Human beings are said to have been sold under sin (7.14); sin rules over humans as over slaves. Because sin rules, Jews cannot keep the Torah, and because they cannot do the will of God, sin rules undeterred.

But this is by no means so only in relation to Jewish women and men. The domination of sin is worldwide and prevents life from being near God. Hence Paul's anguished cry, 'Wretched human being that I am! Who will deliver me from this (enslaved) body of death?' (7.24). Political-contextual reading of the text recognizes in his cry the situation of oppression that prevailed at that time throughout the Mediterranean world. Sin, that is to say, the general practice of life that had developed under Roman rule, holds back from doing the will of God (Torah); it is a life far away from God (ματαιότης) (8.20).

In this analysis of the way of life of huge numbers of people in the *imperium romanum*, Paul formulates his critique of culture from the viewpoint of a Jewish male. According to him, the whole of creation is subjected to the pressure of Roman economic and military laws as well as to the pressure to conform and to keep quiet. Such pressure causes all human beings to groan.

Life under a 'Grievous and Thickly Pressing Pain'

A comparison of Paul and two of his contemporaries shows that he is not alone in hearing groaning cries among the people. Let me show now how Philo Judaeus and Flavius Josephus use the verbs στενάζειν and στενεῖν in order to speak of the suffering of their fellow human beings.

Philo also paints a picture of a groaning world (οἰκουμένη) when speaking of the helpless suffering of the population under the rule of Caligula. 'For all others, men, women, cities, nation, countries, regions of the earth, I might almost say, the whole inhabited world, groaning (στενόντες) though they were at what was happening,

---

16 Luzia Sutter Rehmann, *Vom Mut, genau hinzusehen: Feministisch-befreiungstheologische Interpretationen zur Apokalyptik* (Lucerne: Exodus Verlag, 1998). See Ebach, 'Apokalypse'.
17 Luise Schottroff, 'Die Schreckensherrschaft der Sünde', in *idem, Befreiungserfahrungen: Studien zur Sozialgeschichte des Neuen Testaments* (Munich: Chr. Kaiser Verlag, 1990), p. 63.

flattered him all the same and magnified him out of all proportion and augmented his vanity.'[18] Philo describes the deportment of people who suffered under Caligula and yet continued to support him. Even though all were mere slaves under Caligula's rule, Jews were most affected because they were the most despised of them all (p. 119). The Jewish population suffered from the Emperor's deep mistrust towards them: Caligula looked with disfavor on the Jews alone because they alone opposed him on principle. Of all the nations, the nation of the Jews was exempted from imperial veneration, and this heightened Caligula's suspicion that they were not loyal enough, wishing to counteract his desires (p. 117). The analysis Philo's perspective provides is devastating.

He also uses the verb στενεῖν to describe the suffering of the children of Israel in Egypt (*Leg. All.*, 3.212). But their cry reached the ear of God so that help came to them. In Egypt, Jews lived under a brutal rule that finally moved them to seek liberation and risk the exodus into the desert. But, as Philo knows, groaning is a very intense pain.[19] Only when the groaning stage has been reached does the situation really begin to be unbearable, and then every lever is activated. In relation to the children of Israel, this meant that their groaning had become so loud that God could no longer ignore them.[20] But in his *Legatio ad Gaium*, Philo mentions no option possible for the Jewish people to rid themselves of this 'most grievous and thickly pressing pain' that is behind the verb 'to groan'—unless the intentional use of στενεῖν connects the groaning of the children of Israel of all times to the oppressed Jews under Caligula and leads to a life of religiously motivated resistance.

'Did Not Palestine Groan?'

Flavius Josephus's use of στενάζειν also testifies to the knowledge of God coming to the aid of God's groaning people. In his report on the Jewish–Roman war (66–74 CE),[21] he compares the people's suffering with the suffering endured earlier under Assyrian occupation. 'Morever, did not Palestine groan under the ravage the Assyrians made, when they carried away our sacred ark?' (*War*, 5.384). It was this groaning that caused God to intervene (5.386), since God's heart is always touched by the cries of the children of Israel.

When groaning is suppressed, it takes on an utterly tormented and desolate sound. Josephus tells of the great terror that was upon the Jewish people, when men were crucified and their dead bodies were brought at night to their houses. No one had the courage to weep openly for the dead men or to bury them, for if they did, the same fate awaited those who mourned for others (4.332). Thus, mourning had to be

---

18 Philo, *The Embassy to Gaius: With an English Translation* (ed. T.H. Colson; London: William Heinemann Ltd, 1962), p. 116.

19 In his *Leg. All.* 3, Philo explains the meaning of the verb: 'Now groaning is a violent and intense pain. For we are very often in pain without groaning. But, when we groan, we are under the influence of most grievous and thickly pressing pain' (C.D. Yonge [trans.], *The Works of Philo* [Peabody, MA: Hendrickson, 1995], p. 211).

20 Philo knows that the good and merciful God does not reject suppliants when they, 'groaning at the Egyptian deed and passion, cry to him in sincerity and truth' (*Det. Pot. Ins.*), in Yonge, *The Works of Philo*, p. 93.

21 William Whiston (trans.), *The Works of Josephus* (Peabody, MA: Hendrickson, 1988).

silenced. 'They shed tears in secret, and durst not even groan (στενεῖν) without great caution, lest any of their enemies should hear them ...' (4.331). Can God hear this suppressed groaning? Josephus says nothing about that. No one dares to offer resistance; it seems impossible.

Philo and Josephus make it plain that the times in which the Jewish people and they themselves lived were full of groaning. The whole world (οἰκουμένη) groaned, says Philo, but only Jews dared to resist. Both recall the resisting groaning of the children of Israel in Egypt and Palestine. And Josephus speaks of situations when even groaning was life-threatening.

The Longing of the People ...

We turn to Paul, writing to the young Christian community in Rome. Like Philo and Josephus, he knows of the great, and at times unbearable pressure that weighs upon all human beings, but above all upon Jews, in the Roman Empire. All three writers make use of the forcefulness of the verbs στενεῖν and στενάζειν to show the high level of distress. We have seen that memory of the groaning that elicits aid to the distressed is part of the Jewish relationship with God, that it is integral to the memory of the exodus, the way of liberation of the oppressed. The people's groaning makes its oppression manifest and asks for change, for deliverance. In this sense, groaning is an aspect of resistance.

Paul clearly connects στενάζειν with ὠδίνειν, that is, he does not simply portray helpless, impotent suffering but labor for new life that will change the situation of distress. Groaning that results from the exertion of birthing, and from the pressure of labor pains, will lead to delivery, to release.[22] When Paul speaks of the birthing of a groaning creation, he roots his analysis of his age in the apocalyptic literature of resistance. His talk of creation giving birth is an image of hope!

Many apocalyptic texts live from this hope in the onset of a new, more just and fulfilling time when God's nearness is felt again. At the same time, such texts also announce the impending end of the age when God is far away, the present time full of injustice and suffering (cf. Isa. 24–27; Mk 13.24–29; Lk. 21.25–33; *Ethiopian Enoch* 1.1–6).

... And the Earth as Focus of Transformation and Mystery

Longing for the nearness of God, for a new heaven and a new earth, results, indeed, from an apocalyptic perspective embracing both present and future time. But how will this long-expected change of the quality of time come to pass? How can people longing for justice and God's nearness perceive the transformation? Apocalyptic language focuses on the earth as the center of transformation. The dead sleep in the lap of the earth, resting there until the long-expected change of the new age. The

---

22 Luise Schottroff insists that in the pains of labor and the groans of the mother giving birth, the experience of new life is central. In light of this she also interprets συστενάζειν as groaning that expresses the experience of hard work and of pain. See Schottroff, 'Die befreite Eva', in Christine Schaumberger and Luise Schottroff (eds), *Schuld und Macht: Studien zu einer Befreiungstheologie* (Munich: Chr. Kaiser Verlag, 1988), pp. 15–152 (112–13).

earth guards the dead and with them the injustice they had to suffer. That is why their stories are not lost before God opens the books. And when time is fulfilled, the earth participates in the resurrection of the dead from the dust (Rev. 20.12–13; Dan. 12.1–2; Isa. 26.19–21) by releasing them from its inner region. 'And the earth shall give up those who sleep in it, and the dust those who rest there in silence; and the chambers shall give back the souls entrusted to them' (*4 Esdras* 7.32). 'In those days, Sheol will return all the deposits which she had received and hell will give back all that which it owes. And he shall choose the righteous and the holy ones from among [the risen dead] . . . In those days, mountains shall dance like rams; the hills shall leap like kids satiated with milk. And the faces of all the angels in heaven shall glow with joy, because on that day the Elect One has arisen. And the earth shall rejoice; and the righteous ones shall dwell upon her and the elect ones shall walk upon her'(*1 En.* 51.1–2, 4–5).[23]

The chambers of the earth give back the dead that she had carefully guarded. This image of dwellings in the earth's inner region parallels a view held by gynecologists of antiquity that the uterus has several caves. And those doctors knew well that the muscles of the uterus had to do the work of birthing.[24] The birthing metaphor of apocalyptic puts the stress on the end of the long waiting period, of the arduous time of pregnancy. The long-awaited hour (Jn 16.21), the day full of awe (Jer. 30.7), the day of decision: in spite of being afraid of it, it is a moment long waited for by the people, a moment close to a good ending because the end of pregnancy brings with it active collaboration, cries of release and, finally, deliverance. This is how the experience of innumerable women can be expressed in the terminology of apoca-lyptic, namely that the good ending does *not* happen *without collaboration* and active exertion. The new earth does not simply fall from the sky; justice does not come about without our cooperation. The earth's birthing signals a great transform-ation that needs the involvement of everyone's energies in order to succeed. Fundamental to this worked-for and yet ultimately *mysterious transformation* is the metaphor of the earth's uterus. In the inner region of the earth, there is mystery because from the earth comes forth vegetation; every year new life comes from her. Her inner region harbours power of transformation. That is why the body of the earth is remembered as the place of transformation and her power as that which puts an end to distress (cf. 1 Cor. 15.35–58).

The interpretation that associates the earth's labor pains chiefly with death, demise, and terror suffers from androcentric reductionism in relation to birthing. To the powerful of this world, those who keep humans away from God and whose demands on life subject the whole creation under sin, the labor pains of the end signal that their power is limited. But to the women and men who are groaning and oppressed, the signs of this time of birthing are signs of hope. They let the nearness of God shine through even now; they give cause to employ their energies fruitfully, and support with everything the birth of God's new world.

---

23 E. Isaac (trans.), '1 Enoch', in James H. Charlesworth (ed.), *The Old Testament Pseudepigrapha* (2 vols.; London: Darton, Longman & Todd, 1983), II, pp. 5–100.
24 For example, Hippocrates, Claudius Galenus. For sources, see my *Geh, frage die Gebärerin*, p. 167; Soranus of Ephesus, *Peri gynaikeion*, 1.3.8.

Working Hard ...

Paul not only takes up the image of birthing drawn from women's experiences, but also employs it for his own work and for that of inspired Christians. In her commentary on Romans, Beverly Roberts Gaventa points out the traditional imagery that is contained in Rom. 8.18–25.[25] She too sees that this section of the letter portrays the anguish and the confidence with which believers live in this present age. This present age, she argues, seems to be characterized by 'suffering and decay'. The believers, together with all of creation, 'await the final triumph of God'.

Gaventa adopts the traditional interpretation of this imagery without finding in those images the perspective of women and their experience of giving birth. It is not accidental that she cites only Isa. 13.8 and Jer. 4.31, two passages that connect birthing with punishment and death. But this completely obscures the part played by collaboration, the common exertion and struggle for new life. I do not see Paul and his friends awaiting the final triumph of God; they are working hard for it. Feeling themselves bound up with the suffering of many, they let themselves be urged on by it so that their strengths are doubled.

In the whole section of 8.18–39, Paul talks of the difficulties and hopes that work on behalf of the new world brings with it. He and all with whom he groans and labors together know about the sufferings of this age (8.18). Their work brought about persecution and caused unrest in the already-sensitive position of Jewish congregations in the Roman Empire. And so Paul and his co-workers got themselves into a state of great disharmony with their environment; they experienced this often (cf. Acts). The suffering caused by the persecution that resulted from the work of liberation may be understood within the context of the tradition of Jewish martyrs.[26] This suffering is not comparable to the senseless suffering that results from having to bear injustice. For such passive suffering would only worsen the situation, by daily letting the powerful grow even more powerful, while at the same time reducing the strength of those who suffer.

With the Roar of Torrents ...

Paul does not use traditional apocalyptic imagery only to speak of the coming of the new age. When he hears the groaning of so many as an expression of utter distress, he does not simply offer a report of the situation. His description of the present situation is apocalyptic in that the groaning is both heard and interpreted as a *sign of the coming change*. That is, Paul weaves his perception of suffering together with his engagement for a different common life in a world where God can be near at hand. But as the whole 'inhabited earth' (οἰκουμένη; understood as the regions around the

25 Beverly Roberts Gaventa, 'Romans', in Carol A. Newsom and Sharon H. Ringe (eds), *The Women's Bible Commentary* (Louisville, KY: Westminster/John Knox Press, 1992), p. 318.
26 Even though there were in Paul's days no official persecutions of Christians for reasons of the name 'Christ', there were persecutions arising from local conflicts between Christians and non-Christians, resulting in people being suspected and denounced. Paul himself had experiences with Roman officials, as can be seen not only in Acts but also in 2 Cor. 11.25 and Rom. 8.35. See also Luise Schottroff, 'Gebt dem Kaiser, was dem Kaiser gehört, und Gott, was Gott gehört', in *idem*, *Befreiungserfahrungen*, pp. 184–216.

Mediterranean Sea) moans under the yoke of Roman rule, this moaning comes to his assistance. For it multiplies ten, even one hundred times his own crying and grasping for justice, and it gives him and his co-workers more reason to long for, and thereby hasten, the envisioned coming of a new earth and a new heaven in which God will be all in all (1 Cor. 15.28).

Paul senses the urgency of transformation and is filled with compassion and energy. He describes the power of this energy as 'labor' in Rom. 9.2 as well. His vision of another world is not somehow attached to the reality that is experienced now; it does not fall some day or some night from the sky. This vision is related to great, hard work, and intensive engagement, which in Rom. 8.26 he calls *Spirit-caused birthing*. Here he describes the power of the Spirit who intercedes with groans where words fail, where suffering has become unbearable and one can no longer contain oneself. The moaning of the Spirit is expressed by Paul in the related verb στενάζειν. Στενάζειν does not only mean 'to groan, sigh, wail'; it also describes 'the roar of torrents' or 'the loud breathing of horses galloping'.[27] The related old Indo-European word *stanati* means 'thunder, roar'. The linguistic field has to be kept wide here: from sighing and groaning to mourning and complaining, on to raging, snorting, gasping and thundering.[28] It is a mighty inhaling and exhaling, creating movement and relief. It causes people to tremble and quake; it is the howling of the children of Israel that touches the heart of their God. It is the crying of women birthing in the exertion of labor, in the final pains that bring an end to the birthing process. Change is at hand when the stage of moaning and quaking has been reached.

There is a cosmic dimension in the apocalyptic perspective of the onset of the good age. The whole of creation suffers from the subjection under powers hostile to God (8.20), powers that impose their premises on every human being and every other creature. The Spirit's snorting expresses indignation about this. Paul perceives the 'snorting of the Spirit' as the power or energy of transformation in those who experience the present time as devastating and long impatiently for the nearness of God. He lays great stress on this dimension of togetherness (8.22–23). And so, this apocalyptic perspective on the groaning of the whole creation helps Paul to feel support for himself and his work. He is not alone; the Christian congregations are not alone. The groaning is so loud that it must come from many, many throats.

Apocalyptic is vibrant because it embraces the whole cosmos: its hope for a new heaven and a new earth is far more embracing than hope for a just world. This is often expressed in pictures of the whole cosmos participating, such as stars changing colors, the sun and moon turning dark, the seas roaring, animals rising up from the sea, and the like. This perspective on the cosmos is not based on a dualism of human beings vs. creation, spirit vs. matter. The earth and her heavenly siblings, the stars, etc., work towards a transformation of this world (order) as much as they who have the 'first fruits of the Spirit' (8.23).

27 Cf. LSJ.
28 LSJ.

Summary and Openings

A feminist critical immersion into apocalyptic imagery shows how resistance and hope are interwoven into the metaphor of the laboring creation. It is absolutely inadequate to classify this birthing under the 'traditional imagery of suffering and decay' and to assume uncritically the androcentric and reductionist view. Birthing is not an impotent whimpering of poor female bodies, nor is it passive suffering. Above all, it is *action*.

Let me ask some concluding questions: What does this reading of Rom. 8.22–23 mean for women (and men) today? What could it possibly have meant for Paul's co-workers like Phoebe, Prisca, and Persis (Rom. 16.1, 3, 12)? Does his talk of labor disqualify female bodily experiences? Does he discredit women who have never been mothers?

In Rom. 16.1ff., Paul mentions not only many 'women' but explicitly identifies them as co-workers, apostles, and deacons. That means he acknowledges their work and contributions to the community. Mary (16.6), Tryphaena, Tryphosa, and Persis (16.12) are mentioned in relation to their hard work, their 'labor', κοπιάζειν. Prisca and Aquila stuck out their necks saving the life of Paul (16.4). Here in Romans 16, the themes of Romans 8 are hinted at: hard, bodily exertion, hard work on behalf of the new life, resistance, and the dangers that threaten the lives of those that support or offer the resistance.

The birthing image of Rom. 8.22–23 is, structurally speaking, in the middle of the sixteen chapters of Romans. The groans for deliverance, the arduous transformation of existing conditions, and the collaboration in shaping the new world were quite likely very familiar matters to women like Prisca, Mary, Tryphaena, Tryphosa, and Persis. The image of giving birth keeps alive the memory of their contribution to the transformation of a world far away from God. It expresses, perhaps, something of the bond of the congregations to these women. So we can conclude that in the epistle to the Romans, experiences of women occupy a central place because they shape the apocalyptic metaphor into one that expresses resistance and cooperation. And at the end of the Epistle (16. 1f), Paul resumes and re-affirms the meaning of these female co-workers for the birth of the new world.

OUR MOTHER ST PAUL: TOWARD THE RECOVERY OF A NEGLECTED THEME*

BEVERLY ROBERTS GAVENTA

We begin, not in the first century, but in the eleventh, with a prayer composed by Anselm of Canterbury:

> O St. Paul, where is he that was called
>   the nurse of the faithful, caressing his sons?
> Who is that affectionate mother who declares everywhere
>   that she is in labour for her sons?
>   Sweet nurse, sweet mother,
> who are the sons you are in labour with, and nurse,
> but those whom by teaching the faith of Christ
>   you bear and instruct?
> Or who is a Christian after your teaching
> who is not born into the faith and established in it by you?
> And if in that blessed faith we are born
>   and nursed by other apostles also,
>   it is most of all by you,
> for you have laboured and done more than them all in this;
> so if they are our mothers, you are our greatest mother.[1]

Anselm's prayer, however, is not simply the product of pious imaginings. Anselm may well have been influenced by the medieval theme of Jesus as Mother, but his prayer does not merely play variations on a common melody.[2] Instead, it draws on passages *within* the Pauline letters, passages that from all evidence have faded from our view.

In an effort to correct this situation and restore those texts to their proper place, I am engaged in an examination of maternal imagery in the letters of Paul.[3] In this essay, I intend to sketch in a programmatic way what I understand to be involved in this study. I need to stress the word programmatic, for this is very much a work in progress.

* Inaugural address at Princeton Theological Seminary, originally published in *Princeton Seminary Bulletin* 17 (1996), pp. 29–44. Reprinted by permission.

1 The translation is that of Benedicta Ward in *The Prayers and Meditations of Saint Anselm* (London: Penguin Books, 1973), p. 152.

2 Carolyn Walker Bynum's perceptive analysis of the theme in twelfth-century texts provides a convenient entry into the growing literature on this topic ('Jesus as Mother and Abbot as Mother: Some Themes in Twelfth-Century Cistercian Writing', in *Jesus as Mother: Studies in the Spirituality of the High Middle Ages* [Berkeley: University of California Press, 1982], pp. 110–69).

3 For my earlier work on this topic, see 'The Maternity of Paul: An Exegetical Study of Galatians 4.19', in Robert T. Fortna and Beverly R. Gaventa (eds), *The Conversation Continues: Studies in Paul and John in Honor of J. Louis Martyn* (Nashville: Abingdon Press, 1990), pp. 189–201; and 'Apostles as Babes and Nurses in 1 Thessalonians 2.7', in John T. Carroll, Charles H. Cosgrove, and E. Elizabeth Johnson (eds), *Faith and History: Essays in Honor of Paul W. Meyer* (Atlanta: Scholars Press, 1990), pp. 193–207.

The questions I want to consider are as follows: (1) What passages in the letters of Paul employ maternal imagery? (2) Apart from that imagery itself, what else do these texts have in common that warrants treating them together? (3) What avenues of investigation offer the best prospects for illuminating this particular set of passages? (4) What learnings might be gleaned from such a study? In other words, so what? What difference does it make?

What Passages in the Letters of Paul Employ Maternal Imagery?

In order to answer that question, I need first to identify those passages in which Paul refers to *himself* (and sometimes his co-workers) in maternal terms.[4]

> But we became babes in your midst, as a nurse cherishes her own children (1 Thess. 2.7). Brothers, I was not able to speak to you as to spiritual people but as to fleshly people, as to babes in Christ. I gave you milk to drink, not solid food, for you were not yet able, but even now you are not able[5] (1 Cor. 3.1–2).

> My children, with whom I am in labor again until Christ is formed in you ... (Gal. 4.19).

The metaphor that underlies all three of these passages is 'I am your mother.' In 1 Thess. 2.7, the metaphor serves as a reminder of the loving character of Paul's work ('I am the mother who cared for you'). 1 Cor. 3.2 similarly draws upon the mother's feeding of her child ('I am the mother who was not able yet to wean you to solid food because you were not ready'). In Gal. 4.19, Paul returns to the time of birth itself ('I am the mother who labored to bring you into the world').

In two other instances Paul employs maternal imagery as a way of speaking metaphorically about the eschaton:

> Then sudden destruction will come upon them as labor pangs upon a pregnant woman (1 Thess. 5.3).

> For we know that all creation groans together and labors together even until now (Rom. 8.22).

---

4 All translations are my own unless otherwise indicated.

5 O. Larry Yarbrough has recently attempted to connect this passage with the presence of male nurses in Roman households, men who would assist with the tasks of child care, even including the feeding of milk ('Parents and Children in the Letters of Paul', in L. Michael White and O. Larry Yarbrough [eds], *The Social World of the First Christians: Essays in Honor of Wayne A. Meeks* [Minneapolis: Fortress Press, 1995], pp. 126–41). The study by Keith R. Bradley on which Yarbrough draws, however, analyses inscriptions involving 39 men, of whom only one is identified as a *nutritor lactaneus*, an attendant who fed milk to children. Bradley does not himself argue that males routinely were involved in feeding milk to infants through some precursor to the baby bottle ('Child Care at Rome: The Role of Men', in idem, *Discovering the Roman Family: Studies in Roman Social History* [New York: Oxford University Press, 1991], pp. 37–75). The most obvious reading of 1 Cor. 3.2 is that Paul is the nursing mother whose breasts provide milk to the infant community, not that Paul is the male nurse who administered 'goat's milk sweetened with honey' (Yarbrough, 'Parents and Children', p. 133).

That is, the arrival of the eschaton cannot be predicted or controlled, any more than can the pangs of maternal labor.

Two additional texts employ maternal imagery to refer to Paul's calling to the apostolic vocation:

God ... set me apart from the womb of my mother and called me through his grace ... (Gal. 1.15).

Now last of all, as to something monstrously born, he appeared to me (1 Cor. 15.8).

This last text poses notorious problems because of the difficulties of translating the Greek word ἔκτρωμα.[6] This rare noun refers to the product of an untimely birth or miscarriage, and, thus, it may connote either the untimely character of Paul's calling or his state of being unfit for the calling. However we translate the word, Paul here refers to himself by means of birth imagery.

These seven passages differ from one another, but, at the very least, they all involve *maternal imagery*, whether Paul or someone else is the mother.[7] That observation prompts my second question.

What Else Do these Texts Have in Common that Warrants Treating Them Together?

To grant that each of these passages involves maternal imagery does not necessarily mean that anything else justifies examining them together. Is maternal imagery something that can rightly be called a 'topic' or a 'thread' in the Pauline letters, or is it simply a handful of disparate images? Four considerations prompt me to regard it as a topic.

First, most of these passages involve complex metaphorical movements, movements I have come to think of as 'metaphors squared'. When Paul says in 1 Cor. 4.15 that he begat the Corinthians, he speaks metaphorically. He transfers the fathering act of which he is presumably capable from the begetting of a physical child to the begetting of a spiritual child. Similarly, when he describes himself as a 'skilled master builder' (1 Cor. 3.10) or a farmer who plants a field (1 Cor. 3.6), he employs metaphors that are relatively simple and direct.

All that changes when he writes, 'I gave you milk to drink, not solid food.' While certainly it is within the realm of possibility to imagine Paul as 'a skilled master builder' who laid a foundation, or as a farmer who planted a field, or as a father to children, he could never be a nursing mother. That metaphor involves a kind of

---

6 George W.E. Nickelsburg proposes that ἔκτρωμα be understood in light of the birth imagery in Gal. 1.15; see his discussion and his review of the secondary literature in 'An ἔκτρωμα, Though Appointed from the Womb: Paul's Apostolic Self-Description in 1 Corinthians 15 and Galatians 1', in George W.E. Nickelsburg and George W. MacRae (eds), *Christians among Jews and Gentiles* (Philadelphia: Fortress Press, 1986), pp. 198–205.

7 Another text that might be considered is Gal. 4.21–31, the allegorical interpretation of Sarah and Hagar, especially in light of J. Louis Martyn's important argument that they represent two forms of Christian mission, the law-free Gentile mission associated with Sarah and the law-observant Gentile mission associated with Hagar ('The Covenants of Hagar and Sarah', in Carroll, Cosgrove, and Johnson [eds], *Faith and History*, pp. 160–92).

double switch or what I intend by the expression 'a metaphor squared'. First, he metaphorizes (if you will pardon the barbarism) the gospel as milk, then he squares that by metaphorizing Paul as the mother whose body supplies the milk.

An extrabiblical example may help to clarify this point. Among my dearest friends is a male colleague who is several years younger than me. I have actually introduced him on occasion as my 'little brother'. Had I introduced him as my 'little sister', I would have been squaring the metaphor—taking a friendship, metaphorizing it by means of an appropriate familial relationship, and then metaphorizing the metaphor.

More complex than 1 Cor. 3.2 is 1 Thess. 2.7: 'But we became babes in your midst, as a nurse cherishes her own children.'[8] First Paul speaks of himself and his colleagues as 'babes', and then he abruptly takes up the nurse metaphor. When Paul identifies himself as a nurse caring for her own children, he again speaks metaphorically about his relationship with the Thessalonians. As in all metaphors, the relationship is figurative, but here also the figure has been squared: first Paul metaphorizes the relationship between himself and the Thessalonians as that between family members; then he metaphorizes himself into the role of nurse-mother.

The most complex of these passages, metaphorically speaking, is the one with which I began my investigation, Gal. 4.19: 'My children, with whom I am in labor again until Christ is formed in you . . .'. As in other passages, Paul is the mother. Here he is in the process of giving birth *again*. (How exactly it is possible to give birth again we will not pause to consider.) Paul remains in labor, not until the child is born, but until Christ is born in the child. Anyone who does not see the problem this verse involves should try sketching its dynamics. My point is simply that, time and again, these passages involve complex metaphorical moves.[9]

A second consideration that leads me to connect these texts with one another is that they cannot be dismissed as mere variations on the larger theme of paternal imagery. That would seem to be obvious, since mothers and fathers are not customarily confused with one another, but apparently it is not obvious. Commentaries on these passages regularly say things such as: 'Paul often refers to himself as the father of believers; see also 1 Corinthians 4.15.' That is, the two sets of texts are understood

---

8 The NRSV translates this verse differently, reading 'we were gentle' rather than 'we were babes'. That significant difference arises because of a notorious text-critical problem; see my discussion of the problem in Gaventa, 'Apostles as Babes and Nurses', pp. 194–98. In addition to the literature cited there, see also Stephen Fowl, 'A Metaphor in Distress; A Reading of ΝΗΠΙΟΙ in 1 Thessalonians 2.7', *NTS* 36 (1990), pp. 469–73; Fowl and I come to the same text-critical judgment on different grounds. The text-critical problem is not urgent for the point under discussion since, even if it is resolved in favor of 'gentle', we still have another double metaphorical transference present here.

9 In his discussion of the marriage analogy in Rom. 7.1–6, C.H. Dodd comments that Paul 'lacks the gift of sustained illustration of ideas', probably because of a 'defect of imagination' (*The Epistle of Paul to the Romans* [New York: Ray Long and Richard R. Smith, 1932], p. 103). Generalizing about Paul's use of metaphor is perilous, but my impression is quite different from that of Dodd; Paul employs metaphors well, and his mixed metaphors (the ones Dodd would regard as defective) often appear in settings where he is striving to convey a particular point *and* to avoid another. For example, the analogy in Rom. 7.1–6 logically requires Paul to say that the law has died, but he refuses to do that, affirming instead that believers died to the law.

as being part and parcel of the same phenomenon, and in one sense they are, because both employ metaphors of family to speak of the Christian community.

The distinction between them is an important one, however. At one level, it is important because we have too long neglected any sort of references to women or imagery involving women. Just as we failed to ask about the apostle Junia and the household of Chloe, we failed to notice these astonishing references to the maternity of a male apostle. As one conversation partner, not incidentally a woman, commented in response to my initial work on this problem, 'I have been reading the Bible my entire life, and I never even noticed these texts.'

Beyond this first-level task of retrieval, however, these passages convey something quite distinct from what is conveyed with paternal imagery. Maternal imagery appears in contexts referring to the ongoing nature of the relationship between Paul and the congregations he founded; paternal imagery, by contrast, regularly refers to the initial stage of Christian preaching and conversion.[10]

English translations sometimes render this distinction obscure. In the NRSV, Phlm. 10 says that Paul became the father of Onesimus, a translation that might suggest a protracted period of care and concern. The Greek, however, is more concise: Paul says he begat Onesimus, and the context makes it clear that he refers to the fact that he is the one who introduced Onesimus to the Christian faith. Similarly, in 1 Cor. 4.15, Paul refers to his role in the initial formation of the church at Corinth as an act of begetting and appeals to that role to persuade the Corinthians to continue to listen to him. The biological act of fathering takes place in a single instant, and Paul's references to begetting believers are metaphorically congruent with that biological fact: he refers to a single event in past time.[11]

In addition to these two passages in Philemon and in 1 Corinthians, only two others refer unmistakably to Paul's paternity. In Phil. 2.22, he compares the relationship between himself and Timothy with that between father and son. Since he is referring to a specific working relationship rather than to his relationship to believers in general, that text seems to fall outside our purview. In 1 Thess. 2.11–12 (just following the use of maternal imagery in 2.7), he speaks of the apostles as dealing with the Thessalonians 'as a father with his own children, urging and encouraging you and insisting that you lead a life worthy of God'. Here paternity does involve a process of maturation, of course; in 1 Thessalonians 2, however, Paul is contrasting his mission with those who would flatter and seek praise and make demands (1 Thess. 2.5–7), so that he may have a particular reason for drawing

---

10 Earl J. Richard identifies Paul's use of maternal imagery with his founding visit and his use of paternal imagery with the process of growth and discipline (*First and Second Thessalonians* [Collegeville, MN: Liturgical Press, 1995], pp. 86, 106). In so doing, however, Richard considers only the maternal imagery in 1 Thess. 2.7 and does not take into account the other passages under discussion here. Richard also fails to note that all of 1 Thess. 2.1–12 concerns Paul's founding visit, including the paternal metaphor of 1 Thess. 2.11.

11 J. Louis Martyn rightly characterizes γεννάω, the Greek verb for begetting that appears in Phlm. 10 and 2 Cor. 4.15, as Paul's 'missioning verb' (Martyn, 'The Covenants of Hagar and Sarah,' p. 177). Norman R. Petersen similarly comments on Phlm. 10 that fatherhood is 'a metaphor describing one who brings an individual into the church, whether through the preaching or through baptizing, or through both' (*Rediscovering Paul: Philemon and the Sociology of Paul's Narrative World* [Philadelphia: Fortress Press, 1985], p. 85 n. 69).

attention to 'urging and encouraging' in this context. That is, Paul distances himself from the sophist who manipulates his disciples for his own ends.

Incidentally, the four texts I have just mentioned are the only ones I can identify in which Paul uses paternal imagery, apart, of course from his references to God as father.[12] Statistically, that means that Paul uses maternal imagery more often than he does paternal imagery, a feature that is simply astonishing, especially when we consider its virtual absence from most of our discussions of the Pauline letters.

I have left out of consideration the occasions when Paul addresses believers as his children without clearly depicting himself either as father or as mother. In 2 Cor. 6.13, he writes, 'I speak as to children—open your hearts also.' And in 2 Cor. 12.14, he defends his decision not to be a burden to the Corinthians by analogy with parental responsibilities: 'Because children ought not to lay up for their parents but parents for their children.' Other than perpetuating the familial relationship between apostles and congregation, these texts add little to our understanding of Paul as either father or mother.

To return to the question of the difference between Paul's use of paternal and maternal metaphors, it is striking that none of the instances in which Paul uses maternal imagery can be read as referring to a single event that occurred at one moment in the past. Quite the contrary, when Paul uses maternal imagery, the image always requires the elapse of some extended period of time: a woman who is pregnant, after all, is pregnant for a period of time and does not control when her labor will begin; the process of labor itself generally extends over a period of time; the physical nurture of feeding an infant is seemingly endless; the care of a nurse-mother lasts until the child is able to perform certain tasks independently. Later on, parents may feel as if infancy lasts only moments, but for a nursing mother, a 3:00 a.m. feeding can be a glimpse of eternity!

Whether or not Paul is conscious of the choices he makes, the biological and, to a certain extent, cultural differences between mothering and fathering shape the differences between these two sets of texts. However much the paternal metaphors and the maternal metaphors have in common, they are by no means merely interchangeable with one another. To take a particularly telling example, I cannot imagine how one would rewrite the laboring image of Gal. 4.19 in the language of fathering.

A third factor that connects these texts is that in them Paul describes the apostolic office; that is, he is not referring to himself in general terms but to his vocation. Given that most of Paul's statements of self-reference have to do with his apostolic role, that claim is almost tautological; the distinction is, nevertheless, important. These metaphors do not serve merely to decorate Paul's text or to illustrate a point; instead, they are a vital part of communicating what the apostolic task involves.

The connection between maternal imagery and apostolic task is easy to see in 1 Thess. 2.7, where not only the verse but the passage as a whole describes the work of an apostle. And in Gal. 4.19, Paul explicitly applies the image of a woman's

---

12 A recent essay by John L. White attempts to trace both Paul's Christology and his ecclesiology to his conception of God as father; God's generativity brings about both the son Jesus Christ and the Christian community ('God's Paternity as Root Metaphor in Paul's Conception of Community', *Foundations and Facets Forum* 8 [1992], pp. 271–95). Much in White's article is suggestive, but in my judgment he has not taken adequate account of the presence of maternal imagery (although see p. 280 n. 19).

birth pangs to his work as apostle in sustaining Christians in the Galatian churches. Even in 1 Cor. 3.2, however, where he speaks of feeding with milk rather than with solid food, he is concerned both with the maturity (or the lack of maturity) of the Corinthians *and* with his own task as apostle, as the remainder of the chapter and ch. 4 make clear. And in the strange case of 1 Cor. 15.8, where he speaks of himself as a 'monstrous birth', he is referring to his calling as an apostle and makes that connection explicit in the very next sentence. Something in Paul's understanding of the apostolic task causes him to turn to this language of maternity.

A fourth feature that connects several of these texts is their association with apocalyptic contexts. Obviously, that is the case with 1 Thess. 5.3, where the topic under discussion is the 'day of the Lord'. Similarly, Rom. 8.22 depicts the longing of creation for its future redemption. Although 1 Cor. 15.8 ('something monstrously born') itself does not directly concern the apocalyptic future, certainly the larger discussion of the resurrection and the final triumph of God does concern apocalyptic.

In connection with apocalyptic, Gal. 4.19 is the text that proves most interesting. Paul's comparison of himself to a woman in labor may well derive from the apocalyptic convention of using the birth pangs of a woman to refer to the suddenness of the end time or its unpredictability. By applying that conventional metaphor to himself, to his own work, Paul associates his own apostolic vocation with the anguish anticipated in an apocalyptic era and recalls for the Galatians their crucifixion with Christ. As such, Gal. 4.19 employs a conventional metaphor, that of the anguish of a woman in labor, to identify Paul's apostolic work with the apocalyptic expectation of the whole created order.

By virtue of their unusual metaphoric structure, their distinctiveness from paternal imagery, their association with Paul's apostolic vocation, and their location in apocalyptic contexts, then, these texts merit our attention under the general rubric of maternal imagery. That conclusion brings me to my third question.

What Avenues of Investigation Offer the Best Prospects for Illuminating this Particular Set of Passages?

Of the many approaches that could promote understanding of Paul's use of maternal imagery, three seem essential. First, attention to the history of traditions within these passages will help us see where Paul may have acquired some of these expressions and how he has employed them. Most obvious here is the way in which Gal. 4.19 replays maternal imagery in texts such as Jer. 6.24: 'We have heard the report of it, our hands fall helpless; anguish has taken hold of us, pain as of a woman in travail' (NRSV).[13] And Paul's depiction of himself as a nursing mother in 1 Thess. 2.7 recalls Moses' frustrated complaint to God in Num. 11.12, 'Did I conceive of all this people? Did I give birth to them, that you should say to me, "Carry them in your bosom, as a nurse carries a sucking child"?' (NRSV). Somewhat less aggrieved, in the *Hodayoth* of Qumran the Teacher of Righteousness rejoices:

> Thou has made me to be a father to the sons of grace,
>   and a foster-father to men of marvel;

---

13 See also Mic. 4.10; *1 En.* 62.4; *2 Bar.* 56.6; *4 Ezra* 4.42; and my discussion in Gaventa, 'The Maternity of Paul', pp. 192–94.

they have opened their mouths like little babes
   [at the mother's breast] ...
   like a child playing in the lap of its nurse. (1QH 7.19–23, 25)[14]

The maternal imagery in these and other texts promises to enhance our sense of ways in which biblical and other Jewish traditions shape (consciously or unconsciously) Paul's language, but the history of traditions must be supplemented by attention to the socio-cultural context of Paul's usage. What cultural codes are enforced or violated when Paul images himself as a woman in labor or a nurse caring for her own children? Do other men use such imagery and, if so, when?

These questions are exceedingly complex, not only because of the vast literature that needs to be combed but also because of the difficulty of deciding what constitutes a parallel. To take but one example, commentators often adduce a passage from Epictetus as a parallel to 1 Cor. 3.2. Epictetus asks his audience, 'Are you not even yet willing, like little children, to be weaned and to grasp more solid food, and not to cry for mothers and wet-nurses—the wailings of old women?' (*Discourses* 2.16.39). Epictetus does make use of the distinction between milk and solid food, although his usage differs dramatically from Paul's. Paul places himself in the middle of the analogy (he is the mother who feeds), but Epictetus stands at arm's length from those who must be weaned. Epictetus also scorns the very role of 'mothers and wet-nurses', a role Paul claims for himself.

This last observation moves us from the issue of parallels to the even more elusive question of how Paul's contemporaries might have heard his use of maternal imagery. The emerging literature on gender construction in the Greco-Roman world offers some important clues that will need to be pursued.[15] One of the prominent themes in that discussion is gender hierarchy and the severe loss of pride experienced by a male who was suspected of 'going AWOL from [his] assigned place in the gender hierarchy'.[16] One could go AWOL by wearing women's clothing, by engaging in certain sexual practices, or simply by not being sufficiently 'manly'. It is not difficult to imagine that some would hear Paul's use of maternal imagery as an abandoning of his assigned role.

These are important approaches, but they risk dismantling the metaphors into parts that can be traced and analysed without looking directly at the metaphors themselves and what they accomplish in their contexts. Here I think contemporary work in metaphor can assist us. Again, I need to offer a caveat, for I have only begun to

14 The translation is that of Geza Vermes, in *The Dead Sea Scrolls in English* (London: Penguin Books, 3rd edn, 1987), p. 185. See my discussion of this text in Gaventa, 'Apostles as Babes and Nurses', pp. 202–203.
15 See especially Maud W. Gleason, *Making Men: Sophists and Self-Presentation in Ancient Rome* (Princeton: Princeton University Press, 1995); John J. Winkler, *The Constraints of Desire: The Anthropology of Sex and Gender in Ancient Greece* (New York: Routledge, 1990); David M. Halperin, John J. Winkler, and Froma I. Zeitlin (eds), *Before Sexuality: The Construction of Erotic Experience in the Ancient Greek World* (Princeton: Princeton University Press, 1990); and Thomas Laqueur, *Making Sex: Body and Gender from the Greeks to Freud* (Cambridge, MA: Harvard University Press, 1990). For a recent attempt to read a Pauline letter in conversation with issues of gender and construction, see Dale B. Martin, *The Corinthian Body* (New Haven: Yale University Press, 1995).
16 Winkler, *The Constraints of Desire*, p. 21.

explore this area and do not pretend to be an expert on metaphor theory. In such reading as I have done, however, I find several developments that are particularly helpful in approaching Paul's use of maternal imagery.[17]

First, much contemporary discussion of metaphor, beginning with a pivotal essay by Max Black in 1954, attends to the *cognitive character* of metaphor. Precisely how metaphor influences cognition is hotly debated and is not significant for my present purposes. What is important is to recognize *that* metaphor does not merely decorate or illustrate it; it provokes reflection and even insight. Metaphors ask us to change our minds.[18]

Samuel Levin notes that when we encounter a metaphor, especially one that is either novel or still lively, typically we react by noticing what's wrong with it. We reject it out of hand.[19] An example may prove amusing as well as illustrate my point. An advertising agency was devising a campaign that required some way of ident-ifying the Society of Biblical Literature that would catch the attention of the general public (and I happened to be the contact person for the Society in those negotiations). One draft of a brochure the agency proposed read: 'The SBL is the NFL of biblical scholarship.'[20] Although the advertising people had my great sympathy for a difficult task, I did reject that particular metaphor out of hand. And I have not revised my view.

If a metaphor does work its way with us, however, it forces us to consider things differently. It alters our perspective. Let me offer a somewhat more successful example. During the vile winter of 1994, one that broke many records in the Northeast Corridor, my son's ninth-grade English class was studying metaphor. A teacher who knew how to capitalize on current events asked the students to compose metaphors for snow. As I recall, one metaphor that emerged was 'Snow is the underside of hell'.

That metaphor makes no literal sense. We reject it, seeing initially only the absurd differences between snow and hell. Or we recall other expressions in which snow and hell are treated as opposites, such as 'a snowball's chance in hell'. By thinking through the new metaphor, however, especially by recalling the early months of 1994 in the Northeast, we may think differently about both snow and hell. We may see points of similarity. We may change our judgment. We have gained a new perspective.

Eva Fedder Kittay, speaking metaphorically about this aspect of metaphor, says that a metaphor rearranges the furniture of the mind.[21] Think about the living room

---

17 Perhaps a word of clarification is in order at the outset. Some may already be uncomfortable with my use of metaphor theory for the study of images, some of which, technically speaking, are similes (e.g. 'as a nurse'). Recent work on metaphor regards that distinction as insignificant, and I have followed that lead.

18 Max Black, 'Metaphor', in *idem, Models and Metaphors* (Ithaca, NY: Cornell University Press, 1962), pp. 25–47.

19 Samuel R. Levin, 'Standard Approaches to Metaphor and a Proposal for Literary Metaphor', in Andrew Ortony (ed.), *Metaphor and Thought* (Cambridge: Cambridge University Press, 1979), pp. 124–35.

20 Editor's note: NFL stands for the National Football League, an American association of professional football teams.

21 Eva Fedder Kittay, *Metaphor: Its Cognitive and Linguistic Structure* (Oxford: Oxford University Press, 1987), pp. 316–24.

for a moment. If I move the sofa across the room and add a chair on the opposite wall and place the coffee table between them, something happens to the room. The room may seem larger, or smaller. It becomes more hospitable, or, perhaps, colder. The changes force me to take a new path through the room. Metaphorically speaking, metaphors do all these things also.

Similarly, when Paul says, 'I am in labor [with you] again until Christ is formed in you', he invites the Galatians to contemplate their relationship with him, how he can be their mother, how he can be giving birth a second time, or how Christ can be formed in them. Rather than dismissing this assertion as some sort of odd mistake or unimportant mis-statement, we are provoked (I hope) to look more closely at what exactly he is saying.

To a certain extent, at least, this vivid use of language requires a decision on the part of the hearer or reader. As Wayne Booth puts it, 'To *understand* a metaphor is by its very nature to decide whether to join the metaphorist or reject him [or her], and that is simultaneously to *decide* either to be shaped in the shape [the] metaphor requires or to resist.'[22]

Here Booth touches on a second feature of metaphor theory that proves helpful for reading the maternal imagery in Paul, namely, the relationship between *metaphor and intimacy*. Ted Cohen has proposed that a metaphor is an invitation to intimacy.[23] That insight is helpful *if* we realize that the invitation may be quite unconscious on the part of the speaker or writer. If I say to you, 'Snow is the underside of hell', I am implicitly inviting you to join in my assessment of snow. You may respond negatively (but only if you sat out the winter of 1994 in some southern territory) with something like 'snow is a white cotton blanket'. Or you may concur, 'Snow is a curse from the heavens.' If we find that we agree, a certain relationship has been created, however transient and even silly in this instance.

The relationship between metaphor and intimacy is particularly appropriate when we think about the way in which Paul employs maternal imagery. That connection is easy enough to see in 1 Thess. 2.7, where he is recalling his close relationship with the Thessalonians, or in Gal. 4.19, where he seeks to reestablish a relationship that now seems jeopardized. But even in 1 Cor. 15.8, where he refers to himself as 'monstrously born', he creates a connection between himself and his correspondents. Had he said, 'Even though I did not deserve it, Christ appeared to me', the letter might have been clearer (*if* that is what he means). For the Corinthians, however, the figure of the 'monstrous birth' serves as an invitation to puzzle through Paul's meaning and to draw their own conclusions.

To associate a metaphor with intimacy is not to say, of course, that all metaphoric intimacy is of the happy, collegial sort. Just as jokes can be told with hostile intent, metaphors also can be invitations to hostility. If metaphor creates boundaries around a community, it also creates barriers against outsiders, against those who 'just don't get it'.

The third development in metaphor study that I want to mention concerns a specific category of metaphor, namely, kinship metaphors. Here I am drawing

---

22 Wayne C. Booth, 'Metaphor as Rhetoric: The Problem of Evaluation', in Sheldon Sacks (ed.), *On Metaphor* (Chicago: University of Chicago Press, 1978), pp. 47–70 (63). Italics original.
23 Ted Cohen, 'Metaphor and the Cultivation of Intimacy', in Sacks (ed.), *On Metaphor*, pp. 1–10.

particularly on Mark Turner's book, *Death Is the Mother of Beauty*.[24] Turner analyses the ways in which a vast number of kinship metaphors work. Behind these metaphors he detects ten basic metaphoric inference patterns about kinship. One of the inference patterns Turner identifies is 'what springs from something is its offspring', as in 'a proverb is the child of experience'.[25] Or, to return to snow metaphors, we might say, 'snow is the mother of boredom'. Another of Turner's inference patterns is 'members of a natural group are siblings', as in 'death is the brother of sleep' or 'accuracy is the twin of honesty'.[26] It is this inference pattern that prompts me to refer to my colleague as my 'little brother' because we are members of a 'natural' group.

By definition, Paul's use of maternal imagery belongs in Turner's category of kinship metaphors. What is helpful about Turner's work is that he demonstrates the overwhelming prominence of metaphors involving mothers and sisters within the vast realm of kinship metaphors. And he finds that biological and social expectations drive the creation of these kinship metaphors. To no one's surprise, then, metaphors having to do with nurture are almost exclusively associated with mothers.[27] Turner's work appears to corroborate two points I made earlier: mother-talk relates to nurture over a period of time, and Paul's uses of maternal imagery and paternal imagery are not interchangeable.

What Learnings Might Be Gleaned from Such a Study?

I have pointed to a number of texts and number of research directions without actually doing justice to a single text or investigative strategy. My hope is that this very sketchy presentation has managed to convey the existence of a topic in the Pauline letters that is rightly called the 'maternity' of Paul and to suggest some directions for studying that topic. What remains, of course, is the final question: so what? The answer to that question can only be given when the project itself is completed, but I can say a bit about what I hope and why I regard this project as worthy of my time and energy.

First, I want to retrieve these texts from their place in the footnotes of Pauline studies. Even those passages that have received attention (such as 1 Cor. 15.8) have not been examined—at least to the best of my knowledge—in connection with the topic of maternal imagery as such.

In addition, such a study has implications for the continuing discussion of how to identify and understand Paul's theology and theologizing.[28] Here I am helped by the work Steven J. Kraftchick is doing on metaphor theory as a way into thinking about Paul's theology in general. Kraftchick is working with generative metaphors, those implicit metaphors that may structure large aspects of thought, such as 'War on

24 Mark Turner, *Death Is the Mother of Beauty: Mind, Metaphor, Criticism* (Chicago: University of Chicago Press, 1987).
25 Turner, *Death Is the Mother of Beauty*, p. 24.
26 Turner, *Death Is the Mother of Beauty*, p. 25.
27 Turner, *Death Is the Mother of Beauty*, p. 55.
28 I refer especially to the work carried out in the Society of Biblical Literature's Pauline Theology Group; see the essays in Jouette M. Bassler (ed.), *Pauline Theology*, I (Minneapolis: Fortress Press, 1991) and in David M. Hay (ed.), *Pauline Theology*, II (Minneapolis: Fortress Press, 1993).

Poverty'. In 2 Corinthians, for example, Kraftchick argues that Paul uses the death and resurrection of Jesus as a metaphor that structures his understanding of his own task and challenges his readers to restructure their understandings.[29] What Kraftchick and I have in common is that both of us are moving away from the notion that Paul's theology is only to be found in and described by his use of propositional statements. Paul speaks theologically when he says, 'all have sinned and fall short of the glory of God'. He *also* speaks theologically when he says, 'I am in labor until Christ is formed in you.'[30]

The study of maternal imagery should also enhance our understanding of the social function of Paul's language. Wayne Meeks has helped us to see ways in which Paul's use of familial terminology creates and maintains cohesion within the communities he addresses.[31] I suspect that is particularly true when the language is maternal, precisely because references to the anguish of labor, to childbirth, to nursing, assume a profound intimacy between parties.

Finally, I *wonder* whether a study of Paul's use of maternal imagery may have implications for the interrelated and complex sets of questions regarding Paul's understanding of leadership and his attitudes toward women. One reading strategy that has become conventional in recent decades involves dissecting Paul's letters into texts labeled 'hierarchical' and other texts labeled 'egalitarian'. With that dualistic approach to Paul, the texts in which Paul refers to himself as 'father' fall neatly into the hierarchical pile, and those in which he refers to believers as brothers fall neatly into the egalitarian pile.[32] The result is a conflict between the 'bad' hierarchical Paul and the 'good' egalitarian Paul.

What happens when we take seriously the use of maternal imagery for the apostolic office? Maternal imagery scarcely belongs in the egalitarian pile, for mothers do not treat their children as equals (as my son would be the first to insist that I acknowledge). We might conclude that maternal imagery belongs in the hierarchical pile, but that designation also will not fit. Mothers in Paul's world do not have the authority of fathers. More important, when Paul presents himself as a mother, he voluntarily hands over the authority of a patriarch in favor of a role that will bring him shame, the shame of a female-identified male. Still, maternal imagery becomes effective precisely because it plays on hierarchical expectations: Paul presents himself as the authority who does not conform to standard norms of authority.

Taking seriously the presence of maternal imagery, in fact, subverts the reductionistic dichotomy between hierarchical and egalitarian texts. It nudges us to seek some

29 Steven J. Kraftchick, 'Death in Us, Life in You: The Apostolic Medium', in Hay (ed.), *Pauline Theology*, II, pp. 156–81; see also my response, Beverly Gaventa, 'Apostle and Church in 2 Corinthians', in Hay (ed.), *Pauline Theology*, II, pp. 187–93.

30 This approach may be contrasted with that of Victor Paul Furnish, for whom Paul's theology is located more narrowly in his 'critical reflection on the beliefs, rites, and social structures in which an experience of ultimate reality has found expression' ('Paul the Theologian', in Fortna and Gaventa (eds), *The Conversation Continues*, pp. 19–34 [25]).

31 Wayne A. Meeks, *The First Urban Christians: The Social World of the Apostle Paul* (New Haven: Yale University Press, 1983), pp. 84–94.

32 Even without taking maternal imagery into account, there are problems with this strategy. As Dale B. Martin has observed, Paul sometimes 'uses patriarchal rhetoric to make an anti-patriarchal point' (*Slavery as Salvation: The Metaphor of Slavery in Pauline Christianity* [New Haven: Yale University Press, 1990], p. 142).

other lens through which to view the matter of leadership in the Pauline letters. Here I can only assert rather than demonstrate what that lens might be, but in my judgment, the lens that lies ready-to-hand is that of the cross. The same cross that reveals the criminal as Son of God and the bankruptcy of human wisdom also calls forth leaders who can risk identifying themselves as slaves of Christ Jesus (Rom. 1.1), as the 'refuse of the cosmos' (1 Cor. 4.13), and even as women in labor for the second time with the same child.

These are matters for further research, reflection, and conversation. For the time being, I find it encouraging to recall that earlier generations of Christians read these passages closely and drew upon them when they spoke of Paul. Anselm prays to Paul as 'our greatest mother'. A little-known preacher of the same era proclaims that Paul's conversation changed him from torturer to mother, from executioner to nurse.[33] These views find eerie anticipation as early as the *Acts of Paul*, a second-century text that culminates in an account of Paul's execution. When struck by the executioner's sword, so the story goes, what Paul's body yielded up was not blood—but milk. The narrator concludes: '[T]he soldier and all who stood by were amazed, and glorified God who had given Paul such glory'.[34]

---

33 Guerric of Igny, 'Sermon 45: The Second Sermon for Saints Peter and Paul', in *Liturgical Sermons* (2 vols.; Spencer, MA: Cistercian Publications, 1970–71), II, p. 155. This sermon is an extended interpretation of Song 4.5, in which Guerric identifies Peter and Paul as the breasts of the church.

34 An English translation of the *Acts of Paul* by Wilhelm Schneemelcher and Rodolphe Kasser is conveniently available in W. Schneemelcher (ed.), *New Testament Apocrypha* (2 vols.; Louisville, KY: Westminster/John Knox Press, 2nd edn, 1991–92), II, pp. 237–70.

Women's Inheritance Rights in Antiquity and Paul's Metaphor of Adoption

Kathleen E. Corley

The metaphor of adoption, although infrequent in Pauline literature, becomes a central image of the new relation of the redeemed Christian to God. The legal term υἱοθεσία, 'adoption as a son', occurs three places in the book of Romans, in 8.15, in 8.23, and in 9.4 where this adoption is said to belong to Israel. The only other occurrences of this word in the entire New Testament are in Gal. 4.5, where believers are said to receive sonship rather than to be sons as a consequence of birth, and in Eph. 1.5 where this adoption is said to have been predestined (προορίζω). This relationship is one that is based on faith alone (Romans 4, Gal. 3.27), as Christians are sons by virtue of their belief in Christ, and not because they are lineal descendants of Abraham. In fact, not all those who are natural sons (τὰ τέκνα τῆς σαρκός) of Abraham will inherit the promises of God, but the children of the promise (τὰ τέκνα τῆς ἐπαγγελίας) will (Rom. 9.8). Some of these children who are named as heirs are even aliens to the family of God, but God has mercifully brought them into the family, as branches of a wild olive tree are grafted onto a domestic olive tree (11.17). The metaphor of adoption is therefore a profound one, for in the process of adoption a person completely outside of a family is made to be a true member of that family, with all the rights of a natural child. Such legal terminology has meaning even today, as adoption is a familiar legal process in the modern world.

Some scholars, however, have objected to the repeated translation of υἱοθεσία by 'adoption as sons', as this would necessarily exclude women from the metaphor. The Inclusive Language Lectionary Committee of the National Council of Churches has rendered Rom. 8.22, 23 in the following manner:

> We know that the whole creation has been groaning in travail until now; and not only the creation, but we ourselves, who have the first fruits of the Spirit, groan inwardly as we wait for the adoption as the children of God, the redemption of our bodies.[1]

This rendition is intended to translate υἱοθεσία by 'adoption as children' rather than 'adoption as sons' in order to include both male and female adoptees in the metaphor. In this light, υἱοθεσία is seen as a theological concept that highlights Paul's vision of equality for the early Christian community that was 'egalitarian' in its social organization.[2]

This conclusion, however, can be called into question. Rather than being an inclusive metaphor, υἱοθεσία is indeed a gender-exclusive term that excludes

---

1 Inclusive Language Lectionary Committee, National Council of Churches, *Inclusive Language Lectionary: Readings for Year A* (Atlanta: John Knox Press, 1983), Pentecost 8.

2 Robert A. Atkins, *Egalitarian Community: Ethnography and Exegesis* (Tuscaloosa: University of Alabama Press, 1991), pp. 169–90, esp. p. 188.

women from the experience of being made sons by adoption. The term Paul chooses does indeed mean 'adoption as sons' not 'adoption as children', a point that can be demonstrated with the use of the term in documentary sources and inscriptions. Although women were adopted during the Roman period, the terminology for women's adoption was distinct from the terminology for men's adoption, to the point that the term τεκνοθεσία, 'adopt as a child', is found used of a woman, clearly because υἱοθεσία, 'adopt as a son', would have been inappropriate in reference to a woman. Further, although women were adopted during the Roman period, it would have been rare for a woman to have been adopted in order to make her an heir, since women's right to inheritance was limited, and it was more common for women to be left a legacy and not be named as the principal heir in their parents' wills. As a metaphor for the privileges of Christian salvation, then, Paul's choice of υἱοθεσία is not the center of an egalitarian theology, as women have to imagine themselves as male in order to appropriate the metaphor for themselves.

This matter has been discussed in commentaries in the past. The term υἱοθεσία comes from the two words υἱός (son) and θέσις (a placing), and literally would mean 'to place as a son'. W.E. Vine, a popular conservative commentator, considers any translation besides 'adopt as a son' for υἱοθεσία a mistranslation and 'misleading'. He writes, 'Adoption is a term involving the dignity of the relationship of believers as sons', indicating the entrance of a son into a family rather than a mere child.[3] In their discussion of both Romans 8 and Galatians 4, many commentators emphasize that it is their status as *sons* which brings to believers the privilege of being heirs (Romans: so Godet, Sanday and Headlam, Barth, perhaps Barrett; Galatians: so Black, Guthrie, Lightfoot, Eadie, Ridderbos, Betz). All of these commentators assume that it is the privileges of male children that Paul has in mind. A few commentators on Romans suggest the term 'children' is in view (so Hodge), and F.F. Bruce in his Tyndale commentary on Romans goes so far as to add 'and daughters' to his application of Rom. 8.23 and suggests in an earlier commentary on Galatians that υἱοθεσία is a Greek equivalent to the Latin *adoptio* (which was used of both men and women—although he does not suggest this to make that point).[4] Even so, Bruce still refers to the practice of Roman law which gave rights to an 'adopted son, a son deliberately chosen by an adoptive father to perpetuate his name and inherit his estates'.[5] His comment on Rom. 8.23 makes it clear that he assumes female adoptees are not excluded from the metaphor and that they too have the same rights of inheritance in the kingdom of God.

The question of the status of women adoptees can only be answered by a careful examination of the use of υἱοθεσία in the ancient world in order to determine whether or not both males and females were adopted, what the legal terminology for such a transaction would have been, and whether or not boys and girls would have been adopted for the same reasons. The question of whether or not girls would have been adopted *in order* to make them heirs is a crucial one, as Paul clearly links the

3 W.E. Vine, *An Expository Dictionary of New Testament Words* (Old Tappan, NJ: Fleming H. Revell Co., 1966), p. 32.

4 F.F. Bruce, *The Letter of Paul to the Romans* (Leicester: Intervarsity Press; Grand Rapids, MI: Eerdmans, 1985), pp. 155–57; *idem*, *Commentary on Galatians* (Grand Rapids, MI: Eerdmans, 1982), p. 192.

5 Bruce, *Romans*, p. 157.

purpose of the adoption of believers to their new status as heirs of God (Rom. 8.17; Gal. 4.7). Consequently, we must investigate the various legal forms of adoption in antiquity that might have influenced Paul's metaphor as well as adoption terminology in the documentary sources that are available.

The Question of Adoption within Judaism

The question of whether or not the Jews had any legal form of adoption is a matter of much debate. That adoption was unknown as a legal institution of Jewish law is usually acknowledged,[6] as the system had two other methods of dealing with the need of a childless man to secure a legal heir: legitimation of any of his male children, or the practice of levirate marriage. The need for a male heir was imperative, as daughters were generally excluded from the succession, although they were often provided with dowries or supported by their brothers until the time of their marriage.[7] Estates could be 'transferred' to a daughter, should she be the only surviving natural issue, but she was required to choose a husband within the clan in order to insure that the property would remain within the larger family unit.[8] In such a system, however, any male child of a man could legally continue a line. All that was necessary was the father's acceptance and identification of his son, and only sons of idol-worshiping or slave mothers were excluded.[9] Children of servants were allowed to inherit, as the story of Hagar and Ishmael shows (Gen. 16.2). Ishmael was driven out precisely because he had a legal claim to Abraham's property. Jacob also obtained children through the maids of his wives (Gen. 30.1–13). By Paul's time, however, women were regularly bequeathed property by various means, both as wives and daughters, in spite of biblical precedents which denied women inheritance rights.[10]

The levirate allowed a brother to marry his dead brother's wife and to produce sons to carry on his brother's line. These children would carry on the natural line of the dead man. Again, such a procedure would prevent the property from passing out of the family's jurisdiction.[11] Through the levirate, as through legitimation, the Jews insured that any heir would be related to the father by blood,[12] rather than through artificial means.[13] Both levirate marriage and legitimation therefore produced a

---

6 Ben-Zion Schereschewsky, 'Adoption', in *Enc Jud*, II, p. 301; G. Fohrer, 'υἱός, υἱοθεσία', in *TDNT*, VIII (Grand Rapids, MI: Eerdmans, 1964), pp. 353–54 (343); David R. Mace, *Hebrew Marriage: A Sociological Study* (New York: Philosophical Library, 1953), p. 210.

7 Mace, *Hebrew Marriage*, pp. 210–12. But see S. Joy Osgood, 'Women and Inheritance in Early Israel', in George J. Brooke (ed.), *Women in the Biblical Tradition* (Lewiston, NY: Edwin Mellen Press, 1992), pp. 29–51.

8 Shmuel Shilo, 'Succession', in *Enc Jud*, XV, p. 479. See *Ket.* 68a, 101b, 102b.

9 Ze'ev W. Falk, *Hebrew Law in Biblical Times* (Jerusalem: Wahrmann Books, 1964), p. 168. See also Num. 27.1–11; Tob. 6.10–11; *B. Bat.* 120a.

10 Tal Ilan, *Jewish Women in Greco-Roman Palestine* (Peabody, MA: Hendrickson, 1996), pp. 167–75.

11 Francis Lyall, *Slaves, Citizens, Sons: Legal Metaphors in the New Testament* (Grand Rapids, MI: Academie Books, 1984), p. 71.

12 Lyall, *Slaves, Citizens, Sons*, p. 72.

13 Schereschewsky, 'Adoption', p. 301.

natural son, rather than an heir who was completely unrelated to the family, as in true adoption.

There are those who think that adoption did occur in ancient Israel, and there are various disputed cases in both the Hebrew Bible and other literary documents from the ancient Near East.[14] Possible adoptees that have been discussed are Manasseh, Moses, Genubath, Obed, and Esther. Adoption formulas have been seen in language pronouncing the king of Israel God's 'son' in 2 Sam. 7.14, 'I will be his Father', and Ps. 2.7, 'You are my son', as well as in language describing the Deity as Father in relation to Israel.[15] It is this adoptive terminology that is now thought by many to be the precursor to Paul's use of υἱοθεσία. The background for Paul's metaphor is seen as Jewish or Semitic, not Greek or Roman.[16] Apologetic interests that object to Paul being influenced by foreign forces outside of the stream of official inspiration, however, may be behind these discussions.[17] Still, it is often noted that many of these quasi-adoptions take place outside of Palestine, and even those who argue for a Semitic background to Paul's metaphor admit that the Hebrew Bible contains no clear adoption formulas and that υἱοθεσία is not found in the LXX.[18] Adoptions are considered to be few and equivocal.[19] Also to be considered are Jewish inscriptions in Rome which could indicate adoptions, although if Jewish law did not allow for formal adoption, these inscriptions could be attributed to the influence of Roman law

14 On adoption in ancient Near Eastern sources, see I. Mendelsohn, 'A Ugaritic Parallel to the Adoption of Ephraim and Manasseh', *Israel Exploration Journal* 9 (1959), pp. 180–83; Shalom M. Paul, 'Adoption Formulae: A Study of Cuneiform and Biblical Legal Cases', *Maarav* 2.2 (1979–80), pp. 173–85.

15 Those who argue for there being cases of adoption in the Hebrew Bible are Samuel Feigin, 'Some Cases of Adoption in Israel', *JBL* 50 (1931), pp. 186–200, who argues for the case of Jepthah (Jud. 11.1–3) and in Ezra 10.44; and William H. Rossell, 'New Testament Adoption—Graeco-Roman or Semitic', *JBL* 71 (1952), pp. 233–34, who sees behind Gal. 4.6 and Rom. 8.15 the story of Eliezar in Gen. 15.4. Good arguments against seeing adoption in the Hebrew Bible can be found in Francis Lyall, 'Roman Law in the Writings of Paul—Adoption', *JBL* 88 (1969), pp. 458–66; *idem, Slaves, Citizens, Sons*, ch. 4; and Fohrer, 'υἱός υἱοθεσία'. Note also that υἱοθεσία does not occur in the Septuagint. Boaz Cohen, *Jewish and Roman Law: A Comparative Study* (New York: The Jewish Theological Seminary of America, 1966) does not have any discussion of adoption. Shaye J.D. Cohen (ed.), *The Jewish Family in Antiquity* (BJS, 289; Atlanta, GA: Scholars Press, 1993) has no mention of adoption practices among Jews.

16 Brendan Byrne, *'Sons of God'—'Seed of Abraham': A Study of the Idea of the Sonship of God of All Christians in Paul against the Jewish Background* (Rome: Biblical Institute Press, 1979); James I. Cook, 'The Concept of Adoption in the Theology of Paul', in *idem* (ed.), *Saved by Hope: Essays in Honor of Richard C. Oudersluys* (Grand Rapids, MI: Eerdmans, 1978), pp. 133-44; Rossell, 'New Testament Adoption', pp. 233–34; Martin W. Schoenberg, *'Huiothesia*: The Adoptive Sonship of the Israelites', *The American Ecclesiastical Review* 143 (1960), pp. 261–73; *idem, 'Huiothesia*, the Word and the Institution', *Scripture* 15 (1963), pp. 115–23; James M. Scott, *Adoption as Sons of God: An Exegetical Investigation into the Background of YIOTHESIA in the Pauline Corpus* (Tübingen: J.C.B. Mohr [Paul Siebeck], 1992); M. Vellanickal, 'The Pauline Doctrine of Christian Sonship', *Biblebhashyam* 5 (1979), pp. 187–207.

17 See comments by Vellanickal, 'Pauline Doctrine of Christian Sonship', p. 188. The Old Testament, and not Roman sources, is the proper background for Paul's metaphor.

18 Schoenberg, *'Huiothesia*, the Word and the Institution', pp. 115–23; Rossell, 'New Testament Adoption', pp. 233–34.

19 See comments by Paul, 'Adoption Formulae', pp. 173–74.

on the Jewish community.[20] A Jewish adoption deed has also been found from Elephantine, Egypt.[21] Two wills from Syria in Akkadian may impact the discussion of the question of adoption in the ancient Near East. In both, the testator makes women 'male' so that they might inherit property that otherwise would be denied them. In another will from Nuzi, a father 'adopts' three daughters 'as sons' to whom he bequeaths his estate.[22] In other cuneiform texts, husbands adopt wives as their children in order to bequeath them property.[23]

A possible background for Paul's discussions of adoption from the Hebrew Bible is the adoption of Eliezar in Genesis 15. Abraham designates his slave Eliezar his heir as a possible solution to his dilemma of childlessness. This was apparently a common custom in the ancient Near East, as the Nuzi documents attest to the fact that childless couples adopted slaves so that they might serve them as long as they lived and might mourn their deaths. In exchange for these services, the slave was designated their heir. Should a natural son be born to the couple, however, the adopted slave had to yield the right of inheritance to the natural son. This makes Gen. 15.4 explicable, where God tells Abraham, 'This man will not be your heir, but your own son shall be your heir.' As Abraham was to have a natural son, the natural son would have precedence over an adopted one. If Paul does have the adoption of the slave Eliezar in mind, particularly in Galatians, he also must have in mind some form of adoption that would allow for the adopted son to maintain his rights of inheritance, or an adoption that would form a stronger familial bond. It would seem that these slaves that were adopted were not truly part of the family (in a sense they were still servants) and did not have all the rights of natural children.[24]

The Jewish legal system did allow for the case of an orphaned child, male or female, but this institution of guardianship was purely for the benefit of the underaged child and in no way created a legal heir for the guardian. The word *apotropos* (father, guardian, custodian) indicated that the adult was a legal custodian of the minor's affairs. Unless the child was mentally deficient, such a guardianship would be terminated when the child came of age, at the age of twelve for a young girl, and at the age of thirteen for a boy. The guardian was legally responsible for the child's financial affairs and held a position similar to that of a modern administrator of an estate, executor of a will, or trustee of property. An *apotropos* was appointed by either a father or the court. Although it has been thought that women could not be guardians, new evidence from antiquity shows that they could.[25] The child's relation to natural parents was in no way altered, nor were such children legal heirs of their guardians, although they could be provided for in a will, especially if the guardian

20 Lyall, 'Roman Law', p. 464. These are the only references to adoption of Jews during the Roman period known to Tal Ilan (personal correspondence, 23 Aug. 2002).

21 Scott, *Adoption as Sons of God*, p. 85.

22 John Huehenegard, 'Biblical Notes on Some New Akkadian Texts from Eman (Syria)', *CBQ* 47 (1985), pp. 428–34 (430 n. 9).

23 Jacob Rabinowitz, 'Semitic Elements in the Egyptian Adoption Papyrus Published by Gardiner', *JNES* 17 (Jan.–Oct. 1958), pp. 145–46; John Van Seters, 'The Problem of Childlessness in Near Eastern Law and the Patriarchs of Israel', *JBL* 87 (1968), pp. 401–408, esp. 405–406.

24 For discussions of Eliezar, see Rossell, 'New Testament Adoption', pp. 233–34; Cook, 'The Concept of Adoption in the Theology of Paul', p. 136.

25 Ilan, *Jewish Women in Greco-Roman Palestine*, pp. 172–75.

were to die before the child came of age.[26] The institution of guardianship was therefore not related to the legal institution of adoption, as the child becomes not a member of the new family, but is rather a ward. It would seem therefore that Jewish law or practice does not fully explain Paul's legal metaphor of υἱοθεσία, since although adoptions did occur among Jews, the practice was not prevalent.[27] In any case, if Paul was thinking of the adoption of Israel or the king of Israel (see Rom. 9.4), he was clearly thinking of the adoption of a son, not a daughter.[28]

Adoption in Greek Law

Adoption appears to have been common in ancient Greece. The information concerning such adoptions comes primarily from court orations of Isaeus, who lived in Athens around 375 BCE, and therefore dates almost four centuries before Paul was writing.[29] The motivation for adoptions stemmed primarily from a desire to avoid the usual laws governing succession. If a man left legitimate sons, the sons shared the inheritance equally, and the daughters had no share, except perhaps in the form of a dowry of maintenance until they married. Grandsons of deceased sons could represent their fathers, and such representation could continue until the fourth generation, that is, great-grandsons.[30] If the only descendant living was an unmarried daughter, the estate went with her, not to her, and went to the nearest agnate who would marry her. The ramifications of the laws concerning such heiresses were complicated.[31] By adopting, therefore, a family could avoid the difficulties that the succession of a daughter would produce.[32] Adoption of a male heir could be done in three ways: through a formal ceremony during the lifetime of the adopter, by a will, or by a posthumous adoption.[33] If an heiress was already married, she could see to it that one of her sons was posthumously adopted as his grandfather's son, making it unnecessary for her to procure a divorce if she had not married someone next-of-kin, or if her husband had not been adopted by her father during his lifetime.[34]

Little is known about the status of the adopted person, except that such an adoption did not affect the man's relation to his mother.[35] In any case, daughters

---

26 Ben-Zion Schereschewsky, '*Apotropos*', in *Enc Jud*, III, p. 218. See also references to the rights of orphans and guardianship in *B. Meṣ.*70a; *Giṭ.* 52a; *Ket.* 109b.

27 See now Frederick W. Knobloch, 'Adoption', in *ABD*, I, pp. 76–79.

28 On that those who argue for a Jewish or Semitic background for Paul's metaphor tend to agree—the adoption is of 'sons', not daughters. See Scott, *Adoption as Sons of God*, pp. 268–69; Schoenberg, '*Huiothesia*: The Word and the Institution', *passim*; *idem*, '*Huiothesia*: The Adoptive Sonship of the Israelites', *passim*; Byrne, *'Sons of God'—'Seed of Abraham'*, p. 215.

29 Lyall, *Slaves, Citizens, Sons*, p. 89.

30 J.W. Jones, *The Law and Legal Theory of the Greeks* (Oxford: Clarendon Press, 1956), pp.189–95.

31 Lyall, *Slaves, Citizens, Sons*, p. 262; Sarah Pomeroy, *Goddesses, Whores, Wives and Slaves: Women in Classical Antiquity* (New York: Schocken Books, 1975), pp. 60–62; Douglas M. MacDowell, 'Inheritance: Greek', in S. Hornblower and A. Spawforth (eds), *Oxford Classical Dictionary* (Oxford: Oxford University Press, 1996), p. 454.

32 Jones, *Law and Legal Theory of the Greeks*, p. 196; Lyall, *Slaves, Citizens, Sons*, p. 91.

33 Lyall, *Slaves, Citizens, Sons*, pp. 89–90.

34 Jones, *Law and Legal Theory of the Greeks*, pp. 196–97.

35 Jones, *Law and Legal Theory of the Greeks*, p. 197.

were rarely adopted, as women would not be able to carry on the inheritance of the family,[36] although such an adoption did occur occasionally, even though it would not produce an heir or one capable of representing the family in religious rites.[37] Also, unlike the Jewish method of legitimation, in Greek adoption bastards could not be made legitimate.[38] Adoption could only raise legitimate males to a higher place in the order of succession than they had by birth, as in the cases of adopting a grandson or a cousin.[39] What is similar to the Jewish methods of providing an heir, however, is the intention of keeping the inheritance within the family, and the interest in passing that inheritance on to someone related by blood to the heirless father.[40]

The Greek institution of adoption has been suggested as a source for Paul's metaphor, especially in light of certain adoption inscriptions found in South Galatia which seem to indicate that South Galatia followed Greek and not Roman law.[41] This may be a questionable conclusion, since the point of Paul's metaphor of adoption is that one who is outside the family has been adopted by God. Although the adoption of outsiders could occur under Greek law, it seems to have been the exception, as near relatives, rather than aliens, were usually adopted.[42] Also, under Greek law, one did not completely leave his natural family, as ties remained with the natural mother. Furthermore, if an adoptee died childless, he could not pass on the estate either by adopting a son himself or by drafting a will; upon the death of a childless adoptee, the order of succession would revert to its original order before the adoption occurred.[43] It would seem that the Classical Greek form of adoption did not produce a strong family tie, but was rather similar in purpose to a will.[44] In any case, if Paul's reference to adoption is a reference to the Classical Greek form of adoption, then women probably would not be included in his metaphor, since under the Greek system women were rarely adopted as they could not legally inherit property. Further, since Paul stresses the inheritance rights of those adopted, a Greek background to the metaphor would necessarily exclude women.

During the years of Roman expansion, however, the knowledge of legal systems with which individuals have familiarity would have been diverse. Many Hellenistic cities probably maintained aspects of their private law, as the policy of the Roman Republic tended to favor the autonomy of the Greek cities,[45] and the policy established by Augustus was in no way an attempt to 'romanize' Greek-speaking provinces, although the emperors did establish Roman colonies in the East.[46] The colonies, however, did not alter the essentially Greek culture of these areas, but

---

36 Pomeroy, *Goddesses*, p. 69.

37 Jones, *Law and Legal Theory of the Greeks*, p. 197.

38 Jones, *Law and Legal Theory of the Greeks*, p. 196.

39 Jones, *Law and Legal Theory of the Greeks*, p. 197.

40 Lyall, *Slaves, Citizens, Sons*, p. 91; see also p. 99: 'The adoption of an outsider was rare.'

41 For further on Roman law, see below. W.M. Calder, 'Adoption and Inheritance in Galatia', *JTS* 81 (1930), pp. 372–74, describes two adoption inscriptions in which an adopted son is also called the father's son-in-law. Such a relationship would have been considered incestuous under Roman law.

42 Lyall, *Slaves, Citizens, Sons*, p. 92.

43 Jones, *Law and Legal Theory of the Greeks*, p. 197.

44 Lyall, *Slaves, Citizens, Sons*, p. 82.

45 A.H.M. Jones, *The Greek City* (Oxford: Clarendon Press, 1940), p. 51.

46 Jones, *The Greek City*, pp. 60–61.

rather became Hellenized themselves.[47] Moreover, Imperial policy was to maintain the existing systems of government, so that there was little change, even though the 'major items of government—police, justice, and above all finance—' were in the hands of the central government.[48] The Galatians, therefore, would surely have been aware of Greek adoption; the question would simply be whether or not Roman adoption law had been introduced there by the 50s. Surely any Roman citizens in the area would have been familiar with Roman laws, but might also have understood Greek law as well. The possible overlapping of Greek and Roman law during the years preceding Paul's writing should be kept in mind.

Adoption in Roman Law

The most developed form of adoption is found within the Roman legal system. In a Roman adoption, adoptees were taken out of their previous family and placed under the *potestas* (authority) of a new *paterfamilias*. All the debts of the adopted individuals were canceled, and in a sense they took on a new identity. The jurisdiction of a *paterfamilias* over the adoptee was the same as that over a natural child. The *paterfamilias* legally owned all of the adopted people's property, governed their personal relationships, and had the right to discipline them as he saw fit.[49] The severance with the previous family was complete in cases of adoption, and in cases of adrogation the previous family was dissolved, so both processes were taken seriously.[50]

In the Roman system there were two forms of adoption, *adrogatio* and *adoptatio*. *Adrogatio* was the process by which one who was *sui iuris* was adopted, the adoption, that is, of one who was not under the authority of another.[51] In the case of adrogation, not only the adrogated, but all those under his *potestas* would come under the *potestas* of the new *paterfamilias*. This was done by the permission of both the religious authorities of Rome and the rest of Rome's citizenry (*populi auctoritate*; Gaius, *Inst.* 1.97). Apparently, in the early period of Roman history, all the citizens of Rome met for such an occasion.[52] The *adrogatus* would then renounce his old family cult and would enter into the new family.[53] As this type of adoption could occur only in Rome, and not in the provinces (although sometimes by an imperial rescript), it is unlikely that Paul

---

47 Jones, *The Greek City*, p. 61.

48 Jones, *The Greek City*, pp. 76–77.

49 For *potestas* and the power of the *paterfamilias*, see Gaius, *Inst.* 1.55–107; *Twelve Tables*, 4.1–4; W.W. Buckland, *A Textbook of Roman Law* (Cambridge: Cambridge University Press, 1972), pp. 118–20; A. Berger, 'Potestas', 'Paterfamilias', in *idem* (ed.), *Encyclopedic Dictionary of Roman Law* (Transactions of the American Philosophical Society, NS 43, part 2; Philadelphia: American Philosophical Society, 1953).

50 Lyall, *Slaves, Citizens, Sons*, p. 85.

51 Lyall, *Slaves, Citizens, Sons*, p. 84; See also B. Nicholas and S.M. Treggiari, 'Adoption', in Hornblower and Spawforth (eds), *Oxford Classical Dictionary*, 1996), pp. 12–13; A. Berger, '*Adoptio*', in *idem* (ed.), *Encyclopedic Dictionary of Roman Law*, p. 350; Gaius, *Inst.* 1.99.

52 Lyall, *Slaves, Citizens, Sons*, p. 85.

53 Lyall, *Slaves, Citizens, Sons*, p. 85. Lyall notes the similarity of the process of adoption with early baptismal ceremonies.

would have this type of adoption in his mind, especially when writing to Galatia.[54]

The second form of adoption was the adoption of one who was *alieni iuris*, one who was under the *potestas* of another.[55] In adoption, the *potestas* of one *paterfamilias* was destroyed and another *potestas* was established. The new member of the family was then in the same relationship to the new *paterfamilias* as were his natural children. The process stemmed from the ancient law of the *Twelve Tables* which stated that if a father sold his son three times then that son would be free from *potestas* (approximately 450 BCE). Daughters need only be sold once.[56] Adoption therefore had two parts: first, the destruction of the old *potestas* and second, the declaration of the new *potestas* by a court.[57] Eventually, the repeated sales were no longer necessary, and by the time of Justinian (sixth century CE) merely the appearance before a magistrate was necessary for adoption.[58] This form of adoption could take place anywhere in the Roman Empire.

Gaius reports that both sons and daughters were regularly adopted, although daughters could not be adopted 'by the authority of the people' as in adrogation, as they were seldom *sui iuris*, not under some man's authority. Gaius writes, however, that females were regularly adopted in the provinces, and before a praetor (*Inst.* 1.101). Also, all children, both natural and adoptive, were equally considered *sui heredes*, at least in cases of intestacy. Women and minors, although kept under a tutelage upon the death of their *paterfamilias*, were still heirs.[59]

This does not mean, however, that women were treated equally in the process of the passing on of the family property. Being a system based on the notion of *paterfamilias* and the *potestas* of the male head of household, Roman law was more likely to favor men when it came to testamentary succession. Moreover, a father was only required to raise one first-born daughter, but all of his sons.[60] It was only in cases of intestacy that women were considered heirs equally along with their brothers. Also, in the order of intestate succession, although close male relatives could succeed to the sixth degree, the only female relative who could succeed was the sister of the deceased.[61] Long before classical times, however, intestacy had become unusual, if not a misfortune.[62] Furthermore, because of the restrictions of the *Lex Voconia*, passed in 168 BCE, the amount a woman could inherit by testament was limited. A

---

54 Lyall, *Slaves, Citizens, Sons*, pp. 85–86. Lyall does point out the interesting ramifications of adrogation and its parallels to instances in Acts where entire households are converted (Lk. 19.9; Acts 10; 16.14–16; 16.29–33; 18.8).

55 Nicholas and Treggiari, 'Adoption', pp. 12–13; Berger, '*Adoptio*', p. 350; Buckland, *A Textbook of Roman Law*, pp. 121–23; Lyall, *Slaves, Citizens, Sons*, pp. 86–87.

56 Buckland, *A Textbook of Roman Law*, p. 121; Lyall, *Slaves, Citizens, Sons*, p. 87.

57 Buckland, *A Textbook of Roman Law*, p. 122.

58 Buckland, *A Textbook of Roman Law*, p. 122.

59 David E.L. Johnston, 'Inheritance: Roman', in Hornblower and Spawforth (eds), *Oxford Classical Dictionary*, p. 758; Herbert F. Jolowicz and Barry Nicholas, *Historical Introduction to the Study of Roman Law* (Cambridge: Cambridge University Press, 1972), p. 249; Buckland, *A Textbook of Roman Law*, pp. 290–92.

60 Pomeroy, *Goddesses*, pp. 164–65; Judith P. Hallett, *Fathers and Daughters in Roman Society: Women and the Elite Family* (Princeton, NJ: Princeton University Press, 1984), p. 181.

61 Pomeroy, *Goddesses*, p. 162.

62 Buckland, *A Textbook of Roman Law*, p. 365.

woman could succeed in cases of intestacy, but she could not be willed a large patrimony, and any amount a woman was to inherit was not to exceed what was left to male heirs.[63] The *Lex Voconia*, however, did encounter substantial opposition, particularly in the century immediately following its passage. Various wealthy men who had only female relatives remaining as possible heirs had to find loopholes in order to leave their estates to their daughters, wives or mothers.[64] In fact, an article on women in Roman succession indicates that women were indeed designated *heredes* despite the Voconian law, but if there were sons in the family, fathers had a tendency to institute their sons as *heredes* and disinherit their daughters, wives, and mothers, leaving them a legacy instead.[65]

The question also arises as to who these females mentioned by Gaius were who were being adopted. In a marriage *cum manu* (that is, when a woman had formally passed from her father's family into the power of her husband), a woman would have the legal status of a daughter, and upon the death of her husband would be considered a *sua heres* as a daughter.[66] Could these be the women who were 'adopted daughters'? Probably not. There was no sign that there was adoption involved in the giving of women in marriages *cum manu*.[67] Moreover, although at the time of the *Twelve Tables* marriage ordinarily was accompanied by *manus*, by the end of the Republic marriages *cum manu* were the exception.[68] As Gaius is writing about 167 CE, it is likely that at this time ordinary married women were not related to their husbands in this manner or considered legally their daughters. Gaius's reference to the adoption of females is probably not a reference to wives.

When it occurred, the effect of a marriage *cum manu* on the inheritance rights of a woman, however, was significant. Roman women could not legally be considered part of more than one family at the same time. Should a woman be married with *manus*, she no longer had any rights whatsoever to her father's property, but instead would become part of her husband's family, and would rather have the same right to inherit from her husband that his legal daughters had. Such a woman would probably have come into her marriage with a dowry that would have been her portion of her inheritance from her father.[69] The Roman daughter's right to inherit surely complicated the financial plight of even fathers who did not wish to give female children preferential treatment in their wills.[70]

Male members of a household would still be more likely to be favored in a testamentary succession, however, exception being made for those few wills that favored women.[71] It would therefore be rare for a man to adopt a daughter *in order* to make

---

63 Hallett, *Fathers and Daughters*, p. 93.

64 Hallett, *Fathers and Daughters*, p. 96.

65 J.A. Crook, 'Women in Roman Succession', in Beryl Rawson (ed.), *The Family in Ancient Rome: New Perspectives* (Ithaca, NY: Cornell University Press, 1986), pp. 58–82.

66 Pomeroy, *Goddesses*, pp. 152–54; Jolowicz and Nicholas, *Historical Introduction*, p. 115; Johnston, 'Inheritance: Roman', p. 758.

67 Buckland, *A Textbook of Roman Law*, p. 118.

68 Jolowicz and Nicholas, *Historical Introduction*, p. 234.

69 Hallett, *Fathers and Daughters*, pp. 217; 91–92.

70 Hallett, *Fathers and Daughters*, pp. 91–92.

71 Hallett, *Fathers and Daughters*, p. 91.

her his heir.[72] It would make much more sense for him to adopt a son, should he be bereft of someone to inherit his property. When Augustus adopted heirs, it should be remembered that they all were men or boys, even though his daughter Julia was still living. Why then were girls adopted?

Even though daughters were probably not given as much importance in the Roman family as were the sons, it is clear that they were indeed valued by the family and society, and primarily valued as their father's daughters, at least in the elite family. It was her status as her 'father's daughter' that remained with an elite Roman woman throughout her life.[73] Not only was there cultural importance given to the role of daughter in Roman society, but there was emphasis in the upper classes on ties of blood and marriage through daughters and father's daughters—'chiefly ties of and through such males as daughters' and sisters' sons, maternal grandfathers and maternal uncles, and fathers-in-law, sons-in-law, and brothers-in-law'.[74] The political, social, and economic benefits of having daughters in a family would have been many. Without daughters, fathers could not make important political and economic alliances with other families. Without sisters, brothers would not have the advantage of close personal ties created by such alliances. The benefits of having daughters would also have been personal, as relationships between fathers and daughters as well as brothers and sisters seem to have been particularly strong. It would be the economic advantages, however, which would seem most likely to be reasons to add a daughter to a family where there wasn't one, or to add additional daughters for the purposes of familial alliance. However, even though such adopted daughters would clearly have all the rights of a natural daughter in matters of inheritance, they probably were rarely adopted in order to inherit property, especially since the amount they could inherit was limited, and their brothers would have a certain amount of priority over them in a testamentary succession.

Paul's Source of υἱοθεσία —Greek or Roman?

Paul had at least three systems of legal thought available to him. It would seem that the background to Paul's metaphor of adoption is at least Greek or Roman, rather than Jewish, as both Greek and Roman law allow more clearly for the adoption of children. Both forms of adoption may have been known to him and to the recipients of his letters as he lived and traveled in an empire that was complex in its legal and cultural make-up. There are, however, several reasons for preferring to see behind Paul's legal metaphor of adoption a specifically Roman rather than Greek legal

---

72 Rare, but not unheard of. One example of just this situation can be found. There is Claudia Metrodora of Chios, the illegitimate daughter of Claudius Calobrotus, who was adopted by another man named Skytheinos. See Roz Kearsley, 'Women in Public Life in the Roman East: Iunia Theodora, Claudia Metrodora and Phoebe, Benefactress of Paul', *Ancient Society: Resources for Teachers* 15 (1985), pp. 124–37, (128–30), with more detailed discussion of the inscriptions at p. 135. The information is taken from several fragmentary texts, reconstructed by Louis Robert, 'Inscriptions de Chios du Ier siècle de notre ère', in *idem* (ed.), *Etudes épigraphiques et philologiques* (Paris: Champion, 1938), pp. 128–34 (128–29, 131).

73 This is the main thesis of Hallett's *Fathers and Daughters*.

74 Hallett, *Fathers and Daughters*, p. 263.

background.[75] First of all, Paul was a Roman citizen, which would entail both of his parents being citizens as well. Aspects of his life in a Roman family and living in a Roman province would have necessarily brought Paul into contact with Roman law. Even though Paul was Jewish by religious training, the fact that he mentions adoption indicates his contact with the greater Hellenistic world around him.[76]

The intended destination of the letter to Rome makes an assumption of a knowledge of Roman legal procedure on the part of his recipients most likely, particularly in the case of the Gentile members of the Roman community. Jewish inscriptions in Rome indicate that Jewish families, although not heir to a legal form of adoption, had been influenced by the Roman practice of adoption.[77] It is also most likely that Roman law was known by the time of Paul in Galatia, especially in South Galatia (Pisidian Antioch, Iconium, Derbe, and Lystra) and even in North Galatia, that was familiar with the concept of *patria potestas* (Gaius, *Inst*. 1.55). Ephesus, as a center of Roman administration and the leading city of the province of Asia, would certainly have felt the presence of Roman law. Moreover, Roman adoption was the major method by which great Roman families made their alliances, particularly the emperors.[78] Julius Caesar, Augustus, and Tiberius were all related by means of adoption.[79] Furthermore, it should be pointed out that the major point that Paul is making is that those foreign to a family are being made true members of it, which was not usually the case in Greek adoptions. In Greek adoptions, those lower on the ladder of succession who were already members of the family were raised to a higher place in the succession. Paul wishes to claim that even those not descended from Abraham are made children of promise by means of adoption, and are therefore true sons and true heirs of the Father. Even if Paul knew of Greek adoption, he seems to be drawing on this aspect of Roman adoption, at least in respect to the Gentile believers of the Roman and Galatian communities.

Since Paul is thinking specifically of the privileges of inheritance connected with adoption (which is a privilege of both Greek and Roman adoptees, but only of male adoptees in Greek law), he may not have females as well as males in mind. Even though female adoptees would have rights to succession under Roman law in cases of intestacy, it seems unlikely that a head of a household would adopt a daughter in order to make her his heir. He would be more likely to adopt a daughter so that he could make familial alliances through her marriage and her subsequent progeny. If Paul is simply referring to the consequences of adoption (i.e. that it gives an individual inheritance rights) then he could have both men and women in view. However, it can be shown that the gender-specific nature of the language Paul employs makes even this possibility problematic.

---

75 Here I summarize several of Lyall's arguments in favor of Paul's use of Roman law. See *Slaves, Citizens, Sons*, pp. 82–83; 95–99; see also W.E. Ball, *St Paul and Roman Law* (Edinburgh: T. & T. Clark, 1901), pp. 4–6.

76 Lyall, *Slaves, Citizens, Sons*, pp. 82–83.

77 Lyall, 'Roman Law', p. 464. See n. 11 for further bibliography.

78 Lyall, *Slaves, Citizens, Sons*, p. 82. Against W. Calder. 'Adoption and Inheritance'.

79 Lyall, *Slaves, Citizens, Sons*, p. 83; Appendix 4, pp. 223–38.

Papyrological Evidence for the Adoption Formula

Paul is not the only private writer to utilize the adoption formula in antiquity. That both males and females were adopted during the period of Roman domination of the ancient world can be seen in the inscriptions and documentary papyri of this period. The terminology used for the different sexes, however, is distinct. In inscriptions the word υἱοθεσία is always found in the formula καθ' υἱοθεσίαν δέ: A, son of B, καθ' υἱοθεσίαν δέ son of C. The formula for the adoption of females is κατὰ θυγατ-ροποίαν, which occurs seven times.[80] This separate terminology for the adoption of sons and daughters continues in the extant papyri, in letters and in contracts and other legal documents. In fact, the term υἱοθεσία does not occur in reference to a female, but only when a male adoptee is in view. The following study is based on as exhaustive a collection of documents referring to the adoptive relationship as is possible, utilizing the available indices to published documentary papyri. Many of the dates of these documents are later than we would like to see for comparison with the NT, but a study of such documentary texts can still be illuminative if their relative significance is kept in perspective. It should also be kept in mind that most of these documents come from Egypt, where climate conditions made it possible for them to survive. All date after the Roman takeover of the Egyptian government, and some, though by no means all, show influence of Roman legal practice.

References to Adopted Children in Letters

The adoptive relationship is most often mentioned in letters when persons are ident-ified by name, and familial identification is necessary. There are only four letters which indicate that one of the persons being spoken of is adopted, and all are official in nature.

The first letter comes from Oxyrhynchus in Egypt, and is dated 100 CE.[81] The meaning of this letter is clear. Phanias and Diogenes write to the market clerks that Arthothes the younger, a priest in the temple of Thoeris, Isis, and Sarapis, has ceded to his elder brother Arthothes, the adopted son of Ampendis, also a priest in the same temple, a portion of corn land. The elder Arthothes appears to be the natural son of Petarbebebis, but is being distinguished as the adopted son of another man, Ampendis. The additional identification of the elder Arthothes as an adopted son was probably necessary due to the official nature of the letter.

The letter opens with the common opening formula of letters, 'A- to B- χαίρειν', the opening which usually occurs in familiar letters, business letters and official communications.[82] The letter closes with the common formula ἔρρωσο (ῥώννυμι), also found in familiar letters, business letters, and official documents.[83] Of the letters using this closing, Exler identifies 117 as business letters, 150 as familiar letters, and 17 as official communications.[84] Due to the subject matter of this particular letter, it

---

80 G. Adolf Deissmann, *Bible Studies* (Edinburgh: T. & T. Clark, 1923), p. 239.

81 P Oxy 46 (100 CE). Text and translation in A. Hunt and B. Grenfell (eds), *Oxyrhynchus Papyri* (47 vols.; London: Egyptian Exploration Fund, 1898), I, pp. 103–104.

82 Francis Xavier J. Exler, *The Form of the Ancient Greek Letter: A Study in Greek Epistolography* (Washington: Catholic University of America Press, 1923), p. 23.

83 Exler, *The Form of the Ancient Greek Letter*, p. 70.

84 Exler, *The Form of the Ancient Greek Letter*, p. 70.

should be classified as an official letter, as it notifies the authorities of a land transaction. The motivation of the letter is simply 'in order that' the authorities 'should know'. The adopted party is identified by the simple use of θέσις, by adoption (son of)', occurring directly before the name of the party he was adopted by.

The second letter, also from Oxyrhynchus, is an official receipt in the form of a letter.[85] Again, the letter opens with the usual 'A- to B- χαίρειν' formula, but the letter is lacking a closing formula, and ends instead with only the date. As many business communications in antiquity ended without any closing formula, this is not unusual.[86] Again, the adopted person is identified by the use of θέσις, which occurs directly before the name of the adopter. This letter also should be classified as an official document, as it serves as a business receipt.

The third letter also begins with the usual opening formula, but as the document is cut off and extremely fragmentary, the main provision of the document as well as the ending are lost. It dates from 187 CE.[87] It is a contract in the form of a letter between Platonis (Ophelia) and a woman called Heras concerning a certain inheritance from Hermias, the maternal grandfather of Heras and by adoption the father of Platonis's deceased husband. Portions of this inheritance were to be given to Platonis's two sons. This letter was probably an agreement between the two women. Although the reference to adoption does not occur in the opening lines, as did previous references, it is clear that the official nature of the document necessitated spelling out the lineage of the deceased in order to determine the claim of inheritance. The relationship of adoption included the usual rights to inheritance, so that Platonis and her sons were also entitled to a portion of the inheritance, as by adoption Platonis's sons were the grandchildren of Hermias.

The fourth letter, which contains our first reference to the adoption of a girl, dates from 158–59 CE.[88] In this contract, which also takes the form of a letter, the new tenant of a portion of land assures the daughter of its previous cultivator, now deceased, that she will be free of any responsibility for the future demands for dues on the land, over which he is given full rights, and at the same time agrees never to make any other claims on the rest of the estate. The reference to an adopted woman comes in the identification of the new tenant in the opening lines of the letter, as his mother was the adopted daughter of Ballarus. The letter opens with the usual 'A- to B- χαίρειν', but has no formal closing. Again, the letter is more official in content, necessitating the clear identification of a certain individual.

Of the four letters cited, none is what would be called a familiar letter.[89] All of these references are in official documents, leading one to the conclusion that adoption was not of issue in a personal letter, and the identification there of 'son of', 'daughter of' or 'father of' would be sufficient, without the mention of whether or

85 P Oxy 1719. Text in Hunt and Grenfell (eds), *Oxyrhynchus Papyri*, XIV, p. 165. Translation by Shawn Carruth and Kathleen Corley.

86 Exler, *The Form of the Ancient Greek Letter*, pp. 69, 71.

87 P Oxy 1721. Text in Hunt and Grenfell (eds), *Oxyrhynchus Papyri*, XIV, pp. 165–66. Translation by Shawn Carruth and Kathleen Corley.

88 P Oxy 1123. Text and translation in Hunt and Grenfell (eds), *Oxyrhynchus Papyri*, VIII, pp. 215–16.

89 See Deissmann, *Bible Studies*, pp. 3-59, for a discussion of the difference between a formal and a familiar letter.

not one was adopted. It would seem, then, that the situation of adoption might only have been worthy of mention, or necessary, if the communication was an official document. This fact will become eminently clear as the further references to adoption are enumerated. The other references to adoption, or the adoption formula, occur in strictly official documents, such as contracts, wills, and other legal documents.

As for the phraseology in these four letters, the adoptive relationship is indicated by the use of θέσις with a genitive, and not the υἱοθεσία which Paul uses in the book of Romans. There appears to be no distinction between the adoption of sons and daughters, but we will see that the phrase θέσει (θυγάτηρ) or θέσει (υἱός) is implied in the genitive construction, as it is often spelled out clearly.[90]

Adoption Contracts

There are two actual adoption contracts extant, and one alienation document.[91] The two adoption contracts concern males, whereas the alienation document concerns a female. P Oxy 1206 serves as an example of such an adoption contract. In this document, a husband and wife, Heracles and Isarion, agree to the adoption of their son by Horion, who promises that the boy will be his heir. The document dates from 335 CE.[92] In this text, the phrase εἰς υἱοθεσίαν is used. There appears to be no apparent reason for the adoption, and no apparent relationship between the ones making the contract. This is a private contract, and there is no mention of *potestas*, although its editors note that it is written according to Roman law of the time. The language is not the language of a letter, nor is this a contract written in the form of a letter, although the two parties of the contract wish each other 'mutual greetings'.

The second adoption contract, P Lips 28, dates from about 30 years later, and concerns the adoption of a fatherless boy by his uncle.[93] The boy's grandmother turns the boy over to his uncle, who promises to care for him, to consider the boy as his own son, and to make him his own heir as well as to administer the boy's property, which he received from his parents. In this contract the phrase καθ' υἱοθεσίαν is used.[94] As the boy's uncle, Silvanus, is a hermit, it would be interesting to know if the boy would also be entering into a monastic life. In any case, the reason for the adoption is clear, and there is a definite familiar relationship between the two parties involved. Again, the document is formal in tone, and no greetings are mentioned at the beginning of the contract.

Also pertinent for our study is a document that is by form a letter and implies the adoption of a nine-year-old girl. This is considered an alienation document and is in effect the counterpart to an adoption contract. Subsequently, there probably existed a corresponding adoption contract by the adopters. Aurelia Harais, the mother, has

90 P Strass 4.4 contains such a reference to a θέσει θυγάτηρ. Unfortunately, due to an error in the index of this papyrus collection, this text is unavailable to me.

91 There is one good discussion of these contracts. See Marek Kurylowicz, 'Adoption on the Evidence of the Papyri', *Journal of Juristic Papyri* 19 (1983), pp. 61–75.

92 P Oxy 1206. Text and translation from Hunt and Grenfell (eds), *Oxyrhynchus Papyri*, IX, pp. 242–43.

93 P Lips 28. Text and description in M. David and A. Groningen (eds), *Papyrological Primer* (Leiden: E.J. Brill, 1965), pp. 50–52.

94 David and Groningen (eds), *Papyrological Primer*, pp. 50–52.

been forced to give away her daughter, as the death of her husband has left her financially incapable of supporting her. The document dates from about 554 CE.[95] Here again, as in P Lips 28, there is a clear reason for the adoption. It would appear, then, that the adoption of a girl would not necessarily be for reasons of familial alliance as might be the case in an upper-class family, but could also be for purely economic reasons. The last sentence, 'in reply to the formal question I have given my consent', also indicates that although the document begins with the formal epistolary opening, it is by content an official document and is therefore legally binding.

These three documents, although later in date than we would like to see for the study of the New Testament and Paul, are the only extant examples we have of adoption contracts. In the two formal contracts, the use of υἱοθησία finally occurs, rather than that of the θέσις plus genitive formula found in the letters. The language for the adoption of boys and girls is distinct, and the two boys are sons 'καθ' or εἰς υἱοθεσίαν', made 'sons by adoption', whereas the girl is adopted as a 'θυγάτηρ *nomine*', a 'legal daughter'. Both the contracts concerning boys mention their 'heirship' as a result of their adoption, whereas the alienation document in regards to the girl does not, although the poor social status of the girl may preclude this, as would the fact that it does not deal with the responsibilities of the adopting family, but rather with the relinquishing of rights over the girl by her natural mother.

Other Contracts

There are five remaining contracts in which the language of adoption is used. All of them come from Oxyrhynchus. The earliest of these dates from 161 CE and is a contract giving the power of attorney.[96] In this contract, a deputy has been appointed with the power of attorney for a particular transaction. Three ex-gymnasiarchs, two of whom were also once high priests, appoint the freedman Sarapion to act as their deputy in a case before the prefect of Alexandria. The elder Sarapion, son of Phanias, was adopted by Cleuchares. The formula for adoption in the identification of a person is θέσις before the name of the adoptive parent, as is the case in letters. In such a document it becomes clear that all familiar relationships are minutely spelled out for clear identification of the contracting parties, so that the legal adoption of the elder son of Phanias is mentioned.

Another contract from Oxyrhynchus, P Oxy 502, dated just three years later in 164 CE, deals with the lease of a house.[97] Here again the persons involved in the transaction are carefully identified by their relationships to members of their family. In the course of these lengthy identifications, the fact that a legal adoption took place in the family of Ptolema surfaces. Iulas appears to have been the natural son of Didymus, but the adopted son of Demetrius, whose other names are also enumerated. Again, the familiar θέσις plus the genitive occurs to indicate the adoption. As well as being another example of the formal type of document in which adoption is

95 P Oxy 1895. Text and translation from Hunt and Grenfell (eds), *Oxyrhynchus Papyri*, XVI, pp. 108–10.

96 P Mert 18. Text and translation from H. Idris Bell and C.H. Roberts (eds), *A Descriptive Catalogue of the Greek Papyri in the Collection of Wilfred Merton, FSA* (London: Emery Walker Limited, 1948), I, pp. 73–77.

97 P Oxy 502. Text and translation from Hunt and Grenfell (eds), *Oxyrhynchus Papyri*, III, pp. 223–25.

mentioned, this lease also demonstrates the responsibilities of certain women in Roman Egypt.

A third document from Oxyrhynchus, P Oxy 2583, is a contract between two brothers, Diophantus and Horion, the first adopted and the second not, for the division of their inheritance from the estate of Heraclius, their father. It dates from the second century CE.[98] In this contract between two brothers, we can see that the adopted son was indeed entitled to his equal portion of the estate left by his adopted father. There seems to be no disagreement between the two sons over this, as they have divided everything equally; there were two donkeys so each one receives one and so on. The formula θέσις plus the genitive occurs again, and the father is identified clearly as the same Heraclius who is the natural father of the younger Diophantus.

The fourth document from Oxyrhynchus, P Oxy 3593, mentions an adoption of a male individual, but rather than the formula θέσις plus the genitive we have seen previously, this document, which outlines instructions to a bank about a slave sale, uses the formula καθ' υἱοθεσίαν in reference to several men, who are named after their adoptive fathers. It dates from the third century, around 238–44 CE.[99] Although this text is extremely fragmentary, the formula καθ' υἱοθεσίαν is evident, both in the case of Marcus Aurelius Athanagoras and in the case of Marcus Aurelius Dionysius.

The last contract available with an identified adopted person is P Oxy 504. This papyrus mentions an adopted woman, rather than a man. Although it is not an adoption contract and cannot indicate too much about the actual adoption process, it does have the language of adoption in it. The document concerns the sale of land and dates from the early second century CE.[100] The identification of 'adopted daughter' is here clearly spelled out. Θυγάτηρ is simply added to the usual θέσει plus the genitive construction.

The parents are also identified as being θέσει πατήρ and θέσει ματήρ, 'father' and 'mother' by 'adoption'. That this document also contains the phrase 'adoptive mother' (θέσει ματήρ) and refers to Aphroditous as the adopted daughter of both Epicrates and his wife is interesting,[101] as under Roman law women could not adopt, at least until the time of Diocletian, around 291 CE.[102] Perhaps her husband was the formal adopter, and she gains the title by being his wife. In any case, it is apparent that Thaisous, the adoptive mother, has some rights over the property being sold, as she must add her agreement to the transaction. Θέσει ματήρ occurs in the signature as well, as part of the identification of Thaisous, which may have not been unusual.[103]

---

98 P Oxy 2583. Text and translation from J.W.B. Barns, *et al.* (eds), *Oxyrhynchus Papyri* (67 vols.; London: Egyptian Exploration Society, 1983), XXXI, pp. 135–37.

99 P Oxy 3953. Text and translation from A.K. Bowman, *et al.* (eds), *Oxyrhynchus Papyri* (67 vols.; London: Egyptian Exploration Society, 1983), L, pp. 226–32.

100 P Oxy 504, lines 1–10, in Hunt and Grenfell (eds), *Oxyrhynchus Papyri*, III, pp. 227–29.

101 P Oxy 504 lines 34, 53.

102 Buckland, *A Textbook of Roman Law*, pp. 123–24.

103 See P Oxy 492 where θέσει may also occur in the signature.

Legal Texts

The final category of texts that mention adoption is extant legal documents. One of these texts comes from the so-called *Gnomon of the Idios Logos*, a legal guide probably given to the financial officer in Egypt to use while he worked. The entire text contains 115 paragraphs pertaining to specific legal issues, and they are all difficult to interpret. The *Gnomon* is considered one of the most important documents pertaining to the administration of Egypt in the Roman era, and dates from around 170 CE.[104] In this law, the words υιοθεσία or θέσις do not appear, but rather the verb υιοποιέομαι:[105]

> Whenever an Egyptian takes a child from the rubbish heap and adopts him as a son, after (the Egyptian's) death, his estate shall be docked a quarter.

Exposure of unwanted children was common in antiquity.[106] This law would indicate that in Roman Egypt, should a native Egyptian choose to adopt a foundling found out in the dump, that Egyptian would be taxed when his death was registered and the estate settled. The motive behind this law is unclear.[107] The child is undoubtably a male one, due to the gender of the nominal prefix of the verb. LSJ render υιοποιέομαι 'adopt as a son' along with υιοθετέω and list a comparable verb for females, θυγατροθετέω.[108] Due to the repeated distinct language that we have seen differentiating between the adoption of the two sexes, it seems more likely that this occurrence of the verb υιοποιέομαι should also be rendered 'adopt as a son'.

The second legal document which refers to adoption is an extract from the Registry Law of Succession found in the Dura-Europos excavations, and is dated around 225–50 CE:[109]

> The rights of inheriting from those who have died shall be granted to the next of kin, and these are as follows: if (the deceased) does not leave children or has not legally adopted a son (υιοποιέομαι), then the father (is next in succession) or the mother, provided she has not remarried; if neither of these survives, then brothers (succeed) who are sons of the same father; if none of these exist, but there survives the father's father or father's mother or a male cousin on the father's side, let the inheritance be theirs. But if there be none of these, let the property be the king's.

---

104 David and Groningen, *Papyrological Primer*, p. 110.

105 *Gnom.* 41. Text in Emil Seckel, Wilhelm Schubart, and W. Uxkull-Gyllenband (eds), *Der Gnomon des Idios Logos, I. Der Text* (2 vols.; Ägyptische Urkunden aus den Staatlichen Museen Berline; Griechische Urkunden, 5; Berlin: Weidmannsche Buchhandlung, 1919), p. 21. Translation by Howard Jackson and Kathleen Corley.

106 See the famous letter of P Oxy 744, where a husband informs his wife to expose her soon-to-be-born child should it be a girl.

107 Just why the adoption of foundlings merited such a fine is unclear. It is possible that the government objected to native Egyptians adopting Greek or Roman foundlings. Beryl Rawson goes so far as to say that the adoption of male foundlings is forbidden in this text, but it is more likely that such a practice is simply being discouraged for some reason. See Rawson (ed.), *The Family in Ancient Rome*, p. 200 n. 51.

108 LSJ, pp. 808; 1846.

109 Dur. 12. Text and translation in C. Bradford Welles (ed.), *The Excavations at Dura-Europos: Final Report: The Parchment and Papyri* (New Haven: Yale University Press, 1959), pp. 76–79.

The editors of this text identify this as an example of Hellenistic city-state law, probably dating back to the original city constitution.[110] Again, the use of υἱοποιέομαι indicates the adoption of a male child. Should a man die childless or not have an adopted son to succeed him, then the rest of the family will have the opportunity to inherit. The only women who are in the list of succession are the deceased person's mother or the father's mother. There is a clear preference in the text for male family members.

There is one last document that is very significant and which dates from 47–54 CE, P Oxy 3271. It is the fragment of a petition, that of a woman, Isidora, who is the daughter by adoption (κατὰ τεκνοθεσίαν) of Dionysios. This is the first attestation of this word in Greek, and the Macquarie editors call it a 'ghost word', and suggest that its use may reflect the inappropriateness of υἱοθεσία applied to a woman. Horsley comments further that Paul's usage of υἱοθεσία is expected in that he refers collectively to a group which includes both men and women with a term usually reserved for males. As I have not been able to find such a use of υἱοθεσία outside of Paul to substantiate such a suggestion, both comments of the Macquarie editors cannot be correct. Either υἱοθεσία is inappropriate to apply to a female, and Paul therefore must be referring to only male adoptees, or υἱοθεσία could be used of both male and female adoptees and Paul is referring to a mixed group with both men and women in view. The occurrence of τεκνοθεσία in the context of P Oxy 3271 belies the latter conclusion.[111]

The Adoption Formula: Some Conclusions

From the study of the previous texts, several things become clear. First of all, it would appear that the issue of an adopted member of a family only became an issue in the identification of individuals in more formal communications. There are no references to individuals as 'adopted sons' or 'adopted daughters' in any published familiar letters. That would mean that in all the available indexed letters, no one is identified in the epistolary openings as an adopted person or an adopted parent, but rather simply as 'mother', 'father', 'son', 'sister', 'daughter', or 'brother'.[112] This attests to the personal nature of the familiar form of letter, where a precise identification would not necessarily be of importance. Even though the adoption formula was found in two signatures, these were signatures appended to official documents, whereas no signatures with the adoption formula were found among the familiar letters. The existence of an adoption within a family unit was therefore only part of the identification of a person within a more formal context, when a careful or specific, legal identification became necessary for legal purposes.

Second, the adoption formula in the letters and other documents consists primarily of θέσις plus the name of the adopter in the genitive case: 'by adoption son (or daughter) of'. Sometimes the sex of the child is spelled out by the addition of

---

110 Welles (ed.), *Excavations at Dura-Europos*, p. 76.

111 G.H.R. Horsley, *New Documents Illustrating Early Christianity* (8 vols.; North Ryde, NSW, Australia: Macquarie University, Ancient History Documentary Research Center, 1983), III, pp. 16–17.

112 See Exler, *The Form of the Ancient Greek Letter*, pp. 25–27 for additions to epistolary openings.

θυγατήρ or υἱός. The formula καθ' or εἰς υἱοθεσίαν is also found, but never in reference to a female child. Both occurrences of the verb υἱοποιέομαι also probably refer to adopted boys, not girls. Moreover, there is one occurrence of τεκνοθεσία in reference to a woman, probably because υἱοθεσία would have been inappropriate in reference to a woman. However, it is clear that girls were numbered among those children being adopted in Egypt, and that this relationship was worthy of mention in letters, contracts, and other legal documents. The number of adopted male children outnumbers the number of female children in the documents cited. Only five of the sixteen adoptees are female. The use of υἱοθεσία seems to be primarily the adoption formula found in adoption inscriptions and adoption contracts, as the formula καθ' υἱοθεσίαν occurs in only one document besides the two adoption contracts (although it may be in a lacuna in a third-century diploma as well).[113] This would perhaps indicate that υἱοθεσία is a term more likely to be found in a legal document of adoption, and not in general reference to an adopted person or parent. Of course, there are many published documents not indexed, and many more not published at all, so that in time this conclusion may have to be modified.[114]

Adoption, Inheritance, and Women as Κληρονόμοι in Antiquity

There are various references to the fact that adopted children were entitled to a share of inheritance by their status as sons or daughters in a particular family. This was seen in both P Oxy 2583, where an adopted son receives an equal share of the inheritance along with the natural son, and in P Oxy 1721, where a woman claims the right of inheritance for herself and her sons as her deceased husband was the adopted son of a man who has died. Earlier, I mentioned that women could be heirs under Roman law. This fact is borne out by the papyri, as there are numerous references to women as heirs in letters, particularly in petitions, as well as in wills. Not only are women designated heirs, but they are referred to by the masculine noun κληρονόμος. This is in contrast to the term υἱοθεσία which seems to have been used only in reference to males.

Women as Heirs in Letters and Petitions

The language of inheritance, like that of adoption, is rare in familiar documents, and is common mainly in formal letters, such as petitions, and in wills. There is one personal letter, however, that not only mentions inheritance, but names a woman as having been made an heir. This letter dates from the third century and states, 'You did not do well not to come on account of your brother; you have allowed his burial to be neglected. Know that a strange woman is made his heir (κληρονομέω).'[115] Due to the neglect of one brother, a 'strange woman' has seized the property of the other.

---

113 P Oxy 3954.
114 P Erl is another text which contains the formula κατὰ υἱοθεσίαν with a name in the genitive. It is a petition, but is very fragmentary. For the text, see W. Schubart, *Die Papyri der Universitätsbibliothek Erlangen* (Leipzig: Otto Harrassowitz, 1942), p. 38.
115 P Oxy 1067. Text and translation from Hunt and Grenfell (eds), *Oxyrhynchus Papyri*, VII, pp. 221–22.

One wonders how this woman came to be in possession of the property to begin with—perhaps she lived with the brother of Helene and Petechon?

Note the simplicity of the nomenclature of this personal letter in comparison to the earlier elaborate constructions in the letters and documents mentioning adoption. Even the mention of the matter of inheritance comes about because of the effect of the situation of the personal lives of the family. The noun κληρονόμος is not used, but the use of the verb κληρονομέω is clearly used in reference to this 'strange woman'. This is the only personal letter found so far which mentions this problem of inheritance.

There are several petitions which make the claim of women as heirs, and these do use the masculine noun κληρονόμος in reference to a female. A good example of these is a petition of a woman who is accusing two neighbors of having seized property to which she was entitled. Although this is a letter to an official, it is very passionate and full of life. It is dated from 295 CE.[116] A woman has had her inheritance stolen while she was away attending to the practical matters of dealing with her mother's death. With our previous documents in mind, it should now be clear that this women is most likely the natural daughter of her mother, as in the formal listing of her parents in the epistolary opening no mention of adoption is made. The form of the epistolary opening is not the 'A- to B- χαιρειν' of the letters we have seen, but is rather the 'To B- from A-' of a petition. The petitioner, using the usual form of the Greek petition, gives the background of the situation in detail. She then makes her request of the official, 'requesting' that those who have injured her will have to give a written security of their intent to appear for judgment. The petition closes with the signature and date.[117] What is also clear is that the term κληρονόμος can indeed be used in reference to a woman, despite the masculine gender of the noun. It is also striking that a woman is using this masculine noun in reference to herself, albeit through a scribe. From the signature of the letter, we can also see that the woman is illiterate, as a common illiteracy formula occurs.

There is one other petition which not only contains many of the forms of a regular petition but is a charming defense of the plight of a woman who has lost her inheritance on account of her sex. A woman's uncles, having been entrusted with her inheritance during her childhood, have kept the inheritance for themselves. It also dates from the third century, about 297 CE.[118] The background of the situation is touchingly related, and the request period begins with, 'I make haste to beg you.' It also contains an illiteracy formula, due to the fact that many of these documents were written for women who could not write.[119] The woman's

---

116 P Oxy 1121. Text and translation in Hunt and Grenfell (ed.), *Oxyrhynchus Papyri*, VIII, pp. 211–13.

117 Exler, *The Form of the Ancient Greek Letter*, pp. 72–73. For a complete discussion of the form of the Greek petition, see John Lee White, *The Form and Structure of the Official Petition: A Study in Greek Epistolography* (Atlanta: Scholars Press, 1972).

118 P Oxy 2713. Text and translation from L. Ingrams *et al.* (eds), *Oxyrhynchus Papyri* (London: Egyptian Exploration Society, 1968), XXXIV, pp. 101–103. See also Exler, *The Form of the Ancient Greek Letter*, p. 74; chart p. 66.

119 In her MA thesis, Katherine Evans has determined that many women who wrote letters were not able to write them themselves. See 'Women's Greek Papyrus Letters and a Study of the Opening Formula' (MA thesis, Claremont Graduate School, n.d.), pp. 71–77.

mother, along with her mother's two brothers, had been designated a κληρονόμος. Aurelia Didyme's mother therefore was entitled to an equal third of the estate left by her father to his three children. Aurelia, as her daughter, by succession gains the right to that third as well. Her rights, however, were easily denied, due to the fact that she was under age (in this case, probably not much more than an infant) and also a woman, a fact which she herself bemoans. She also demands to be given the profits which have accumulated from the time her uncles confiscated her estate.

Women are also commonly referred to in wills by the masculine term κληρονόμος. A good example of this is P Oxy 105, which names a woman, Ammonous, as heir. It dates from the early second century, around 117–37 CE.[120] It would appear that even though Pekusis has many children by his wife Ptolema, he leaves his property to his daughter Ammonous, who comes before her half-brother Antas. His wife shall still have the right of using his house and its fixtures for the duration of her life. The reference to Ammonous as an heir by means of the noun κληρονόμος, is once again clear.

The occurrences of κληρονόμος in reference to women can be multiplied. In BGU 326 (189–94 CE), two women slaves are ordered freed upon the death of a man and then named his heirs.[121] P Oxy 2857 refers to a certain Claudia who is to be the heir of her father, should she comply by registering her claim within 100 days of her father's death.[122] Another will from Oxyrhynchus, P Oxy 907, names five children as heirs, three sons and two daughters, and parcels out certain items to each.[123] There are numerous references to women as κληρονόμοι in other legal documents as well.[124] One woman writes a letter to the strategos asking to be removed from the responsibility of inheriting her father's property, as he is ill and on the verge of death.[125] There is continued use of κληρονόμος in reference to women in letters, both formal and official, petitions, wills, and other documents, despite the masculine gender of the noun.

Women as Heirs: Some Conclusions

We have seen that women were regularly designated heirs in the various letters, petitions, and wills found among the documentary papyri. Not only are they called heirs, but they are also referred to by the masculine noun κληρονόμος. They are sometimes designated equal heirs with brothers, and have the right to petition the government when their rights to property have been violated. They are sometimes designated sole heirs even when there are other children in the family. The language concerning inheritance also seems to be found primarily in formal letters and

---

120 P Oxy 105, in Hunt and Grenfell (eds) *Oxyrhynchus Papyri*, I, pp. 171–72.
121 BGU 326.
122 P Oxy 2857.
123 P Oxy 907.
124 P Oxy 2231; P Oxy 3103; P Oxy 132 (memorandum); P Oxy 1114 (declaration); P Oxy 1034 (will); P Oxy 3117 (court proceedings); *Gnom.* 22 (legal); P Cairo 29 (legal); P Strass 41; P Oxy 3638. On children in general see P Oxy 491; P Oxy 2709. Also, see P Mich 659.60 in Horsley (ed.), *New Documents Illustrating Early Christianity*, II, p. 92.
125 P Oxy 74. See also P Oxy 899 (petition).

petitions or wills, as there is only one personal letter that deals with the problem of inheritance.

It is therefore clear that women both could be adopted and could be made heirs under the Roman legal system. As we have seen previously, however, women probably did not have equal access to their father's estates except in cases of intestacy (which was unusual). Fathers would also be more likely to will large sums of money and large estates to their sons, rather than to their daughters, and indeed were not allowed to give daughters a large patrimony. Therefore, although a woman, if adopted, would be equally an heir with her adoptive brothers if her father died intestate, it would be unlikely that he would have adopted her with a view to will her his estate. It is also evident that although the language describing the adoption of female children was different from that describing male children, language concerning heirship was not. That such discrepancy exists in the use of Greek language should warn us away from making assumptions about word meaning purely on the basis of the gender of a particular word unless that meaning can be documented.

The Translation and Interpretation of Romans 8.15ff.

In Rom. 8.15ff. Paul is discussing an adoptive relationship of believers to God that will be fulfilled by an eschatological adoption and the redemption of believers' physical bodies. This adoption is based on the relationship of the believers to the Son of God, Christ Jesus. As believers are in Christ (8.1) they have the Spirit of Christ (8.9), which is also the Spirit of God (8.14). By this Spirit, believers are the sons (υἱοί) of God (8.15) and have therefore received a spirit of 'adoption as sons' (υἱοθεσία). The τέκνα in vv. 16–17 is probably synonymous with υἱοί, as has been suggested by Käsemann.[126] As believers are transformed into the image of God's Son (τοῦ υἱοῦ αὐτοῦ) (8.29), they number among the υἱοί that are the κληρονόμοι of God and number among the πολλοὶ ἀδελφοί. In Gal. 4.1ff. Paul uses similar terminology, as believers are υἱοί because of their relationship to the υἱός of God, through whom they receive υἱοθεσία. Since they are υἱοί they are also κληρονόμοι. As Paul seems to be keying into the terms *son* of God and *sons* of God, it is more likely that he has the adoption of male children in mind when he uses the term υἱοθεσία, rather than the adoption of children in general. This seems particularly probable since he links this 'sonship' to the privilege of sons as heirs. As Jesus the Son is an heir, so also believers as sons are heirs, even though they are adopted sons. The priority of men over women in the laws of succession in antiquity as well as the gender-specific use of υἱοθεσία in inscriptions and documentary papyri supports this interpretation, especially as it would have been rare in Paul's time for someone to adopt a girl in order to make her an heir.

It is possible that Paul did not intend for his metaphor to be applied to women in the congregations he writes to. As he is writing to entire congregations which

---

126 E. Käsemann, *Commentary on Romans* (trans. G.W. Bromiley; Grand Rapids, MI: Eerdmans, 1980), p. 229; C.E.B. Cranfield, *A Critical Exegetical Commentary on the Epistle to the Romans* (ICC; 2 vols.; Edinburgh: T. & T. Clark, 1982), I, p. 406, also uses 'sons' and 'children' interchangeably.

undoubtedly include both men and women, however, it is more likely that he does intend for the female believers in the congregation to appropriate the metaphor of adoption for themselves. Romans 16 enumerates many women who are singled out for their services within the Pauline mission, including a διάκονος (Phoebe) and an ἀπόστολος (Junia). Moreover, although he omits such language in 1 Cor. 12.13, in Gal. 3.28 Paul asserts that there is to be no distinction made between men and women in Christ (although that may not be his point).[127] Furthermore, since Paul calls women συνεργοί, 'co-workers', in the mission field (Phil. 4.3), it would be hard to imagine that he would not consider them to be συνκληρονόμοι, 'co-heirs', in the eschatological kingdom that they had helped to establish on earth, particularly as κληρονόμος has been established to be a gender-inclusive term. Women can therefore be granted the status of sonship equally alongside their fellow-believers.

The evidence suggests, however, that Paul's metaphor is a gender-specific one, as it probably presupposes the priority of the privileges of sons over those of daughters. Even though Paul may not intend to exclude women from the ranks of the sons of God, for a woman to appropriate this metaphor, there is one more step to be taken before she can participate in the 'adoption' Paul describes. She must have maleness conferred on her before she can be made a son. She must take an additional step up the hierarchical ladder, which for Paul ascends woman, man, Christ, God. The editors of the *Inclusive Language Lectionary*, by rendering υἱοθεσία in Rom. 8.23–24 as 'adoption as children', are attempting to deal with this problematic language by introducing a phrase which is more easily appropriated by women on the congregational level. It may not be a faithful rendering of Paul's metaphor, which seems to have been gender specific, and not gender inclusive. The soteriological language of Paul is therefore not wholly egalitarian, in spite of his declaration of Gal. 3.28: 'in Christ there is neither male nor female'.

127 See Elisabeth Schüssler Fiorenza, *In Memory of Her* (New York: Crossroad, 1983), pp. 205–42.

PHILEMON AND THE PATRIARCHAL PAUL

SARA B.C. WINTER

For centuries, and until quite recently, it was assumed that Onesimus, the newly baptized slave mentioned in the letter to Philemon, was a fugitive, and that Paul wrote on his behalf to ask for clemency—a scenario called for brevity 'the fugitive slave interpretation'.[1] Christians turned to Philemon for scriptural support for slavery. In the United States after the passage of the fugitive slave law of 1850 the Northern churches saw in Philemon a biblical requirement to return fugitives to slavery.

Twentieth-century biblical scholarship, however, has shown the fugitive slave interpretation to be erroneous. Philology and analysis of the historical context of Philemon demonstrate that for two reasons Onesimus cannot have been a fugitive. First, the structure of the letter shows that the slaveowner knew that Onesimus was with Paul,[2] and second, even if Onesimus had run away (unlikely because the slave-owner knew he was with Paul), according to Roman law he was not a fugitive because he went to the residence of a friend.[3] Paul's letter to Philemon cannot have been a plea for clemency, because there was no need for one. An alternative scenario, the 'sent-slave interpretation', asserts that Onesimus had been sent to assist Paul in prison (Philippians refers to a similar situation with Epaphroditus), where Paul baptized him; Paul subsequently wrote this letter asking that the newly baptized Onesimus be manumitted and released from obligations so that he could work with Paul for the church.

The sent-slave interpretation challenged long-held assumptions that Paul supported the rights of slaveholders, if not the practice of slavery as well. This challenge came at a time when scholarship on Romans, 1 and 2 Corinthians, and Galatians was re-envisioning equally long-held views concerning Paul and women, Paul and Judaism and how much authority Paul was accorded during his lifetime. From these recent decades of Pauline scholarship emerges the 'new' Paul for whom the baptismal formula of Gal 3.28, 'neither male nor female, Jew nor Greek, slave nor free', was no empty slogan, but a program to be lived out in the church.

There is no consensus, however, concerning this 'new' Paul, and presently in scholarship the new Paul coexists with the patriarchal Paul. Regarding Philemon

---

1 Margaret Mitchell traces the fugitive slave interpretation back to Athanasius, Basil of Caesarea, the Marcionite Prologs, Ambrosiaster and the *Apostolic Constitutions* (Margaret M. Mitchell, 'John Chrysostom on Philemon: A Second Look', *HTR* 88 [1995], pp. 145–47).

2 Full argument in S.C. Winter, 'Paul's Letter to Philemon', *NTS* 33 (1987), pp. 1–15. That the recipient of the letter knew Onesimus was with Paul is clear from the thanksgiving (see P. Schubert, *Form and Function of the Pauline Thanksgiving* [BZNW, 20; Berlin: Töpelmann, 1939]).

3 McGregor Gray, 'Slave Crimes and Slave Punishment in Roman Society' (seminar report presented at Columbia University Seminars, 1942); Peter Lampe, 'Kein Sklavenflucht des Onesimus', *ZNW* 76 (1985), pp. 135–37.

there is no consensus on the precise purpose of the letter, or on whether Paul asked for the manumission of Onesimus. The question is, in 'no longer as a slave ... a brother beloved ...' (Phlm. 16)[4] are slave and brother mutually exclusive? Or was Paul asking that Onesimus, while remaining a slave, be treated in 'a brotherly fashion'? And more generally, what precisely does Philemon tell us about Paul's view of slavery, and by extension social equality in general?

The letter to Philemon has attracted little scholarly attention, indeed disproportionately little considering its social impact. Addressed to individuals, yet uncontestedly genuine, it is a short letter, and in recent centuries treated in the literature as something of a special case. Scholars study Philemon largely in isolation from the rest of the Pauline corpus. Many of the uncertainties regarding Philemon, however, can be resolved precisely by looking at it in the wider context of Pauline scholarship.

The analysis that follows looks at Philemon in light of scholarship on Romans 16 and Colossians for Part 1; and recent work on Pauline apocalyptic, especially Galatians, for Part 2. Interpreting Philemon in a context of the Pauline corpus brings out two points to be explained in the discussion that follows: (1) Paul made his request not from a position of authority, but from one of weakness. Indeed 'groveling' might be the appropriate word here. That Paul would venture to ask 'for' Onesimus (Phlm. 9a) in these circumstances shows his deep conviction on the matter: a baptized person cannot 'own' another baptized person; a baptized person cannot be the slave of another baptized person. (2) Although Paul 'asks' in Philemon, he couches his request in apocalyptic categories in which slave and brother are polar opposites. Paul makes his argument in language that suggests that he held just as strongly for the equality of men and women in the church. The first section of this article looks at the individuals named in Philemon.

What Is Apphia? Who Is She?

Literary correspondences between Philemon and Colossians are striking. Almost all of the individuals named in Philemon are also mentioned in Colossians. The opening greetings of both letters have Timothy with Paul in prison. The closing greetings of both letters list the same companions. Philemon gives them as Epaphras, Jesus, Mark, Aristarchus, Demas, and Luke, my fellow workers. Col. 4.10–14 has all of these names, and except for interchanging Aristarchus and Epaphras, retains Philemon's order. Colossians also mentions Onesimus (4.9) and closes with an instruction to Archippus, one of the three addressees of Philemon ('and say to Archippus, take care that you fulfill the ministry [διακονία] which you have received in the Lord'; Col. 4.17). There are also correspondences in phrasing between the thanksgivings of the two epistles with Phlm. 4–5 and Col. 1.3–4.[5]

In previous centuries this close literary connection between Colossians and Philemon no doubt played a part in Philemon being read as a support for slavery. But

---

4 Translations are mine throughout.

5 Colossians also makes use of the other prison epistle, Philippians. The correspondences are summarized clearly in Mark Kiley, *Colossians as Pseudepigraphy* (Sheffield: JSOT Press, 1986), pp. 76–91.

the now widely accepted thesis that Colossians is deutero-Pauline sets the literary connection between the two letters in a new light with useful consequences for interpreting Philemon.[6]

Tradition and Paul's authority are central to the argument made in Colossians. In Philemon Paul conveyed greetings from co-workers. The deutero-Pauline Colossians invokes the names of the same co-workers to establish its authority. Although the names in the closing greetings to Philemon and Colossians are practically identical, the list in Philemon gives few details. Eduard Lohse concludes from this that Philemon's list must predate the list in Colossians because the latter is embellished, giving more information with each name.[7] Lohse has explored this aspect of Colossians by comparing the closing greetings of Philemon with those of Colossians, and the closing greetings of Colossians with Romans 16. Both Colossians and Romans were written to congregations not founded by Paul, which he had never visited.[8]

Colossians, Lohse points out, makes no effort to establish a personal connection between Paul and the Colossae church, in sharp contrast to Romans. For in Romans, Lohse observes, Paul strives to establish a personal connection. 'Since he [Paul] thus far had not been able to visit Rome, it is particularly important to him to emphasize that he already knows several Christians who belong to the congregation, and through them to some extent he already has personal connection with the entire congregation.'[9]

Lohse points out further that the Colossians list does not open with greetings from Paul but with a mention of Onesimus and Tychicus who will bring the congregation some details concerning Paul. Indeed, unlike the genuine Philippians (Phil. 1.12) in which Paul writes about what has happened to him, Col. 4.7 tells the readers that they will hear about what has happened to him from the messenger Tychichus.[10] The

---

6 Walter Bujard made a thorough stylistic analysis (Walter Bujard, *Stilanalytische Untersuchungen zum Kolosserbrief als Beitrag zur Methodik von Sprachvergleichen* [Studien zur Umwelt des Neuen Testaments, 11; Göttingen: Vandenhoeck & Ruprecht, 1973]). Wayne Meeks, for example, states, 'Walter Bujard's thorough stylistic analysis ought to put to rest the long debate whether Paul himself could have written the letter: he did not ... although the close similarities between the greetings at the end of Philemon and in Col. 4.7–14 could suggest that the two letters were dispatched at about the same time (Wolf-Henning Ollrog, *Paulus und seine Mitarbeiter: Untersuchungen zu Theorie und Praxis der paulinischen Mission* [Wissenschaftliche Monographien zum Alten und Neuen Testament, 50; Neukirchen: Erziehungsverein, 1979], pp. 219, and excursus 1, pp. 236–42), what is said about Onesimus (Col. 4.9) is more easily understood on the assumption that the author both uses and consciously imitates the letter to Philemon and also knows that the slave's case had a happy outcome' (Wayne Meeks, *The First Urban Christians: The Social World of the Apostle Paul* [New Haven and London: Yale University Press, 1983], p. 125).

7 A conjecture of Zahn argues that the name Jesus (Justus) also belongs in the Philemon list before Mark (T. Zahn, *Einleitung in das Neue Testament*, I [2 vols.; Leipzig: Erlangen, 3rd edn, 1924], p. 321).

8 Eduard Lohse, 'Die Mitarbeiter des Apostels Paulus im Kolosserbrief', in Otto Böcher and Klaus Hacker (eds), *Verborum Veritas: Festschrift für Gustav Staehlin zum 70. Geburtstag* (Wuppertal: Theologishcher Verlag Rolf Brockhaus, 1970), pp. 189–94.

9 My translation. Lohse writes, 'Daß bisher nicht hat nach Rom kommen können, ist es ihm besonders wichtig zu betonen, dass er etliche Christen, die zur Gemeinde gehören, bereits kennt und durch sie gewissermassen schon persönlich Verbindung zur ganzen Gemeinde besitzt' (Lohse, 'Mitarbeiter', p. 190).

10 Kiley, *Colossians*, p. 90.

greetings that conclude Colossians, unlike Romans 16, are not extended *to* individuals known to Paul, but *from* Paul's co-workers, the same mentioned in Philemon.

Lohse observes that the purpose of the closing greetings in Colossians differs from that of the closing greetings in Romans. In Romans, he explains, the greetings function to establish closer ties between Paul and the congregation, but in Colossians the closing greetings function to recommend Paul's co-workers as reliable and faithful.[11] Furthermore, Colossians singles out some individuals. In Philemon, as Lohse observes, all the people on the list are called Paul's fellow worker, but in Colossians only the first three, Aristarchus, Mark, and Jesus Justus, receive this privileged designation, and the writer identifies them as 'from the circumcision'.[12] In Colossians, however, Epaphras has special importance.[13] The epistle, Lohse writes, 'explicitly empowers [Epaphras] as representative of the apostle'.[14]

Lohse concludes that the ending of Colossians assumes a situation where Paul is no longer living (perhaps shortly after his death), and gives evidence of how the Pauline mission proceeded and continued after his death.[15]

Specifically, Colossians transmits Paul's legacy to some of his fellow workers, primarily Epaphras and secondarily Aristarchus, Mark (and Barnabas), and Jesus Justus. Colossians, therefore, differs strikingly from 1 and 2 Timothy and Titus as pseudepigraphy. One purpose of Colossians—to absorb Paul's authority into the authority of Epaphras and Mark (and Barnabas), Aristarchus and Jesus Justus—argues that we have no reason to doubt the concrete facts that Colossians recounts. Although the accuracy of the representation of Paul's theology is questionable, the writer of Colossians would have deployed factual information to convey reliability. Colossians' facts include the reference to 'Onesimus the faithful and beloved brother who is from among you' (Col. 4.9), which we may take as historically accurate, as it generally is. Colossians' appropriation of Philemon's personnel and setting allows us to make use of Colossians to shed light on the addressees of Philemon, otherwise unknown to us.

Colossae was one of three cities in the Lycus Valley of Asia Minor, all three home to Christian congregations in the time of Paul. Colossae was twelve miles south-east of Hierapolis, and about six miles west of Laodicea, the latter two, 'both with several magnificent theater and gymnasia'.[16] Evidently Colossae declined in importance as Laodicea grew.[17] Laodicea was destroyed in an earthquake in 60–61,[18] but

---

11 '[W]erden im Kolosserbrief die Mitarbeiter des Apostels der Gemeinde als zuverlässig und treu empfohlen' (Lohse, 'Mitarbeiter', p. 193).

12 Lohse observes that the mention hints at Paul's break with Judaism. That the three did not abandon him is a 'comfort' to him (Lohse, 'Mitarbeiter', p. 192).

13 Lohse notes the stronger reading that reinforces Epaphras's standing (Lohse, 'Mitarbeiter', p. 192 n. 8).

14 'Sie soll darum wissen, dass er als Vertreter des Apostels ausdrücklich bevollmächtigt ist' (Lohse, 'Mitarbeiter', p. 193).

15 'Der letzte Abschnitt des Kolosserbriefes setzt daher eine Situation voraus, wie sie nicht mehr zu Lebseiten, sonder bald nach dem Tode des Apostels bestand, und biete ein ausschlussreiches Zeugnis dafür, wie die paulinische Mission nach Paulus ihren Fortgang nahm' (Lohse, 'Mitarbeiter', p. 193).

16 Marcus Barth and Helmut Blanke, *Colossians* (AB, 34B; New York: Doubleday, 1994), p. 9.

Hierapolis remained prominent in Christianity for centuries. Significantly, for example, Hierapolis was the city of Papias, who sometime between 80 and 130 CE compiled oral traditions about the apostles and other disciples into his five-volume *Interpretations of the Oracles of the Lord*.[19]

Paul had never been to Colossae, and presumably neither to Laodicea nor Hierapolis, although the letter is not explicit on that matter. The writer of Colossians greets only two individuals not named in Philemon—Tychicus (Col. 4.7), who with Onesimus will be a messenger, and Nympha who is from Laodicea (Col. 4.15). Yet strangely the names in Colossians differ from Philemon in another respect as well. Colossians mentions only one (Archippus) of the three people to whom Paul addresses Philemon. Colossians omits any mention of Philemon and Apphia. Colossians' instruction to Archippus is a final comment after the greetings to Laodicea and the request concerning an exchange of letters to be read in the churches. Archippus, evidently residing in Colossae, is the only individual from Colossae that the writer of Colossians singles out for mention. By contrast, as noted above, in Romans Paul names a great number of people.

Epaphras, whom the writer of Colossians empowers with Paul's legacy, and whom Paul himself calls 'my fellow prisoner of war' (Phlm. 23), evidently founded all three Lycos Valley churches, Colossae, Laodicea, and Hierapolis. The writer of Colossians praises Epaphras effusively, mentioning his work in the three cities (Col. 1.7; 4.12). Interestingly, however, the closing greetings of Colossians mention Laodicea, but fail to convey greetings to Hierapolis.

Several questions emerge from these observations, not all of which can be pursued here. Most important for the purposes of this study, why is there no greeting to Philemon and Apphia in Colossians? This question proves to be a key to another question, never satisfactorily answered, and which I take up here: to whom did Paul write 'Philemon'?

Paul addresses his letter to 'Philemon, our beloved fellow worker' (v. 1), 'Apphia, the sister' (v. 2), 'Archippus our fellow-soldier' (v. 2), and 'the church in your house' (v. 2). How these three individuals are connected and whose house hosts the church is unclear. 'Your' in 'the church in your house' is singular; the phrase is literally, 'house of [singular] you'. This singular 'you' indicates that the house where the congregation meets belongs to only one of the three named.

Paul addresses most of the letter to only one person. He employs second-person singular forms in the thanksgiving ('love and faith of you [sing.]' [v. 5]; 'faith of you [sing.]' [v. 6]) and in the main body of the letter ('I ask you [sing] ...' [v. 10]; '[you, sing.] receive him as me' [v. 17]). Only towards the end of the letter when he mentions his hope for release ('through your prayers' ... 'released to you [plural]'; v. 22) and in the closing benediction does Paul employ 'you' plural. Paul's use of the

---

17 'Despite its favorable position, Colossae lost its prominence in the course of time. The reason for this is found chiefly in the fact that Laodicea, only a short distance away, had developed into a prosperous city during the first century BC (Strabo 12.8.16)' (Eduard Lohse, *Colossians and Philemon* [ET; Hermeneia; Philadelphia: Fortress, 1971], pp. 8–9).

18 In the seventh year of Nero, as reported by Tacitus (*Ann.* 14.27).

19 Unfortunately further exploration of the character of Lycos Valley Christianity lies outside the scope of this article. But see Ulrich H.J. Körtner, *Papias von Hierapolis* (Göttingen: Vandenhoeck & Ruprecht, 1983), pp. 88–96.

singular in the main body of the letter indicates that only one of the three people addressed is principally involved with the fate of Onesimus.

The owner of the house must also be the owner of the slave.[20] The masculine form of 'brother' (vocative ἀδελφέ in vv. 7 and 20) and the masculine pronoun 'yourself' (σεαυτόν; v. 19) show that the owner is one of the men. Meeks, who takes Philemon to be the owner of the slave and house, writes, 'he has a house large enough to accommodate a meeting of Christians (Phlm. 2) and guests (22) and has been a patron of Christians in other ways as well (5–7). He owns at least one slave, probably a number of them, for Paul's strongly implied request to send the slave Onesimus back to work with him (8–14) evidently is not expected to be a great hardship....'[21]

The house belongs to one of the men, but which one? And how are the others connected with the owner of the house? Why are they mentioned? It had been taken for granted that the owner of the slave and the house was Philemon until John Knox challenged that assumption in his 1935 *Philemon among the Letters of Paul.*[22] Knox argued from the epithet 'fellow soldier' (συστρατιώτῃ, v. 2) that Archippus must be the owner of the slave and the house. He studied the epithet 'fellow soldier' that Paul gives also to Epaphroditus (in Phil. 2.25) and from that concluded that Archippus was the owner of the slave.[23] Unfortunately Knox linked identifying Archippus to an argument that Philemon was the lost letter to the Laodiceans, a scenario that has proved untenable, and that made it easy to dismiss his thesis on Archippus. Commentators since Knox for the most part simply assert without explanation that Philemon was the recipient of the letter.[24] Knox's contention concerning Archippus, however, proves to be the logical option, as some attention to Apphia, the woman named in the greeting, will show.[25]

Until recently it was assumed that Apphia was the wife of the owner of the house and the slave, mentioned because she would have been in charge of the household.[26] Lohse, for example, writes, 'Since her name follows immediately after Philemon's,

20 The request to 'prepare [singular] guest lodgings' (v. 22) and other factors, to be discussed below, essentially rule out the possibility that the owner of the slave was not the owner of the house.
21 Meeks, *First Urban Christians,* p. 60.
22 John Knox, *Philemon among the Letters of Paul: A New View of its Place and Importance* (New York: Abingdon, 1935).
23 Knox argued that the relatively rare term 'fellow soldier' (elsewhere in the NT only Phil. 2.25) refers to a 'helper in time of need', especially someone who offers financial assistance. Philemon's epithet 'fellow worker' is restricted to those who have dedicated their lives to working for the church (Knox, *Philemon,* ch. III, esp. pp. 67–68). Lightfoot proposed that Archippus was the adult son of Apphia and Philemon (J.B. Lightfoot, *St Paul's Epistles to the Colossians and to Philemon: A Revised Text with Introductions, Notes, and Dissertations* [London: Macmillan, 1904], pp. 304–307).
24 Lohse, for example, comments on Archippus, 'the beginning of Phlm. lends no support to the thesis that Archippus, not Philemon, was the master of the runaway slave Onesimus. Although Apphia, Archippus and the "house community" are mentioned along with Philemon as the addressees of the letter, there is no doubt that when the Apostle later addresses the letter's recipient in the singular (vss 2, 4), he has only Philemon in mind' (Lohse, *Colossians and Philemon,* p. 186).
25 In my 1987 article I agreed with Knox that Archippus must be the recipient, although I rejected his thesis on the Laodiceans (Winter, 'Paul's Letter to Philemon', p. 2). I hope the more thorough discussion of the recipient of Philemon in this chapter will settle the question.
26 Lightfoot, for example, writing in 1879, speculated at length about Apphia and Archippus and Onesimus (Lightfoot, *St Paul's Epistles,* pp. 304–307).

one can assume that she is his wife. The lady of the house had to deal daily with the slaves. Therefore, she also had to give her opinion when the question of taking back a runaway slave was raised.'[27] And Meeks observes, 'Apphia is usually taken to be Philemon's wife, but she is mentioned in her own right as "the sister".'[28] Although more recent scholars eschew the wife assumption, her name in the greeting of Philemon has generated little interest. Callahan, for example, writing more recently, simply calls her 'an authority figure in Philemon's house assembly'.[29]

The presence of a woman's name among the three, however, and the order of the names (man–woman–man), provides a key to the circumstances under which Paul wrote Philemon. For one, the singular 'your' of 'church in your house' makes it virtually impossible that Apphia was the wife of the owner of the house. Paul employs a plural to refer to the house church of Priscilla and Aquila, 'the church in their house' (Rom. 16.4; 1 Cor. 16.19). And Paul does mention households, congregations, and house churches of individuals, both men and women, who were apparently, as far as the house church was concerned, unattached—perhaps because they were unmarried, perhaps because their spouse did not belong to the house church and hence was of no interest to Paul: 'the household of Crispus' (1 Cor. 1.14; also Acts 18.8), 'Chloe's people' (that is, 'slaves or freedmen or both';[30] 1 Cor. 1.11), Gaius 'my host and host of the whole church' (Rom. 16.23). Colossians has 'the church in Nympha's house' (Col. 4.15). If Apphia had been the wife of the owner of the house (he calls her 'the sister'; she clearly is baptized), Paul surely would have mentioned her in the body of the letter if not in the matter of Onesimus directly, certainly in Phlm. 22 where he asks to 'prepare guest lodgings' and in the closing greetings, 'Epaphras greets you' (v. 23). But both the request for lodging and the closing greetings are in the singular. Hence it is safe to conclude that Apphia was not the wife of the owner of the house and slave.

On Archippus, recent commentators may note Knox's points, but they give his thesis no credence, and leave the enigma of Archippus unexplored.[31] Yet the placing of his name last is logical. If Archippus is the owner of the house and slave, his name is next to 'church in your house' and the subsequent portion of the letter is addressed to him alone.[32] Might Philemon be the owner of the house? If so, Paul has named Apphia before Archippus, signaling that she is either of higher social status or of more importance in the church. Both possibilities are unlikely, however, because she

---

27 Lohse, *Colossians and Philemon*, p. 190. Onesimus's occupation had a bearing on whether his fate concerned the wife of the slaveowner. Although outside the scope of this discussion, scholars' retrojection of a nineteenth-century concept of the household into antiquity deserves a closer look. A nineteenth-century concept of the role of women in the household has been pivotal to the misinterpretation of Philemon.

28 Meeks, *First Urban Christians*, p. 60.

29 Allen Dwight Callahan, *Embassy of Onesimus: The Letter of Paul to Philemon* (Valley Forge, PA: Trinity Press International, 1997), p. 25.

30 Meeks, *First Urban Christians*, p. 59.

31 'Apphia, Archippus and the entire "house community" are named along with Philemon as recipients of the letter. Their names are mentioned because the matter that the Apostle is dealing with is not just a personal affair that concerns Philemon alone … [it] is a concern of the entire community' (Lohse, *Colossians and Philemon*, p. 190).

32 Knox offers a similar example from the papyri (Knox, *Philemon*, pp. 60–63).

receives only the neutral epithet 'sister' in contrast to Archippus's 'fellow soldier', and Colossians omits news of her while singling out Archippus.

Knox emphasized Philemon's standing as 'fellow worker'.[33] Philemon and Apphia may have been a missionary pair. The list of individuals in Colossians is consistent with Knox's thesis, because Colossians includes all the significant individuals from Philemon except the pair Philemon and Apphia. The omission may be explained by the supposition that they were traveling missionaries, not residents of Colossae. By the time Colossians was written, as Meeks notes, the Onesimus matter had been resolved.[34] In the meantime Philemon and Apphia had moved on.[35]

From Colossians we know that Paul had never visited Colossae. The wording of Paul's opening greetings in Philemon conveys a striking point. Paul writes Philemon *'our'* fellow-worker, and Archippus *'our'* fellow soldier. Paul uses this plural, 'our', instead of 'my' for co-workers he has not met personally, as commentators on Romans 16.9 point out, 'Greet Urbanus our fellow worker in Christ and my beloved Stachys.'[36] Paul knew personally none of the three people to whom he addressed Philemon. Indeed 'our' fellow soldier for Archippus suggests that Onesimus was not sent to assist Paul. Perhaps the Colossians sent Onesimus principally to assist Epaphras and secondarily to the others who had closer ties with Colossae.

The closing greetings of Philemon, alongside those of Colossians, offer yet another angle on the circumstances of Paul's writing. Knox pointed out that 'hearing of your love' in Phlm. 5 indicates that Paul did not know the slaveowner personally.[37] In Philemon Paul extends greetings to 'you' (singular) from 'my fellow workers' Epaphras, Jesus,[38] Mark, Aristarchus, Demas, and Luke. Colossians changes the order slightly, and conveys greetings first from Aristarchus, Mark, Jesus, then Epaphras. The writer of Colossians adds a comment that Aristarchus, Mark, and Jesus are the only fellow workers from the circumcision who were a comfort to him (Col. 4.11). The writer of Colossians thereby depicts a rapprochement between Paul and co-workers preaching to Jews that may well have occurred at the end of Paul's life, but was not characteristic of his early years. A closer look at the names is informative.

---

33 Knox, *Philemon*, pp. 64–67.

34 Meeks, *First Urban Christians*, p. 125.

35 Of course it is possible that either or both Apphia and Philemon died between the writing of Philemon and Colossians. The argument that Philemon cannot be owner of the house and slave, which is based on the order of Apphia's and Archippus's names, holds nevertheless.

36 Cranfield writes, 'The reason for the use of ἡμῶν rather than μου is perhaps that Urbanus had not been a colleague of Paul personally, though, as a worker for Christ he was a colleague of all gospel-workers generally' (C.E.B. Cranfield, *A Critical Exegetical Commentary on the Epistle to the Romans* (2 vols.; ICC; Edinburgh: T. & T. Clark, 1979), II, pp. 790–91; also Otto Michel, *Der Brief an die Römer* (MeyerK; Göttingen: Vandenhoeck & Ruprecht, 1978); John Murray, *The Epistle to the Romans* (NICNT; Grand Rapids, MI: Eerdmans, 1959–65); H. Schlier, *Der Römerbrief Kommentar* (HTKNT; Freiburg: Herder, 1977). If Paul had known Apphia, we can be sure he would have addressed a comment to her personally.

37 Knox, *Philemon*, p. 64.

38 'Epaphras my fellow prisoner in Christ, Jesus, Mark ...' must be the reading, not 'Epaphras, fellow prisoner in Christ Jesus, Mark ...' (Lohse, *Colossians and Philemon*, p. 207; and 'Mitarbeiter').

Aristarchus, like Tychichus, whom Colossians also mentions, according to Acts, accompanied Paul bringing the collection to Jerusalem (Acts 19.29; 20.4; 27.2). Although Tychichus and Aristarchus were not unusual names for the time and region, the combination of Tychichus with Aristarchus during Paul's imprisonment argues that they are the same two mentioned in Acts. Colossians groups Mark, whom Colossians identifies as the cousin of Barnabas, and Jesus with Aristarchus as 'those of the circumcision who gave me [Paul] comfort' (4.11). According to both Galatians and Acts, however, Barnabas and Paul had had a bitter parting of the ways, which Galatians attributes to requiring law observance of Gentile converts (Gal. 2.11–14). But according to Acts 15.37 Paul and Barnabas split because Barnabas wanted to take John Mark with them and Paul did not, precipitating what Acts 15.39 calls παροξυσμός, 'a sharp disagreement'. Acts may be technically accurate—that is, perhaps John Mark was going to preach law observance for Gentile converts, and that would have made it two against one. Nevertheless Acts avoids mentioning the issue underlying the split. Acts usually harmonizes differences, especially between Paul and others on the matter of law observance, and here Acts has the passive, thereby assigning no blame for the παροξυσμός. Nevertheless the use of the strong term παροξυσμός hints at a very deep divide.

Going more deeply into the historical reasons behind the split between Paul and Barnabas lies outside the scope of this discussion. Of importance here, however, is that in Philemon Paul uses Mark as a reference, despite Mark's involvement, either marginally or centrally, with the rift between Paul and Barnabas. In Philemon Paul put aside his differences with Mark to add weight to his request, and Colossians builds on that gesture to represent Paul closely tied to those with whom he was previously at odds.[39] By making the connection between Barnabas and Mark explicit, Colossians presents a Paul who has moved beyond the conflicts of his early years.

Demas and Luke (who in Colossians is called 'the beloved physician') are mentioned in canonical literature only in Colossians, Philemon, and in the deutero-Pauline 2 Tim. 4.10–12 (then Luke, Mark, Tychichus here probably a borrowing from Colossians). Two opposing traditions recount a split between Paul and Demas. The *Acts of Thecla* and 2 Tim. 4.10–12 agree that Demas 'abandoned', or as *Acts of Thecla* would have it, betrayed Paul, suggesting that Paul's alliance with Demas, like that with Mark, was fragile.

Some scholars, for example John Howard Schultz, have argued that Paul did not have the stature in his own time that his writings acquired for him with later generations.[40] Certainly Galatians and the Corinthian correspondence testify to differences within the churches. In Philemon Paul was writing to people he did not know and he names co-workers with whom, according to the tradition, he had differences. But these co-workers evidently did carry weight with the Colossians. One conclusion that we may draw is that Colossians may have functioned to represent Paul's views as more in line with those of the Colossians and Laodiceans. The inclusion of the

---

39 The history behind this is lost to us of course. Determining whether Colossians represents the 'truth' of a reconciliation or simply coalition building after Paul's death requires deeper inquiry and probably new sources.

40 John Howard Schütz, *Paul and the Anatomy of Apostolic Authority* (Cambridge: Cambridge University Press, 1975).

household code in Colossians, which so overtly relies on Philemon for its claim to Pauline authorship, serves to isolate Paul's plea for Onesimus as a special case, not a commitment to social equality. The Colossians probably disagreed with Paul both on law observance and on social equality. Whatever Paul's strengths, humility evidently was not one of them. His humble dependence on the good will of co-workers with whom he had had sharp disagreements in the past, and co-workers whom he had never met and who may well have heard ill of him, gives a measure of how much he cared about this request 'for' Onesimus. Section 2 of this paper revisits the substance of the request.

Slavery Passes with 'This Present Evil Age': Pauline Apocalyptic in Philemon

Section 1 above argued that Paul had tenuous authority, if any, with the Colossians. This section explores how he makes his argument. The main body of Philemon comprises a mere fifteen verses (vv. 8–22), a request divided into three parts: First Paul makes his request, 'I ask you for my child ... so that he might serve (διακονέω) with me in the bonds of the gospel ...' (vv. 8–16). Second, Paul offers to cover outstanding debts, guaranteed with his signature, 'If he owes you anything ... I will pay, I, Paul, write with my hand, I will pay' (vv. 17–20). Finally, he expresses confidence that the recipient will do as Paul asks (vv. 21–22). Paul's offer to cover Onesimus's debts is an offer to cover outstanding financial obligations Onesimus might have, presuming that Onesimus will be leaving the household in which he served (to stay with Paul). The expression of confidence is another strategy with which to pressure the slaveowner. The question about Paul's view of slavery centers on the first part of his request, 'that you might have him in full, no longer as a slave, but as a brother ...' (vv. 15–16). Were 'slave' and 'brother' mutually exclusive for Paul, or could a slave be treated in a 'brotherly' fashion? This problem must be analyzed from within a Pauline theological framework, and indeed Paul sets his request in Philemon theologically.

That Paul situates his request for Onesimus theologically is signaled immediately by his use of 'but now' (νυνὶ δέ) both to describe himself and to describe Onesimus. Paul calls himself 'an old man, *but now* (νυνὶ δέ) a prisoner of Christ Jesus' (Phlm. 9).[41] And in reference to Onesimus: 'formerly useless, *but now* his true Christ-full self' (Phlm. 11).[42]

The expression νυνὶ δέ, 'but now', is used to draw a contrast, which may be between two time periods, between two conditions, or between two things. Paul's usage in Phlm. 11 describes what Stählin calls 'the Now of the new life'. The phrase νυνὶ δέ sets up an antithesis between Onesimus before baptism and Onesimus now in Christ. Stählin explains, 'the Now of the new relation to God implies a radical and factual transformation of Christian life. This [life] is no longer lived in bondage to sin (Rom. 6.20, also 5.8) ... but in righteousness (Rom. 3.21; 5.9) and freedom (Rom. 6.22) under the renewing power of the Spirit (Rom. 7.6)'.[43]

---

41 'Old man' has proved puzzling to commentators who often emend it to 'an ambassador'.
42 Paul makes a complicated pun here, explained briefly below.
43 *TDNT*, IV, p. 1117.

Elsewhere Paul employs νυνὶ δέ very clearly in connection with apocalyptic transformation, most notably in Rom. 3.21, 'but now (νυνὶ δέ) the righteousness of God has been revealed separate from the law ...' and 1 Cor. 15.20, 'but now (νυνὶ δέ) Christ has been raised from the dead'. Paul uses νυνὶ δέ to set in relief a new reality, new conditions that obtain in Christ. Concerning Rom. 3.21 Ernst Käsemann writes, 'For Paul the new aeon has already broken into the old aeon in Christ and it is spread abroad with his death. The presence of Christ's lordship gives definitiveness to the "now".'[44] Paul's double usage of νυνὶ δέ signals theological discourse, and, indeed, discourse of Pauline apocalyptic, signaled also by his use of oppositions, for example, slave/ brother.

'But now' (νυνὶ δέ), according to Stählin, may have the sense 'in actuality'[45] and this may be its sense in Phlm. 9, 'but now a prisoner of Christ Jesus' ('in actuality' a prisoner ...). Paul may be employing νυνὶ δέ in a temporal sense, referring to his own impending death with apocalyptic overtones. The context that Reitzenstein identifies is very likely the correct context in which to understand Paul's language here. Reitzenstein discusses Paul designating himself 'prisoner' in the context of Hellenistic mystery religions in which the initiand undergoes a period of probation, 'retained' or imprisoned (κατοχή cf. κατέχειν [to detain] which is used in Phlm. 13) in the sacred precincts.[46] Paul writes of himself as 'prisoner' (δέσμιος) of his Lord also in Philippians (cf. Phil. 1.23).

Paul's use of νυνὶ δέ immediately, and twice, is the first indication that he sets his request for Onesimus theologically. The second indication is the use of oppositions to frame the request. Paul's theological exposition often turns on constructing novel oppositions.[47] He may use standard oppositions, for example strong/weak (e.g. Rom. 15.1). He also may invert the valuation of standard pairs, for example, foolish is valued over wise in Corinthians (e.g. 1 Cor. 1.20–25). Often, as, for example, slave and brother in Philemon, Paul casts as opposites terms that ordinarily would not be so. In 1 Cor. 1.18, Paul contrasts folly with power[48] and in Galatians he contrasts slaves and sons.

Phlm. 15–16 is replete with such oppositions. Two adverbial expressions in opposition ('temporarily'—'for eternity') modify the two verbs, so 'he has been

44 Ernst Käsemann writes, 'νυνὶ δέ characterizes both the logical antithesis and especially the eschatological turn (Stählin, *TDNT*, IV, p. 1117) ... But the antithesis is not captured with the categories of the old, new aeons (Nygren) ... For Paul the new aeon has already broken into the old aeon in Christ and it is spread abroad with his death ... the presence of Christ's lordship gives definitiveness to the "now"' (*Romans*, p. 92).
45 Stählin notes that νυνὶ δέ, 'can also have a very heavy stress when used to oppose something factually valid to a hypothetical but erroneous assumption or an incorrect idea. There is here a shift of meaning from "in the present" to "in actuality"... [T]he NT statements with νυνὶ δέ show particularly impressively what the NT reckons, and would have reckoned, as decisive realities in the world. Almost always we find that facts are set in opposition to a supposition ...' (*TDNT*, IV, p. 1109).
46 Richard Reitzenstein, *Hellenistic Mystery Religions: Their Basic Ideas and Significance* (trans. J.E. Steely; Pittsburgh Theological Monograph Series, 15; Pittsburgh: Pickwick, 1978), pp. 240–42.
47 Detailed examples in A.R. Brown, *The Cross and Human Transformation* (Minneapolis: Augsburg–Fortress, 1995), ch. 4; and N. Schneider, *Die Rhetorische Eigenart der paulinischen Antithese* (Tübingen: Mohr/Siebeck, 1970).
48 See discussion in Brown, *The Cross and Human Transformation*, pp. 75–76.

separated from you temporarily' contrasts with 'you will receive in full for eternity'.[49] The passive form of the verb ἐχωρίσθη, 'he has been separated,' signifies divine agency.[50] And (divine) 'separated' contrasts with (human) 'receive in full'.

The oppositions in vv. 15–16 are the culmination of pairs of oppositions in which Paul couches the first part of his request (vv. 8–14). He explains, he could command (ἐπιτάσσω, v. 8) but instead he asks (παρακαλῶ, v. 9); formerly Onesimus (the name 'Onesimus' means 'useful') was useless (ἄχρηστον, v. 11) but is now 'useful' or 'Christful' (εὔχρηστον, v. 11).[51] Paul wants the good deed of the slaveowner to be not compulsory (κατὰ ἀνάγκην, v. 14) but voluntary (κατὰ ἑκούσιον, v. 14). In sum, Paul delineates two modes of action, setting 'commanding–useless–compulsory' against 'asking–Christful–voluntary'. Two modes of action correspond to what J.L. Martyn calls ... 'two opposed orbs'.[52] In the one even beneficial actions count as compelled and in the other the good is voluntary.

Central to apocalyptic is the idea of two aeons; as Sturm summarizes, apocalyptic thinking includes, '(1) the idea of two aeons, (2) the embattled sovereignty of God over time and history, (3) the revelation of an imminent eschaton'.[53] J.L. Martyn has linked Paul's use of oppositions to apocalyptic. Traditionally, Martyn points out, philosophers and rabbis envisioned the world as constructed of four elements aligned in opposing pairs; hence everything in creation also lined up in opposing pairs.[54] For the rabbis, the pairs circumcision/uncircumcision, law/flesh, male/female, slave/free, and Jew/Gentile structure the religious world. Paul understands the crucifixion of Christ, Martyn observes further, to have realigned the foundation of the cosmos in a new creation brought into being through the giving of the spirit, and polarized into two domains. Martyn writes, '[the two domains are] two opposed orbs of power, actively at war with another *since* the apocalyptic advent of Christ and the spirit'.[55]

For Paul, according to Martyn, what has been revealed (ἀποκάλυψις) is the new creation in Christ. Paul envisioned two opposing domains under different lordship; the one, a domain under Christ's lordship, which is the domain of the spirit, and the other, a domain not yet under Christ's lordship, which is the domain of the

---

49 Indeed ἀπέχω and κατέχω (v. 13) are also set in opposition.

50 Lightfoot, *St Paul's Epistles*, p. 340. What Martyn calls 'divine passive' (Gal. 3.16, 19), is a 'circumlocution used to avoid direct reference to God' (J. Louis Martyn, *Galatians* [AB, 33A; New York: Doubleday, 1977], p. 354).

51 This pair is a complicated play on the name Onesimus. 'Useless' (ἄχρηστον) would have been pronounced 'non-Christ'; εὔχρηστον, the adjective, would have been pronounced 'well-Christ', or 'Christful'.

52 J. Louis Martyn, 'Apocalyptic Antinomies in Paul's Letter to the Galatians', *NTS* 31 (1985), pp. 410–417.

53 R.E. Sturm, 'Defining the Word "Apocalyptic"', in J. Marcus and Marion Soards (eds), *Apocalyptic and the New Testament: Essays in Honor of J.L. Martyn* (Sheffield: JSOT Press, 1989), pp. 17–48 (36). See excellent discussion of Martyn, Käsemann, and Beker on Pauline apocalyptic, in Brown, *The Cross and Human Transformation*, pp. 3–12.

54 Martyn, *Galatians*, pp. 403–404 and comment # 51, pp. 570–74.

55 Martyn, 'Apocalyptic Antinomies', p. 417. Within the domain of the spirit, those who are in Christ, Paul envisioned what Martyn calls 'the advent of anthropomorphic unity in Christ' (Martyn, 'Apocalyptic Antinomies', p. 415). Hence in the baptismal formula of Gal. 3.28, pairs thought to be opposite, for example male/female, slave/free, Jew/Greek, have been made one in Christ (Gal. 3.27–28).

flesh.[56] For Paul, the 'new creation' in Christ under the lordship of the spirit is diametrically opposed to 'this evil age', which is under the lordship of the flesh. Martyn writes, '[a]lthough Paul himself never speaks literally of "the coming age," his numerous references to "the present age" (in addition to Gal. 1.4, see Rom. 12.2, 1 Cor. 1.2; 2.6; 2.8; 3.18; 2 Cor. 4.4) reflect his assumption of eschatological dualism. In Paul's vocabulary the expression that stands opposite "the present evil age" is "the new creation" (Gal. 6.15).'[57]

Paul's understanding of the shift from domain of the flesh to domain of the spirit, 'the turn of the ages', underlies his use of oppositions in Philemon. The old pairs of oppositions between male and female, Jew and Greek, slave and free still hold in the domain of the flesh, but the new creation in Christ, for Paul, dissolves these distinctions. Paul's bitter argument in Galatians is against those whom he sees attempting to preserve the old distinctions inside the new creation. For Paul, requiring circumcision of Gentile converts is a practice belonging to the domain of the flesh, 'this present evil age'. And for Paul slavery characterizes the domain of the flesh. In Gal. 4.21–5.1 he sets in opposition *sons*, those who are in Christ, and *slaves*, those who are under the domain of the flesh. He builds on traditional oppositions, Abraham's two sons, but classifies the requirement of law observance for Gentile converts as slavery.

Furthermore, for Paul, as noted above, this shift from the domain of the flesh to the domain of the spirit has already taken place. The problem (in Galatians, for example) is that his opponents fail to recognize Christ's lordship in the new creation, a recognition which, according to Martyn, 'entails recognizing that Christ's death has effected a rearrangement of … apocalyptic antinomies'[58]—in 'the new creation … embodied in Christ, in the church, and in the Israel of God'.[59]

Identifying the apocalyptic framework in Philemon elucidates Paul's views of slavery in three ways. First, as A.R. Brown points out in a study of 1 Corinthians,[60] for Paul, the transformed life in community is an embodied life. Brown writes, '[h]aving the mind of Christ describes more than an intellectual position; it reflects the comprehensive condition of unity in the Body of Christ, or reconciliation, toward which the entire discourse labors'.[61] She explains further, '[f]reed from the dominating powers of the world, this one is remade in Christ'.[62] Physical life, Brown points out, is also involved. In Rom. 8.11 'Paul discloses the vital connection between spiritual and bodily life … So too in 1 Corinthians mystical union with the Spirit leads to transformed bodily life.'[63]

In Philemon it is striking that Paul writes pointedly that the baptized Onesimus should be received as Paul 'both in the flesh (ἐν σαρκί) and in the Lord' (Phlm. 16).

---

56 J. Louis Martyn, 'Epistemology at the turn of the Ages: 2 Corinthians 5:16', in W.R. Farmer, C.F.D. Moule, and R.R. Niebuhr (eds), *Christian History and Interpretation: Studies Presented to John Knox* (Cambridge: Cambridge University Press, 1967) and Martyn, 'Apocalyptic Antinomies'; Brown, discussion of Käsemann, *The Cross and Human Transformation*, pp. 2–8.

57 Martyn, *Galatians*, p. 98.

58 Martyn, *Galatians*, pp. 404–405 (comment # 41, pp. 393–406).

59 Martyn, *Galatians*, p. 573.

60 Brown, *The Cross and Human Transformation*.

61 Brown, *The Cross and Human Transformation*, p. 165.

62 Brown, *The Cross and Human Transformation*, p. 165.

63 Brown, *The Cross and Human Transformation*, p. 166.

Here 'in the flesh' is a neutral phrase, meaning roughly 'in his bodily existence'. Paul does not refer here to the domain of the flesh, which he designates κατὰ σάρκα.

Second, in Galatians Paul's concept of dissolving the differences between male and female, Jew and Greek, slave and free is linked to equality in community. An argument of Hyam Maccoby sheds light on the connection between the Galatian situation and equality in community.[64] From the account in Acts of the decision of the Jerusalem council Maccoby proposes that some early Christians envisioned—and presumably practiced—a two-tiered community whose inner circle comprised 'Jews practicing the whole Torah' and outer circle comprised 'Gentiles practicing the Noahide laws only.'[65] In a mixed community of Jews and non-Jews partial ritual observance would lead to inequality, with Gentile adherents constituting a second tier.

Third, within Pauline apocalyptic the social distinction slave/free is symptomatic of the present evil age. And slavery is a metaphor for existence in the domain of the flesh. Within Pauline apocalyptic the gap between slave and brother could not be greater.

Conclusions

This chapter has explored which individuals Paul mentioned in Philemon and concluded that Paul went out on a limb to ask that Onesimus might stay to work with him. This chapter also explored the Pauline apocalyptic that framed the request in Philemon. Within this framework the divide between slave and brother is immeasurable, it is the divide between the old and new aeons.

Philemon strengthens the case for the 'new Paul', not simply because Paul argues for manumission of the baptized Onesimus, but because his situating his argument within his apocalyptic links this concrete instance of a baptized slave to the baptismal formula of Gal. 3.28. We possess no genuine Pauline writing arguing for equality between men and women. Yet neither in Galatians nor in Philemon does Paul concern himself with social equality in the Roman Empire as a whole; he concerns himself with behavior within the worshiping community. The significant representation of women leaders in Pauline churches uncovered by feminist scholarship of recent decades puts the burden of proof on those who would argue Paul was indifferent to or opposed to equality of women within the churches.

---

64 H. Maccoby, *The Mythmaker: Paul and the Invention of Christianity* (New York: Harper & Row, 1986), p. 144.

65 Maccoby writes of the account in Acts, 'James's remark thus implies his own unquestioning adherence to Judaism, and his confidence that Judaism would continue. There is therefore a tension in our passage between two opposing interpretations of the debate in Jerusalem. One interpretation (evidently that of the author of Acts) is that this debate marked the breakdown of all distinctions between Jews and Gentiles in the Christian movement. The other interpretation (which can be discerned as the substratum of the discussion, and is thus the authentic and original meaning of the incident) is that it was decided that the Jesus movement should consist of two categories of people: Jews, practising the whole Torah; and Gentiles, practising the Noahide laws only ... It was quite in accordance with Judaism to make a distinction between the two kinds of believers in monotheism, Torah-practisers and Noahides' (*The Mythmaker*, p. 144).

Paul does not write as fully and explicitly as we would wish about issues of equality. Nevertheless, the apocalyptic framework in which he sets Philemon makes explicit his petition for manumission in this instance of a baptized slave of a baptized slaveowner. No text is immune to harmful misinterpretation. Indeed the history of interpretation offers few more striking instances than Philemon and Galatians. Let them remind us of the responsibilities we face as scholars, and perhaps these two epistles can assist in each other's restoration.

Paul on the Relation between Men and Women*

Richard B. Hays

Sex is a minor concern within the foundational logic of Paul's moral vision. One sees this clearly in Romans: apart from the rhetorically charged depiction of sexual immorality as an outward and visible sign of humanity's alienation from God in Rom. 1.24–27, Paul has very little to say about sexual conduct in this most extensive of his teachings.

Nonetheless, Paul was compelled by circumstances to deal with issues of sexual behavior in his churches, particularly at Corinth; his responses in 1 Corinthians have been of fateful import historically for Christian teaching about sex. Furthermore, as issues of sexual conduct are hotly debated at the end of the twentieth century, Paul is alternately invoked or inveighed against by various disputants. Consequently, we cannot avoid asking how his understanding of sex fits into his larger moral vision.[1]

Sex at the Turn of the Ages: 1 Corinthians 7

People who know nothing else about the apostle Paul may know that he wrote, 'It is well for a man not to touch a woman' (1 Cor. 7.1b). This statement, however, is surely one of the most widely misinterpreted texts in the New Testament. Precisely for that reason, it offers an excellent illustration of the importance of careful descriptive exegesis as the first step in the construction of New Testament ethics. On the basis of 1 Cor. 7.1, lifted out of its context, Paul is often castigated as a misogynistic character with pathological attitudes about sex. While the apostle's ideas certainly do not correspond to conventional late twentieth-century notions of 'healthy sexuality', it would be a serious mistake to treat this text as a polemic against sex. Let us examine the passage carefully.

First of all, we must remember that we are reading one side of a conversational exchange. Paul is not setting out to write a general treatise on sex and marriage; rather, he is responding to a Corinthian concern. This is made explicit at the beginning of the sentence: 'Now concerning the matters about which you wrote ...' (1 Cor. 7.1a). This is a major structural transition in the letter. Through the first six chapters, Paul has been responding to reports about the Corinthian community (1.11; 5.1); now he turns to questions they have raised directly in correspondence. Therefore, in order to understand Paul's response, we need to reconstruct the question they have asked and the situation it presupposes.

* Originally published in Richard B. Hays, *The Moral Vision of the New Testament: Community, Cross, New Creation: A Contemporary Introduction to New Testament Ethics* (San Francisco: HarperSanFrancisco, 1996), pp. 46–59. Reprinted by permission.

1 The topics of divorce and homosexuality are more thoroughly treated in Part 4 of *The Moral Vision of the New Testament* (pp. 347–406); consequently, they will not be the focus of attention here.

Several times in 1 Corinthians Paul quotes a slogan popular among some of his readers in order to correct or qualify it, or to challenge the conclusions that the Corinthians were drawing from it. For example, in 1 Cor. 6.12–14, just a few lines before the passage we are considering, Paul scripts the following exchange:

Corinthians: 'All things are lawful for me.'
      Paul: 'But not all things are beneficial.'

Corinthians: 'All things are lawful for me.'
      Paul: 'But I will not be dominated by anything.'

Corinthians: ' "Food is meant for the stomach and the stomach for food", and God will
      destroy both one and the other.'
      Paul: 'The body is meant not for fornication but for the Lord, and the Lord for
      the body. And God raised the Lord and will also raise us by his power.'[2]

In ancient Greek manuscripts there were no quotation marks to set off the Corinthians' lines from Paul's responses, but readers at Corinth who were familiar with the slogans would have had no trouble in following the dialogical characters of this passage. The NRSV translators have provided quotation marks to help us read the dialogue rightly.

In 1 Cor. 8.1, which is structurally analogous to 7.1, we encounter a similar pattern: 'Now concerning food sacrificed to idols: we know that "all of us possess knowledge". Knowledge puffs up, but love builds up' (cf. also vv. 4–6, 8–9). Paul does not attack the Corinthian slogan; he first accepts it, then deflates it. He is quoting (or perhaps characterizing) their position in order to set up a foil for his response.

Once we recognize this rhetorical pattern in the letter, it becomes clear that 1 Cor. 7.1 is another instance of the same technique:

Corinthians: 'It is well for a man not to touch a woman.'
      Paul: 'But because of cases of sexual immortality, each man should have his wife
      and each woman her own husband.'

Thus, we see that the antisex slogan almost certainly comes from the Corinthians rather than from Paul himself.[3] This is one of 'the matters about which you wrote' (7.1a). As the punctuation in the NRSV indicates, Paul is quoting a statement from their letter back to them to identify the topic of discussion.

Paul does not directly challenge the slogan; indeed, he is sympathetic with it (cf. v. 8). Nonetheless, he poses a corrective to it. What exactly is he trying to correct?

---

2 For analysis of the structure of vv. 13-14, see Gordon D. Fee, *The First Epistle to the Corinthians* (NICNT; Grand Rapids: Eerdmans, 1987), pp. 253–57, who argues persuasively that the phrase 'God will destroy both one and the other' expresses not Paul's view but 'the Corinthian view of spritiuality, which looked for a "spiritual" salvation that would finally be divested of the body' (p. 257).

3 For a thorough exegetical defense of this interpretation, see Fee, *The First Epistle to the Corinthians*, pp. 266–86. See also Victor P. Furnish, *The Moral Teaching of Paul: Selected Issues* (Nashville: Abingdon Press, rev. edn, 1985), pp. 29–38.

The key lies in the proper interpretation of v. 2: '... each man should *have* his own wife and each woman her own husband'. The sentence is often read as an encouragement for unmarried people to pair up and get married. Careful reflection will show, however, that this interpretation is impossible: Paul's advice to the unmarried in this same chapter is that they should remain unmarried if at all possible (vv. 8–9, 20, 24, 25–27, 39–40). What, then, does v. 2 mean? The passage makes perfect sense when we recognize that the verb ἐξεῖν ('to have') is a common euphemism for sexual intercourse. For instance, it occurs in this sense in 1 Cor. 5.1: 'It is actually reported that there is sexual immorality among you, and of a kind that is not found even among Gentiles: for a man to *have* his father's wife.' If this is the sense of the verb 'have' in 1 Cor. 7.2, then Paul must be speaking to those who are already married and urging them to continue to have sexual intercourse. This same exhortation is explicitly repeated in v. 3.

But why would such advice be necessary? To readers at the end of the twentieth century, this counsel to married couples may appear foolishly superfluous, as though Paul had written to remind his churches to breathe and eat. But in the first-century context, such teaching about sex was not at all unnecessary. In the first place, the correlation between piety and celibacy was a common feature of Hellenistic culture. The physical body, belonging to the material world, was deprecated and regarded as inferior to the rational soul; the goal of the wise philosopher was to discipline the body by bringing its animal urges under the control of reason. We find a reaction against such teachings in the letter to the Colossians:

> Why do you submit to regulations: 'Do not handle, do not taste, do not touch?' All these regulations refer to things that perish with use; they are simply human commands and teachings. These have indeed an appearance of wisdom in promoting self-imposed piety, humility, and severe treatment of the body, but they are of no value in checking self-indulgence (Col. 2.20b–23).

In many circles, ascetic wisdom was understood to entail sexual abstinence. Celibacy was seen as a sign of spiritual power, because it symbolized freedom from attachment to the crude realm of the material. In short, we might say aphoristically that in the ancient world celibacy had 'sex appeal'.

Second, it is not implausible that there were factors within the earliest Christian traditions that made sexual abstinence appear attractive or even mandatory for participants in this new faith. The baptismal formula that Paul cites in Gal. 3.28 declares that in Christ 'there is no longer male and female'. In other words, Gen. 1.27 ('So God created humankind in his image; ... male and female he created them') has been superseded by the new creation, in which sexual differences are abolished.[4] How then can Christian couples continue to indulge their sexual desires? Is sex not incompatible with life in the new creation? (It is probably not coincidental that when Paul cites the baptismal formula to the Corinthians in 1 Cor. 12.13, he omits the 'no longer male and female' phrase.) Particularly if—as some scholars have argued—some of the Corinthians believed that they were already

4 For an account of the diverse ways in which this symbolism was interpreted in early Christianity, see Wayne A. Meeks, 'The Image of the Androgyne: Some Uses of a Symbol in Earliest Christianity', *HR* 13.1 (1974), pp. 165–208.

living in the state of resurrection life (cf. 4.8), they might well have concluded that married couples should cease having sex. Consider the saying of Jesus reported in Lk. 20.34–36:

> Those who belong to this age marry and are given in marriage; but those who are considered worthy of a place in that age and in the resurrection of the dead neither marry nor are given in marriage. Indeed they cannot die anymore, because they are like angels and are children of God, being children of the resurrection.

It is not at all improbable that some of the Corinthians, who understood themselves to be capable of speaking in 'the tongues of angels' (1 Cor. 13.1), might have regarded themselves as having been translated into such an angelic state.[5]

Thus, we propose the hypothesis that *Paul is seeking to counteract radical Corinthian asceticism*. Against an idealistic hyperspirituality that forswears sexual union even within existing marriages, Paul urges that married couples may and *must* continue to have sexual relations:

> Let the husband give to his wife what is owed her, and likewise the wife to the husband. For the wife does not have authority over her own body, but the husband does. Likewise also the husband does not have authority over his own body, but the wife does (1 Cor. 7.3–4).

The emphasis here on mutuality is striking. In contrast to a patriarchal culture that would assume a one-way hierarchical ordering of the husband's authority over the wife, Paul carefully prescribes *mutual submission*.[6] Neither marriage partner controls his or her own body: in the marriage covenant, one surrenders authority over one's own body to the spouse. (In passing, we should note how sharply this picture of mutual submission contrasts to the twentieth-century notion of the sexual autonomy of each individual.) Those who have already entered marriage relationships, Paul directs, should continue to honor their commitments; to do otherwise is to deprive the spouse of what he or she might legitimately expect from a marriage partner.

Indeed, withdrawal into celibacy is not only a breach of faith with the spouse, it is also dangerous. Why? Because Satan may tempt the superspiritual ascetic to find sexual fulfillment elsewhere (7.5), perhaps through fornication with a prostitute. (Paul has just spoken sternly against such practices in 1 Cor. 6.12–20.) In order to understand Paul's concern, we must picture the sadly comic scenario in which a Christian married couple plays a charade of sexual abstinence with one another while indulging in clandestine extramarital affairs. Though the prospect seems ridiculous,

---

5 There is no indication in the letter that the Corinthians knew this specific tradition of Jesus' teaching or that their self-imposed sexual abstinence was based on appeal to dominical tradition. The point is simply that the Lukan saying gives independent expression to the wider cultural assumption that sexuality is alien to eschatological existence.

6 Peter J. Tomson, *Paul and the Jewish Law: Halakha in the Letters of the Apostle to the Gentiles* (Compendia Rerum Iudaicarum ad Novum Testamentum, 3.1; Assen: Van Gorcum; Minneapolis: Fortress Press, 1990), p. 107, while noting that Paul's teaching is parallel to rabbinic traditions that stress the wife's marital rights on the basis of Exod. 21.10, also observes that the 'remarkable reciprocity' of Paul's statements transcends 'the accepted Rabbinic conception'.

Paul is a realistic observer of the deceitfulness of the human heart,[7] and he knows—as we have seen in recent sex scandals involving television evangelists—that hyperspiritual people are hardly immune to sexual temptations. Thus, he thinks it safer to counsel the continuance of normal sexual relations within marriage:

> Do not deprive one another except perhaps by agreement (ἐκ συμφρώνου) for a set time, to devote yourselves to prayer, and then come together again, so that Satan may not tempt you because of your lack of self-control (7.5).

Marriage partners may agree 'with a common voice' (ἐκ συμφώνου) to temporary abstinence—analogous to fasting—for a special season of prayer, as long as the time is strictly bounded, with the understanding that they will resume sexual relations. This permission for a temporary moratorium on sex is the 'concession' mentioned in v. 6: 'This I say by way of concession, not of command.' Traditionally, the text has been interpreted to mean that Paul grudgingly concedes the legitimacy of sex within marriage. In view of the foregoing exegesis, however, the passage makes better sense if the pronoun τοῦτο ('this') in v. 6 is understood to refer to the immediately preceding v. 5: Paul's concession to the Corinthian ascetics is his cautious approval of a temporary suspension of sexual relations.

In light of these exegetical observations, we can construct a paraphrase of 1 Cor. 7.1-9, filling in some of the silences and gaps in the conversation. The words in italics are supplied as explanatory expansions to show how Paul's advice seeks to address the particular issues raised by the Corinthians.

> (1) Now I will respond to the matters about which you wrote. You propose that, for the sake of holiness and purity, married couples should abstain from sexual intercourse. As you say, 'It is a fine thing for a man not to touch a woman.' (2) But—since that is unrealistic—let each husband have sexual intercourse with his own wife, and let each wife have sexual intercourse with her own husband. (3) Marriage creates a mutual obligation for a couple to satisfy one another's needs; therefore, let the husband give the wife what he owes her, and likewise let the wife give what she owes to her husband. (4) For the wife does not rule her own body; the husband does. Likewise, the husband does not rule his own body; the wife does. (5) Do not deprive one another, unless you decide—in harmony with one another—to abstain from intercourse for a time so that both of you can devote yourselves to prayer. But *(when the time is up)* come together again, so that Satan will not be able to tempt you. (6) I am not commanding this *practice of temporary abstinence*; rather, I am saying this as a concession *to your proposal* (see v. 1, above). (7) I wish that everyone could be *in control of sexual desire* like me. *Obviously, however, that is not the case.* But each person has his/her own gift from God: *if not celibacy, then something else*, one in one way and another in some other way.
>
> (8) To the unmarried and to the widows, on the other hand, I say that it is a fine thing for them to remain *unmarried* as I am. (9) But if they are not in control of themselves, let them marry, for it is better to marry than to burn *with passion*.

It is important to note what is *not* said in this passage about sex within marriage. Perhaps most striking is the absence of any reference to sexual union as an expression

---

7 See Dan O.Via, Jr, *Self-Deception and Wholeness in Paul and Matthew* (Minneapolis: Fortress Press, 1990).

of love. As we have already noted, Paul appeals to love as a motive for behavior when he addresses the problems of idol-meat and speaking in tongues, but he does not do so when he speaks of sex. Perhaps love is implied in Paul's call for mutual submission of marriage partners, but he does not make the point explicit. Second, nothing is said here about the procreative purpose of sex. Husband and wife are to continue having intercourse because sexual union is a part of the obligation of marriage and because it protects them against temptation, but nothing is said here about conceiving children. Presumably, Paul's belief in the imminent eschaton made him relatively indifferent to the raising of families; in this respect his teaching stands in stark contrast to Jewish tradition and to later Christian teaching about procreation as the fundamental purpose of marital sex. Finally, there is no suggestion whatever of differing standards for clergy and laity; indeed, the distinction is anachronistic. Paul knew nothing of a special class of 'ordained' persons who were subject to special standards of sexual behavior.

In sum, we see that the passage has been subject to drastic interpretation. Rather than deprecating women or sex, Paul is actually arguing *against* those who regard sexual intercourse as inappropriate for Christians. He stoutly and realistically affirms the necessity of mutual sexual satisfaction within marriage.[8]

Why, then, does Paul advise the unmarried to remain unmarried (7.8)? At this point, we see the effects of his apocalyptic eschatology:

> I mean, brothers and sisters, the appointed time has grown short; from now on, let even those who have wives be as though they had none, and those who mourn as though they were not mourning, and those who rejoice as though they were not rejoicing, and those who buy as though they had no possessions, and those who deal with the world as though they had no dealings with it. For the present form of this world is passing away (7.29–31).

If the present order of things is about to be swept away, why enter into marriage? Paul's rule of thumb is stated clearly and insistently in 7.17–24: 'Let each of you remain in the condition in which you were called.' The only thing that matters in the present time between the times is 'unhindered devotion to the Lord'. Marriage inevitably brings with it a concern for the 'affairs of the world' and thereby hinders total devotion to the mission of the church at the turn of the ages (7.32–35). That mission is 'the present necessity'[9] that leads Paul to opine that singleness is

---

8 This reading differs in emphasis from Daniel Boyarin's incisive and nuanced interpretation of the same passage (D. Boyarin, *A Radical Jew: Paul and the Politics of Cultural Identity* [Berkeley: University of California Press, 1994], pp. 180–200). Boyarin stresses more heavily Paul's preference for a genderless, spiritualized ideal of Christian existence (as articulated in Gal. 3.28); thus, Paul's statements in 1 Corinthians 7 must be read as a reluctant compromise: 'Paul settled for something else, something less than his vision called for, and thus the continuation of the domestic slavery of marriage for those not called to the celibate life' (p. 193). My difference from Boyarin on the reading of this text is part of a larger debate between us about the extent to which Paul's anthropology parallels the systematic dualism expressed more clearly in Philo of Alexandria. Nonetheless, the differences are primarily matters of where to place the accents in Paul's discourse. I can agree entirely with Boyarin when he writes, 'Paul maintains a two-tiered system of thought regarding sexuality: celibacy as the higher state but marriage as a fully honorable condition for the believing Christian' (p. 192).

9 The translation 'impending crisis' (7.26), despite its appearance in the RSV and NRSV, is indefensible. The participle ἐνεστῶσαν clearly means 'present', as in 1 Cor. 3.22, where it is juxtaposed to μέλλοντα, 'things to come'.

preferable as his own opinion on a matter where he has no command of the Lord (7.25).

At the same time, Paul knows that the power of the present age still exercises influence over the lives of believers. They are subject to temptation and to burning physical desire. Unlike the hyperspiritual enthusiasts that he seeks to correct, he knows that the resurrection remains a future hope rather than a present reality. Consequently, the 'not yet' pole of his eschatology leads him to give sober realistic counsel to the Corinthians, permitting marriage and encouraging sexual relations within marriage. The important thing is that the members of the community, whether married or unmarried, remain in a state of watchful readiness and obedience.

Women and Men in the Ministry of the Pauline Churches

Apart from the questions of sex and marriage, what role did women play in the social organization and worship life of the Pauline churches? The letters seem to send mixed signals. On the one hand, we find the radical egalitarian declaration of Gal. 3.26–28:

> For in Christ Jesus you are all children of God through faith. As many of you as were baptized into Christ have clothed yourselves with Christ. There is no longer Jew or Greek, there is no longer slave or free, there is no longer male and female; for all of you are one in Christ Jesus.

On the other hand, we find in 1 Cor. 14.34–35 a stringent suppression of the public role of women in the worshiping community:

> Let women be silent in the churches. For it is not permitted to them to speak, but let them be subordinate, just as the Law also says. And if they want to learn something, let them ask their own husbands at home. For it is a shameful thing for a woman to speak in church.

How is the tension between these texts to be understood? Are women equal partners with men within the community of faith, or does Paul assign them a subordinate role?

The best way to approach this question is to examine the evidence concerning the roles *actually* played by women in the Pauline communities. Since this matter has been studied extensively in recent New Testament scholarship, we can summarize the pertinent findings briefly here.[10]

First, we know from 1 Cor. 11.3–16 that Paul expected women to pray and prophesy in the community's worship. His major concern in this passage is that they should arrange their hair (or cover their heads)[11] in a seemly manner while

---

10 For more detailed discussion, see Elisabeth Schüssler Fiorenza, *In Memory of Her: A Feminist Theological Reconstruction of Christian Origins* (New York: Crossroad, 1983), pp. 226–30; Furnish, *The Moral Teaching of Paul*, pp. 83–114; Ben Witherington III, *Women in the Earliest Churches* (SNTSMS, 59; Cambridge: Cambridge University Press, 1980).

11 For discussion of this disputed passage, see Schüssler Fiorenza, *In Memory of Her*, pp. 226–30; Furnish, *The Moral Teaching of Paul*, pp. 94–101; Dale B. Martin, *The Corinthian Body* (New Haven: Yale University Press, 1995).

praying and prophesying. Wayne Meeks summarizes the thrust of the passage aptly: 'In brief, he leaves unquestioned the right of women, led by the Spirit, to exercise the same leadership roles in the assembly as men, but insists only that the conventional symbols of sexual difference, in clothing and hair styles, be retained.'[12] Thus, this passage seems to stand in contradiction to the directive of 1 Cor. 14.34–35, which mandates silence for women in the assembly.

Second, numerous incidental references in Paul's letters show that women were included among Paul's co-workers. Some of these women exercised leadership roles in the communities. For example, Paul describes Phoebe as 'a deacon (διάκονος) of the church at Cenchreae' (Rom. 16.1). It is not clear whether the term διάκονος should be understood as designating a formal office in the church (as in Phil. 1.1), or whether it is simply a generic term for 'servant/minister', as in 1 Cor. 3.5 and 2 Cor. 3.6, where Paul uses exactly the same word to describe his own role. In either case, Paul thinks of Phoebe as having some important work to do at Rome, and he instructs the Romans to help her 'in whatever she may require of you', adding that 'she has been a benefactor (προστάτις) of many and of myself as well' (Rom. 16.2). The term προστάτις (literally 'one who stands before') can be used to describe one who leads or presides over a group; here it probably has the more general sense of 'patron' or 'benefactor'.

Prisca and Aquila, a wife and husband team, are among Paul's 'co-workers in Christ Jesus'. Paul mentions that 'all the churches of the Gentiles' give thanks for their ministry, and he mentions that they host a house-church in their home (Rom. 16.3–4; cf. Acts 18.18–28). None of Paul's comments about them suggests any subordination of the wife to the husband; she appears to be a full participant in ministry. Several other women appear as 'workers in the Lord' in Paul's long list of salutations in Rom. 16.1–16, including Mary, Tryphaena, Tryphosa, Persis, and Junia, who along with Andronicus (perhaps her husband) is described as 'prominent among the apostles' (16.7). In Phil. 4.2–3 Paul urges the women Euodia and Syntyche—who have 'struggled beside me in the work of the gospel'—to mend their differences and 'be of the same mind in the Lord'. They are not explicitly described as leaders of the Philippian church, but the prominence that Paul accords them in this letter addressed to the whole church suggests that they are persons with an important role in the community.

The cumulative weight of this evidence suggests that women did play a significant role in the ministry of the Pauline churches, including serving as members of the apostolic mission teams. Certainly, women participated in the activity of prophecy, which had as its purpose the upbuilding of the church (1 Cor. 14.1–25). In many respects, women in these communities enjoyed a greater measure of freedom and dignity than they could have experienced in Greco-Roman society outside the Christian fellowship. Indeed, the relatively egalitarian social structure of the Pauline communities made them particularly attractive to 'upwardly mobile' urban women whose education or economic position ('achieved status') exceeded their hereditary position ('attributed status').[13]

---

12 Wayne A. Meeks, *The First Urban Christians: The Social World of the Apostle Paul* (New Haven: Yale University Press, 1983), p. 220 n. 107.
13 Meeks, *First Urban Christians*, pp. 70–73.

How, then, are we to understand the injunction to silence in 1 Cor. 14.34–35? At least four different explanations have been proposed by scholars.

(1) The passage does not forbid women from exercising leadership or speaking in edifying ways to the community; rather, it forbids disruptive speech during the community's worship. Perhaps the women at Corinth, moving into a new position of freedom in the church, were interrupting worship with questions (v. 35) and creating disorder. Thus, the injunction is not a general rule but a pastoral directive aimed at a specific situation. This explanation makes sense of v. 35 ('If they want to learn something, let them ask their own husbands at home'), but it overlooks the generalizing force of v. 34b ('Let them be subordinate, just as the Law also says') and requires a special narrow sense for the common verb λαλεῖν ('speak') in vv. 34 and 35; it would have to mean something like 'chatter'. If v. 33b ('as in all the churches of the saints') is read with v. 34, this argument becomes impossible, because Paul would be asserting female silence and subordination as a rule for all communities, not just for some particular problematical situation at Corinth.

(2) The passage refers only to married women, whereas the women who are permitted to pray and prophesy (1 Cor. 11.3–16) must be unmarried.[14] Women who marry become subordinate to their husbands and should keep quiet. This interpretation resolves the apparent contradiction, but it requires us to supply a condition not stipulated in 1 Cor. 11.3–16 (that female prophets must be unmarried), and it overlooks the evidence that married women such as Prisca and Junia did play leadership roles in the Pauline communities.

(3) The passage is an interpolation,[15] not written by Paul but added to his letter by a later scribe or editor, such as the author of the Pastoral Epistles (cf. 1 Tim. 2.8–15). This hypothesis finds some support in the existence of a number of ancient manuscripts that place vv. 34–35 at the end of the chapter rather than between vv. 33 and 36. The verses do appear intrusive in Paul's discussion of order in the exercise of prophetic gifts; when they are removed, the passage reads smoothly. Furthermore, on material grounds it is difficult to imagine these words coming from Paul's hand: the Paul who wrote 1 Cor. 11.3–16 certainly did not think that it was 'shameful for a woman to speak in church'. There are, however, no extant manuscripts that omit vv. 34–35; if these verses were added to the text secondarily, they were added at a very early stage.[16]

(4) Antoinette Wire, rejecting the interpolation theory, has recently argued that 1 Cor. 14.34–35 is the rhetorical goal and climax of the entire letter, which is constructed to lead up to Paul's silencing of female prophets at Corinth.[17] (She leaves open the question of whether Paul intentionally structures the whole argument to

---

14 Schüssler Fiorenza, *In Memory of Her*, pp. 230–33.

15 For an extended defense of this argument, see Fee, *The First Epistle to the Corinthians*, pp. 699–708. For a counterargument defending the authenticity of the verses, see Antoinette Clark Wire, *The Corinthian Women Prophets: A Reconstruction through Paul's Rhetoric* (Minneapolis: Fortress Press, 1990), pp. 149–52.

16 Significantly, however, a recent article by Philip Payne, 'Fuldensis, Sigla for Variants in Vaticanus, and 1 Cor. 14.34–35', *NTS* 41 (1995), pp. 240–62, identifies previously unnoticed evidence from the sixth-century Codex Fuldensis suggesting that vv. 34–35 were regarded as an interpolation by Bishop Victor of Capua, under whose authority the manuscript was produced. My thanks to Dr Payne for allowing me to consult a prepublication of his essay.

17 Wire, *Women Prophets*, pp. 135–58.

lead to this conclusion or whether he arrives at it through wrestling with the community's problems.) On this reading, 1 Cor. 11.3–16 is interpreted not as an endorsement of prophecy by women but as a preliminary restriction on the dress and behavior of the female prophets; having gained an inch rhetorically in ch. 11, Paul takes a mile in ch. 14, promulgating a far more comprehensive restriction on the Corinthian women. Of the four options considered here, this is the least plausible: it depends on an elaborate speculative reconstruction of the role of women prophets at Corinth, it construes the whole letter as an instance of manipulative and repressive rhetoric, and—most tellingly—it clashes flagrantly with the evidence enumerated above concerning the actual roles of women in Paul's churches.

All things considered, the third of these explanations—the interpolation theory—is the likeliest, the one most consistent with the picture that Paul's letters otherwise convey of the role of women in worship and ministry. Whether Paul wrote these words or not, however, they give expression to a theological judgment that appears again in the Pastoral Epistles; consequently, a New Testament ethic that seeks to be responsive to the full witness of the canonical New Testament must take 1 Cor. 14.34–35 into account in the synthetic and hermeneutical stages of normative reflection. In other words, we cannot end our consideration of this text by saying, 'Paul did not write it.' In a later stage of our work, we will have to deal with the New Testament's differing attitudes concerning the role of women in the church.

Regardless of our judgment concerning the interpretation of 1 Cor. 14.34–35, we must recognize a certain built-in tension concerning the role of women in Paul's symbolic world. The deepest logic of his gospel declares that men and women are one in Christ and ought to live in relations of loving mutuality. His instructions on marriage are remarkable for their time in their careful, egalitarian balancing of the obligations of husband and wife. In his missionary work he joyfully acknowledges the contributions of female colleagues, fellow 'workers in the Lord'. Yet in some passages, such as 1 Cor. 11.3–16, he insists—with labored and unpersuasive theological arguments—on the maintenance of traditional markers of sexual distinction; despite the ingenious efforts of exegetes at the end of the twentieth century, it is impossible to deny the hierarchical implications of such symbolic markers. Indeed, Paul seems to have found the Corinthian church's experiments in gender equality somewhat unsettling; consequently, he sought to constrain what he saw as excesses.

In this matter as in so many others, Paul's ethical stance is comprehensible only in light of his dialectical eschatology: already men and women enjoy equality in Christ; however, not yet can that equality sweep away all the constraints and distinctions of the fallen order. Sexual distinctions do persist, and sexual relations are fraught with danger. The transformation of gender roles was not a programmatic emphasis of Paul's mission; rather, it was an unintended consequence, as the Spirit worked in the churches. The calling of Christians at the turn of the ages, according to Paul, is to live sacrificially within the structures of marriage and community, recognizing the freedom of the Spirit to transform institutions and roles but waiting on the coming of the Lord to set all things right. In the meantime, apostle and community find themselves poised on a tightrope, seeking to discern the will of God in circumstances where old norms no longer hold. 'Do not be conformed to this age, but be transformed by the renewing of your minds, so that you may discern what is the will of God—what is good and acceptable and perfect' (Rom. 12.2).

How does this exhortation work itself out in the community's understanding of the right relation of women and men? Perhaps on no other issue do we see Paul struggling so visibly to get it right. In that respect, the church today stands to learn something from Paul, since—as he wrote to the Philippians in another context—'you are having the same struggle that you saw I had' (Phil. 1.30).[18] Any sexual ethic that takes its bearings from Paul will shape the community's discernment with respect to the three fundamental theological motifs that we have identified in Paul's thought: How do our actions manifest the presence of the new creation in a sin-dominated world, how do our actions correspond to the self-sacrificed love of the cross, and how do our actions serve the good of the community? We rightly understand Paul's particular teachings about sex only when we see them as attempts to answer these questions for the communities that he was forming.

18 As Boyarin remarks, 'People in the late antiquity had not thought their way out of a dilemma which catches us on its horns even now—in *very* late antiquity' (Boyarin, *A Radical Jew*, p. 200).

Virgins, Widows, and Wives: The Women of 1 Corinthians 7

Margaret Y. MacDonald

There are two passages in 1 Corinthians where Paul deliberately makes parallel statements about the respective obligations of men and women: 1 Corinthians 7 and 1 Cor. 11.2–16.[1] That the latter places most emphasis on the female has frequently led to the conclusion that the Corinthian women were donning the attire of the opposite sex,[2] and that the problem underlying the instructions about head attire in 1 Corinthians 11 is with women.[3] No such consensus exists with respect to 1 Corinthians 7.[4] The fact that the parallelism in 1 Corinthians 7 is even more extensive than in 1 Corinthians 11 might suggest that in his discussion of marriage and celibacy, Paul was equally concerned with the practices of men and women. Or, does this well-crafted parallelism mask signs of women's initiative? Is there a connection between the activities of the women of 1 Cor. 11.2–16 and Paul's exhortations in 1 Corinthians 7?

This chapter addresses these questions by means of socio-historical analysis. It seeks to reconstruct the social context of 1 Corinthians 7 by drawing upon comparative material from the ancient world. Insights from anthropological studies of Mediterranean society are used as an analytical tool to uncover the values that shaped Paul's response in 1 Corinthians 7 and to explore the concomitant effect of these values on the lives of women. But before turning to issues of context, it will first be necessary to study Paul's parallel statements carefully, paying close attention to his terminology and to interruptions in the usual patterns of his language.

Behind the Parallelism of 1 Corinthians 7

At a quick glance, 1 Corinthians 7 reveals a number of almost monotonously parallel statements about the mutual obligations of men and women. Yet a closer reading discloses several interruptions of the rhetorical parallelism, offering indications of a special interest in the behavior of women. The first of these occurs in 1 Cor. 7.

---

1 See Wayne Meeks, 'The Image of the Androgyne: Some Uses of a Symbol in Earliest Christianity', *HR* 131 (1974), pp. 165–208 (199-200); for further discussion of parallelism in 1 Corinthians see David L. Balch, '1 Cor. 7.32–35 and Stoic Debates about Marriage, Anxiety, and Distractions', *JBL* 102.3 (1983), pp. 436–37.

2 Meeks, 'Image of the Androgyne,' p. 201.

3 See Dennis R. MacDonald, *There Is No Male and Female: The Fate of a Dominical Saying in Paul and Gnosticism* (HDR, 20; Philadelphia: Fortress Press, 1987), p. 73 n. 22.

4 Note that I argued that 1 Corinthians 7 reveals a special concern for the behavior of women in my earlier article, 'Women Holy in Body and Spirit: The Social Setting of 1 Corinthians 7', *NTS* 36 (1990), pp. 161–81. The present chapter constitutes further development of my ideas on this matter and includes a more detailed social-scientific analysis of Paul's response to the Corinthian women. On women in 1 Corinthians 7 see also Antoinette Clark Wire, *The Corinthian Women Prophets: A Reconstruction through Paul's Rhetoric* (Minneapolis: Fortress Press, 1990), pp. 82–90.

10–11. Paul applies the command from the Lord against divorce equally to believing men and believing women.[5] Yet, surprisingly, he admits parenthetically that some women have indeed separated from their husbands and states that either these women should become reconciled to their husbands or they should remain unmarried. Because the exhortation concerning women is longer and precedes the corresponding instruction concerning men (cf. 7.12–13), it is reasonable to conclude that women were the main instigators of the separations.[6] As discussed further below, there are indications in 1 Corinthians 7 that a strongly ascetic teaching had taken root in the community and women were among its most fervent proponents. When married women became attracted to this teaching, they may have sought to dissolve unions with their husbands on the basis of the fact that sex desecrated their holiness. Abstinence from sex within marriage would not be enough if the husband did not share his wife's passion for celibacy and found the temptation of living with her too great. He may have been tempted to seek sexual fulfillment elsewhere, falling captive to the sexual immorality that Paul feared (cf. 1 Cor. 7.2–5).

A similar interruption of the rhetorical parallelism occurs at the end of 1 Corinthians 7. Here we find an instruction to widows without reference to male counterparts (1 Cor. 7.39–40; cf. 1 Cor. 7.8). As in many other societies, widows in Greco-Roman society could find themselves alone and destitute; the early church seems to have offered them support from the beginning (e.g. Acts 6.1; 1 Tim. 5.16). But it is also the case that these women could sometimes possess a relatively large amount of autonomy in society at large, especially if they were financially independent. This meant that they were in a position to make a substantial contribution to the leadership of early church communities as single women (cf. 1 Tim. 5.13–14).[7] It is evident that the initiative of widows (including their determination to remain unmarried even if widowed at a very young age) was perceived as highly problematic by the author of 1 Timothy, writing about the beginning of the second century CE (1 Tim. 5.3–16). Decades earlier Paul indirectly acknowledged the resolve of these women by giving the impression that he expected to be contradicted on the basis of some claim to spiritual authority. Although it is not obvious in many English translations that eliminate 'also', a literal translation of the Greek text

---

5 Note that Paul is using the terms 'to separate' (χωρίζειν) and 'to divorce' (ἀφιέναι) interchangeably in 1 Cor. 7.10–16; see the discussion in Jerome Murphy-O'Connor, 'The Divorced Woman in 1 Cor 7.10–11', *JBL* 100 (1981), pp. 601–606 (605).

6 Murphy-O'Connor notes that the structure of Paul's argument indicates that the apostle may have had a particular case in mind. But Murphy-O'Connor believes that men were the main instigators of divorce here, arguing that, contrary to the usual reading, 1 Cor. 7.10b should be translated as 'the wife should not allow herself to be separated from her husband'; see 'The Divorced Woman', pp. 601–603. See the response to Murphy-O'Connor's hypothesis in O. Larry Yarbrough, *Not Like the Gentiles: Marriage Rules in the Letters of Paul* (Atlanta: Scholars Press, 1985), p. 111 n. 67.

7 Note that Augustan legislation encouraged widows and divorced women to remarry. But the legislation does not seem to have hampered the activity of wealthy widows who chose to remain in control of their affairs and were in fact praised for remaining faithful to the memory of their dead husbands; see S. Pomeroy, *Goddesses, Whores, Wives and Slaves: Women in Classical Antiquity* (New York: Schocken Books, 1975), pp. 149–50, 158, 161; J.P.V.D. Balsdon, *Roman Women: Their History and Habits* (London: Bodley Head, 1962), pp. 76–77, 89–90, 220–22; Jo Ann McNamara, *A New Song: Celibate Women in the First Three Centuries* (New York: The Haworth Press, Inc., 1983), p. 59.

reveals the anticipation of resistance: 'I think that I, too (κἀγώ), have the Spirit of God' (1 Cor. 7.40; cf. 7. 25).[8] Paul's response may well constitute a rejoinder to widows who insisted on remaining unmarried based on their experiences of the Spirit. Perhaps they sought to impose their view of holiness on widows who found celibate life unattractive or economically difficult. Paul could agree that a widow is happier if she remains as she is, but he acknowledged that this may not always be possible. His reaction to celibacy was positive, though somewhat cautious. He may have been dealing with some of the same issues encountered by the author of 1 Timothy, but he stopped short of laying down regulations dictating under what circumstances a woman might remain a widow in the early church.

Paul's use of the term παρθένος (virgin) throughout 1 Cor. 7.25–38 offers probably the strongest evidence for a special concern for the behavior of women in 1 Corinthians 7. Although there is nothing to indicate gender the first time the term is employed (1 Cor. 7.25), the other uses of παρθένος (1 Cor. 7.28, 34, 36–38) in the passage refer to women. The process of translation has in fact masked the significance of this terminology to a certain extent. Although the NRSV sought to rectify the situation, the RSV used three different English words for this Greek term: unmarried (v. 25), girl (vv. 28, 34), and betrothed (vv. 36–38).[9] It is evident that Paul intended his eschatological perspective to speak to the lives of men and women (1 Cor. 7.26–34), but the use of παρθένος in 1 Cor. 7.28, 34 and 36–38 implies that women's virginity was of special significance in Corinth and was also of particular concern to the apostle.

One of the most confusing features of 1 Cor. 7.25–38 is the ambiguous terminology Paul uses to address the unmarried. Here again there are interruptions in Paul's parallelism. For example, Paul speaks of the unmarried man (ὁ ἄγαμος) in 1 Cor. 7.32–33, but of both the unmarried woman and the virgin (ἡ γυνὴ ἄγαμος καὶ ἡ παρθένος) in 1 Cor. 7.34. It is impossible to be certain about what Paul means by these two categories. If he were trying to distinguish virgins from other unmarried women such as widows, one would have expected more specific terminology.[10] It may be that Paul was employing the category 'unmarried' to refer to women who did not qualify as either virgins or widows, such as women separated from their husbands (1 Cor. 7.10–11) or women abandoned by non-believing husbands (1 Cor. 7.12–16). Antoinette Clark Wire has argued that the puzzling terminology is intended to describe 'a cross-generational group that would provide mutual support among consecrated women'.[11] But once again, this proposal does not account for the lack of specific terminology. C.K. Barrett has offered the most convincing explanation. Paul appears to have clarified the term 'unmarried' to be sure that his audience was aware that he was addressing a specific issue. It is as if Paul was

8 C.K. Barrett, *A Commentary on the First Epistle to the Corinthians* (London: Adam & Charles Black, 1968), p. 186. See also H. Conzelmann, *1 Corinthians: A Commentary on the First Epistle to the Corinthians* (trans. James W. Leitch; Hermeneia; Philadelphia: Fortress Press, 1975), p. 136. Note that in contrast to many earlier translations, the NRSV includes the word 'too'.

9 Note that the only use of παρθένος to refer to male virgins in the literature of the first century appears to be Rev. 14.4.

10 See Barrett, *1 Corinthians*, pp. 180–81 for consideration of possible meanings.

11 Wire, *Women Prophets*, p. 92.

saying: 'By "unmarried", yes I mean the virgins, those who strive to be holy in body and spirit' (1 Cor. 7.34).[12]

It is important to note that in 1 Cor. 7.32–34 Paul's parallelism is interrupted not only by the unusual terminology used to describe unmarried women, but also by the description of the 'anxiety' (μεριμνάω) that characterizes their lives. In Paul's balancing of references to married and unmarried men and women, the anxiety involves a kind of 'pleasing' (ἀρέσκω) in all but the instruction to unmarried women. This is probably a sign that a more specific problem comes to mind when he discusses unmarried women. Instead of stating that the unmarried woman or virgin is anxious about the affairs of the Lord and how to please the Lord, Paul states that she is anxious about the affairs of the Lord and how to be holy in body and spirit (1 Cor. 7.34). 1 Cor. 7.32–34 is often read as Paul contrasting marriage, characterized by worldly anxiety, with unmarried life, characterized by a positive kind of anxiety—anxiety to please only the Lord. However, what is said about the unmarried woman or virgin makes it much more probable that Paul is arguing that anxiety to please the Lord can actually stand in the way of devotion to the Lord.[13] Since elsewhere in Paul's letters holiness is an attribute of the married state (e.g. 1 Thess. 4.14; 1 Cor. 7.14), it is unlikely here that Paul seeks to contrast the holiness of the unmarried woman with the worldliness of the married woman.[14] As Barrett has noted, it seems that 'she may be holy in body and spirit' are words quoted from the Corinthian ascetic party.[15] In light of the extremist tendencies of some members of the Corinthian congregation, it is likely that Paul is worried that those who seek to live a celibate life, and who are not thus gifted, might be so anxious in their efforts that they will become distracted from their devotion to the Lord and might even fall prey to immorality. In other words, while married life can be subject to anxiety, there is an anxiety that comes from striving to be holy through compulsory celibacy. Members of the community have lost their true focus on the Lord in their efforts to shed all of the marks of earthly imperfection, including sexuality.

1 Cor. 7.36–38 offers further evidence that the category 'virgin' was popular in Corinth and was causing the apostle concern. Here Paul offers instructions to the man who feels he is not behaving properly towards his 'virgin' and advises marriage 'if it has to be'. But scholars have long puzzled over the nature of the relationship between the man and the woman. Some argue that the text refers to 'spiritual marriages' (i.e. couples living together without physical union). However, we have no evidence outside of 1 Corinthians for this phenomenon in this early period, and it is difficult to harmonize such an interpretation with 1 Cor. 7.2–5 where Paul rejects perpetual celibacy within marriage. More likely, the relationship is between a father and a daughter, or between an engaged couple.[16] Favoring the latter interpretation, Barrett

---

12 Barrett, *1 Corinthians*, p. 180.
13 See the discussion in Barrett, *1 Corinthians*, p. 179.
14 On holiness in the Christian community, see Barrett, *1 Corinthians*, p. 181.
15 Barrett, *1 Corinthians*, p. 181.
16 Note, however, that it is sometimes argued by scholars who favor the 'spiritual marriage' interpretation that 1 Cor. 7.36–38 refers to cohabitation in marriages which have never been consummated. Some have also understood Paul's reference to a 'sister wife' in 1 Cor. 9.5 as a reference to a spiritual marriage. On the history of interpretation of 1 Cor. 7.36–38 and the notoriously difficult problems of interpretation see discussions in Wire, *Women Prophets*, pp. 224–25; Conzelmann,

suggests the following about the convictions of Paul's ascetic opponents: 'perhaps it is significant of their point of view that a fiancée should be described as a virgin—the implication being that this is the important thing about her and that she would do well to remain as she is'.[17]

Although the parallelism of the text is never interrupted and no special categories are used to describe women, 1 Cor. 7.12–16 should nevertheless also be considered briefly to uncover what lies behind the balancing of references to men and women in 1 Corinthians 7.[18] It must be admitted that because Paul offers no direct evidence that he primarily has women in view in 1 Cor. 7.12–16, our conclusions must remain highly tentative. However, there is a good deal of external evidence suggesting that the treatment of marriage between believers and non-believers in this text masks problems that largely affected the women of the community. First, it should be noted that in recommending that such marriages (including those between believing women and non-believing men) be preserved if possible, Paul was in fact sanctioning a type of marital infidelity within the context of Greco-Roman society. A Greco-Roman wife's faithfulness to her husband included faithfulness to his gods. The wife and the children were expected to share in the religion of the household.[19] The influence of this norm can actually be detected in the conversion patterns of early church groups. There are various accounts of male believers and their households entering church groups (e.g. Acts 16.32–33; 18.8; 1 Cor. 1.16). Given the social arrangements of Greco-Roman society, one would expect wives to have shared their husbands' Christian allegiances from the outset. Despite Paul's parallelism, it is difficult to believe that many of the 'mixed' marriages involved believing men and non-believing women. We do know, however, that women entered church communities without their partners despite cultural expectations to the contrary. An extensive body of later evidence, including 1 Pet. 3.1–6, refers almost exclusively to believing women involved in such arrangements.[20] We also know that sometimes early Christian women tried to extricate themselves from marriages to non-believers. The second-century apologist Justin Martyr tells the tale of a church woman who initiated a divorce against her husband after previous attempts to preserve the union. Her motives are described in a manner that recalls the efforts of the unmarried women of 1 Corinthians 7 who strove to be holy in body and spirit (1 Cor. 7.34). She no longer wished 'to

---

Corinthians, pp. 134–36; J.C. Hurd, *The Origin of 1 Corinthians* (London: SPCK, 1965), pp. 169–75; J.D.M. Derrett, 'The Disposal of Virgins', in *idem, Studies in the New Testament: Glimpses of the Legal and Social Presuppositions of the Authors* (Leiden: E.J. Brill, 1977), pp. 184–91. On 'spiritual marriages' see also Elizabeth Castelli, 'Virginity and its Meaning for Women's Sexuality in Early Christianity', *JFSR* 2 (1986), pp. 61–88.

17 Barrett, *1 Corinthians*, p. 185.

18 See full discussion of this text in Margaret Y. MacDonald, *Early Christian Women and Pagan Opinion: The Power of the Hysterical Woman* (Cambridge: Cambridge University Press, 1996), pp. 189–95.

19 See for example Plutarch, *Moralia* 140D (trans. F.C. Babbitt; 16 vols.; LCL; Cambridge, MA: Harvard University Press, 1927–69). See M.Y. MacDonald, *Early Christian Women*, pp. 49–126.

20 See Margaret Y. MacDonald, 'Early Christian Women Married to Unbelievers', *Studies in Religion* 19.2 (1990), pp. 221–34, reprinted in Amy-Jill Levine (ed.), *A Feminist Companion to the Deutero-Pauline Epistles* (London: T. & T Clark, 2003), pp. 14–28.

participate in his sinful and impious acts by continuing to live with him by sharing his table and his bed'.[21]

Paul provides us with no specific information about the circumstances that led to his instructions concerning marriage between believers and non-believers in 1 Cor. 7.12–16. But that there were serious problems with such households is beyond a doubt. Paul reassures believers that in the case where the non-believer is no longer willing to live with the believer, 'the brother or sister is not bound'. A veiled reference to conflict is probably contained in the phrase, 'God has called you to peace!' (1 Cor. 7.15). Women may have been seeking to guarantee their own sanctity by avoiding sex with a non-believing partner or even by separating themselves from their partners altogether (cf. 1 Cor. 7.10–11). On the other hand, they frequently may have been abandoned by non-believing mates. Read from the perspective of church women, 1 Cor. 7.12–16 offers insight both into the initiative of women, and into the suffering they probably endured.

Thus, behind the parallelism of 1 Corinthians 7 lie many indications of women's initiative and of a special concern on the part of Paul and the Corinthian community for the behavior of women. This comes as somewhat of a surprise since the impression given by the Corinthian slogan quoted at the beginning of Paul's discussion is one of male initiative: 'It is well for a man not to touch a woman' (1 Cor. 7.1). Yet, one would expect an acknowledgment of male prerogatives in this first-century setting even if the ascetic impulse came mainly from women. The celibate efforts of these traditionally subordinate members would most likely require the blessing of males if the community was to continue as a mixed group. Certainly Paul acknowledges the authority of men in marriage arrangements throughout 1 Corinthians 7 (e.g. 1 Cor. 7.28, 36).[22]

The Corinthian slogan quoted in 1 Cor. 7.1 actually reflects the Mediterranean values of honor and shame. The man's honor is tied to the active protection of the woman's chastity. The male members of the community understand their own holiness as fundamentally related to the preservation of the sexual purity of females.[23] Paul qualifies the Corinthian slogan in order to respond to the ascetic extremism that took root in Corinth, but his teaching also reflects traditional Mediterranean values. For example, if the 'engaged couple' translation of 1 Cor. 7.36–38 is preferred, Paul may be describing a man's hesitancy to take as his wife a woman who reminds him that she is doing far more for his sanctity by remaining his virgin than by becoming his bride. But in response to this hesitancy, Paul warns that if there is danger that the man will 'shame his virgin'—violate her virtue—he then is free to marry (1 Cor. 7.36). In Paul's view, sexual immorality must be avoided at all costs. If a man is to marry, he should take a wife in holiness and honor, not in the passion of lust like the pagans who do not know God (1 Thess. 4.4).

---

21 Justin, *Second Apology* 2, in Thomas Falls (trans.), *Saint Justin Martyr* (FC, 6; Washington: Catholic University of America Press, 1948). See discussion in M.Y. MacDonald, *Early Christian Women*, pp. 205–12.

22 See Barrett, *1 Corinthians*, p. 176; Wire, *Women Prophets*, pp. 88–89.

23 See the anthropological discussion by J. Pitt-Rivers, 'Honour and Social Status', in J.G. Peristany (ed.), *Honour and Shame: The Values of Mediterranean Society* (London: Weidenfeld & Nicolson, 1965), p. 45; see also the discussion in B. Malina, *New Testament World* (London: SCM Press, 1983), pp. 42–48. On the Corinthian slogan see n. 26 below.

Asceticism in Corinth

The problems of interpreting 1 Corinthians 7 are compounded by the presence of contradictory attitudes towards sexuality in Corinth.[24] On the one hand there was libertinism (1 Corinthians 5–6). As illustrated perhaps most dramatically by the incest case described in 1 Corinthians 5, it seems that the Corinthians' new-found freedom in Christ (cf. 1 Cor. 4.8; 15.12) was leading some to the conviction that all things were permissible with respect to sex. On the other hand there was asceticism. Some Corinthians felt that their transcendence of the material world was best lived out in complete abstinence from sex—both the avoidance of intercourse within marriage and the rejection of marriage altogether (1 Cor. 7.1–9).[25] There is a growing consensus that the words, 'It is well for a man not to touch a woman' do not reflect Paul's opinion, but are a quotation from the Corinthians' letter to Paul.[26] In 1 Corinthians 7, Paul offers a qualified endorsement of celibacy that is intended to respond to the more extreme ascetic tendencies of some members of the congregation.

Whatever the precise historical relationship between the two contradictory attitudes towards sexuality in Corinth, it is clear that Paul regarded them as two sides of the same coin. They both triggered the same reaction in him. Fear of immorality (πορνεία) frames his discussion from the mention of the incest case in 1 Cor. 5.1 to his instructions concerning what a man should do with his virgin in 1 Cor. 7.36–38. It is because of the temptation of immorality that marriage should take place among those who do not possess the gift of celibacy and that physical union must remain an integral part of the couple's life (1 Cor. 7.1–7, 9). Modern readers have often been disheartened by Paul's presentation of marriage as a means of 'containing' passions. The chasm between marriage and celibacy as the preferred option has seemed impossibly wide. But it is helpful to keep in mind that while we tend to read 1 Corinthians 7 as setting forth a dramatic contrast between marriage and celibacy—a contrast that continues to have significant meaning in our own time—Paul's main interests are somewhat different. For him, the more important opposition seems to have been between celibacy/marriage and immorality. Celibacy might allow for a more perfect representation of the freedom of the eschaton, but marriage is also good, and for some, because of the temptation to immorality, it is the only desirable choice.

While he describes no specific case of abstinence leading to indulgence in 1 Corinthians 7, Paul seems to have feared that the rigid asceticism of some Corinthians could lead to disaster—precisely the kind of immoral behavior they may well have sought to avoid in the first place. Paul's reaction to the incest case gives us a sense of what was at stake if immorality penetrated the boundaries of the

24 Scholars are divided with respect to the exact nature of the problems in Corinth. For example, compare the hypothesis of W. Schmithals who believes the main problem involved a libertine attitude (*Gnosticism in Corinth* [Nashville: Abingdon Press, 1971], p. 234) with that of Yarbrough who believes that 'ascetic' elitism was the main issue (*Not Like the Gentiles*, pp. 124–25).
25 See Hurd, *1 Corinthians*, pp. 155–57.
26 See Jouette M. Bassler, '1 Corinthians', in Carol A. Newsom and Sharon H. Ringe (eds), *The Women's Bible Commentary* (Louisville, KY: Westminster/John Knox, 1992, pp. 321–29[323]). See also D.R. MacDonald, *No Male and Female*, pp. 69–72, esp. p. 70. For a summary of the debate see R. Scroggs, 'Paul and the Eschatological Woman', *JAAR* 40 (1972), pp. 295–96. Note that 'to touch a woman' is a euphemism for sexual intercourse; see Hurd, *1 Corinthians*, p. 158.

community: 'Such immorality is not even found among the Gentiles!' (1 Cor. 5.1). Paul uses the standards of the outside world as a basis for comparison in order to make his point about the laxity of the Corinthians. One gets the impression that community boundaries have been compromised. The threat of immorality looms over Corinth. Paul's teaching on marriage and celibacy in 1 Corinthians 7 is designed to prevent any further defiling of the holy community and perhaps also to guard against expressions of disrespect on the part of outsiders.[27] It is interesting to note that similar concerns seem to have shaped the response to widows given by the author of the Pastoral Epistles (1 Tim. 5.3–16). Writing in Paul's name at about the beginning of the second century, this author spoke to a community where an office of widows was in place (1 Tim 5.9–11). The author's efforts to restrict membership in this office to older women is an indication of the seriousness of the problem. The references to violation of the celibacy pledge and straying after Satan suggest that the author was convinced immorality and apostasy were occurring, even though the women themselves may have understood their actions quite differently (1 Tim. 5.11–15). Like Paul, the author of 1 Timothy kept his eye on the outside world. The author was convinced that the activity of these women resulted in the slander of the community's good repute (1 Tim. 5.14). They had apparently become attracted to ascetic teaching (2 Tim. 3.6) that included a command to abstain from marriage (1 Tim. 4.3). Moreover, as in the Corinthian letter, we find evidence that ascetic tendencies were probably related to the belief that one had already transcended the boundaries of the material world; the false teachers proclaimed that the resurrection had already happened (2 Tim. 2.18; cf. 1 Cor. 4.8; 1 Cor. 15.12).[28]

Given the differing contexts, a straightforward correlation between the Corinthian situation and the situation in the community of the Pastorals cannot be drawn. However, the above analysis makes it clear that 1 Corinthians 7 reflects women's initiative and attraction to strongly ascetic teaching, anticipating the later situation of the Pastorals. Widows, who are also instructed in 1 Cor. 7.39–40 (without reference to male counterparts), had become a source of serious concern for the author of the Pastorals. Comparison of 1 Corinthians 7 to 1 Tim. 5.3–16 alerts us to possible motives for Paul's response. In particular, we have been alerted to the need to attend to community values and priorities concerning relations between the church and the outside world. Before turning to a detailed analysis of Paul's response in 1 Corinthians 7 and its consequences for the lives of women, however, it is important to consider the scholarly discussion concerning the roots of the Corinthian asceticism and to explore possible correlations between the initiative of women we have uncovered in 1 Corinthians 7 and the text where female initiative emerges most boldly in the epistle: 1 Cor. 11.2–16.

1 Cor. 11.2–16 has figured prominently in investigations of women in Corinth.[29] Moreover, the fact that in contrast to Gal. 3.28, Paul omitted the male/female pair

27 That Paul's instructions on marriage and sexual morality reveal an interest in the relationship between church communities and the outside world is suggested by 1 Thess. 4.3b–5. Yarbrough has noted the similarity between Paul's language and Jewish paraenesis which served to distinguish the community of the Diaspora from the outside world. See *Not Like the Gentiles*, pp. 86–87.

28 On the widows of 1 Timothy see Dennis R. MacDonald, *The Legend and the Apostle: The Battle for Paul in Story and Canon* (Philadelphia: Westminster Press, 1983).

29 On this notoriously complicated text see the groundbreaking work of Elisabeth Schüssler Fiorenza, *In Memory of Her: A Feminist Theological Reconstruction of Christian Origins* (London:

when he spoke of unity in Christ with reference to Gentiles/Jews and slaves/free in 1 Cor. 12.13 has sparked considerable debate. The omission may have been deliberate on the apostle's part, given his knowledge of the situation in the community. Perhaps Paul had previously told the Corinthians that in Christ 'there is no longer male and female' and they had sought to put this message into practice by eliminating the distinction between the sexes.[30] A second link with Gal. 3.28 is suggested by the very structure of 1 Corinthians 7. In 1 Cor. 7.17–28 Paul follows a discussion of the social divisions of circumcision/uncircumcision (vv. 17–19) and slave/free (vv. 21–23) with consideration of the desirability of marriage (vv. 25–28).[31] Although it is impossible to arrive at firm conclusions about the relationship between Gal. 3.28 and the activity of the Corinthian women, it is most often to this relationship that scholars turn when discussing the origin of the theology that inspired them.[32] *There Is No Male and Female* by D.R. MacDonald, a work on the background of Gal 3.26–28 and its significance for understanding 1 Corinthians, proves to be especially valuable. Although MacDonald does not undertake a thorough analysis of 1 Corinthians 7 (he concentrates instead on 1 Cor. 11.2–16), his study is especially suggestive for uncovering what inspired the initiative of the women behind the parallelism of 1 Corinthians 7.[33]

MacDonald believes that Gal. 3.27–28 originated in the saying of Jesus recorded in the *Gospel of the Egyptians*: 'When you tread upon the garment of shame and when the two are one and the male with the female neither male nor female' (Clement of Alexandria, *Strom.* 3.13.92, and found in similar versions in *2 Clem.* 12.2 and *Gos. Thom.* 37, 21a, 22b).[34] Both the *Gospel of the Egyptians* and Gal. 3.27–28 contain garment imagery ('putting on Christ'—Gal. 3.27), speak of unification, and mention the pair of opposites male/female. After a careful study of the occurrences of the saying, MacDonald offers the following explanation: 'When you tread upon the garment of shame' calls for trampling on the body in order that the believer might achieve perfection. 'When the two are one' refers to the reunification of the sexes, the return to the perfection of the androgyne. Finally, 'the male with the

---

SCM Press, 1983), pp. 226–33. For a very thorough recent investigation of this text see Wire, *Women Prophets*, pp. 116–34. See also Ross S. Kraemer, *Her Share of the Blessings: Women's Religions among Pagans, Jews, and Christians in the Greco-Roman World* (Oxford: Oxford University Press, 1992), pp. 146–49. Discussions of women in Corinth sometimes also focus on 1 Cor. 14.34–35. But many scholars believe that these verses represent a marginal gloss, perhaps intended to harmonize Paul's teaching with 1 Tim. 2.11–12. See discussion in Bassler, '1 Corinthians', pp. 327–8 and Wire, *Women Prophets*, pp. 149–52.

30 See J.P. Meier, 'On the Veiling of Hermeneutics (1 Cor. 11.2–16)', *CBQ* 40 (1978), pp. 212–26 (217).

31 On the relationship between Gal. 3.28 and 1 Cor. 7.17–28 see S.S. Bartchy, *Mallon Chresai: First Century Slavery and the Interpretation of 1 Cor. 7.21* (SBLDS, 11; Missoula, MT; Scholars Press, 1973), p. 174.

32 For a summary of the literature linking the situation in Corinth with Gal. 3.28 see D.R. MacDonald, *No Male and Female*, pp. 87–88 n. 75.

33 See especially D.R. MacDonald, *No Male and Female*, pp. 65–111.

34 See D.R. MacDonald, *No Male and Female*, pp. 17–21. Note that the *Gospel of the Egyptians* here should not be confused with its namesake from Nag Hammadi. Note also that MacDonald argues that the relationship between these versions is oral not literary; see p. 21. See also MacDonald's arguments in favour of the Dominical Saying being more primitive than Gal. 3.27–28, pp. 114–26.

female neither male nor female' constitutes a description of the consequence of the reunification—abstinence from sexual relations.[35] A study of the circles he identifies with the saying, Valentinian Gnosticism and early Syrian Christianity, leads MacDonald to conclude that the saying was rooted in a baptismal setting.[36]

MacDonald argues that Paul was aware of the saying that later became recorded in the *Gospel of the Egyptians* or a very similar saying but disagreed with the anthropology and soteriology it presupposed.[37] For Paul, the putting on of Christ at baptism did not mean bodily escape and return to androgynous perfection. The notion of being 'in Christ' that runs throughout Gal. 3.26–28 tied the experience of faith to the creation of a new community. 'There is no longer male and female' referred to the ideal of social unification—membership in Christ's body where antagonisms were eliminated. The church was a new entity where alienated social groups— Jews/Greeks, slaves/free, and men/women—could come together.[38]

The relationship between Paul's proclamation 'there is no longer male and female' and the saying of Jesus recorded in the *Gospel of the Egyptians*, coupled with the links between Gal. 3.28 and the text of 1 Corinthians described above, leads MacDonald to ask: Did a theology similar to that implied by the saying of Jesus inspire the Corinthians? 1 Cor. 11.2–16 offers evidence that this may well have been the case. It seems that during ecstatic worship, pneumatic Corinthian women believed that they had transcended sexual differentiation.[39] These women acted out their status by becoming like men: they removed their veils—symbols of the inferiority and subordination that characterized their day-to-day living.[40] Indeed, when they did return to their daily lives, one would expect that they would symbolize their new status by means of celibacy. The link between the notion of salvation as a return to androgynous perfection and abstinence from sexual relations implied by the saying of Jesus is reinforced by other passages in the sources where it is cited. For example, the *Gospel of the Egyptians* contains the following question and answer: 'Salome said, "How long will people die?" Jesus answered, "As long as women bear children"' (Clement, *Strom.* 3.9.64). Similarly, the following passage might be interpreted as a plea for sexual asceticism: 'Jesus said, "I have come to destroy the works of the female"' (Clement, *Strom.* 3.9.63).[41] MacDonald understands the activity of

---

35 D.R. MacDonald, *No Male and Female*, p. 50; MacDonald traces the long history of the images of putting off garments and of making the two one in anthropological discussions among Greek philosophers. He argues: 'It is within the context of this philosophical tradition and its religious permutations in hellenized Judaism and Gnosticism that we should interpret the imagery of the Dominical Saying' (p. 25).

36 See D.R. MacDonald, *No Male and Female*, pp. 50–63. On the relation between baptism and asceticism in the early church see A. Vööbus, *Celibacy: A Requirement for Admission to Baptism in the Early Syrian Church* (Stockholm: Papers of the Estonian Theological Society in Exile, 1951) and R. Murray, 'The Exhortation to Candidates for Ascetic Vows at Baptism in the Ancient Syriac Church', *NTS* 21 (1974), pp. 59–80.

37 D.R. MacDonald, *No Male and Female*, pp. 113–26.

38 D.R. MacDonald, *No Male and Female*, pp. 119–26, esp. pp. 121, 126.

39 The exact nature of the problem addressed in this passage has long been debated. See the discussion of the various possibilities in D.R. MacDonald, *No Male and Female*, pp. 81–91.

40 D.R. MacDonald, *No Male and Female*, pp. 72–98; see pp. 108–109.

41 D.R. MacDonald, *No Male and Female*, pp. 30–31. See also *Gos. Thom.* 37, 49, 75, 79, 104, 112, 114; *2 Clem.* 12.5. On sexual asceticism in the *Gospel of Thomas* see for example the

the Corinthian women as one of many examples from antiquity of women imitating the male appearance in an effort to become androgynous.[42] Paul responded to their efforts (which seem to have included some devaluation of what is particularly female) by speaking of the indispensability of women as women (1 Cor. 11.11–12), but also by reinforcing the subordinate status of women in the community on the basis of his understanding of Genesis.[43]

It is impossible to know for certain whether the saying of Jesus recorded in the *Gospel of the Egyptians* or something like it was known by the Corinthians. But the content of 1 Corinthians 7 actually supports MacDonald's theories. 1 Corinthians 7 reveals a remarkable interest in the sayings of Jesus with respect to sexuality, and so implies that the Corinthians were using such sayings to support their position (1 Cor. 7.10, 12, 25).[44] In fact, the synoptic tradition includes sayings that might justify a radically ascetic attitude (e.g. Lk. 14.26; 17.26–27; 18.29–30; 20.34–35). On the basis of MacDonald's work, it seems reasonable to conclude that the women who removed their veils mentioned in 1 Corinthians 11 may well also have been of primary concern in 1 Corinthians 7.[45] But if this is case, why does Paul himself not link celibacy with women baring their heads? Paul's independent treatment of the two issues was probably related to the difficulty of his own position. He wished to offer qualified approval of celibacy but to reject the idea of women removing their veils categorically. From 1 Corinthians 7 it is clear that Paul cherished the gift of celibacy if it was exercised by the truly gifted. Therefore, he was convinced of the need to break the link between celibacy and a theology with which he fundamentally disagreed. He sought to do this by rooting his discussion of marriage in his own eschatological position—a theology suited to a world on the verge of transformation, but that was still very much capable of inducing troubles in community life.

In order to shed light upon the origins of asceticism in Corinth, one final aspect of the social setting of church life needs to be considered: the link between continence and the ritual context of 1 Cor. 11.2–16, for the removal of the head covering of the Corinthian women took place while the community gathered for prayer and prophecy (1 Cor. 11.4–5). Social scientists have stressed that ritual is extremely important for the development of a religious worldview. Clifford Geertz, for example, argues that for the participant in a religious performance the ritual becomes both a model of what is believed and a model for believing it.[46] In a manner

discussion of the contrast between logion 79 and Lk. 11.27–28; 23.29 in J.É. Ménard, *L'Évangile selon Thomas* (NHS, 5; Leiden: E.J. Brill, 1975), pp. 180–81. On the similarities between the *Gospel of the Egyptians* and the *Gospel of Thomas* see D.R. MacDonald, *No Male and Female*, p. 49 n. 105. On asceticism in *2 Clement* see D.R. MacDonald, *No Male and Female*, pp. 41–43.

42 D.R. MacDonald, *No Male and Female*, pp. 98–102.

43 D.R. MacDonald, *No Male and Female*, pp. 108–10.

44 For an excellent treatment of the relationship between 1 Corinthians 7 and the sayings of Jesus congenial to asceticism in the Synoptics see D.L. Balch, 'Backgrounds of 1 Cor VII: Sayings of the Lord in Q; Moses as an Ascetic ΘΕΙΟΣ ΑΝΗΡ in II Cor III', *NTS* 18 (1972), pp. 351–58.

45 D.R. MacDonald's hypothesis that the theology of the saying of Jesus recorded in the *Gospel of the Egyptians* inspired the Corinthian 'pneumatics' allows for a direct connection to be made between Paul's response to the problems involving women in 1 Corinthians 11 and his comments against obligatory celibacy in 1 Corinthians 7. In fact, MacDonald identifies such a connection, but does not discuss it in detail; see *No Male and Female*, esp. pp. 69–72, 110.

46 See C. Geertz, 'Religion as a Cultural System', in M. Banton (ed.), *Anthropological Approaches to the Study of Religion* (London: Tavistock, 1966), pp. 1–46, esp. p. 29.

that recalled the momentous event of their baptism, the Corinthian women who removed their veils were probably simultaneously experiencing and expressing their relationship with the Divine, their transformation into a new perfect creation.[47] Ritual is 'consecrated behavior' taking place during times set apart from the regular course of events. Eventually women's ritual performance would have come to an end, and they would have needed to function in the everyday world once more. They may have been willing to cover their heads again, but they nevertheless had been profoundly transformed.[48] Their new status was visible to themselves, to other church members, and even to outsiders as it was reflected in their continence. As will be explored further in the next section, this visibility played a central role in Paul's response to the Corinthian women.

In an effort to situate 1 Corinthians 7 within the broader context of Paul's world, Richard Horsley draws attention to the connection between celibacy and ecstatic experiences of worship in Philo's description of the ascetic sect, the Therapeutae.[49] The devotion of the Therapeutae culminates in a vision of the Divine (*Vit. Cont.* 12). Philo describes their 'sacred vigil', involving the fusion of a male choir with a female choir. The ecstatic worship of the Corinthians comes to mind:

> ... they sing hymns to God composed of many measures and set to many melodies, sometimes chanting together, sometimes taking up the harmony antiphonally, hands and feet keeping time in accompaniment, and rapt with enthusiasm reproduce sometimes the lyrics of the procession, sometimes of the halt and of the wheeling and counter-wheeling of a choric dance. Then when each choir has separately done its own part in the feast, having drunk as in the Bacchic rites of the strong wine of God's love they mix and both together become a single choir, a copy of the choir set up of old beside the Red Sea in honour of the wonders there wrought (*Vit. Cont.* 84–85).

The group that comes together to form a single unified choir follows a strict ascetic way of life in keeping with a dualistic vision of the world (*Vit. Cont.* 34–37). Choosing this contemplative identity means that homes and, at times, even spouses must be left behind (*Vit. Cont.* 13, 18). With respect to their suitability as celibates, it is striking that Philo shares none of Paul's worry about the danger of some lacking the required self-control. Particularly relevant for the present discussion is that when Philo speaks of sexual asceticism, his attention turns especially to the admirable behavior of women:

---

47 On the relationship between baptism and 'pneumatic' activities in Corinth see D.R. MacDonald, *No Male and Female*, pp. 67–69.

48 See Geertz, 'Religion', p. 38.

49 See R.A. Horsley, 'Spiritual Marriage with Sophia', *VC* 33 (1979), pp. 40–43; see Philo, *De Vita Contemplativa* (trans. F.H. Colson; 10 vols.; LCL; Cambridge, MA: Harvard University Press, 1929–62). A connection between asceticism and spiritual experiences is also discussed by Horsley in relation to Philo's description of Moses (*Vit. Mos.* 2.66–70), the Wisdom of Solomon, and devotion to Isis; see pp. 33–34; 43–46. For an excellent discussion of this group see also Kraemer, *Her Share of the Blessings*, pp. 113–17. See also Ross S. Kraemer, 'Monastic Jewish Women in Greco-Roman Egypt: Philo on the Therapeutrides', *Signs: A Journal of Women in Culture and Society* 14.1 (1989), pp. 342–70.

The feast is shared by women also, most of them aged virgins, who have their chastity not under compulsion, like some of the Greek priestesses, but of their own free will in their ardent yearning for wisdom. Eager to have her for their life mate they have spurned the pleasures of the body and desire no mortal offspring but those immortal children which only the soul that is dear to God can bring to the birth unaided because the Father has sown in her spiritual rays enabling her to behold the verities of wisdom (*Vit. Cont.* 68).

Similarly, when Galen of Pergamum described a Christian group in the second century CE, he spoke of them as having attained 'a pitch not inferior to that of genuine philosophers' and drew attention to the presence of women.[50] Both descriptions come as a reminder that the asceticism of women in antiquity could be greatly admired under certain circumstances.

The Corinthian 'ascetics' are clearly not identical to either the Philo-like mystics or the gnostics of the second and third centuries. But drawing upon Jewish sources, gnostic texts, and early Christian writings for comparison can provide much valuable material for understanding the religious mentality of those who championed the slogan, 'It is well not to touch a woman.'[51] As in the case of the Therapeutae, the asceticism of the Corinthians was probably related to their ecstatic experiences in the midst of worship. However, both their sexual ethics and their ritual behavior were shaped by, and indeed helped to shape, a theology that may well have included the saying of Jesus recorded in the *Gospel of the Egyptians*.[52] In Corinth Paul seems to have encountered the conviction that believers have transcended the material world (1 Cor. 4.8; 15.12). Perhaps they understood their rising with Christ at baptism as a return to primordial perfection (1 Cor. 1.21–2.16; 3.18–23) which included a new sexless state (1 Cor. 11.2–16). Worshiping women were inspired to symbolize their new status by removing their veils. With the ritual ended, they looked for a way to concretize the profound transformation they had experienced. Convinced that 'the male was now with the female', they set out to avoid sex altogether.[53]

Commentators have often described the belief system of Paul's opponents in 1 Corinthians as one of 'realized eschatology'.[54] Having studied the doctrine of the androgyne, Mircea Eliade argued that symbols depicting the abolition of opposites and conflicts are eschatological symbols par excellence. They denote '... that the "profane" Universe has been mysteriously replaced ... by a World purely spiritual in nature'.[55] The reunification of opposites could indeed serve as a most effective

50 See Richard Walzer, *Galen on Jews and Christians* (London: Oxford University Press, 1949), p. 15. For a full discussion of the significance of Galen's reference to early Christian women and its relationship to Philo's description of monastic Jewish women see M.Y. MacDonald, *Early Christian Women*, pp. 82–94.

51 See D.R. MacDonald, *No Male and Female*, pp. 65–66.

52 On the dialectical relationship between human thought and the social context in which it arises see the valuable treatise on the sociology of knowledge by P.L. Berger and T. Luckmann, *The Social Construction of Reality* (Garden City, NY: Doubleday, 1967).

53 See D.R. MacDonald, *No Male and Female*, p. 60. But note that spiritual transcendence for some in Corinth seems to have meant freedom to perform any sexual act (1 Cor 5.2; 6.12). See pp. 69–70.

54 See, for example, Meeks, 'Image of the Androgyne', pp. 202–203.

55 M. Eliade, *Mephistopheles and the Androgyne* (New York: Sheed & Ward, 1965), p. 121.

way for Paul to legitimate the new pattern of relating between Gentiles and Jews in this new age (Gal. 3.28). But Paul's opponents in Corinth seem to have pushed his thought one step further. Some seem to have been convinced that the old universe had already been replaced by a world purely spiritual in nature and that celibacy was vital to the spiritual perfection of the entire community. Paul responded with powerful eschatological language (e.g. 1 Cor. 7.26–31). The apostle was convinced that the world was on the brink of transformation and that the celibacy of men and women was a sign of the transformation. But for Paul the conditions of the old world were still binding to a certain extent—the kingdom was not as yet perfectly realized. Immorality was an ever-present danger, and community members could still lose control.

Paul's Response: Stability and Honor

Paul's desire to encourage a sense of eschatological reservation within the Corinthian community—a sense of 'not yet'—is often noted by commentators. It can be seen most clearly in his statements designed to reduce the anxiety of community members and to ensure that they behave in a seemly fashion.[56] As noted earlier in this chapter, Paul saw both celibate and married life as possible sources of negative anxiety. This is supported by his statement in 1 Cor. 7.35.[57] Here Paul states that he does not wish to impose an arbitrary rule upon the Corinthians about marriage and celibacy; he places the onus upon them to do what is expedient in relation to their own circumstances and gifts.[58] It would be difficult to avoid the conclusion that Paul was indeed creating a rule if 1 Cor. 7.32–34 were read as proclaiming celibacy conducive to pleasing the Lord and condemning marriage as inevitably worldly. Were this what Paul meant, he would be lending support to the argument of those Corinthians who viewed sexual asceticism as essential for all believers. However, it appears more likely that Paul warned community members of the anxiety that could dominate both married and celibate life.

Not only does 1 Cor. 7.35 express Paul's reluctance to constrain the Corinthians, but it also communicates the intention of his exhortation in 7.32–35, and perhaps also of his teaching throughout the chapter. Paul wishes to promote seemliness (or good order) and desires that the Corinthians wait upon the Lord without hindrance. 'Seemliness' (εὐσχήμων) might strike the modern reader as a mundane priority, rather in sharp contrast to the call for 'undivided devotion to the Lord'. A concern for propriety and social respectability is implied. An echo of this concern is also found in 1 Cor. 7.36 where a cognate of εὐσχήμων appears (cf. 1 Thess. 4.12; 1 Cor. 14.40). Paul gives instructions about one who feels he is not behaving honorably (ἀσχημονεῖν) towards his virgin (ἐπὶ τὴν παρθένον αὐτοῦ) and goes on to advise

56 On eschatological reservation see D.R. Cartlidge, '1 Corinthians 7 as a Foundation for a Christian Sex Ethic', *JR* 55 (1975), pp. 220–34.
57 On the similarities between Paul's position and the thought of his day see Balch, '1 Cor 7.32–35 and Stoic Debates', pp. 429–39 (436–37).
58 Note, however, that with respect to new marriages, it appears that Paul believed that they should take place among members of the church. This is implied by his instruction that remarriage was acceptable for widows, but only 'in the Lord' (1 Cor. 7.39). See Malina, *New Testament World*, pp. 115–16.

that a marriage should take place 'if it has to be'. Reflecting the Mediterranean values of honor and shame, Paul is actually referring to the risk of 'shaming' one's virgin in 1 Cor. 7.26. An understanding of these values can help explain why 'seemliness' is such a priority both at the level of the whole community and at the level of particular interactions between believers.

'Seemliness' is a term used to confer honor—the public acknowledgment of worth. Public recognition of reputation is a central means of establishing identity in the ancient Mediterranean world. In the concrete interactions between men and women, honor is seen most often as embodied by males, and shame (in a positive sense, as concern for reputation) as embodied by females. Men become the defenders of women's chastity.[59] Similar 'honor/shame' language occurs in 1 Cor. 12.23–24 where Paul is aiming to inspire the proper attitude towards charismatic gifts and calling for relations between community members that reflect the harmonious workings of the physical body. According to Paul, dishonorable (ἀτιμότερα) parts require an investment of greater honor (τιμή) and unseemly parts (ἀσχήμων) need to be treated with a seemliness (εὐσχημοσύνη) which the more seemly (εὐσχήμων) do not require (cf. Rom. 1.27). Jerome Neyrey understands this text as offering an example of the Bible's characteristic link between nudity and shame. The nudity of a woman was the ultimate conveyor of shame; it was a dramatic sign that her chastity had been compromised.[60]

Such considerations illustrate what is at stake with women removing their head coverings (1 Cor. 11.2–16). But they also shed light upon the teaching concerning virgins in 1 Corinthians 7. Whatever the precise shape of the man's dishonorable actions in 7.36, he is obviously in danger of forfeiting his responsibilities to the woman as an honorable community member. The virgin's chastity is somehow threatened, and he must ensure that it remains protected. If the father/daughter translation of 7.36 is preferred, Paul is acknowledging that the honor of the father may require the marriage of a daughter who is passing the reasonable age of marriage.[61] Although less obviously than in the case of the father/daughter rendering, the engaged-couple translation of this passage might also disclose a concern for the reputation of the couple and the church. Unbridled desire (7.36, 37) can lead to behavior that will not mirror the purity of the *ekklesia* to the outside world (cf. 1 Cor. 5.1). If the man violates his fiancée's virtue, he will in essence be stripping her naked, exposing her before the male members of the community and the world outside. She will be reduced to the level of the prostitute or adulteress! Moreover, the man's natural inclination to go through with the marriage might be aggravated by social pressure—the honor of the household may well depend upon the marriage.[62]

---

59 See J. Plevnik, 'Honor/Shame', in John J. Pilch and Bruce J. Malina (eds), *Biblical Social Values and their Meaning: A Handbook* (Peabody, MA: Hendrickson, 1993), pp. 95–104.

60 Jerome H. Neyrey, 'Nudity', in Pilch and Malina (eds), *Biblical Social Values*, p. 120.

61 On the involvement of parents in arranging marriages for their children in Greco-Roman society see Balsdon, *Roman Women*, pp. 173–77; on the role of the *paterfamilias* in relation to his daughter see P.E. Corbett, *The Roman Law of Marriage* (Oxford: Clarendon Press, 1930), pp. 1–6.

62 On the process of betrothal in the Roman world, see Corbett, *Law of Marriage*, pp. 1–23; Balsdon, *Roman Women*, pp. 177–79; on betrothal and Augustan legislation see esp. Pomeroy, *Goddesses*, p. 166.

For example, if the virgin was part of an unbelieving household, on what basis might the struggling celibate delay the union?

As is often recognized, Paul was striving to curtail social disruption in Corinth. Thus his recommendation 'to remain as one is' and his identification of situations when this might not be possible (such as in the case of 7.36–38). Disruption could distract the community from its focus on the Lord. But, as illustrated above, Paul's response to the Corinthians was also shaped by the core Mediterranean values of honor and shame. The reputation of the community was of central importance and Paul was wary of disorderly behavior that could bring unnecessary suspicion on a group seeking to embrace the whole world. There is in fact one passage where Paul explicitly expresses his fear that unnecessary suspicion will fall upon the group. In 1 Cor. 14.23–25 we hear of Paul's worry that outsiders who witness the worship of the Corinthians and perceive a frenzy of tongues will conclude that they are mad. Such a perception might prevent the possibility of the outsider worshiping the one true God. Paul clearly understands the rituals of the community as being publicly visible and subject to the curious evaluations of neighbors. The concern for social respectability expressed in 1 Cor. 14.23–25 is found within a longer passage that aims to instill order in Corinthian worship. If Paul was worried about the impression that the Corinthian style of worship would make upon unbelievers, would he not also have been anxious about how the community's sexual/marriage practices would have been perceived? It must be admitted that Paul does not explicitly tell us this. However, as one so actively involved in the initial organization of communities, he was well aware that communal behavior with respect to the highly visible institution of marriage would have some repercussions in the realm of relations with outsiders. Already the marriages between believers and non-believers were causing concern in community life.

In first-century society, the question of whether or not to marry caused considerable controversy. Philosophers in particular raised arguments and practical considerations against marriage, and at times their line of reasoning was very similar to Paul's thought.[63] For example, although Epictetus does link marriage with the obligations of citizenship for people in general (*Discourses* 3.7, 19–22, 25–6), his comments about the ideal Cynic closely resemble Paul's observations about the anxiety that accompanies married life: 'But in such an order of things as the present, which is like that of a battle-field, it is a question, perhaps, if the Cynic ought not be free from distraction (ἀπερίσπαστον), wholly devoted to the service of God' (3.22, 69, cf. 3.22, 69–72).[64] But in response to these objections against marriages, there were also strong endorsements of marriage and societal measures to encourage marriage and bearing of children. Among the most famous of these are the marriage laws promulgated by Augustus and his successors. These laws included penalties for non-marriage and childlessness and rewards for fecundity.[65]

---

63 See Yarbrough, *Not Like the Gentiles*, pp. 31–33; more recently Will Deming has interpreted 1 Corinthians 7 in light of the Stoic–Cynic debate on the desirability of marriage. See *Paul on Marriage and Celibacy: The Hellenistic Background of 1 Corinthians 7* (Cambridge: Cambridge University Press, 1995).

64 Trans. W.A. Oldfather, *Discourses and Encheiridion* (2 vols.; LCL; Cambridge, MA: Harvard University Press, 1966–67).

65 The moral legislation of 19/18 BCE was consolidated and to some extent modified in 9 CE. For the details of this legislation see Yarbrough, *Not Like the Gentiles*, pp. 45–46 n. 78; Balsdon, *Roman Women*, pp. 75–79, 89–90, 202, 230; Corbett, *Law of Marriage*, pp. 119–21; Kraemer, *Her Share of the Blessings*, pp. 115–16. On the enforcement of the Augustan legislation during the course of the first three centuries CE see Pomeroy, *Goddesses*, p. 166.

Remaining unmarried and childless could mean restrictions on inheritance and the thwarting of the privileges of legal independence for women.[66] However, these laws affected only Roman citizens and seemed to have been aimed specifically at an aristocracy plagued by a falling birthrate. There are many questions about the success of this legislation, and it is doubtful that any member of Paul's communities would have been affected by them directly. However, this legislation nevertheless reveals something important about the type of society where early Christianity was born: it was a society that offered rewards 'to married couples who gave Rome the children which the State—in particular its hungry legions—needed'.[67] Strong, traditional households were a microcosm of a healthy empire. The historian Dio Cassius attributes to Tiberius (emperor 14–37 CE) a speech in which he responds negatively to a plea to repeal the law concerning the unmarried and childless. Tiberius proclaims the benefits of marriage and children both for the individual and the state.[68]

Given this complex picture, it is very difficult to know how a young widow or virgin determined to remain 'holy in body and spirit' (7.34) would have fared in urban Corinth. The remarks of Galen cited earlier indicate that second-century non-believers could praise ascetic church women. Because they are much closer in date to Paul's writings, the admiring remarks of Philo about the Therapeutae are even more striking in this regard (even though Philo cannot be considered an outside critic of the Therapeutic society in the way that Galen was an outside critic of the early Christians). In her study of this Jewish sect who lived on the shore of Lake Mareotis outside Alexandria, Ross Kraemer discusses the implications of the group's radical separation from normal social relations. Philo treats the female members like unusual philosophers, while at the same time endorsing traditional gender distinctions governing the lives of men and women. Moreover, in addition to what is implied about their educational opportunities, Philo's description of the women members as 'aged virgins' suggests that these women were exceptional: highly educated, perhaps in control of significant financial resources before they entered the community, and beyond the years of childbearing.[69] Unlike the isolationist sectarians Philo describes, the Corinthians remained at home in the Greco-Roman city. They were not protected by physical barriers from societal tensions created by a refusal to marry. They remained constantly visible in a society with watchful eyes. Moreover, one of the most remarkable features of Paul's teaching in 1 Corinthians 7 is that it is so unqualified; the implication is that women of all ages and backgrounds are to remain unmarried if possible. This means that Paul's position on women and celibacy is significantly different from that of the author of the Pastoral Epistles who sought to limit celibacy to an option for older women alone (1 Tim. 5.3–16).

Because the social context of 1 Corinthians 7 was a society that drew a connection between the virtue of women and the welfare of the broader community, it is highly likely that both women who were determined to remain unmarried and those who

---

66 Balsdon, *Roman Women*, p. 202.
67 Balsdon, *Roman Women*, p. 14; see also pp. 75 and 197–98. On the relationship between wealth and the rejection of marriage see Polybius's invective, *Histories* 36.17, 5–10 (trans. W.R. Paton; 6 vols.; LCL; Cambridge, MA: Harvard University Press, 1960).
68 Dio Cassius, *Roman History* 56.1–10 (trans. E. Cary; 9 vols.; LCL; Cambridge, MA: Harvard University Press, 1914–27). See also Polybius, *Histories* 36.17, 5–10.
69 Kraemer, *Her Share of the Blessings*, pp. 113–15.

entered the church without their spouses would have caused controversy.[70] Anthropologists working on women and culture in the Mediterranean world have frequently noted the tendency to view a woman's body as a reflection of a corporate entity. The woman's behavior, especially her chastity, comes to be viewed as the primary indicator of the reputation of the house and/or broader social group. Houses, villages, and groups are understood as symbolically female.[71] This dynamic seems also to have been at work in Greco-Roman society. Among its more interesting manifestations is the way in which women's behavior was used as a yardstick to measure the legitimacy of religious groups and how characterizations of female behavior were a means of articulating the reputation of the whole group. Women's religious activities deemed illegitimate in Greco-Roman society were connected with moral degeneracy. Because descriptions of the involvement of women were often a stereotypical means of casting aspersions on the reputation of a group, however, it is very difficult to judge the actual extent of female involvement.[72] Such authors as Juvenal and Plutarch state that the women of Greco-Roman society were especially susceptible to bizarre religious impulses that could break through household boundaries.[73] On numerous epitaphs, women were praised in conventional terms for domestic virtues that included being religious without being fanatical.[74] Analysis of the Roman appraisals of the Dionysus and Isis cults and of Judaism reveals certain stereotyped criticisms: these groups produced immorality among Roman women and sedition in society.[75] By the second century, the members of the early church were similarly criticized for the effect they had on the household and the wider social order.

Various second-century pagan authors attacked early Christian groups by drawing attention to their propensity to attract women. These women were alternately presented as gullible (cf. 2 Tim. 3.6–7) and devious.[76] Particularly striking are the detailed comments of Celsus. This pagan intellectual aims to deride early Christianity by drawing attention to the heavy involvement of women, including the adulterous mother of Jesus, a hysterical woman who claimed to witness the resur-

---

70 See Pomeroy's description of the efforts of Emperor Domitian (reigned 81–96 CE) who perceived a connection between popular morality and female degeneracy, including the enforcement of the Augustan marriage legislation, the restoration of the shrine of Plebeian Chastity, and making public examples of the Vestals by holding capital trials of Vestals and their lovers. See Pomeroy, *Goddesses*, p. 212; see also Balsdon, *Roman Women*, pp. 13, 241–42.

71 See remarks of Carol Delaney concerning life in a Turkish village in 'Seeds of Honor, Fields of Shame', in David Gilmore (ed.), *Honor and Shame and the Unity of the Mediterranean* (AAA Special Publication no. 22; Washington: American Anthropological Association, 1987), p. 44. See also Juliet du Boulay's comments concerning Greek village life in *Portrait of a Greek Mountain Village* (Oxford: Clarendon Press, 1974), pp. 131–33.

72 On evaluating the evidence for the involvement of women in cults see Wayne Meeks, *The First Urban Christians: The Social World of the Apostle Paul* (New Haven: Yale University Press, 1983), pp. 24–25.

73 See Juvenal, *Satires* 6.511; on Juvenal see Pomeroy, *Goddesses*, p. 221. See Plutarch, *Moralia* 140D.

74 Balsdon, *Roman Women*, pp. 206–207.

75 D.L. Balch, *Let Wives Be Submissive: The Domestic Code in 1 Peter* (SBLMS, 26; Chico, CA: Scholars Press, 1981), p. 74; see also pp. 65–80.

76 See full discussion of remarks of Pliny, Marcus Cornelius Fronto, Lucius Apuleius, Lucian of Samosata, and Celsus in M.Y. MacDonald, *Early Christian Women*, pp. 49–82.

rection (probably Mary Magdalene) and dubious women who were generally involved in the evangelizing efforts of church groups. According to Celsus, Christians lure children who are accompanied by stupid women to a private place and teach them to disobey their fathers and school teachers.[77] There is every reason to suspect that such impressions circled around early Christian groups long before they were recorded in the works of pagan intellectuals and officials. The remarks of Celsus and others reflect conventional attitudes concerning women and religion that permeated both the first and second centuries CE.

It is against this background that one should understand Paul's cautious advice concerning marriage and celibacy in 1 Corinthians 7. Celibacy is clearly the better option, but marriage is not a sin; it is even good and sometimes absolutely necessary. Paul desires to make known his preference for the freedom of celibacy in a world that is passing away without contributing to the unseemliness that might destroy the community. Paul must speak to a world imbued with the values of honor and shame. The ever-present threat of immorality (the threat that community members will dishonor each other and, ultimately, the whole community) leads him to reject any tendency to advocate compulsory celibacy as essential to life in the Spirit. Moreover, while we cannot be certain of his motives, the apostle was probably aware of the difficulties faced by celibate believers in a society where marriage, the virtue of women, and the stability of the state were seen as interrelated. Controversy was almost inevitable despite the fact that the moral rectitude of these believers might have won them admiration in certain circles. If a young virgin determined to remain unmarried, how could she avoid the appearance of staging a rebellion against her household (cf. *Acts of Paul and Thecla*)? How could a female believer survive the treacherous position of living in a pagan household (cf. 1 Cor. 7.12–16)? If her behavior was considered in any way out of the ordinary—even if her absences from her house were too frequent—how quickly would the problem be blamed on a strange religion? It is in light of such very real and pressing concerns that we must understand Paul's interest in promoting seemliness. For a new religious group open to new members in an urban setting the need to stabilize the place of the group within the wider context of society was nothing less than urgent.

Conclusion

Behind the parallelism of 1 Corinthians 7 lies a special concern for women that is revealed by Paul's instructions concerning virgins, widows, and wives. There are various indications of women's initiative in the text. In particular, it seems that women were among the main supporters of a radically ascetic teaching that promised spiritual perfection. Therefore, it is important to reflect upon what Paul's teaching would have meant for them.

The activities of certain wealthy widows and other exceptional Greco-Roman women remind us of the opportunities for those who were not bound to males in permanent relationships to remain in control of their own affairs. The women of the Corinthian church who remained unmarried had much in common with Jewish and

---

77 Origen, *Contra Celsum* 3.55; for full discussion on Celsus and early Christian women see M.Y. MacDonald, *Early Christian Women*, pp. 94–120.

pagan women in similar circumstances. But what is most striking about Paul's instructions in 1 Corinthians 7 is that they do not limit celibacy to women of certain age or status, or with a certain number of progeny; Paul extended to 'ordinary' women the possibility of remaining unmarried.[78] It is, however, by no means easy to assess the significance of this acceptance of women's celibacy. This chapter argues that in many respects, 1 Corinthians 7 reflects traditional values and concepts of gender. Paul's instructions reveal the dominant values of honor and shame which operate by linking male honor to the protection of the chastity of women as the most valuable resource. In a group that came to see celibacy as a potent symbol of the kingdom, one would expect special attention to be given to women's purity. Yet there is also a sense in which the old basis for honor is rejected in favor of a new standard. The instructions concerning the widows in 1 Cor. 7.39–40 illustrate this most dramatically. The values of honor and shame call for women to be protected by male guardians (e.g. fathers, husbands). By approving a widow's choice (even a very young widow's choice) to remain unmarried, Paul sanctioned a life where the woman was removed from immediate male protection and made responsible for protecting her own honor and for presenting her own honor and the honor of her community to the outside world.

Paul would not allow this extension of independence and responsibility under all circumstances, however. His cautious remarks, probably directed mainly at women for whom celibacy was an essential representation of their freedom in the Lord, warn women that they may not always be able to do what they wish. In effect, these remarks restrict choices. For example, the father who suffered under social pressure might call his virgin daughter to marry despite her own preference to remain free from the marriage bond.[79] The woman engaged to a man troubled by desire could unwittingly contribute to the desecration of the community if she persisted in her determination to remain unmarried. This woman would need to sacrifice the privileges of virginity. To some women Paul offered no choice at all. The woman married to the non-believer was free to separate from her husband only if he no longer desired to be with her. He may have been living out everything that she despised, but she was instructed to remain as she was. The potential of her role as evangelist in her own home had been recognized.

Paul's teaching and implicit attitude to women need to be understood in light of the social tensions created by the combination of efforts to preserve a group's distinct identity with the goal of evangelization. Such a combination inevitably leads to considerable dialogue between church and world and considerable maneuvering to preserve reputation.[80] That such social dynamics occurred in a society that linked

78 On the implications of Paul's offer to women of the privileges of the marriage-free life see Schüssler Fiorenza, *In Memory of Her*, pp. 224–26. Schüssler Fiorenza relies here on the conclusions of Pomeroy, *Goddesses*, pp. 210–14.

79 On the complexities of the Roman law of marriage in relation to the role of the father see Pomeroy, *Goddesses*, pp. 150–63; S.B. Pomeroy, 'The Relationship of the Married Woman to her Blood Relatives in Rome', *Ancient Society* (1976), pp. 215–27; J. Carcopino, *Daily Life in Ancient Rome* (New Haven: Yale University Press, 1940), p. 96.

80 As Bryan Wilson's sociological work illustrates, concern for social respectability necessarily accompanies an effort to evangelize in religious sects; see 'An Analysis of Sect Development', in *idem* (ed.), *Patterns of Sectarianism* (London: Morrison & Gibb, 1967), pp. 22–45.

honor with the public demonstration of the reputation of women only heightened the tensions. The dialogue between early Christianity and Greco-Roman society did not have uniform consequences for women and early Christian literature does not offer a monolithic, straightforward response to virgins, widows, or wives.[81] Nevertheless, an awareness of the social tensions related to a desire both to remain distinct from the world and to 'win' the world sheds light on the gradual trend in later Pauline circles to squeeze women out of leadership roles and to define more clearly their position in the patriarchal household (e.g. 1 Tim. 5.3–16). The visibility of women caused increasing concern in church groups that were appearing subversive to curious onlookers and officials alike. The Deutero-Pauline writings and writings of the Apostolic Fathers are far more cautious about the marriage-free life and far more insistent upon the importance of a believing wife's subjection to her husband in the household than are Paul's writings. From a writing composed at the end of the first century, we gain a sense of the changing Corinthian landscape. When Clement of Rome wrote to Corinth, he remembered not the virgins and the widows, but spoke of the reputation of the community as a church which instructed wives '... to remain in the rule of obedience and to manage their households with seemliness, in all circumspection' (*1 Clem.* 1.3; cf. *1 Clem.* 21.6–7).[82]

81 See, for example, Kate Cooper, *The Virgin and the Bride: Idealized Womanhood in Late Antiquity* (Cambridge, MA: Harvard University Press, 1996).
82 Trans. K. Lake, *The Apostolic Fathers* (2 vols.; LCL; Cambridge: Harvard University Press, 1912–13).

DOES PAUL MAKE A DIFFERENCE?

FAITH KIRKHAM HAWKINS

Had the Apostle [Paul] enjoined upon women to do good works without envy or jealousy, it would have had the weight of a Divine command. But that, from the earliest record of human events, woman should have been condemned and punished for trying to get knowledge, and forbidden to impart what she has learned, is the most unaccountable peculiarity of masculine wisdom ... It cannot be admitted that Paul was inspired by infinite wisdom in this utterance.[1]

Our question is double-edged. On the one hand, it asks whether (and how) Paul is relevant to feminist biblical interpretation at the beginning of the twenty-first century. On the other, it asks whether (and how) Paul draws distinctions between groups, distinctions which themselves may remain relevant. A hundred years ago, a colleague of Elizabeth Cady Stanton anticipated a firm answer to the first aspect of the question by suggesting that on matters such as the 'proper' place of women, Paul's views are best dismissed as 'unilluminated [and] biased by prejudice'.[2] After reflecting upon this and similar responses to the question of Paul's relevance, I will begin to respond to the second side of our question.

However attractive it might be, the dismissive approach is not without drawbacks. While many may wish to ignore or dismiss Paul, we cannot do so—at least not without significant risk. Because others continue to rely on Paul to shape their view of women and men, sexual roles and sexual ethics, ecclesial organization and theology, Paul does indeed make a difference: his ideas matter as long as significant numbers of people believe they do. It is not enough to dismiss his ideas as 'merely human' rather than the product of 'infinite wisdom', for not all biblical readers recognize such distinctions. In their awareness of the ongoing influence and thus the need to address Paul's views, Stanton and her colleagues are worthy models for current feminist readers, however frequently they resorted to the sort of dismissal evidenced above. The continuing appropriation of his ideas in faith communities, whether to justify the exclusion of women from ecclesiastical leadership or to prescribe gender roles within 'Christian' households, makes ongoing feminist readings of Paul both necessary and, often, controversial.

Paul makes a difference as well in our understanding of earliest Christianity. Whether or not we focus specifically upon the Pauline or Deutero-Pauline letters, Paul's importance in the recorded history of the earliest Christian communities is undeniable. The relatively large collection of his extant writings, testimonies to his importance in Acts and in patristic sources, and his often disconcerting statements

---

1 Lillie Devereux Blake, 'Comments on Timothy', in Elizabeth Cady Stanton, *The Woman's Bible* (2 vols.; Boston: Northeastern University Press, 1993), II, p. 163.

2 This was evidently the unilluminated utterance of Paul, the man, biased by prejudice (Blake, 'Comments on Timothy').

about the role of women within the churches combine to make Paul the particular and necessary focus of feminist historical reconstruction,[3] literary and rhetorical analyses,[4] and ideological interpretations.[5]

It is no coincidence that many feminist readings of Paul focus upon his correspondence with the church at Corinth, for these letters offer the most concentrated glimpse of his views of gender.[6] Women and—as they are often somewhat derisively called within the North American political context—'women's issues' appear at several points in this correspondence. For example, in 1 Cor. 11.2–16 and 14.34b–36, Paul delineates the natural and theological bases of gender roles as they are or, in his opinion, should be expressed in worship settings.

In 1 Cor. 11.2–16, he argues for gendered forms of headdress, although his conclusion is perhaps less important two millennia later than the means by which he justifies it. Paul combines appeals to theology with appeals to natural law or common sense,[7] a blending that continues to shape justifications of gender roles to this day. In Paul's view, because 'Christ is the head of every man, and the husband is the head of his wife, and God the head of Christ' (v. 3), there are certain things patently appropriate and inappropriate for men and women to do. While 'a woman should wear a veil', and not pray or prophesy with her head uncovered (v. 5), 'a man ought not to have his head veiled, since he is the image and reflection of God' (v. 7). In 11.11–12, Paul makes a somewhat belated attempt to soften his appeal to theological premises that subordinate women, but this attempt is undercut by his appeal to 'nature itself' (v. 14). Paul's obvious vexation on this issue may seem out of proportion to modern readers, but it reflects his sense that external markers are important manifestations of proper gender roles and their place in the order of God's creation. As Elizabeth Castelli notes, 'gender differences are borne by the physical body. They can be read by observers, they matter, and *they function as signs that stand for deeper ethical essences*. To blur the lines between male and female . . . violates some more essential set of differentiations . . .'[8]

---

3 Most notably, perhaps, Antoinette Wire's *The Corinthian Women Prophets: A Reconstruction through Paul's Rhetoric* (Minneapolis: Fortress Press, 1990).

4 See, for instance, Margaret Mitchell's *Paul and The Rhetoric of Reconciliation: An Exegetical Investigation of the Language and Composition of 1 Corinthians* (Louisville, KY: Westminster/John Knox Press, 1991), which though not explicitly feminist in perspective, is an important study setting Paul's discussion of 'divisions' within Corinth in its political and rhetorical contexts.

5 Elizabeth Castelli's *Imitating Paul: A Discourse of Power* (Lousiville, KY: Westminster/John Knox Press, 1991) is one example of this type of reading of particular statements within Paul's letters; another example, focusing more specifically upon 1 Corinthians, is Dale B. Martin's *The Corinthian Body* (New Haven: Yale University Press, 1995).

6 Such 'glimpses' occur in references to women co-workers (Romans 16; 1 Corinthians 16; Philippians 4), in metaphorical and analogical examples that rely on gender roles (Rom. 7.2–4; 8.21ff.; Gal. 4.21ff.; 1 Thess. 5.3), statements about the behavior of women (generally and specifically, Rom. 1.26; 1 Cor. 5; 11: 14.34–36), as well as explicit statements regarding gender and gender roles (1 Cor. 11; 14.34–36; Gal. 3.28, and the household codes in the Deutero-Pauline Eph. 5.22–33 and Col. 3.18–19).

7 Of course, one person's common sense is another's nonsense, but Paul is appealing here to views he assumes his audience shares.

8 'Paul on Women and Gender', in Ross Shepherd Kraemer and Mary Rose D'Angelo (eds.), *Women and Christian Origins* (Oxford: Oxford University Press, 1999), pp. 221–35 (228–29), emphasis added.

Similarly, in 1 Cor. 14.33b–36, Paul offers a parenthetical remark on the behavior of women in worship that seems to speak to 'a more essential set of differentiations'.[9] Again relying upon a combination of theology and common sense to prescribe specific gender roles within the Christian community, he asserts, 'Women should be silent in the churches', and he advises 'they should be subordinate, as the law also says' (v. 34). This appeal to Torah, the law given by God, is thus an attempt to justify theologically his proscription against women's speech in church.[10] An appeal to common sense, similar to the exhortation in 11.13 to 'judge for yourselves', arises in 14.35, where he contends that 'it is shameful for a woman to speak in church'. The lack of argument supporting the characterization of such speech as 'shameful' indicates that this view is, for Paul, simply common sense. In both passages, therefore, Paul conjoins theological claims and invocations of common sense or natural law. The effect is to cast gender differentiation, and a hierarchical relationship between men and women, as ordained by God.[11]

However, feminist interpretations of 1 Corinthians need confine themselves neither to these particular passages nor to statements about women or 'women's issues'. Indeed, feminist interpreters of Paul have much to gain from considering other aspects of the epistle. While Paul's remarks on women's roles are of obvious interest, his remarks on other groups within the community (such as slaves) and indeed on the existence of such groups in general can also provide insight into his views on the group 'women'. Gender is, like race, ethnicity, religious affiliation, and sexual orientation, a marker of human particularity.[12] Within the logic of identity[13] and the ideology of patriarchy, which together form the conceptual nucleus of Western thought and culture, such markers of particularity are always markers of *difference* from the perceived, idealized, and privileged 'norm': the white, heterosexual, male.[14] Gender therefore is not a unique interpretive category but is rather

---

9 Some interpreters see these verses as an interpolation by a later editor, a view that attractively displaces their authority. However, there are strong arguments against this view, and in either event, the appearance of these verses in a genuine Pauline letter requires us to take them more seriously than such a dismissal allows.

10 Paul's use of Christological appeals in ch. 11, and his rhetorically similar appeal to Torah in ch. 14, reveal the theological continuity he sees between God's action in Torah and God's action in Christ. This in turn must discourage us from concluding that Christology (or, writ large, the religions of the New Testament) is a more feminist-friendly ideology than the ideology of Torah (or, writ large, the religions of the Hebrew Bible).

11 The rhetorical effect, in short, is much the same as Paul's rhetoric elsewhere in 1 Corinthians where he asserts, 'I give this command—not I, but the Lord' (1 Cor. 7.10).

12 See, for instance, Iris Marion Young, *Justice and the Politics of Difference* (Princeton, NJ: Princeton University Press, 1990), especially pp. 98–102 and pp. 122–30.

13 The logic of identity values sameness above difference, and 'seeks to reduce differences to a unity', according to Young (*Justice and the Politics of Difference*, p. 97). Following postmodern thinkers such as Derrida, Adorno, and Irigaray, Young argues that this logic 'denies or represses difference' because difference challenges the hegemony of identity (*Justice and the Politics of Difference*, p. 98).

14 Young notes that within societies structured by 'hierarchical relations of race, gender, class, and nationality ... the privileged groups lose their particularity' (*Justice and the Politics of Difference*, p. 127). This loss of particularity, perceived as *freedom from* particularity, signals the negative value assigned by the dominant groups to particularity—and leads to the denigration and oppression of those who are defined by their particularity, and its difference from the norms of the dominant groups.

one of many interrelated interpretive categories. Attentiveness to the ramifications for individuals and groups of all markers of difference is both necessary and helpful to feminist analysis of biblical texts.

There are important distinctions in the circumstances and oppressions experienced by differently marked individuals and groups, distinctions that result directly or indirectly from the particularities of gender, race, ethnicity, class, and sexual orientation. However, as Iris Young argues, 'To say that there are differences among groups does not imply that there are not overlapping experiences, or that two groups have nothing in common. The assumption that real differences in affinity, culture, or privilege imply oppositional categorization must be challenged. Different groups are always similar in some respects, and always potentially share some attributes, experiences, and goals.'[15] Young's view suggests that some similarities arise precisely from the marking of particular groups as 'different' or as 'other'. Her comments on relationships among contemporary social groups are relevant to the study of the ancient church. For instance, we can identify several groups perceived as 'different' by the dominant voice(s) of early Christianity: Gentiles and Gentile Christians are marked as different from Jewish Christians; Christians who follow Torah are marked as different from those who do not; Jews who do not believe in Jesus (as) the Christ are marked as different from Jews (and Gentiles) who do follow 'the Way'; women and slaves are marked as different from men and freemen, respectively. Because all of these groups are so marked, statements about any one of them can inform our understanding of the experience of, and attitudes toward, the others. Although the distinctive nature of each marker (and of the oppressions each experienced) precludes an exact one-to-one transfer, systems of differentiation function similarly even when directed at distinct groups.

We arrive, therefore, at the other edge of our opening question: Does Paul make a difference? Does he draw distinctions among groups that shape his understanding of all groups? And might his view of difference in general help us deepen our understanding of his view of gender in particular? To explore these questions, and to demonstrate the value to feminist analysis of focusing on passages where gender is not the central issue, we will consider as a test case Paul's remarks on the matter of εἰδωλόθυτος, 'things sacrificed to idols', in 1 Corinthians 8.

Making a Difference in 1 Corinthians 8

Paul responds to a question raised by the Corinthians in their letter to him, as indicated by his use of the περὶ δε formula at 8.1: περὶ δε εἰδωλοθύτον ...[16] While it is difficult to know exactly what they had asked about sacrifices (or things sacrificed) to idols, a minimalist reconstruction of their query would be, 'Is it acceptable to eat things which have been sacrificed to idols?' This concern would result from

15 Young, *Justice and the Politics of Difference*, p. 171. Indeed, the failure to recognize the common ground on which different groups stand in their relationships to dominant ideologies is in effect to conclude that any difference is absolute otherness—thereby submitting to the logic of identity.

16 In 1 Cor. 7.1, Paul writes, 'concerning the things about which you wrote ...'. The περὶ δε formula appears also at 7.25 and 12.1, indicating that chs. 7 through 10, as well as 12, are at least in part responses to specific questions raised by the Corinthians.

the common practices of daily life in a Greco-Roman city: food left over from sacrifices in pagan temples was sold in the public markets, and many social and civic events would include (perhaps token) sacrifices to one or another deity. The question is therefore important for several reasons, not least of which is that it reflects a more general problem facing early Christians, the question of assimilation to and differentiation from the larger society. A central goal of the question is to determine the practical ramifications of a monotheistic faith in Jesus the Christ.

As has long been observed, however, Paul gives this question a second level of importance: his response suggests that Christian practice must be established not only in consideration of one's faith, but in consideration of one's membership in a community of believers. In other words, Paul recognizes that the uncertainty about boundaries between faithful and unfaithful practice has close connections to larger questions of differentiation. Certainly one of these is the question of how differentiated from the broader culture Christians must be, but another is how much (and what kinds of) differentiation can reasonably coexist within the Christian community. Paul's response focuses on this second question, but it relies as well upon some assessment of the first.

Paul's argument is based upon his recognition not only of the importance of practice as an expression of Christian faith, but also that the community itself is, as he states it in 1 Corinthians 12, 'many members, but one body'. Thus, 'if one member suffers, all suffer together with it' (12.26). The tension between the behaviors of individuals and the 'health' of the community emphasized in his response to the question about eating food offered to idols is one Paul neither dismisses nor dispels: he does not offer a simple 'Yes, it is acceptable to eat these foods' or 'No, it is not acceptable'. Such a response would erase, or significantly limit, differences within the community. Rather, Paul considers carefully the views of those on each side of the issue (especially in ch. 8) as well as the contingencies under which the issue might arise (ch. 10). His reluctance to offer a single, universally valid response suggests a sort of *Realpolitik*, or better, a recognition that differences among members are an unavoidable aspect of community life. To this recognition he adds the imperative that the community itself must thrive with, rather than in spite of, these differences. Although this imperative is most poetically expressed through the body metaphor of 1 Corinthians 12, it is equally important to 1 Corinthians 8.

A close reading of this chapter, one attuned in particular to the question of difference, indicates that Paul's argument in response to the question of εἰδωλόθυτος is quite thoroughly shaped by the ways in which he *constructs* differences among members—or, better, reconstructs them. This reconstruction yields insight into Paul's view of the distinctions between those with knowledge (8.1–6) and those without (8.7–13), and it also helps us better understand his view of differences among people more generally, such as between women (who should wear veils) and men (who should not) (11.2–16).

The first element of this reconstruction of difference is the broader context of Paul's comments about different groups. As noted above, in Paul's view the groups are subgroups of the larger—and ultimately more important—Corinthian Christian community. The primary context for his discussion of difference is therefore a particularized sameness, traits all members of his audience share. Paul establishes the importance of this context in several ways within 1 Corinthians 8. The first is his use of the term εἰδωλόθυτος (things sacrificed to idols) to identify the issue under consideration. The term occurs only within Jewish and Christian literature of this era, drawing a contrast with the term ἱερόθυτος ('things sacrificed in temples', which Paul does use at 10.28). It is a deeply monotheistic term, already biased and weighted against that which it names. Εἰδωλόθυτος makes explicit the monotheistic perspective of those who use it—and so names all of those who use it as sharing this view. The presence of the term here suggests that Paul is interested at the outset in establishing, or reminding the Corinthians of, the similarities within which their conflict arises. The knowledge implicit in the term εἰδωλόθυτος also indicates a certain distinction—accepted by Paul if not originally drawn by him—between those who know that ἱερόθυτος is really εἰδωλόθυτος, and those who do not recognize this. It is here drawing a distinction between 'insiders' and 'outsiders', a boundary between members of the community and those (pagans) who are not members. But there is no suggestion of a corresponding distinction within the community between those not bothered by the eating of εἰδωλόθυτος and those who object to it. Such a suggestion arises only much later, at 8.7, although most treatments of the passage take such an intra-community distinction for granted.[17] Rather at this point, as suggested by the term εἰδωλόθυτος, the community as a whole is defined by the shared perspective toward pagan sacrifices, temples, and idols.[18] Paul's first rhetorical move thus names the issue in a way that also names the entire community. At this stage, the true status of ἱερόθυτος (as εἰδωλόθυτος) is the 'common knowledge' shared by *all* within the community.

As a point of contrast indicating the similar 'insider knowledge' εἰδωλόθυτος conveys, we may look briefly to the second phase of Paul's discussion of things sacrificed to idols in ch. 10. There he offers advice on how believers should respond when someone makes available 'something offered in a temple' (10.28). 'Something offered in a temple' in this instance is *not* εἰδωλόθυτος, but ἱερόθυτος ('temple-offering')—a term which does not specify that the temple involved is one for an 'idol'. The use of ἱερόθυτος at 10.28 suggests that the hypothetical situation is a discussion between believer and non-believer; the terminology itself indicates such boundaries. In contrast then, the use of εἰδωλόθυτος at 8.1 indicates that all of those involved in the discussion share knowledge that these temples are idolatrous.

A second way in which Paul emphasizes the communal context within which the disagreement occurs is through his comments in 8.1b–3 on knowledge and the believer's relationship to God. Paul's response to the Corinthian maxim (πάντες γνῶσιν ἔχομεν, 'we all have knowledge') suggests that he sees a focus on knowledge as a potential basis for drawing distinctions between church members, distinctions he characterizes negatively.[19] 'Knowledge puffs up' (ἡ γνῶσις φυσιοῖ),

17 Assuming the presence of some degree of factionalism within the community on this issue is related to assuming that πάντες γνῶσιν ἔχομεν is a 'slogan', and indicates more about the interpreter than about the situation in Corinth addressed by Paul. See further on this point below.

18 As the remainder of the discussion will indicate, exactly how widely this perspective is shared within the community is uncertain.

19 So Mitchell, who notes that the only way to explain the 'apparent contradiction between 8.1 and 8.7' is to recognize that 'γνῶσις is one of the precious commodities claimed as an exclusive possession by some, contributing to community division' (Mitchell, *Paul and the Rhetoric of Reconciliation*, p. 126).

he replies, in contrast to love, which builds (οἰκοδομέω) community. Although 'puffing up' is often understood as pointing to arrogance, the contrast is not between arrogantly 'puffing up' and 'building up', but rather between tearing apart and building up, and thus it relies on the metaphor of the community as a building.[20] Margaret Mitchell notes that this metaphor is 'a *topos* in literature urging unity on divided groups'.[21] Moreover, the metaphor seldom appears in literature where such divisions are considered irreconcilable or inherent.[22] That is, the metaphor itself presumes that the 'divided groups' are divisions of a whole: subgroups within a larger group. Thus while Paul's use of the term does 'urge unity' upon the Corinthians, he is in fact appealing for unity resumed, rather than for something new.[23]

Paul's presumption that this unity existed previously is indicated by his comments in 8.3: 'if anyone loves God, this one is known by him [God]' (εἰ δὲ τις ἀγαπᾷ τὸν θεόν, οὗτος ἔγνωσται ὑπ' αὐτοῦ). 'To love God' is a remarkably rare phrase in Paul's letters; it appears only twice in 1 Corinthians (2.9 and here) and once in Romans (8.28). 1 Cor. 2.9 helps to set the context for 8.3. In 1 Corinthians 2, Paul is contrasting 'God's wisdom, secret and hidden' (2.7), prepared for and revealed to believers, with the wisdom of the world, which does not recognize God's wisdom (2.8). In this section of 1 Corinthians, Paul is distinguishing between 'those who love God' (the believers) and those who do not ('the rulers of this age'). The distinction is between insiders and outsiders, rather than among community members. Paul thus uses 'those who love God' to indicate the entire Christian community, as a community. Given this context, there is no reason to think that at 8.3 Paul is using

---

20 Although most interpreters of Paul understand 'puffing up' in terms of simple conceit or arrogance, these translations of the term do not capture the connotations found in Paul's use of it. The verb used at 8.1 is found only in 1 Corinthians and in Col. 2.18. Within 1 Corinthians, it appears in various forms six times, suggesting it is particularly appropriate to the Corinthian situation at this time, when internal divisions and disagreements threaten the entire community. This indicates that the term is directed toward *internal* affairs: 'puffing up' is how Paul characterizes some dynamics internal to the community at Corinth. Although here we cannot address the details of Paul's use of the term throughout the letter, its appearances elsewhere in 1 Corinthians confirm this interpretation. Suffice it to say that in all of its previous uses in 1 Corinthians, the term describes situations and behaviors clearly felt by Paul to be negative. For our purposes, the most important element of Paul's use of the term elsewhere is suggested in 1 Corinthians 5, where Paul chides the entire community for its blindness to ongoing sin among them. Here, Paul suggests that ignorance of how one's actions affect the community is characteristic of being puffed up—and this will be an argument he includes in his response to the question of foods offered to idols in 1 Corinthians 8.

21 Mitchell, *Paul and the Rhetoric of Reconciliation*, pp. 99–100.

22 Mitchell cites passages from Cicero and Lucan, among others. Both of these authors use the metaphor to dissuade their audiences from engaging in civil war—that is, political/military division of a previously unified whole. See Mitchell, *Paul and the Rhetoric of Reconciliation*, pp. 100–103, especially n. 219.

23 This view diverges somewhat from that of W. Jaeger, who suggests that 'the Christian community at Corinth ... had to be "edified", i.e., literally constructed like an edifice, so that its members would join together to form an organic whole' ('Tyrtaeus on True Arete', in Werner Jaeger, *Werner Jaeger: Five Essays* [trans. A.M. Fiske; Montreal: Casaline, 1966], pp. 103–42 [140]; quoted in Mitchell, *Paul and the Rhetoric of Reconciliation*, p. 101). Closer to my view is another cited by Mitchell, that of Elliot on οἶκος, which he considers 'a central image of human unification and reunification' (J.H. Eliott, *A Home for the Homeless* [Philadelphia: Fortress Press, 1981], pp. 165–266, quoted by Mitchell, *Paul and the Rhetoric of Reconciliation*, p. 101).

the idea of loving God in a more partial fashion, to refer to only some of those in the community at Corinth. Rather, the language of loving God at 8.3 is reminiscent of its use at 2.9, and it serves much the same purpose of reaffirming the love of God shared by all Corinthian believers.

Combined with the use of εἰδωλόθυτος, the idea of 'loving God' suggests that to love God is to recognize God monotheistically, that is, to recognize that meat offered in pagan temples is not merely food offered in temples (ἱερόθυτος), but is food offered to idols (εἰδωλόθυτος). 'All' (πάντες, v. 1) within the community, Paul suggests, love God, for all recognize the true nature of such meat. As a result, none can claim privileged knowledge, and distinctions drawn within the community on this basis are without merit.

Paul also emphasizes the similarities among the Corinthians through kinship language. Although not dominant, this language ('brother', ἀδελφός [8.11, 12, 13]) appears at crucial moments within Paul's argument, usually following verses in which Paul has identified points of distinction between members of the Corinthian community. In vv. 7 and 9, Paul distinguishes between 'some' who lack knowledge (defined as 'weak', ἀσθενέσιν) and others (addressed directly as 'you' [plural], ὑμεῖς) who have 'freedom' (ἐξουσία) and, by implication, knowledge. In 8.11, 12, and 13, the language of kinship in Christ offsets some of the potentially divisive effects of such distinctions, and it does so rather emphatically through repetition. The climax of Paul's advice to those with knowledge and freedom hinges upon the familial relationship between them and their 'weak brothers [and sisters]' in Christ. 'When you sin against the brothers [and sisters] (εἰς τοὺς ἀδελφοὺς) ... you sin against Christ' (8.12). The strategic usage of the language of kinship suggests that Paul's primary assumption, as well as his primary goal, is a familial model of community in which difference need not be divisive.

However, in addition to emphasizing the similarities and shared beliefs among members, Paul also acknowledges their differences. This acknowledgment has long been the focus of scholarly analysis, such that the community in Corinth has been under-stood to be virtually severed by irreconcilable disagreements between 'the Weak' and 'the Strong'. Without disputing that Paul does draw distinctions between groups, it is important to note the ways in which he does *not* do so: the categories of 'Weak' and 'Strong', for instance, are imposed upon the community (and upon Paul's construction of the community) by his interpreters. Within ch. 8, no such oppositional language appears: those who are 'weak' are contrasted with 'you who have knowledge' (8.10) rather than with 'the strong'. Like Paul's emphasis on shared beliefs, this contrast may indicate that he places a premium upon the attributes shared by the groups, rather than the oppositions between them. It is perhaps overstated to suggest that Paul does not subscribe to the 'logic of identity' and its oppositional understanding of difference, and yet his language expresses this logic less forcefully than most modern interpreters suggest.

On what bases, then, and with what effects, does Paul construct difference within this chapter? Three elements of his argument stand out: the content and value of 'knowledge', the consciences of the believers, and the practical results of eating food offered to idols within the communal context. The three are wholly intertwined within Paul's comments, and each relies upon related distinctions which Paul draws.

Paul's response to the maxim 'we all have knowledge' is first to draw distinctions between different ways of knowing (vv. 2–3), and then to distinguish between different kinds of knowledge (vv. 4–6, 7). As we have seen, Paul begins by asserting that knowledge is not necessarily good; in contrast to love, which 'builds up' the community, knowledge 'puffs up' and so threatens it (8.1c). This immediately suggests the need for a revision in the Corinthian view of knowledge, a revision Paul attempts to effect in vv. 2–6. Verse 2 ('If anyone supposes himself to know something, that one does not yet know as it is necessary to know') marks a distinction between two forms of knowing: supposing (oneself) to know something (δοκεῖ ἐγνωκέαι τι), and knowing as it is necessary to know (ἔγνω καθὼς δεῖ γνῶναι). Used as a transitive verb, δοκέω almost always implies misapprehension, 'knowledge' or certainty that is suspect at best, wholly untenable at worst.[24] The New Testament use of the term δοκέω thus follows the sense in classical Greek, most importantly in the construction of an antithesis between δοκεῖν and εἶναι, between that which is thought to be true and that which actually is true, between appearance and reality.[25] Paul's use of δοκέω suggests that the claim to knowledge made by the Corinthians is illegitimate, a point refined through the contrast with 'necessary' ways of knowing.[26]

This distinction continues in 8.3: 'If anyone loves God, that one is known by [God]'. Paul here asserts that 'necessary' knowledge is not the believers' possession, but is based on God's activity. The shift in 8.2-3 from a focus upon the believer as 'knower' to the believer as 'known' is somewhat abrupt, but it can be partially clarified through attention to a small, but important detail: Paul's use of οὔπω ('not yet') in 8.2. This term contrasts present, mundane knowledge with some other, not-worldly way of knowing, and so introduces eschatological consciousness into the discussion.[27] The injection of the eschatological framework of 'necessary' ways of knowing therefore both further discredits the Corinthians' view and also (in 8.3) displaces them from the Subject position by presenting God as Subject. The assertion that God is the one who knows effectively renders any claim to knowledge on the part of the Corinthians as a form of idolatry, for it claims as the possession of humans something rightfully possessed only by God. Paul thus shifts the governing

---

24 Two strong exceptions to this characterization of δοκέω occur in 1 Cor. 4.9 and 7.4. In both instances, Paul says of his own opinion, 'δοκῶ ...' (e.g. 7.40, 'I think that I too have the Spirit of God'). This formulation may be pragmatic, Paul's attempt to take the sharp edge off of his own judgment. Or it may be a simple use of δοκέω in its least judgmental form, which nonetheless still suggests 'subjective opinion' (so BAGD, p. 201). The central point is that the verb stresses the subjectivity of the opinion it introduces. When Paul uses this verb to characterize others' opinions, it takes on a more negative connotation than when he uses it to introduce his own views.

25 Plato (in *Rep.*, 2.361b) cites Aeschylus, *Seven against Thebes*, as coining the distinction between a man wishing to seem (δοκέω) good and to be (εἶναι) good. Aeschylus actually writes of a man who 'does not wish to seem (δοκέω) the most brave, but to be (εἶναι) the most brave' (*Seven against Thebes*, 592), but the point is nonetheless the same: here as in Plato's *Republic* and *Gorgias*, the distinction between outer appearance or perception and real character is of central importance in classical Greek ethical thought.

26 In drawing this contrast, Paul makes a distinction not only between forms of knowing, but between himself and the Corinthians, or at least those Corinthians who would claim (or accept as legitimate the claims of others regarding) knowledge as expressed in the maxim of 8.1.

27 Again, the term is rare within Paul's letters, appearing only in 1 Cor. 3.12 and 8.2, and Phil. 3.13. In Philippians, it has an obviously eschatological effect, while in 1 Corinthians 3 it appears in the midst of a discussion contrasting worldly and divine views—a contrast that is characteristic of eschatological discourse.

consciousness of the discussion[28] from the Corinthians' perspective to God's perspective. This move is crucial to Paul's overall discussion for—once he has established the 'necessity' of seeing as God sees—he will move in the remainder of the chapter to explicate how God views the situation, and to advise the Corinthians to act accordingly.

Having distinguished between ways of knowing, Paul then moves to the 'content' of the knowledge at issue. This knowledge is articulated in two other apparent excerpts from the Corinthians' letter to Paul, quoted in 8.4: 'no idol [is] in the world' and '[there is] no God except one'. Left unchallenged, these statements would lead one to conclude that because idols do not really exist, eating food offered sacrificially to them is a wholly unimportant practice. Paul does not leave this view unchallenged. Working from the ostensible perspective of God, who knows all who love God (v. 3), Paul argues that the worldly reality of idols is not as easily dismissed as the Corinthian maxims suggest. Paul attempts to correct their view by arguing that 'there are so-called gods in heaven and on earth, just as there are many gods and many lords' (8.5). These 'so-called gods ... and lords' are precisely those worshiped in the temples, to whom the foods under discussion are offered. Intriguingly, Paul does not here call them idols, as the Corinthians did. His refusal to do so suggests that he sees, and urges the Corinthians to see, that these 'so-called gods ... and lords' cannot be dismissed as figments of the religious imagination. They may not exist, but for some people they are real—a point he will clarify further in 8.7ff. In effect, Paul has redefined the Corinthians' term 'idol' in a way that acknowledges the real effects of these 'so-called gods and lords' upon some members of the community. Thereby, he delineates a tension that is the hallmark of his distinction between members of the Corinthian community: the tension between the shared recognition that sacrifices in temples are offered to idols (εἰδωλόθυτος), on the one hand, and divergent views on the ongoing relevance of 'many gods and many lords'—that is, idols—on the other.

By pointing to those divergent views, Paul enters the first stages of drawing distinctions between groups. In 8.5–6 he juxtaposes the reality of 'many gods and many lords' and the striking monotheistic confession of 'one God ... and one Lord'. This marks a distinction between those affected by the reality of 'many gods and many lords' and those ('us', in Paul's language) for whom there is but one God and one Lord. On one level, this is again a distinction between believers and non-believers. But it is also a distinction among believers, as 8.7 makes clear: 'This knowledge is not in all. Some, accustomed until now to idols, eat as a sacrifice to idols, and their consciences, being weak, are defiled.' As before, the appearance of εἰδωλόθυτος indicates that the focus of Paul's discussion is the community itself. Thus 8.5–7 draws a distinction between two groups of believers which may mark

---

28 Here we follow Danna Nolan Fewell and David Gunn, who differentiate between 'the subject' and 'the Subject'. They write, 'We are not looking for an answer to the question, What is the subject? Rather we mean the governing consciousness (and unconsciousness), the point of view whose interest this text expresses, or better, constructs. That is, we are seeking to answer the question, Who is its subject (Or, to avoid confusion, Subject).' Quoting Chris Weedon, Danna Nolan Fewell and David Gunn note that subjectivity within a text refers to 'the conscious and unconscious thoughts and emotions of the individual, her sense of herself and her ways of understanding her relation to the world'. See D.N. Fewell and D. Gunn, *Gender, Power, and Promise: The Subject of the Bible's First Story* (Nashville: Abingdon Press, 1993), pp. 16–17.

points on a wider spectrum of views, a distinction based on knowledge, specifically that regarding 'so-called gods and lords'.

That the practical status of idols, the various forms of knowledge, and the consciences of believers are tied together in Paul's response to the Corinthians' initial question is indicated by 8.7. His redefinition of idols in 8.5 (as 'many gods and many lords', which influence at least some believers) allows him to claim that some within the community eat food offered to idols (εἰδωλόθυτος) as food offered, in effect, to 'so-called gods and lords'. There are three reasons for this, all identified in 8.7: the knowledge that 'is not in them'; that they have been 'accustomed until now to idols'; and their 'weak consciences'. These believers, it seems, are unable to agree with the maxim '[there is] no idol in the world'. Rather, for them, idols (so-called gods and lords) *do* exist. As Paul describes it, these believers do not understand idols as non-existent, but rather see them as 'false gods'. They may 'know' that these idols are merely false gods, but they seem not to know (within their consciences, at least) that these false gods, in fact, exist not at all.

Their belief in the ongoing relevance of these so-called gods and lords arises from prior custom and gives rise to 'weak consciences'. Exactly what Paul means by 'conscience' is a point of significant debate,[29] but for our purposes, we can follow Ben Witherington's description: 'its root meaning is "awareness" or "reflective consciousness"'.[30] The former of these possibilities makes particular sense here: the 'awareness' of the true status of idols is 'weak' within some believers. Not knowing God and Jesus with the thoroughgoing certainty expressed in 8.6, these believers are as yet unaware that idols are irrelevant. Indeed, as long as they are thus unaware and weak in conscience, 'so-called gods and lords' are relevant, because they continue to exert influence upon some members of the congregation. However, in 8.12, Paul suggests that this weakness of conscience need not be permanent. As the NRSV translation indicates, one may see Paul as warning the knowledgeable Corinthians not to 'wound [another's] conscience *when it is weak*',[31] a phrasing that suggests those consciences will not always be so, though Paul makes no effort to encourage anyone to attempt such strengthening. His goal is not to erase the differences in 'strength' of conscience among believers, but to enable the community itself to be strengthened by the differences among them. In order to do so, he attempts to convince the 'knowledgeable' Corinthians to take a different viewpoint from that with which they began. This is where the imposition of God's perspective (in 8.3) returns: God knows even those believers who are not certain of the nonexistence of idols and, Paul

---

29 For discussion of the meaning of the Pauline term 'conscience', see C.A. Pierce, *Conscience in the New Testament: A Study of* Syneidesis *in the New Testament* (Studies in Biblical Theology; London: SCM, 1955); R. Jewett, *Paul's Anthropological Terms: A Study of their Use in Conflict Settings* (AGJU, 10; Leiden: Brill, 1971); J. Stepien, 'Syneidesis: la conscience dans l'anthropologie de Saint-Paul', *Revue d'histoire et de philosophie religieuses* 60.1 (1980), pp. 1–20; P.W. Gooch, 'Conscience in 1 Cor. 8 and 10', *NTS* 33 (1987), pp. 244–54; J.A. Davis, 'The Interaction between Individual Ethical Conscience and Community Ethical Consciousness in 1 Corinthians', *Horizons in Biblical Theology* 10 (December, 1988), pp. 1–18.

30 Ben Witherington III, *Conflict and Community in Corinth: A Socio-Rhetorical Commentary on 1 and 2 Corinthians* (Grand Rapids, MI: Eerdmans, 1995), p. 199.

31 Here, τὴν συνείδησιν ἀσθενοῦσαν is understood to be a dative of attendant circumstance, a construction that suggests that the attendant circumstance may be temporary.

suggests, attends to their 'weak consciences'. So too, then, should those knowledgeable Corinthians. A central element of the reasoning behind this view is implicit here, but it is expressly stated in 12.22ff.: 'the members of the body that appear to be weaker are indispensable ... If one member suffers, all suffer together with it.'

Paul's argument in favor of such a shift in perspective is grounded in his description of the effects of eating εἰδωλόθυτος. He does not disagree with the idea that this food has no bearing upon the relationship of some to God, an idea (possibly originating in the Corinthians' letter) expressed in 8.8: 'Food will not bring us close to God. If we do not eat we will not be made further from God, nor if we eat will we be closer.' In spite of his apparent agreement, the focus of his response is his concern for those in whom 'this knowledge is not' (8.7). Those 'accustomed until now to idols' (that is, to so-called gods and lords) are affected within 'their consciences, [which] being weak, are wounded' (8.7). If 'encouraged' by the example of others to eat εἰδωλόθυτος, they 'are destroyed' (8.10) and can be 'caused to fall' (σκανδαλίζω, 8.13), presumably away from God and Christ. If food is (for the knowledgeable ones) a matter of no consequence, how can it have such disastrous effects upon those with weak consciences? It is precisely this weakness of conscience that makes the difference: they would still 'eat as if sacrifices to idols' were in fact sacrifices to so-called gods and lords, and in so doing, would violate the monotheistic knowledge they do have.

An intriguing element of Paul's argument is the apparent equation of wounding a conscience, destroying a 'brother', and 'causing a brother to fall'. The second term in the trio indicates precisely how seriously Paul views this matter: although one might have qualms about 'wounding [another's] conscience' or even about 'causing a brother to fall' or 'stumble', it is quite another matter to 'destroy the brother for whom Christ died' (8.11). Should the knowledgeable Corinthians eat εἰδωλόθυτος, each of these is an equally likely result. The equation, and indeed the admonition to avoid such results, is based again in the 'God's eye' view of the situation first established in 8.3, and governing the discussion from that point forward. God knows the 'weak consciences' of some and fully recognizes the effects that consumption of εἰδωλόθυτος may have upon them. The influence of this divine perspective filters through Paul's final comment as well: 'if food causes my brother [and sister] to fall, then I will not eat meat for eternity, so that I might not cause my brother [and sister] to fall' (8.13). Again, echoes of eschatological language, and the divine perspective it conveys, are apparent in the phrase εἰς τὸν αἰῶνα, 'for eternity'.

Through this brief exploration, we see that Paul does draw distinctions between groups within the Corinthian community, and also draws distinctions between ways of knowing and forms of knowledge: indeed, his entire response to the question of εἰδωλόθυτος is shaped by the differences he constructs. Perhaps the overriding distinction is that between the Corinthians' perspective and God's perspective: once he has shifted the 'governing consciousness' of the discussion away from the Corinthians to God (in 8.3), he is able to construct differences as God sees them. The link he draws between his perspective and God's grants Paul an authority he fully expects the Corinthians to acknowledge. We can recognize in Paul's construction of difference several elements of considerable importance. First, the distinctions he draws are (ostensibly) based not in human understanding but in the love of God— and as such, come within the shared context of all believers' love of God. 'If anyone loves God, that one is known by God'—and known in all one's weakness as well as one's faith. This statement of God's knowledge of all members of the community is implicitly followed by the assertion that anyone who loves God will also attempt to know others as God does, for this is knowing 'as it is necessary to know'.

Second, the hierarchies suggested by so many scholarly interpretations of this passage, most frequently expressed through the characterization of the groups as 'the Strong' and 'the Weak', are certainly not the focus of Paul's emphasis. His discussion does not oppose the two groups in dichotomous, hierarchy-producing fashion. Rather, by placing the discussion of group differences firmly within the context of group sameness, Paul suggests that neither group can or should claim superiority over the other. Nor should they focus on their differences to the extent that their similarities are overlooked. The third point is closely related: Paul's initial focus upon all that members of the community share, coupled with his later remark about wounding another's conscience 'when it is weak', suggests that his view of the various groups is neither static nor rigid. The possibility that those with weak consciences may somehow strengthen their monotheistic faith is a real one for Paul, for it is based in his sense that weakness is not a matter of essence, but of previous custom and insufficient knowledge. Moreover, the emphasis upon the relationship to God that all believers share suggests that Paul views the different groups primarily in terms of their relationships to God, rather than in terms of their relative 'weakness' or 'knowledge'.

Paul thus couples a dynamic understanding of each group's identity with an awareness of large areas of overlap and similarities, which for him are ultimately more determinative than the differences he draws among them. For Paul, the most important things that members of each group must recognize about members of the other are that all love God and are equally known by God (8.3), and that Christ died on behalf of them all (8.11). Only by an awareness of this interrelationship, which is far more significant than are their distinctions, can the community of believers flourish in the midst of the differences.

Implications

The ways in which any particular group is marked as different from a perceived norm can inform our view of all other groups that are so marked. Consequently, Paul's marking of group differences within 1 Corinthians 8 adds to our understanding of Paul's view of other groups within the community, such as women (in 11.2–16).

Our brief review of Paul's discussion of head coverings in worship indicated that Paul's sense of gender differentiation is quite hierarchical. This is in contrast to the lack of hierarchical distinctions between the groups involved in the disagreement over εἰδωλόθυτος. The contrast between a hierarchical understanding of group differentiation and a less hierarchical one is a fertile area for research into Paul's view of difference in general and gender in particular. Is the ostensibly innate character of gender the basis for his more hierarchical view? In what ways might his reliance in that discussion on 'common sense', strikingly absent from his discussion of εἰδωλόθυτος, shape his conceptions along more hierarchical lines? Explorations of other passages in which Paul draws distinctions between groups may well help us determine if his view of gender is especially hierarchical, or if his view of the groups in 1 Corinthians 8 is anomalously egalitarian.

A second area in which our discussion of 1 Corinthians 8 suggests options for further feminist research is Paul's discussion of 'ways of knowing'. Feminist theories of epistemology may enhance our understanding of the role and function of knowledge in Paul's thought. The links that Paul makes in 1 Corinthians 8 between 'knowledge', 'custom' (that is, previous experience), and 'conscience' are links that feminist epistemology also emphasizes, which suggests that his understanding of knowledge may be the locus of fruitful interaction with these epistemologies.

Finally, feminist theologians and ethicists may find the (ostensibly) divine perspective on group differentiation ground for reflection. As contemporary faith communities struggle with difference—both between and within groups—further discussion of divine perspective on difference is both inevitable and necessary. There is much to be said for including biblical theology in these discussions. Paul's attempt to replace a human view of difference with a divine view in 1 Corinthians 8 suggests that his thought on this topic may prove a helpful prototype to guide discussions of difference in the future.[32]

These are merely a few ways in which feminist interpretation can further explore how, and why, Paul 'makes a difference'. As generations of feminist interpreters have noted, there are certainly areas of his thought that we must challenge and even refute. However, there are also ways in which Paul may be a helpful and intriguing dialogue partner, particularly as we continue to move beyond minimalist conceptions of the topics and tasks of feminist interpretation. Paul will continue to make a difference in more ways than we can currently imagine, while feminists also can and should make a difference in understandings of Paul.

---

32 I follow here Elisabeth Schüssler Fiorenza's distinction between the Bible as 'archetype' and the Bible as 'prototype'.

'LAW-FREE GENTILE CHRISTIANITY'—
WHAT ABOUT THE WOMEN?
FEMINIST ANALYSES AND ALTERNATIVES*

LUISE SCHOTTROFF

The Concept of 'Gentile Christianity'

To this day, Second Testament scholarship and Christian dogmatics are governed by the assertion that the Christian gospel is 'law-free'. In relation to how Paul is interpreted, it means that Paul rejects the law, that is to say, the Torah of the Jewish people, as a way to salvation. Men of non-Jewish origin who believe in Jesus as the Messiah are not to seek circumcision; being circumcised would mean to submit to the law that leads to death. The concept of 'law-free Gentile Christianity' represents a depiction of Christian identity in historical as well as theological perspective. It determines the Christian interpretation of the Jesus-tradition, of Paul, and the portrayal of early Christian history. Therefore, I intend to submit this concept to a fundamental theological and historical critique. The majority of current scholarly commentaries on the Second Testament, textbooks, and lexica assume this concept. I will not provide a detailed list here of such works.[1]

In summary, these are the stereotypes of that concept:

- the Christian gospel is law-free. At the heart of the gospel is God's saving act in Jesus Christ (Christocentrism);
- Judaism is legalistic;
- seeking to achieve salvation on one's own (through the law) is sin;
- Paul's repudiation of circumcision signifies the fundamental abrogation of the law;
- even Jesus himself tends to represent a law-free position (cf. Mk 2.27);
- the Pharisees are opponents of Jesus and represent a calculating, legalistic position.

* Originally published as ' "Gesetzesfreies Heidenchristentum"—und die Frauen? Feministische Analysen und Alternativen', in Luise Schottroff and Marie-Theres Wacker (eds), *Von der Wurzel Getragen: Christlich-feministische Exegese in Auseinandersetzung mit Antijudaismus* (BIS, 17; Leiden: E.J. Brill, 1996), pp. 227–45. Reprinted by permission. Translated by Barbara and Martin Rumscheidt.
1 For detailed documentation, see Christine Schaumberger and Luise Schottroff, *Schuld und Macht: Studien zu einer feministischen Befreiungstheologie* (Munich: Chr. Kaiser Verlag, 1988), pp. 17ff. Again, the concept of 'law-free Gentile Christianity' also forms the basis of very recent articles of the *Theologische Realenzyklopädie* (e.g. on 'Judenchristentum') or of new textbooks (such as François Vouga's history of early Christianity, *Une théologie du Nouveau Testament* [Le monde de la Bible, 43; Geneva: Labor et Fides, 2001]).

I want to analyze this concept from a feminist perspective. Here, I will draw on feminist discussion of the Christian understanding of sin, Christology, and anti-Judaism in feminist theology, as well as in studies of anti-Judaism in Jewish–Christian dialogue.[2] As a concept, 'law-free Gentile Christianity' is anti-Jewish, misogynist, and dominating. It presupposes an imperialist perspective: by paying no attention to Jewish self-understanding and to contradictory assertions by Jews, Christians define Judaism from their own perspective. The concept presupposes that Christianity has the power to define Judaism. In its concentration on circumcision, 'law-free Gentile Christianity' is also androcentric. Western theology and the church manifest an *imperialist perspective* that, when exercising their power, employs this concept to define which movements within the church are sanctionable by the church. I cite the 1985 theses of the bishops of the North German Lowlands (*Nordelbien*) on feminist theology. They judged that feminist theology advocates self-liberation and asserts an existence of human beings free of sin.[3] It is the same allegation that discounts both Jewish religion and feminist theology. The imperialist perspective of a Christocentric Christology reduces human beings to objects and obscures the mutuality in the relationship to Jesus found, for example, in the narrative parts of the Jesus-tradition.[4] In other words, from its roots, the concept of law-free Gentile Christianity is anti-Jewish: it devalues the Jewish religion. Moreover, it is misogynist in its androcentrism, its understanding of sin, and, of course, its interests of domination.

What follows is further analysis of the *misogyny* of 'law-free Gentile Christianity', which is so closely related to its anti-Judaism. First, I question the role that this concept assigns to women if—other than in the presentation of Pauline theology and its androcentrism—they are mentioned at all. The concept of law-free Gentile Christianity depicts women as the alleged *victims* of the legalistic religion. Jewish regulations concerning impurity and purity are said to discriminate against women in worship and in everyday life. Contrary to this, Jesus is shown to be the liberator of women. I name some of the Second Testament 'hooks' on which this thesis is hoisted: Jn 4.27, Mk 5.25–34 and Gal. 3.28. The latter is always contrasted with *tBer*. 7.18, 'Praise to the One who did not make me a heathen, a woman, an ignoramus' (in the translation of Holtzmann).[5]

---

2 I confine myself to citing just one title for each aspect addressed. On the Christian understanding of sin and the anti-Judaism in the traditional interpretation of Paul, see Schaumberger and Schottroff, *Schuld und Macht*. On feminist Christology, see Doris Strahm and Regula Strobel (eds), *Vom Verlangen nach Heilwerden: Christologie in feministischer Sicht* (Fribourg/Lucerne: Exodus Verlag, 1991). On anti-Judaism in feminist theology, see Leonore Siegele-Wenschkewitz (ed.), *Verdrängte Vergangenheit, die uns bedrängt: Feministische Theologie in der Verantwortung für die Geschichte* (Munich: Chr. Kaiser Verlag, 1988). On Christian anti-Judaism from the traditional androcentric perspective within Christian–Jewish dialogue, see the journal *Kirche und Israel*.

3 For the bishops' text and a feminist analysis of their theses, see Schaumberger and Schottroff, *Schuld und Macht*, pp. 26ff.

4 Cf. in particular Carter Heyward, *The Redemption of God: A Theology of Mutual Relation* (Lanham, MD: University Press of America, 1982).

5 On anti-Judaism in the interpretation of Jn 4.27, see Martina Gnadt, ' "Und die Jünger wunderten sich …" ': Christlicher Antijudaismus in der Auslegung von Joh 4,27', in Leonore Siegele-Wenschkewitz (ed.), *Christlicher Antijudaismus und Antisemitismus: theologische und kirchliche Programme Deutscher Christen* (Frankfurt am Main: Haag & Herchen, 1994), pp. 235–59. On Gal.

However, in this concept there is also the depiction of women as *active agents* in contrast to their role as victims. A. Oepke speaks of the 'feminism of the Jewish and Gnostic propaganda' and says that the Christian congregation is differentiated from this.[6] The historical fact that many non-Jewish women at that time chose, on their own, to follow the Jewish God and to embrace the Jewish way of life is what Oepke calls 'Jewish feminism'. In Oepke's view, it is Jewish propaganda that accounts for this phenomenon. Here, Judaism is discounted for being a religion of women.

There is yet another internal contradiction. Christian exegetes present *Judaism as decidedly a religion of men* and make no value-judgment of this phenomenon. To me, the Christian depiction of Phariseeism as a fraternity of men and of synagogue worship is tantamount to Judaism becoming a surrogate for particular Christian desires. With great zeal Christians assert (cf. Acts 16.13) that a legitimate service of worship in a synagogue cannot be celebrated by women alone[7] and that there was no such thing as a female Pharisee (cf. Acts 23.6).[8] In my view, such zeal seems to be fueled more by Christian conceptions of what legitimate worship is,[9] and by the Christian guild of theologians as a male entity, than from a critique of Judaism.

Therefore, not only are anti-Judaism and discrimination of women to be addressed, but also self-contradictions within Christian exegesis, even by one and the same author. These contradictions can be readily explained. All such statements about Judaism and women, from Christian perspective, proceed from an uncritical assumption that the Christian congregation does everything properly. In addition, there is no critical self-consciousness that would acknowledge androcentrism and an oppressive, patriarchal order of values and praxis. From a Christian perspective one can identify with Judaism as an alleged religion of men and view women as victims; at the same time, with impunity, one may perceive Jewish women as active agents and, in response, completely devalue Judaism as a religion of women.[10]

How does feminist theology deal with the concept of a law-free Gentile Christianity? In relation to the question of Jesus and women, or Gal. 3.28 and Judaism, there soon arose a great and very necessary critique of the uncritical adoption of Christian stereotypes of anti-Judaism on the part of feminist theology.[11]

3.28 and *tBer*. 7.18, cf. Luise Schottroff, *Lydia's Impatient Sisters: A Feminist Social History of Early Christianity* (Louisville, KY: Westminster/John Knox Press, 1995), p. 255 n. 24; on Mk 5.25–34, cf. Evi Krobath, 'Brief der Anonyma, einer von Jesus geheilten Frau, an Luise, die Weise und Gelehrte', in Dorothee Sölle (ed.), *Für Gerechtigkeit streiten: Theologie im Alltag einer bedrohten Welt* (Gütersloh: Gütersloher Verlagshaus, 1994), pp. 15–21.

6 A. Oepke, 'δυνή,' TWNT 1, pp. 776–89 (784). Cf. Luise Schottroff, *Befreiungserfahrungen: Studien zur Sozialgeschichte des Neuen Testaments* (Munich: Chr. Kaiser Verlag, 1990), pp. 292–93.

7 For a critical analysis of the exegetical tradition, see Bernadette Brooten, *Women Leaders in the Ancient Synagogue* (Chico, CA: Scholars Press, 1982), pp. 139–40.

8 Many commentaries set out not to read Acts 23.6 as a statement about Paul's mother being a Pharisee herself.

9 Cf. Schottroff, *Befreiungserfahrungen*, p. 295.

10 On this see Luise Schottroff, *Let the Oppressed Go Free: Feminist Perspectives on the New Testament* (Louisville, KY: Westminster/John Knox Press, 1993), pp. 65–67.

11 A survey is found in Marie-Theres Wacker, 'Historical, Hermeneutical, and Methodological Foundations', in Luise Schottroff, Silvia Schroer, and Marie-Theres Wacker (eds), *Feminist Interpretation: The Bible in Women's Perspective* (Minneapolis: Fortress Press, 1998), pp. 55–62.

A more detailed examination of that discussion is not required at this point. Without noticing it, feminist theologians incorporated Christian stereotypes of Judaism in addressing the issue of women and male circumcision. Here, the discussion is still very much in its initial stages. Christian tradition speaks of women being discriminated against in Judaism because only men are circumcised. It also argues that it was easier for women to convert to Judaism than for men because they did not have to bear the yoke of circumcision.[12] It was against this background that Elisabeth Schüssler Fiorenza concluded that the Christian repudiation of circumcision brought liberation to women. 'If it was no longer circumcision but baptism which was the primary rite of initiation, then women became full members of the people of God with the same rights and duties.'[13] In contrast, Judith Lieu has demonstrated convincingly that male circumcision did not mean that women were not members of the Jewish congregation in the full sense. Women do not have the negative status of the uncircumcised.[14]

The difficult, lengthy process of recognizing Christian anti-Judaism in oneself is more apparent in feminist theology than in traditional theology; it is pursued more openly. Feminists may indeed be proud of this if such pride keeps them moving on the road of critical self-knowledge. For myself, I consider 'law-free Gentile Christianity' to be a powerful and pervasive concept in the Christian consciousness. Therefore, when dealing with particular points that I cannot comprehend sufficiently, I cannot rule out falling into its trap again. Because I am a Gentile Christian who does not want to live law-free, I fundamentally reject the concept of a law-free Gentile Christianity. All the historical assumptions that I have mentioned thus far concerning Judaism on the part of Christian theology and historiography need to be recognized as expressions of Christian anti-Judaism. A new understanding of the history and theology of Judaism is utterly essential for Christian theology. In what follows I try to address some aspects of this.

Feminist Alternative: The Relationship of Judaism and Christianity until 135 CE

Jewish Women, Female Proselytes, and God-Fearers as Bearers of the Young Christian Movement

I do not find it necessary to substantiate that women were significant to the early Christian movement. After more than 20 years of feminist research, I can take for granted here that this young movement was shaped decisively by autonomously acting women—married, unmarried, and widowed. Women like Prisca and Junia were Jewish; Lydia and Phoebe were from Gentile nations. The questions I raise are these: (1) *What did it mean for a non-Jewish woman to become Christian?* (2) *What did it mean for a Jewish woman to become Christian?* The traditional concept of Gentile Christianity provides no satisfactory answers to these questions. It does indeed give the positive answer that these women now believe in Jesus as the Messiah of the Jewish people. Yet negative answers also abound: the law is not a

---

12 Cf. Schottroff, *Befreiungserfahrungen*, p. 299.

13 Elisabeth Schüssler Fiorenza, *In Memory of Her: A Feminist Theological Reconstruction of Christian Origins* (New York: Crossroad, 1983), p. 210.

14 Cf. Judith M. Lieu, 'Circumcision, Women and Salvation', *NTS* 40 (1994), pp. 358–70.

way of salvation for them; in accordance with Paul's views, they should reject circumcision for non-Jewish males. I pursue my questions with material from the Second Testament.

Case One. 1 Cor. 7.15—I shall use the word 'Christian' even though it evokes the erroneous impression that an institutional Christian religion already existed. A (nameless) Christian woman—more precisely, a Gentile-Christian woman married to a non-Christian/non-Jewish man—faces divorce because she has changed so much since becoming a Christian. Her everyday life must have changed fundamentally. She is under pressure from her Christian congregation to prevent the divorce. What needs to be noted even now is what a wide range of choices she is assumed to have open to her. She has become a Christian independent of her husband. She can influence his intention to obtain a divorce. On the other hand, Paul's text presupposes that for this woman the suffering caused by marital strife is a great burden. Paul decides to support this woman's wish to have the divorce even though he actually rejects divorce for Christian women (1 Cor. 7.10): '... in these circumstances, the ... sister is not tied; God has called you to a life of peace. If you are a wife, it may be your part to save your husband, for all you know ...' (1 Cor. 7.15–16). A portrait of this marital strife may be gleaned, for example, from Tertullian (ca. 160–220 CE): if the Christian woman wishes to keep a regular fast on two days of the week, the husband arranges for a bath early in the day, either to prevent her from participating in Christian worship or because fasting included abstaining from taking a bath. Tertullian's list of issues in marital strife provides the following information about a Gentile-Christian woman's way of life: she keeps regular fasts and other fast days; she leaves the house and her domestic work to visit the huts of poor Christian families in other parts of the city; she attends Christian gatherings during the night, participates in the Christian meal celebration, visits prisoners in jail, exchanges the kiss of peace with fellow brothers, fetches water for washing the feet of the saints, and uses food from the marital household to feed Christian women and men in transit (cf. Tertullian, *Ad uxorem* 2.4). Elsewhere in Tertullian, one finds that Christian women attended Christian gatherings in make-up and jewelry (*De cultu fem.* 2.4). This list of contentious points passed through a filter of androcentrism, namely Tertullian's. Still it shows that the sphere of conflict was constituted by the practice of Christian love and what happened outside the home related to that activity. Consequences of becoming Christian had to do with the conviviality of the congregation and the results of the Christian conduct of life.

In 1 Cor. 7.15, compelled by what seems to be bold liberality on his part in the matter of a Christian woman's divorce, Paul inserts an excursus on 'the basics' into his *halachah* on the regulation of sexual relations (1 Cor. 7.17–24). He wants to elucidate the criteria according to which *halachic* decisions are to be made.

For Paul, the criterion is to live in accordance with God's call. In relation to the case in point, this means that God's peace can be realized only through a divorce. Neither the family status (divorced or not), nor religious origin ('circumcision', that is, Jewish or non-Jewish origin), nor even the legal status (slave or free) is decisive.

It is God's call that is decisive,[15] and that means the observance of God's command-ments (1 Cor. 7.19). In Paul's view, under certain circumstances it is not a commandment of God to preserve a marriage, nor to circumcise a non-Jewish male because he desires to observe God's commandments. For Paul, to observe the commandments of God means to live according to God's will, that is, the Torah. Read literally, this text says that what matters is the Jewish way of living and that circumcision of non-Jewish men is *not* part of it, other than for its significance for Jewish men. In the case of this Christian woman, what leads to marital strife is her observing God's commandments in her way of living. The details of this way of living which I have named with the help of Tertullian may without exception be corroborated from sources of the Second Testament period.

Case Two. Acts 9.36–43—Tabitha is a Jewish woman who becomes Christian and is called a disciple. It is reasonable to assume that like other women she is a pupil of Jesus and that from her teacher she learns to read and to interpret Scripture. In addition, the text refers to her as a just Jewish woman: 'never tired of doing good or giving in charity' (9.36).[16] An aspect of her exemplary life-praxis becomes apparent from the narrative: she wove tunics and clothes (9.39), and with her work contributed to the economic foundation of a women's community within the Christian congre-gation (cf. 1 Tim. 5.16). As Ivoni Richter Reimer notes: 'Jewish pious practices on behalf of the poor are neither challenged nor overthrown by this story. On the contrary: such a spirituality is both confessed and practiced by Tabitha, who is at the very center of the story. A Jewish-Christian woman had no need to repudiate her roots.'[17]

The narrative shows Tabitha embraced by a network of people who relate to and honor her as a justice-living Jewish woman. It reveals how they are all related in a specific manner to the Jew Jesus. She quite likely belongs to those who believe in Jesus' resurrection and in his being the Messiah of the Jewish people. As a Jewish Christian she lives in a Christian congregation.

Here I want to call attention to Jewish traditions indicating that Jewish women, as a result of their charitable activities, deported themselves with great self-awareness in relation to their husbands; in other words, there exists a distinctive history of Jewish and, subsequently, Christian women and their works of love.[18]

But the question to be addressed now is this: What really distinguishes the nameless Gentile-Christian woman (case no. 1) from a Jewish proselyte woman, one who fears God? What is the Christian difference?

---

15 This interpretation of 1 Cor. 7.17–24 has to overcome the widely held, traditional view that the word κλῆσις in 1 Cor. 7.20 refers to one's 'state' or 'condition' (RSV) in patriarchal society and not God's calling. Such a reading turns 1 Cor. 7.17–24 into the manifesto of a status-quo theology: 'Let each of you remain in the state (condition) in which you were called', meaning that being Christian does not change being woman or slave. For an interpretation of 1 Cor. 7.17–24, see Schottroff, *Lydia's Impatient Sisters*, pp. 121–35.

16 See Ivoni Richter Reimer, *Women in the Acts of the Apostles: A Feminist Liberation Perspective* (Minneapolis: Fortress Press, 1995), pp. 33–62, on Tabitha's discipleship and practice of living.

17 Reimer, *Women in the Acts of the Apostles*, p. 61.

18 Cf. Luise Schottroff, 'Dienerinnen der Heiligen: Der Diakonat der Frauen im Neuen Testament', in Gerhard K. Schäfer and Theodor Strohm (eds), *Diakonie—biblische Grundlagen und Orientierungen* (Heidelberg: Heidelberger Verlagsanstalt, 1994), pp. 222–42.

In biblical times there were no autonomous conversions of women to Judaism. A non-Jewish woman who married a Jewish man left behind her former deities, became a Jew and the mother of Jewish children.[19] It is only in the first century CE that we encounter autonomous conversions of women to Judaism (and to other religions). The chief witnesses are Josephus, the Second Testament and *Joseph and Aseneth*. At that time, there were no clear regulations as to what constitutes a proselyte or a God-fearing woman. Shaye Cohen speaks of 'chaos' in this issue.[20] Conversion was a personal matter; in individual cases very different points emerge relating to a woman's conversion. By the second century CE baptism for female proselytes (circumcision and baptism for male proselytes) seems to have become the accepted practice.[21] Even the distinction between proselyte and God-fearing women is unclear at this time and seems not to have been firmly fixed.[22] After the defeat of Bar Kokhba in 135 CE, as struggle about Jewish identity intensified, separation and hostility on the part of Christianity emerged. Only then did rabbis endeavor to regulate conversions and to clarify which children from a Jewish/non-Jewish mixed marriage were actually Jewish, applying the principle of matrilinearity.[23] The picture often implicitly conveyed in Christian histories of the first century, that there were courts that ruled in a legally binding way on withdrawal from Judaism and entry into Christianity (or Judaism), does not correspond to historical reality. Instead, it appears that being Jewish was decided by membership in the local Jewish or Jewish-Christian congregation. There may have been differences among congregations about what was expected of proselyte women or men and how they related proselytes, God-fearers, and Jews by birth, and how they and God-fearers were classified in relation to the civil community or the state (e.g. after 70 CE in the matter of *fiscus judaicus*). In cases of political conflict between Jewish or Jewish-Christian congregations and Rome it would have been decisive whether a man was circumcised, or whether men and women referred *to themselves* as Jewish or Christian. Calling oneself Christian was to identify oneself as a follower of the Jewish Messiah, which as such (*nomen ipsum*) rendered one suspect of desiring to undermine and do away with Roman political rule.[24]

Tabitha was a Jewish woman who believed Jesus was the Messiah. The anonymous woman whose marital strife I tried to portray was of non-Jewish origin. She had committed herself to the God of Israel and to the commandments of that God, believing also in Jesus as the Messiah of the Jewish people. On account of her faith in Jesus, she is a special case among proselyte/God-fearing women, but she

---

19 Cf. Shaye J.D. Cohen, 'The Origins of the Matrilineal Principle in Rabbinic Law', *Association of Jewish Studies Review* 10 (1985), pp. 19–53.

20 Cf. Shaye J.D. Cohen, 'The Rabbinic Conversion Ceremony', in *JJS* 41 (1990), p. 195. For a survey of scholarship on on the God-fearers, see Bernd Wander, *Trennungsprozesse zwischen frühem Christentum und Judentum im 1. Jh. n. Chr.* (Texte und Arbeiten zum Neutestamentlichen Zeitalter, 16; Tübingen: Francke Verlag, 1994).

21 Cohen, 'The Rabbinic Conversion Ceremony', p. 195.

22 Lieu, 'Circumcision, Women and Salvation', pp. 364f. A valuable source of information and editions of the inscription at Aphrodisias is found in Joyce Reynolds and Robert Tannenbaum, *Jews and God-Fearers at Aphrodisias: Greek Inscriptions with Commentary* (Cambridge: The Cambridge Philological Society, 1987).

23 Cf. Cohen, 'The Origins of the Matrilineal Principle'.

24 Cf. Shaye J.D. Cohen, 'Crossing the Boundary and Becoming a Jew', *HTR* 82 (1989), pp. 13–33.

practices the Jewish way of life, which is also the Christian way of life. However, as already indicated, the question as to what the Jewish or Christian way of life was had not been uniformly regulated in detail nor made legally binding.

The history of Jewish-Christian and of Gentile-Christian women (just as that of the corresponding men) in the course of the first and into the second century CE is part of the history of Judaism in the Diaspora and the Jewish homeland. Gentile-Christians are part of the large group of Jewish proselytes/God-fearers. They opted for the God of Israel and the Jewish way of life in its different forms while placing the Messiah Jesus at the center of their relationship with God. In their own perspective, in that of Rome and of the Jewish and Jewish-Christian congregations, these people are to be counted as part of the Jewish people or, at least, as a marginal group with Judaism. From the very outset, there were conflicts between Jews and Jewish-Christians, but these conflicts did not at all presuppose a definite separation.

A hermeneutical observation is necessary here: I am a German Christian writing after Auschwitz. When I look at the Second Testament and early Christianity as part of the history of Judaism, I open myself to the misunderstanding that my hypothesis is meant to excuse the Second Testament for its anti-Judaism. I am indeed of the opinion that the Second Testament is not anti-Jewish. Even the so-called anti-Judaism of the Gospel of John can be read as an intra-Jewish conflict.[25] Later I refer to Paul in relation to this matter. When I want to understand early Christianity as part of the history of Judaism, it could appear that I am attempting to usurp Judaism or, conversely, that I am presenting anti-Judaism once again as a problem of Jewish people. But in spite of the danger of such misinterpretation, I feel compelled to advance my hypothesis.

Certainly, it would be simpler to assert that there are anti-Jewish passages in the Second Testament from which we need to distance ourselves with informed criticism. But such a thesis would unjustifiably incorporate the Second Testament and other early Christian texts into the Christian anti-Judaism of later ages. Hence, for me the necessary consequence that arises from my historical perspective is to respect the Second Testament as a Jewish book[26] and to respect the deep abyss of Christian anti-Judaism that exists between myself and that book. I am aware of the many centuries of Christian persecution and murder of Jews, and particularly of the murder of millions of Jews on the part of my people during my lifetime. That means that I have irrevocably lost the non-critical way Christians tend to appropriate the Second Testament as a Christian document and even as the word of the Christians' God. Yet the Second Testament, as well as the First Testament, were the texts that my parents loved as God's word, and that I love as God's word. The way toward a new Christian identity and toward accepting both Testaments can only be the development of a new Christian theology and a biblical exegesis that step by step critically

---

25 On the persecution visited upon Jewish messianism by Rome and Rome's perception of Christianity as a form of Jewish messianism, see e.g. Hegesippus in Eusebius, *Hist. eccl.* 3.19–20 and Schottroff, *Befreiungserfahrungen*, pp. 184ff.

26 Cf. Klaus Wengst, *Bedrängte Gemeinde und verherrlichter Christus: Ein Versuch über das Johannesevangelium* (Munich: Chr. Kaiser Verlag, 2nd edn, 1990); Schottroff, *Befreiungserfahrungen*, pp. 226–28; Barbara Nathanson, 'Toward a Multicultural Ecumenical History of Women in the First Century/ies CE', in Elisabeth Schüssler Fiorenza (ed.), *Searching the Scriptures*, I. *A Feminist Introduction* (New York: Crossroad, 1993), pp. 272–98.

reassess Christian anti-Judaism and anti-Semitism. This new Christian theology will differ in substance from the one I have lived with most of my life. I see myself and my companions only at the very beginning of the journey.

A New Reading of Paul

Part of the continuing development of any new word and just Christian theology is a new reading of Paul. There has been relatively little work done on this aspect in feminist theology because, justifiably, the focus has been on Paul's androcentrism and obstinate patriarchalism. His theological conceptions of law, sin, justification, and Christ were read by women in essentially the traditional way and critiqued in terms of feminism. I do not doubt that this feminist critique of Paul's sexism and anti-Judaism is applicable to the Christian *exegesis* of Paul. Nor do I doubt the validity of the feminist critique of his sexism and oppression of women. But I do doubt his anti-Judaism. For Paul does not say that righteousness ἐξ ἔργων νόμου (from the works of the law) has been annulled by the gospel. A new reading of Paul's theology must be a component of the feminist project. Feminist Christian women, too, have understood him to be an authoritarian, oppressive churchman and theology professor who renounced his Judaism. I believe that valuable insights may be gained by feminists from Paul's theology—though clearly not from what he says about women and about sexuality. Even for feminist Christian women, there is something to learn from Brother Paul, fallible and deserving of critique as he is.

Let me proceed by trying out this new reading in relation to one of Paul's central statements. It is one that according to the Christian and anti-Judaistic habit of reading seems to declare the traditional thesis of the law-free gospel. I choose Gal. 2.16.

> ... but we know that no one is justified on the basis of works of the law but only through faith in Jesus the Messiah. We too came to faith in the Messiah Jesus in order to be justified on the basis of faith in the Messiah Jesus and not on the basis of the law's works. For, on the basis of works of the law no being of flesh can be justified.

Traditional reading says this: it is on the basis of works of the law that the 'Jew' seeks to become justified before God. That is why *the law leads to sinning, which is a pious performance that through its own power wants to achieve salvation*, thereby wresting oneself from (or rising up against) God. Through the death and resurrection of Christ, God has intervened in favor of this human being entangled in sin. God has made the godless righteous and the law is now annulled as a way of salvation. For Christian tradition, the law's significance is restricted to its ethical tradition. Ritual law and, in particular, circumcision have ceased to remain in force for Christians. Circumcision of non-Jewish Christian men places them under the law but does not lead to righteousness before God.

A *new reading* proposes that the key to looking at Paul's theology in a new way is the understanding of sin. Nowhere does Paul say that the *will* to fulfill the law is sin. He says that all humans sin because, without exception, all transgress the law, that is to say, no one lives according to God's will (cf. only Rom. 2.17–24; 3.9ff.; 7.14–25).

It is *the false practice of living* that destroys the life God wills. And this living falsely comes from the structural sin[27] whose power is present everywhere and turns people into murderers. The death and resurrection of the Messiah signify God's intervention in favor of humanity alienated from life. We are set free now (νυνί) from the coercive domination of false praxis. We can 'walk in the new life' (Rom. 6.4), that is, live according to the Torah. Paul rigorously argued the position that living according to God's will, as written in the Torah, is not possible without faith in Christ. Much to his sorrow, most Jews of his time did not accept this position, if they knew it at all. But holding that position meant not that Paul did no longer regard himself as a Jew.

Paul developed an analysis of the human situation in his historical period that is particularly close to the analysis of 2 Esdras. Paul's insight into humankind's false way of living arose from his experience of liberation through faith in the Messiah and how that liberation was manifest in messianic communities. In the analyses of Paul and 2 Esdras, despite their androcentrism, I see sources of inspiration for a feminist analysis of the entanglement of women and men in the structures of domination that thwart their lives, even taking their lives, literally as well as figuratively.[28]

It is often said that the position Paul takes on circumcision is unthinkable within Judaism.[29] It is argued that Jewish congregations could not recognize his stance as Jewish. I do not want to enter the discussion here about first-century Jews who did not consider circumcision an irreplaceable practice. For example, what Josephus writes in his *Ant.* 20.34ff. is subject to polemical debate on this subject. As I have already stated, Paul thought of himself as a Jew (see Phil. 3.3; Gal. 2.15).

Nowhere in Paul's letters do I detect that his repudiation of the need for circumcision for Gentile-Christian men meant that he abrogated God's law or was moving beyond the scope of Judaism. Even within Christianity his view was not undisputed, just as, according to Josephus, the corresponding view of the Jewish merchant Ananias was not beyond dispute. That a century later his view would become a brick in the wall that separated Christianity from Judaism is something Paul could not have known.

---

27 On the feminist-liberation theological concept of structural sin, see Schaumberger and Schottroff, *Schuld und Macht,* pp. 251ff.

28 Here I provide merely a sketch of the traditional reading of Paul's theology and the attempt of a feminist new reading of it. For a more extensive treatment of this, see Schaumberger and Schottroff, *Schuld und Macht.*

29 In her article, 'Paul and the Law: How Complete was the Departure?', *The Princeton Seminary Bulletin* (Supply Issue No. 1, 1990), pp. 71–89, Bernadette Brooten rightly calls for a more differentiated perception 'of various schools of Jewish legal thinking' for classifying Paul's treatment of the law (p. 89). Lieu ('Circumcision, Women and Salvation') and Cohen ('Crossing the Boundary') consider that already in the first century, circumcision is imperative for truly being Jewish. Cf. Lieu, 'Circumcision, Women and Salvation', on sources supporting the view that even independent of Christianity in the first century CE there was a debate within Judaism about the necessity of circumcision which implies, of course, that it was also rejected.

The Emergence of 'Law-Free' Gentile Christianity and of Christian Anti-Judaism

In this final section I want to sketch out in what period of time I locate the separation of Christianity and Judaism, how I picture the emergence of the concept of 'law-free' Gentile Christianity, and, correspondingly, the rise of Christian anti-Judaism. I consider this development to be a consequence of Hadrian's bloody war against the Jewish people under Bar Kokhba's leadership and the expulsion of the surviving Jewish population from Jerusalem and surroundings in 135 CE. Unfortunately, we know all too little about that war's brutality. For that period a historian like Josephus is missing.

Eusebius recounts that until the suppression of the Jews by Hadrian, fifteen bishops succeeded one another in Jerusalem. Though all were said to have been Hebrews by birth, they had sincerely accepted the teaching of Christ. For this reason they were declared worthy of the episcopal office by those appropriate to do so. After Hadrian's victory over the Jews in 135 CE, there were no more bishops from the circumcision (*Hist. eccl.* 4.5.1–4). As a result of Hadrian's reconstruction of Jerusalem as *Aelia Capitolina*, his expulsion of the surviving Jewish population from the city and his prohibition of Jews visiting or settling in Jerusalem, a Gentile-Christian congregation came into being in Jerusalem (*Hist. eccl.* 4.6.4). Now, how do those fifteen bishops from the circumcision fit into the picture of history painted by Christians? Even Eusebius himself accommodates them to his perception by assuming that they required legitimation from Gentile-Christian males in leadership positions. According to the traditional Christian view of history, the year 70 and the destruction of Jerusalem by Titus saw the diminution of Jewish Christianity to an insignificant left-over in relation to the 'real' Christianity. It is said to have existed subsequently as a Jewish-Christian sect. Those fifteen Jewish bishops do not quite fit into the traditional picture Christians have painted of history. For they signal the existence of a sizeable Jewish-Christian church in Jerusalem whose voice needed to be heard by the Gentile-Christian congregations in the Diaspora. As long as there was a strong Jewish Christianity, an anti-Jewish Gentile Christianity could hardly come into being.

Before and during the second Jewish–Roman war, there was great conflict between the Jewish-Christian congregations in Jerusalem and in the remaining territory under Bar Kokhba's rule and Bar Kokhba's government. He and the Jewish people with him were fighting for the existence of the people. Bar Kokhba regarded Jewish Christians as *Jews* who as such were obliged to serve in the war against Rome. Since he saw himself as the Messiah and was so understood also by the people, for Jewish Christians military service against Rome was tied to the recognition of Bar Kokhba as the Messiah. Thus, they refused to fight alongside him.[30]

---

30 For information on Jewish-Christian refusal to serve in Bar Kokhba's army, see Orosius, *History* 7.13 where it is said that they did not everywhere support him and his army against Rome, or Justin Martyr, *First Apology* 31 (cf. Eusebius, *Hist. eccl.* 4.8) who suggests that it would have been a denial and a mockery of Jesus to serve in that army, or, finally, Eusebius, in his chronology of the seventeenth year of Hadrian's reign: Jewish-Christians refused to help Bar Kokhba in his fight against Roman soldiers. On the Jewish–Roman conflict as a whole, see Michael Avi-Jonah, *Geschichte der Juden im Zeitalter des Talmud*, II (Berlin, de Gruyter, 1962). Cf. Schottroff, *Lydia's Impatient Sisters*, p. 12. Justin Martyr, in *Dial. Tryph* 47, depicts a Gentile Christianity that no longer feels it necessary to pay attention to Jewish demands that the law be observed.

Together they died with the many other Jews who lost their lives in Hadrian's war. Only *after* that did Jewish Christianity essentially disappear. It declined with the last prince of Judah even though it did not fight with him against Rome. Only *after* that could a Gentile Christianity arise 'law-free' and anti-Judaistic, denying its Jewish roots. Justin and Marcion are the first to give testimony to this Gentile Christianity. Only after 135 CE is there an increase in the number of Christian voices maintaining that being Christian means not to be Jewish.

John Chrysostom (d. 407 CE) frets about Christian women who attend Jewish worship services.[31] His demarcation of Christianity from Judaism is based on Judaism having been discounted. Reflecting on what Christian identity is and formulating one's creeds at the expense of others, in particular of Jews, was and is an expression of Christian power politics. Around Chrysostom there were women who did not go along with this. For my part, I want to join in and live out a confession to Jesus as the Messiah that is not based on an unholy separation while denying Jews, Muslims, and people of other faiths their way to God. I consider strengthening one's identity in everyday life to be a central task in a society that is dissolving in injustice and consumerism. But an identity that is detrimental to others is a murder weapon exchanged for the path to life. As a Gentile Christian woman, I want to live in accordance with God's law, the Torah. In doing so I do not want to blur my Christian identity. Part of that identity involves a long history of Christian anti-Judaism/anti-Semitism and the task of reflecting about a Christology that is no longer imperialistic. As a Gentile Christian I want to think with my Jewish and Christian sisters and brothers about what it means to live in our endangered world today according to God's will, and then to live that life together with them.

---

31 Chrysostom, *Adv. Judaeos* 2.3–6; 4.3 (in Ross S. Kraemer, *Maenads, Martyrs, Matrons, Monastics: A Sourcebook on Women's Religions in the Graeco-Roman World* [Philadelphia: Fortress Press, 1988]. According to the Syrian *didaskalia*, Christian women engaged autonomously in active resistance against the power-politics of excluding people from the bishop's church; cf. Schottroff, *Lydia's Impatient Sisters*, p. 143. The notion of a clear ideology that functions to fix boundaries and the practice of exclusion with the help of such an ideology are part and parcel of the history of unjust structures of domination.

Aland, K., *Neutestamentliche Entwürfe* (Munich: Kaiser, 1979).

Aspegren, K., *The Male Woman: A Feminine Ideal in the Early Church* (ed. René Kieffer; Stockholm: Almqvist & Wiksell, 1990).

Atkins, R.A., *Egalitarian Community: Ethnography and Exegesis* (Tuscaloosa: University of Alabama Press, 1991).

Atwood, M., *Dancing Girls and Other Stories* (New York: Simon & Schuster, 1978).

Aune, D.E., 'Romans as a *Logos Protreptikos* in the Context of Ancient Religious and Philosophical Propaganda', in Hengel and Heckel (eds), *Paulus und das antike Judentum*, pp. 91–124.

Avi-Jonah, M., *Geschichte der Juden im Zeitalter der Talmud in den Tagen von Rom und Byzanz* (Studia Judaica; Forschungen zur Wissenschaft des Judentums, 2; Berlin: De Gruyter, 1962).

Baeck, L., *Das Evangelium als Urkunde der jüdischen Glaubensgeschichte* (Berlin: Schocken Verlag, 1938).

Balch, D.L., 'Backgrounds of 1 Cor VII: Sayings of the Lord in Q; Moses as an Ascetic ΘΕΙΟΣ ANHP in Cor III', *NTS* 18 (1972), pp. 351–58.

—— '1 Cor. 7.32–35 and Stoic Debates about Marriage, Anxiety, and Distractions', *JBL* 102.3 (1983), pp. 429–39.

—— *Let Wives Be Submissive: The Domestic Code in 1 Peter* (SBLMS, 26; Chico, CA: Scholars Press, 1981).

Balch, D.L., E. Ferguson, and W. Meeks (eds), *Greeks, Romans, and Christians: Essays in Honor of Abraham J. Malherbe* (Minneapolis: Fortress Press, 1990).

Ball, W.E., *St Paul and Roman Law* (Edinburgh: T. & T. Clark, 1901).

Balsdon, J.P.V.D., *Roman Women: Their History and Habits* (London: Bodley Head, 1962).

Barber, E.W., *Women's Work: The First 20,000 Years* (New York: W.W. Norton, 1994).

Barns, J.W.B. *et al.* (eds), *Oxyrhynchus Papyri, XXXI* (67 vols.; London: Egyptian Exploration Society, 1983).

Barrett, C.K., *A Commentary on the First Epistle to the Corinthians* (London: Adam & Charles Black, 1968).

Bartchy, S.S., *Mallon Chresai: First Century Slavery and the Interpretation of 1 Cor. 7.21* (SBLDS, 11: Missoula, MT: Scholars Press, 1973).

Barth, M., and H. Blanke, *Colossians* (AB, 34B; New York: Doubleday, 1994).

Bassler, J.M., '1 Corinthians', in Newsom and Ringe (ed.), *The Women's Bible Commentary*, pp. 321–29.

—— 'Divine Impartiality in Paul's Letter to the Romans', *NovT* 26 (1984), pp. 43–58.

—— *Divine Impartiality: Paul and a Theological Axiom* (SBLDS, 59; Chico, CA: Scholars Press, 1982).

Bassler, J.M. (ed.), *Pauline Theology*, I (3 vols.; Minneapolis: Fortress Press, 1991).

Beavis, M.A.,' 2 Thessalonians,' in Schüssler Fiorenza (ed.), *Searching the Scriptures*, II, pp. 263–72.

Belenky, M.F., *et al.* (eds), *Women's Ways of Knowing: The Development of Self, Voice, and Mind* (New York: Basic Books, 10th anniversary edn, 1997).

Bell, H.I., and C.H. Roberts (eds), *A Descriptive Catalogue of the Greek Papyri in the Collection of Wilfred Merton, FSA* (London: Emery Walker Limited, 1948).

Berger, A. (ed.), *Encyclopedic Dictionary of Roman Law* (Transactions of the American Philosophical Society, NS, 43; Philadelphia: American Philosophical Society, 1953).

Berger, K., *Formgeschichte des Neuen Testaments* (Heidelberg: Quelle & Meyer, 1984).

—— *Hellenistische Gattungen im Neuen Testament: Principat 25,2* (*ANRW*, II.25/2; Berlin: Walter de Gruyter, 1984), p. 1140.

Berger, P.L., and T. Luckmann, *The Social Construction of Reality* (Garden City, NY: Doubleday, 1967).

Betz, H.D., *Galatians: A Commentary on Paul's Letter to the Churches in Galatia* (Hermeneia; Philadelphia: Fortress Press, 1979).

Black, M., *Models and Metaphors* (Ithaca, NY: Cornell University Press, 1962).

Blake, L.D., 'Comments on Timothy', in Stanton, *The Woman's Bible* (2 vols.; Boston: Northeastern University Press, 1993), II, p. 163.

Boesak, A., *Comfort and Protest: Reflections on the Apocalypse of John of Patmos* (Philadelphia: Westminster Press, 1987).

Booth, W.C., 'Metaphor as Rhetoric: The Problem of Evaluation', in Sacks (ed.), *On Metaphor*, pp. 47–70.

Boswell, J., *Christianity, Social Tolerance, and Homosexuality* (Chicago: University of Chicago Press, 1980).

—— 'Revolutions, Universals, and Sexual Categories', in Duberman (ed.), *Hidden from History: Reclaiming the Gay and Lesbian Past 17* (New York: New American Library, 1989), pp. 21–25.

Boucher, M., 'Some Unexplored Parallels to 1 Cor. 11.11–12 and Gal. 3.28: The New Testament on the Role of Women', *CBQ* 31 (1969), pp. 50–58.

Bowman, A.K., *et al.* (eds), *Oxyrhynchus Papyri*, L (67 vols.; London: Egyptian Exploration Society, 1983).

Boyarin, D., 'Allegoresis against Difference: The Metalinguistic Origins of the Universal Subject', *Paragraph* (forthcoming).

—— 'Apostles as Babes and Nurses in 1 Thessalonians 2.7', in Carroll, Cosgrove, and Johnson (eds), *Faith and History*, pp. 193–207.

—— ' "Behold Israel according to the Flesh": On Anthropology and Sexuality in Late Antique Judaism', *Yale Journal of Criticism* 5 (1992), pp. 25–55.

—— *Carnal Israel: Reading Sex in Talmudic Culture* (New Historicism, 25; Berkeley: University of California Press, 1993).

—— 'Internal Opposition in Talmudic Literature: The Case of the Married Monk', *Representations* 36 (1991), pp. 87–113.

—— 'The Maternity of Paul: An Exegetical Study of Galatians 4.19', in Fortna and Gaventa (eds), *The Conversation Continues*, pp. 189–201.

—— *A Radical Jew: Paul and the Politics of Cultural Identity* (Berkeley: University of California Press, 1994).

Boyarin, D., and C. Ocker (eds), *Galatians and Gender Trouble: Primal Androgyny and the First-Century Origins of a Feminist Dilemma* (Berkeley: Center for Hermeneutical Studies, 1995).

Bradley, K.R., 'Child Care at Rome: The Role of Men', in *idem.*, *Discovering the Roman Family: Studies in Roman Social History* (New York: Oxford University Press, 1991), pp. 37–75.

Brawley, R.L., *Biblical Ethics and Homosexuality: Listening to Scripture* (Lousville, KY: Westminster/John Knox Press, 1996).

Brooke, G.J. (ed.), *Women in the Biblical Tradition* (Studies in Women and Religion, 31; Lewiston, NY: Edwin Mellen Press, 1992).

Brooten, B., *Love Between Women: Early Christian Responses to Female Homoeroticism* (Chicago Series on Sexuality, History, and Society; Chicago: University of Chicago Press, 1996).

—— 'Paul and the Law. How Complete was the Departure?' *The Princeton Seminary Bulletin* (Supply Issue No. 1, 1990), pp. 71–89.

—— *Women Leaders in the Ancient Synagogue* (BJS; Chico, CA: Scholars Press, 1982).

Brown, A.R., *The Cross and Human Transformation* (Minneapolis: Augsburg–Fortress Press, 1995).

Brown, P., *The Body and Society: Men, Women, and Sexual Renunciation in Early Christianity* (Lectures on the History of Religion; NS, 13; New York: Columbia University Press, 1988).

Bruce, F.F., *Commentary on Galatians* (Grand Rapids, MI: Eerdmans, 1982).

—— *The Letter of Paul to the Romans* (Leicester: Intervarsity Press; Grand Rapids, MI: Eerdmans, 1985).

Bruns, J.E., 'Philo Christianus: The Debris of a Legend', *HTR* 66 (1973), pp. 141–45.

Buckland, W.W., *A Textbook of Roman Law* (Cambridge: Cambridge University Press, 1972).

Bujard, W., *Stilanalytische Untersuchungen zum Kolosserbrief als Beitrag zur Methodik von Sprachvergleichen* (Studien zur Umwelt des Neuen Testaments, 11; Göttingen: Vandenhoeck & Ruprecht, 1973).

Butler, J. *Gender Trouble: Feminism and the Subversion of Identity* (London: Routledge, 1990).

Bynum, C.W., *Jesus as Mother: Studies in the Spirituality of the High Middle Ages* (Berkeley: University of California Press, 1982).

Byrne, B., *'Sons of God'—'Seed of Abraham': A Study of the Idea of the Sonship of God of All Christians in Paul against the Jewish Background* (Rome: Biblical Institute Press, 1979).

Caizzi, F.D., 'The Porch and the Garden: Early Hellenistic Images of the Philosophical Life', in A.W. Bulloch, *et al.* (eds), *Images and Ideologies: Self Definition in the Hellenistic World* (Berkeley: University of California Press, 1993), pp. 303–29.

Calder, W.M., 'Adoption and Inheritance in Galatia,' *JTS* 81 (1930), pp. 372–74.

Callahan, A.D., *Embassy of Onesimus: The Letter of Paul to Philemon* (Valley Forge, PA: Trinity Press International, 1997).

Carcopine, J., *Daily Life in Ancient Rome* (New Haven, CT Yale University Press, 1940).

Carroll, J.T., C.H. Cosgrove, and E.E. Johnson (eds), *Faith and History: Essays in Honor of Paul W. Meyer* (Atlanta: Scholars Press, 1990).

Carson, A., 'Putting Her in her Place: Women, Dirt, and Desire', in Halperin, Winkler, and Zeitlin (eds), *Before Sexuality*, pp. 135–69.

Cartlidge, D.R., '1 Corinthians 7 as a Foundation for a Christian Sex Ethic', *JR* 55 (1975), pp. 220–34.

Castelli, E., '"I Will Make Mary Male": Pieties of the Body and Gender Transformation of Christian Women in Late Antiquity', in J. Epstein and K. Staub (ed.), *Body Guards: The Cultural Politics of Gender Ambiguity* (London: Routledge, 1991), pp. 29–50.

—— *Imitating Paul: A Discourse of Power* (Louisville, KY: Westminster/John Knox Press, 1991).

—— 'Paul on Women and Gender', in Kraemer and D'Angelo (eds), *Women and Christian Origins*, pp. 221–35.

—— 'Romans', in Schüssler Fiorenza (ed.), *Searching the Scriptures*, II, pp. 273–300.

—— 'Virginity and its Meaning for Women's Sexuality in Early Christianity', *JFSR* 2 (1986), pp. 61–88.

Charlesworth, J.H. (ed.), *The Old Testament Pseudepigrapha* (2 vols.; London: Darton, Longman & Todd, 1983).

Chesnut, G., 'The Ruler and the Logos in Neopythagorean, Middle Platonic, and Late Stoic Political Philosophy', *Principat 16,2* (*ANRW*, II.16/2; ed. W. Haase; Berlin: Walter de Gruyter, 1978).

Clark, E., 'Ascetic Renunciation and Feminine Advancement: A Paradox of Late Ancient Christianity', in *idem* (ed.), *Ascetic Piety and Women's Faith: Essays in Late Ancient Christianity* (Studies in Women and Religion, 3; Lewiston, NY: Edwin Mellen Press, 1986), pp. 75–208.

Cohen, B., *Jewish and Roman Law: A Comparative Study* (New York: The Jewish Theological Seminary of America, 1966).

Cohen, J., *'Be Fertile and Increase, Fill the Earth and Master It': The Ancient and Medieval Career of a Biblical Text* (Ithaca, NY: Cornell University Press, 1989).

Cohen, S.J.D., 'Crossing the Boundary and Becoming a Jew', *HTR* 82 (1989), pp. 13–33.

—— 'The Origins of the Matrilineal Principle in Rabbinic Law', *Association of Jewish Studies Review* 10 (1985), pp. 19–53.

—— 'The Rabbinic Conversion Ceremony', *JJS* 41 (1990), pp. 177–203.

Cohen, S.J.D. (ed.), *The Jewish Family in Antiquity* (Atlanta, GA: Scholars Press, 1993).

Cohen, T., 'Metaphor and the Cultivation of Intimacy', in Sacks (ed.), *On Metaphor*, pp. 1–10.

Colish, M., *The Stoic Tradition from Antiquity to the Early Middle Ages* (Studies in the History of Christian Thought; Leiden: E.J. Brill, 1985).

Collins, J., 'Towards the Morphology of a Genre', *Semeia* 14 (1979), pp. 1–20.

Conzelmann, H., *1 Corinthians: A Commentary on the First Epistle to the Corinthians* (trans. James W. Leitch; Hermeneia, Philadelphia: Fortress Press, 1975).

Cook, J.I., 'The Concept of Adoption in the Theology of Paul,' in *idem* (ed.), *Saved by Hope: Essays in Honor of Richard C. Oudersluys* (Grand Rapids, MI: Eerdmans, 1978), pp. 133–44.

Cooper, K., *The Virgin and the Bride: Idealized Womanhood in Late Antiquity* (Cambridge, MA: Harvard University Press, 1996).

Corbett, P.E., *The Roman Law of Marriage* (Oxford: Clarendon Press, 1930).

Corley, K.E., and K.J. Torjesen, 'Sexuality, Hierarchy, and Evangelism', *TSF Bulletin* (March–April 1987), pp. 23–27.

Cranfield, C.E.B., *A Critical Exegetical Commentary on the Epistle to the Romans* (ICC; 2 vols.; Edinburgh: T. & T. Clark, 5th edn, 1975–79; repr. with corrections, 1983–86; repr. 2001).

Crook, J.A., 'Women in Roman Succession,' in Rawson (ed.), *The Family in Ancient Rome*, pp. 58–82.

Crook, R.H., *An Introduction to Christian Ethics* (Upper Saddle River, NJ: Prentice Hall, 3rd edn, 1999).

Crouzel, H., *Origen: The Life and Thought of the First Great Theologian* (trans. A.S. Worrall; San Francisco: Harper & Row, 1989).

D'Angelo, M.R., 'Veils, Virgins, and the Tongues of Men and Angels: Women's Heads in Early Christianity', in Eilberg-Schwartz and Doniger O'Flaherty (ed.), *Off with Her Head!*, pp. 131–64.

David, M., and A. Groningen (eds), *Papyrological Primer* (Leiden: E.J. Brill, 1965).

Davies, S., *The Revolt of the Widows: The Social World of the Apocryphal Acts* (Carbondale, IL: Southern Illinois University Press, 1980).

Davis, J.A., 'The Interaction between Individual Ethical Conscience and Community Ethical Consciousness in 1 Corinthians', *Horizons in Biblical Theology* 10 (1988), pp. 1–18.

Dawson, D., *Allegorical Readers and Cultural Revision in Ancient Alexandria* (Berkeley: University of California Press, 1992).

Deissmann, G.A., *Bible Studies* (Edinburgh: T. & T. Clark, 1901; 2nd edn, 1909; repr. 1923).

Delaney, C., 'Seeds of Honor, Fields of Shame', in D. Gilmore (ed.), *Honor and Shame and the Unity of the Mediterranean* (AAA Special Publication no. 22; Washington DC: American Anthropological Association, 1987), pp. 35–48.

Deming, W., *Paul on Marriage and Celibacy: The Hellenistic Background of 1 Corinthians 7* (Cambridge: Cambridge University Press, 1995).

Derrett, J.D.M., 'The Disposal of Virgins', in *idem, Studies in the New Testament: Glimpses of the Legal and Social Presuppositions of the Authors* (Leiden: E.J. Brill, 1977), pp. 184-91.

Dixon, S., *The Roman Family* (Baltimore, MD: Johns Hopkins University Press, 1992).

Dodd, C.H., *The Epistle of Paul to the Romans* (New York: Ray Long and Richard R. Smith, 1932; London: Hodder & Stoughton, 1949).

Dover, K.J., *Greek Homosexuality* (Cambridge, MA: Harvard University Press, 1989).

du Boulay, J., *Portrait of a Greek Mountain Village* (Oxford: Clarendon Press, 1974).

Dunn, J.D.G., *Romans 1–8* (WBC, 38A; Dallas, TX: Word, 1988).

Ebach, J., 'Apokalypse—zum Ursprung einer Stimmung', in F.W. Marguardt *et al.* (eds), *Einwürfe* (2 vols; Munich: Chr. Kaiser Verlag, 1985), II, pp. 5–61.

Eilberg-Schwartz, H., and W. Doniger O'Flaherty (eds), *Off with Her Head! The Denial of Women's Identity in Myth, Religion, and Culture* (Berkeley: University of California Press, 1995).

Eliade, M., *Mephistopheles and the Androgyne* (New York: Sheed & Ward, 1965).

Elliott, J.H., *A Home for the Homeless* (Philadelphia: Fortress Press, 1981).

Engberg-Pedersen, T., *Paul and the Stoics* (Louisville, KY: Westminster/John Knox Press, 2000).

—— '1 Corinthians 11.16 and the Character of Pauline Exhortation', *JBL* 110 (1992), pp. 679–89.

Evans, K., 'Women's Greek Papyrus Letters and a Study of the Opening Formula', (MA Dissertation, Claremont Graduate School [n.d.]).

Exler, F.X.J., *The Form of the Ancient Greek Letter: A Study in Greek Epistolography* (Washington DC: Catholic University of America Press, 1923).

Falk, Z.W., *Hebrew Law in Biblical Times* (Jerusalem: Wahrmann Books, 1964).

Farmer, W.R., C.F.D. Moule, and R.R. Niebuhr (eds), *Christian History and Interpretation: Studies Presented to John Knox* (Cambridge: Cambridge University Press, 1967).

Fee, G.D., *The First Epistle to the Corinthians* (NICNT; Grand Rapids, MI: Eerdmans, 1987).

Feigin, S., 'Some Cases of Adoption in Israel,' *JBL* 50 (1931), pp. 186–200.

Fewell, D.N., and D. Gunn, *Gender, Power, and Promise: The Subject of the Bible's First Story* (Nashville: Abingdon Press, 1993).

Fitzmyer, J., 'Another Look at ΚΕΦΑΛΗ in 1 Corinthians 11.3', *NTS* 35 (1989), pp. 503–11.

—— *Romans* (AB, 33; New York: Doubleday, 1993).

Fohrer, G., 'υἱός, υἱοθεσία', in *TDNT*, VIII (Grand Rapids, MI: Eerdmans, 1964), pp. 343–54.

Ford, D.C., 'Misogynist or Advocate?: St John Chrysostom and his Views on Women' (PhD dissertation. Drew University, 1989).

Fortna, R.T., and B.R. Gaventa (eds), *The Conversation Continues: Studies in Paul and John in Honor of J. Louis Martyn* (Nashville: Abingdon Press, 1990).

Fowl, S., 'A Metaphor in Distress: A Reading of ΝΗΠΙΟΙ in 1 Thessalonians 2.7', *NTS* 36 (1990), pp. 469–73.

Fraade, S.D., 'Ascetical Aspects of Ancient Judaism', in Green (ed.), *Jewish Spirituality* (2 vols.; New York: Crossroad, 1986), I, pp. 253–88.

Furnish, V.P., *The Moral Teaching of Paul: Selected Issues* (Nashville: Abingdon Press, rev. edn, 1985).

—— 'Paul the Theologian', in Fortna and Gaventa (eds), *The Conversation Continues*, pp. 19–34.

Gamble, H.A., Jr, *The Textual History of the Letter to the Romans* (Grand Rapids, MI: Eerdmans, 1977).

Gaston, L., 'For *All* the Believers: The Inclusion of Gentiles as the Ultimate Goal of Torah in Romans', in *idem*, *Paul and the Torah* (Vancouver: University of British Columbia, 1987), pp. 116–34.

Gaventa, B.R., 'Apostle and Church in 2 Corinthians', in Hay (ed.), *Pauline Theology*, II, pp. 187–93.

—— 'Apostles as Babes and Nurses in 1 Thessalonians 2.7', in Carroll, Cosgrove, and Johnson (eds), *Faith and History*, pp. 193–207.

—— 'The Maternity of Paul: An Exegetical Study of Galatians 4.19', in Fortna and Gaventa (eds), *The Conversation Continues*, pp. 189–201.

—— 'Romans', in Newsom and Ringe (eds), *The Women's Bible Commentary*, pp. 313–20.

Gebara, I., 'The Face of Transcendence', in Schüssler Fiorenza (ed.), *Searching the Scriptures*, I, pp. 172–86.

Geertz, C., 'Religion as a Cultural System', in M. Banton (ed.), *Anthropological Approaches to the Study of Religion* (London: Tavistock, 1966), pp. 1–46.

Gerson, L., '*Isa ta hamartemnata:* The Stoic Doctrine "All Errors are Equal"', in D.V. Stump, *et al.* (eds), *Hamartia: The Concept of Error in the Western Tradition: Essays in Honor of John M. Crossett* (TextsSR, 16; New York: Edwin Mellen Press, 1983), pp. 119–30.

Gleason, M.W., *Making Men: Sophists and Self-Presentation in Ancient Rome* (Princeton, NJ: Princeton University Press, 1995).

—— 'Semiotics of Gender: Physiognomy and Self-Fashioning in the Second Century CE', in Halperin, Winkler, and Zeitlin (eds), *Before Sexuality,* pp. 389–415.

Gnadt, M., 'Und die Jünger wunderten sich . . .': Christlicher Antijudaismus in der Auslegung von Joh 4,27', in Siegele-Wenschkewitz (ed.), *Christlicher Antijudaismus und Antisemitismus*, pp. 235–59.

Gooch, P.W., 'Conscience in 1 Cor. 8 and 10', *NTS* 33 (1987), pp. 244–54.

Gray, M., 'Slave Crimes and Slave Punishment in Roman Society' (Seminar report presented at Columbia University Seminars, 1942).

Greenberg, D., *The Construction of Homosexuality* (Chicago: University of Chicago Press, 1988).

Guerric of Igny, 'Sermon 45: The Second Sermon for Saints Peter and Paul', in *Liturgical Sermons* (trans. Monks of Mount Saint Bernard Abbey; 2 vols.; Spencer, MA: Cistercian Publications, 1970–71), II, p. 155.

Gundry, R.H., *Sôma in Biblical Theology: With Emphasis on Pauline Anthropology* (Grand Rapids, MI: Academie Books, 1987).

Haase, W., (ed.), *Aufstieg und Niedergang der Römischen Welt: Geschichte und Kultur Roms im Spiegel der Neuren Forschung. II. Principat 36,3: Philosophie, Wissenschaften, Technik: Philosophie (Stoizismus)* (*ANRW*, II.36/3; Berlin: Walter de Gruyter, 1989).

Hallett, J.P., *Fathers and Daughters in Roman Society: Women and the Elite Family* (Princeton, NJ: Princeton University Press, 1984).

Halperin, D., *One Hundred Years of Homosexuality and Other Essays on Greek Love* (New York: Routledge, 1990).

Halperin, D., J. Winkler, and F. Zeitlin (eds), *Before Sexuality: The Construction of Erotic Experience in the Ancient Greek World* (Princeton, NJ: Princeton University Press, 1990).

Hanson, A.E., 'The Medical Writers' Woman', in Halperin, Winkler, and Zeitlin (eds), *Before Sexuality*, pp. 309–38.

Harrison, V.E.F., 'Male and Female Cappadocian Theology', *JTS* 41 (October 1990), pp. 441–71.

Hay, D.M. (ed.), *Pauline Theology*, II. *First and Second Corinthians* (3 vols.; Minneapolis: Fortress Press, 1993).

Hays, R.B., *Echoes of Scripture in the Letters of Paul* (New Haven CT: Yale University Press, 1989).

—— *The Faith of Jesus Christ* (SBLDS, 56; Chico, CA: Scholars Press, 1983).

—— *The Moral Vision of the New Testament: A Contemporary Introduction to New Testament Ethics* (San Francisco: HarperSanFrancisco, 1996).

—— 'Relations Natural and Unnatural: A Response to John Boswell's Exegesis of Romans 1', *Journal of Christian Ethics* 14 (1986), pp. 184–215.

—— ' "The Righteous One" as Eschatological Deliverer: A Case Study in Paul's Apocalyptic Hermeneutics', in M.L. Soards and J. Marcus (eds), *Apocalyptic and the New Testament* (Sheffield: JSOT Press, 1989).

Hengel, M., and U. Heckel, *Paulus und das antike Judentum* (WUNT, 58; Tübingen: J.C.B. Mohr [Paul Siebeck], 1991).

Heyward, C., *The Redemption of God: A Theology of Mutual Relation* (Lanham, MD: University Press of America, 1982).

Hock, R.E., ' "By the Gods, It's My One Desire to See an Actual Stoic": Epictetus' Relations with Students and Visitors in his Personal Network', *Semeia* 56 (1991), pp. 121–42.

Hock, R.F., *The Social Context of Paul's Ministry: Apostleship and Tentmaking* (Philadelphia: Fortress Press, 1980).

Hornblower, S., and A. Spawforth (eds), *Oxford Classical Dictionary* (Oxford: Oxford University Press, 1996).

Horsley, G.H.R., *New Documents Illustrating Early Christianity* (8 vols.; North Ryde, NSW, Australia: Macquarie University Ancient History Documentary Research Center, 1983).

Horsley, R.A., 'Spiritual Marriage with Sophia', *VC* 33 (1979), pp. 40–43.

Huehenegard, J., 'Biblical Notes on Some New Akkadian Texts from Eman (Syria)', *CBQ* 47 (1985), pp. 428–34.

Hultgren, A.J., and R. Aus, *I–II Timothy, Titus, II Thessalonians* (Minneapolis: Augsburg, 1984).

Hunt, A., and B. Grenfell (eds), *Oxyrhynchus Papyri* (47 vols.; London: Egyptian Exploration Fund, 1898).

Hurd, J.C., *The Origin of 1 Corinthians* (London: SPCK, 1965).

Ilan, T., *Jewish Women in Greco-Roman Palestine* (Peabody, MA: Hendrickson, 1996).

Inclusive Language Lectionary Committee, National Council of Churches, *Inclusive Language Lectionary: Readings for Year A* (Atlanta: John Knox Press; New York: Pilgrim Press; Philadelphia: Westminster Press, 1983).

Ingrams, L., *et al.* (eds), *Oxyrhynchus Papyri*, XXXIV (London: Egyptian Exploration Society, 1968).

Isaac, E., '1 Enoch', in Charlesworth (ed.), *The Old Testament Pseudepigrapha*, II, pp. 5–100.

Jaeger, W., *Werner Jaeger: Five Essays* (trans. A.M. Fiske; Montreal: Casaline, 1966).

Jewett, R., *Paul's Anthropological Terms: A Study of their Use in Conflict Settings* (AGJU, 10; Leiden: E.J. Brill, 1971).

Johnson, E.E., '2 Thessalonians,' in Newsom and Ringe (eds), *The Women's Bible Commentary*, pp. 351–52.

Johnston, D.E.L., 'Inheritance: Roman', in Hornblower and Spawforth (eds), *Oxford Classical Dictionary*, p. 758.

Jolowicz, H.F., and B. Nicholas, *Historical Introduction to the Study of Roman Law* (Cambridge: Cambridge University Press, 1972).

Jones, A.H.M., *The Greek City* (Oxford: Clarendon Press, 1940).

Jones, J.W., *The Law and Legal Theory of the Greeks* (Oxford: Clarendon Press, 1956).

Jordan, M.D., 'Ancient Philosophical Protreptic and the Problem of Persuasive Genres', *Rhetorica* 4 (1986), pp. 309–33.

Judge, E.A., 'St Paul and Classical Society', *JAC* 15 (1972), pp. 19–36.

Käsemann, E., *An die Römer* (Tübingen: J.C.B. Mohr, 1973).

—— *Commentary on Romans* [translation of *An die Römer*] (trans. G. W. Bromiley; Grand Rapids, MI: Eerdmans, 1980).

Kearsley, R., 'Women in Public Life in the Roman East: Iunia Theodora, Claudia Metrodora and Phoebe, Benefactress of Paul', *Ancient Society: Resources for Teachers* 15 (1985), pp. 124–37.

Kee, H.C., and I.J. Borowsky (eds), *Removing Anti-Judaism from the Pulpit* (Philadelphia: North American Publishing and Trinity Press International; New York: Continuum, 1996).

Kessler-Harris, A., *Out to Work* (New York: Oxford University Press, 1982).

Kiley, M., *Colossians as Pseudepigraphy* (Sheffield: JSOT Press, 1986), pp. 76–91.

Kittay, E.F., *Metaphor: Its Cognitive and Linguistic Structure* (Oxford: Oxford University Press, 1987), pp. 316–24.

Klassen, W., 'The King as "Living Law", with Particular Reference to Musonius Rufus', *SR* 14.1 (1985), pp. 63–71.

Knobloch, F.W., 'Adoption', *ABD*, I, pp. 76–79.

Knox, J., *Philemon among the Letters of Paul: A New View of its Place and Importance* (New York: Abingdon Press, 1935).

Körtner, U.H.J., *Papias von Hierapolis* (Göttingen: Vandenhoeck & Ruprecht, 1983).

Kraemer, R.S., *Her Share of the Blessings: Women's Religions among Pagans, Jews, and Christians in the Greco-Roman World* (Oxford: Oxford University Press, 1992).

—— *Maenads, Martyrs, Matrons, Monastics: A Sourcebook on Women's Religions in the Graeco-Roman World* (Philadelphia: Fortress Press, 1988).

—— 'Monastic Jewish Women in Greco-Roman Egypt: Philo on the Therapeutrides', *Signs: A Journal of Women in Culture and Society* 14.1 (1989), pp. 342–70.

Kraemer, R.S., and M.R. D'Angelo (eds), *Women and Christian Origins* (Oxford: Oxford University Press, 1999).

Kraftchick, S.J., 'Death in Us, Life in You: The Apostolic Medium', in Hay (ed.), *Pauline Theology*, II, pp. 156–81.

Krobath, E., 'Brief der Anonyma, einer von Jesus geheilten Frau, an Luise, die Weise und Gelehrte', in D. Sölle (ed.), *Für Gerechtigkeit streiten: Theologie im Alltag einer bedrohten Welt* (Gütersloh: Gütersloher Verlagshaus, 1994), pp. 15–21.

Kurylowicz, M., 'Adoption on the Evidence of the Papyri', *Journal of Juristic Papyri* 19 (1983), pp. 61–75.

Kürzinger, J., 'Frau und Mann nach 1 Kor. 11.11f', *BZ* 22 (1978), pp. 270–75.

Lampe, P., *Die stadtrömischen Christen in den ersten beiden Jahrhunderten* (WUNT, 2.18; Tübingen: J.C.B. Mohr [Paul Siebeck], 1989).

—— 'Kein Sklavenflucht des Onesimus', *ZNW* 76 (1985), pp. 135–37.

Laqueur, T., *Making Sex: Body and Gender from the Greeks to Freud* (Cambridge, MA: Harvard University Press, 1990).

Levin, S.R., 'Standard Approaches to Metaphor and a Proposal for Literary Metaphor', in Ortony (ed.), *Metaphor and Thought*, pp. 124–35.

Levine, A.-J. (ed.), *A Feminist Companion to the Deutero-Pauline Epistles* (London: T. & T. Clark, 2003).

—— *'Women Like This': New Perspectives on Jewish Women in the Greco-Roman World* (Early Judaism and its Literature, 1; Atlanta: Scholars Press, 1991).

Lieu, J.M., 'Circumcision, Women and Salvation', *NTS* 40 (1994), pp. 358–70.

Lightfoot, J.B., *St Paul's Epistles to the Colossians and to Philemon: A Revised Text with Introductions, Notes, and Dissertations* (London: Macmillan, 1904).

Lloyd, G., *The Man of Reason: 'Male' and 'Female' in Western Philosophy* (Minneapolis: University of Minnesota Press, 1984).

Lohse, E., *Colossians and Philemon* (Hermeneia; Philadelphia: Fortress, 1971).

—— 'Die Mitarbeiter des Apostels Paulus im Kolosserbrief', in O. Böcher and K. Hacker (eds), *Verborum Veritas: Festschrift für Gustav Staehlin zum 70. Geburtstag* (Wuppertal: Theologischer Verlag Rolf Brockhaus, 1970), pp. 189–94.

Long, A.A., *Hellenistic Philosophy: Stoics, Epicureans, and Skeptics* (Berkeley: University of California Press, 1986).

Lyall, F., 'Roman Law in the Writings of Paul—Adoption', *JBL* 88 (1969), pp. 458–66.

—— *Slaves, Citizens, Sons: Legal Metaphors in the New Testament* (Grand Rapids, MI: Academie Books, 1984).

Maccoby, H., *The Mythmaker: Paul and the Invention of Christianity* (New York: Harper & Row, 1986).

MacDonald, D.R., 'Corinthian Veils and Gnostic Androgynes', in K.L. King (ed.), *Images of the Feminine in Gnosticism* (Philadelphia: Fortress Press, 1988), pp. 276–92.

—— *The Legend and the Apostle: The Battle for Paul in Story and Canon* (Philadelphia: Westminster Press, 1983).

—— 'The Role of Women in the Production of the Apocryphal Acts of the Apostles', *Iliff Review of Theology* 40 (1984), pp. 21–38.

—— *There Is No Male and Female: The Fate of a Dominical Saying in Paul and Gnosticism* (HDR, 20; Philadelphia: Fortress Press, 1987).

MacDonald, M.Y., *Early Christian Women and Pagan Opinion: The Power of the Hysterical Woman* (Cambridge: Cambridge University Press, 1996).

—— 'Early Christian Women Married to Unbelievers', *Studies in Religion* 19.2 (1990), pp. 221–34, reprinted in Levine (ed.), *A Feminist Companion to the Deutero-Pauline Epistles* (London: T. & T. Clark, 2003), pp. 14–28.

—— 'Women Holy in Body and Spirit: The Social Setting of 1 Corinthians 7', *NTS* 36 (1990), pp. 161–81.

MacDowell, D.M., 'Inheritance: Greek', in Hornblower and Spawforth (eds), *Oxford Classical Dictionary*, p. 454.

Mace, D.R., *Hebrew Marriage: A Sociological Study* (New York: Philosophical Library, 1953).

Malherbe, A.J., *Moral Exhortation: A Greco-Roman Sourcebook* (Philadelphia: Westminster Press, 1986).

Malina, B., *The New Testament World* (London: SCM Press, 1983).

Maloney, L.M., 'The Pastoral Epistles', in Schüssler Fiorenza (ed.), *Searching the Scriptures*, pp. 361–80.

Martens, J.W., 'Romans 2.14-16: A Stoic Reading', *NTS* 40 (1994) 55–67.

Martin, D.B., '*Arsenokoitês* and *Malakos*: Meanings and Consequences', in Brawley (ed.), *Biblical Ethics and Homosexuality*, pp. 117–36.

—— *The Corinthian Body* (New Haven: Yale University Press, 1995).

—— 'Heterosexism and the Interpretation of Rom. 1.18–32', *BibInt* 3.3 (1995), pp. 332–55.

—— *Slavery as Salvation: The Metaphor of Slavery in Pauline Christianity* (New Haven: Yale University Press, 1990).

Martyn, J.L., 'Apocalyptic Antinomies in Paul's Letter to the Galatians', *NTS* 31 (1985), pp. 410–24.

—— *Galatians* (AB, 33A; New York: Doubleday, 1977).

—— 'The Covenants of Hagar and Sarah', in Carroll, Cosgrove, and Johnson (eds), *Faith and History*, pp. 160–92.

—— 'Epistemology at the Turn of the Ages: 2 Corinthians 5:16', in Farmer, Moule, and Niebuhr (ed.), *Christian History and Interpretation*.

Massey, L., *Women in the New Testament: An Analysis of Scripture in the Light of New Testament Era Culture* (Jefferson, NC: McFarland & Co., 1989).

McNamara, J.A., *A New Song: Celibate Women in the First Three Centuries* (New York: The Haworth Press, Inc., 1983).

Meeks, W.A., *The First Urban Christians: The Social World of the Apostle Paul* (New Haven: Yale University Press, 1983).

—— 'The Image of the Androgyne: Some Uses of a Symbol in Earliest Christianity', *HR* 13.1 (1974), pp. 165–208.

Meier, J.P., 'On the Veiling of Hermeneutics (1 Cor. 11.2–16)', *CBQ* 40 (1978), pp. 212–26.

Ménard, J.É., *L'Évangile selon Thomas* (NHS, 5; Leiden: E.J. Brill, 1975).

Mendelsohn, I., 'A Ugaritic Parallel to the Adoption of Ephraim and Manasseh', *Israel Exploration Journal* 9 (1959), pp. 180–83.

Michel, O., *Der Brief an die Römer* (MeyerK; Göttingen: Vandenhoeck & Ruprecht, 1978).

Mitchell, M.M., 'John Chrysostom on Philemon: A Second Look', *HTR* 88 (1995), pp. 145–47.

—— *Paul and the Rhetoric of Reconciliation: An Exegetical Investigation of the Language and Composition of 1 Corinthians* (Louisville, KY: Westminster/John Knox Press, 1991).

Murphy-O'Connor, J., 'The Divorced Woman in 1 Cor. 7.10–11', *JBL* 100 (1981), pp. 601–606.

Murray, J., *The Epistle to the Romans* (NICNT; Grand Rapids, MI: Eerdmans, 1959–65).

Murray, R., 'The Exhortation to Candidates for Ascetic Vows at Baptism in the Ancient Syriac Church', *NTS* 21 (1974), pp. 59–80.

Nathanson, B., 'Toward a Multicultural Ecumenical History of Women in the First Century/ies CE', in Schüssler Fiorenza (ed.), *Searching the Scriptures*, I, pp. 272–98.

Newsom, C.A., and S.H. Ringe (eds), *The Women's Bible Commentary* (Louisville, KY: Westminster/John Knox Press, 1992).

Neyrey, J.H., 'Nudity', in Pilch and Malina (ed.), *Biblical Social Values*, p. 120.

—— *Paul, in Other Words: A Cultural Reading of his Letters* (Louisville, KY: Westminster/John Knox Press, 1990).

Nicholas, B., and S. M. Treggiari, 'Adoption', in Hornblower and Spawforth (eds), *Oxford Classical Dictionary*, pp. 12–13.

Nickelsburg, G.W.E., 'An ἔκτρωμα, Though Appointed from the Womb: Paul's Apostolic Self-Description in 1 Corinthians 15 and Galatians 1', in *idem* and MacRae (eds), *Christians among Jews and Gentiles*, pp. 198–205.

Nickelsburg, G.W.E., and G.W. MacRae (eds), *Christians among Jews and Gentiles Essays in Honor of Krister Stendahl on his Sixty-Fifth Birthday* (Philadelphia: Fortress Press, 1986).

Nussbaum, M., 'The Stoics on the Extirpation of the Passions', *Apeiron* 20 (1987), pp. 129–77.

—— *The Therapy of Desire* (Princeton, NJ: Princeton University Press, 1994).

Ollrog, W.-H., 'Die Abfassungsverhältnisse von Röm 16', in D. Lührmann and G. Strecker (eds), *Kirsch: Festschrift für Günther Bornkamm zum 75. Geburtstag* (Tübingen: J.C.B. Mohr, 1980), pp. 221–44.

—— *Paulus und seine Mitarbeiter: Untersuchungen zu Theorie und Praxis der paulinischen Mission* (Wissenschaftliche Monographien zum Alten und Neuen Testament, 50; Neukirchen: Erzieheungsverein, 1979).

Ortny, A., *Metaphor and Thought* (Cambridge: Cambridge University Press, 1979).

Osgood, S.J., 'Women and Inheritance in Early Israel', in Brooke (ed.), *Women in the Biblical Tradition*, pp. 29–51.

Paul, S.M., 'Adoption Formulae: A Study of Cuneiform and Biblical Legal Cases', *Maarav* 2.2 (1979–80), pp. 173–85.

Payne, P., 'Fuldensis, Sigla for Variants in Vaticanus, and 1 Cor. 14.34–35', *NTS* 41 (1995), pp. 240–62.

Petersen, N.R., *Rediscovering Paul: Philemon and the Sociology of Paul's Narrative World* (Philadelphia: Fortress Press, 1985).

Phillips, J.F., 'Stoic "Common Notions" in Plotinus', *Dionysius* 11 (Dec. 1987), pp. 33–52.

Philo, *The Embassy to Gaius: with an English Translation* (ed. T.H. Colson; London: William Heinemann Ltd, 1962).

Pierce, C.A., *Conscience in the New Testament: A Study of* Syneidesis *in the New Testament* (Studies in Biblical Theology, 15; London: SCM Press, 1955).

Pilch, J.J., and B.J. Malina (eds), *Biblical Social Values and their Meaning: A Handbook* (Peabody, MA: Hendrickson, 1993).

Pitt-Rivers, J., 'Honour and Social Status', in J.G. Peristany (ed.), *Honour and Shame: The Values of Mediterranean Society* (London: Weidenfeld & Nicolson, 1965).

Plevnik, J., 'Honor/Shame', in Pilch and Malina (eds), *Biblical Social Values*, pp. 95–104.

Pomeroy, S., *Goddesses, Whores, Wives and Slaves: Women in Classical Antiquity* (New York: Schocken Books, 1975).

—— 'The Relationship of the Married Woman to her Blood Relatives in Rome', *Ancient Society* (1976), pp. 215–27.

Rabel, R.J., 'Diseases of the Soul in Stoic Psychology', *GRBS* 22 (Winter 1981), pp. 385–93.

Rabinowitz, J., 'Semitic Elements in the Egyptian Adoption Papyrus Published by Gardiner', *JNES* 17 (Jan.–Oct. 1958), pp. 145–46.

Räisänen, H. 'Galatians 2.16 and Paul's Break with Judaism', *NTS* 31 (1985), pp. 543–53.

—— 'Legalism and Salvation by the Law: Paul's Portrayal of the Jewish Religion as a Historical and Theological Problem', in S. Pedersen (ed.), *Pauline Literature and Theology* (Teologiske Studier, 7; Århus, Finland: Århus Universitet; Göttingen: Vandenhoeck & Ruprecht, 1980), pp. 63–84.

Rapoport-Alpert, A., 'On Women in Hasidism', in *idem* and S.J. Zipperstein (eds), *Jewish History: Essays in Honour of Chimen Abramsky* (London: P. Halban, 1988), pp. 495–525.

Rawson, B. (ed.), *The Family in Ancient Rome: New Perspectives* (Ithaca, NY: Cornell University Press, 1986).

Reimer, I.R., *Women in the Acts of the Apostles: A Feminist Liberation Perspective* (Minneapolis: Fortress Press, 1995).

Reinhartz, A., 'From Narrative to History: The Resurrection of Mary and Martha', in Levine (ed.), *'Women Like This'*, pp. 161–85.

Reitzenstein, R., *Hellenistic Mystery Religions: Their Basic Ideas and Significance* (trans. J.E. Steely; Pittsburgh Theological Monograph Series, 15; Pittsburgh: Pickwick Press, 1978).

Reuters, F.H.Y., 'De Anacharsidis epistulis' (Inaugural dissertation; University of Bonn 1957).

—— *Die Briefe des Anacharsis* (Schriften und Quellen der Alten Welt, 14; Berlin: Akademie Verlag, 1963).

Reynolds, J., and R. Tannenbaum, *Jews and God-Fearers at Aphrodisias: Greek Inscriptions with Commentary* (Cambridge: The Cambridge Philological Society, 1987).

Ribbeck, O., *ALAZON: Ein Beitrag zur antiken Ethologie* (Leipzig: Teubner, 1882).

Richard, E.J., *First and Second Thessalonians* (Collegeville, MN: Liturgical Press, 1995).

Richard, P., *Apokalypse: Das Buch von Widerstand und Hoffnung* (Lucerne: Exodus Verlag, 1998).

Richardson, C.C., *The Gospel of Thomas: Gnostic or Encratite?* (Rome: [publisher unknown], 1973).

Richlin, A., 'Not before Homosexuality: The Materiality of the *Cinaedus* and the Roman Law against Love between Men', *Journal of the History of Sexuality* 3.4 (1993), pp. 523–73.

Rist, J.M., *Stoic Philosophy* (Cambridge: Cambridge University Press, 1969).

Robert, L., 'Inscriptions de Chios du Ier siècle de notre ère,' in *idem* (ed.), *Etudes épigraphiques et philologiques* (Paris: Champion, 1938), pp. 128–34.

Roberts, A., and J. Donaldson (eds), *The Fathers of the Second Century* (Grand Rapids, MI: Eerdmans, 1989).

Rosenberg, R., *Beyond Separate Spheres* (New Haven, CT: Yale University Press, 1982).

Rossell, W.H., 'New Testament Adoption—Graeco-Roman or Semitic', *JBL* 71 (1952), pp. 233–34.

Rudd, N., *Themes in Roman Satire* (Oklahoma: University of Oklahoma, 1986).

Sacks, S. (ed.), *On Metaphor* (Chicago: University of Chicago Press, 1978).

Sanday, W., and A.C. Headlam, *The Epistle to the Romans* (ICC; Edinburgh: T. & T. Clark, 3rd edn, 1898; 5th edn, 1902, repr. 1980).

Sandbach, F.H., *The Stoics* (London: G. Duckworth, 2nd edn, 1994).

Schaumberger, C., and L. Schottroff (eds), *Schuld und Macht: Studien zu einer feministischen Befreiungstheologie* (Munich: Chr. Kaiser Verlag, 1988).

Schereschewsky, B.-Z., 'Adoption', in *Enc Jud*, II, p. 301.

—— 'Apotropos', in *Enc Jud*, III, p. 218.

Schlier, H., *Der Römerbrief Kommentar* (HTKNT; Freiburg: Herder, 1977).

Schmithals, W., *Gnosticism in Corinth* (Nashville, TN: Abingdon Press, 1971).

Schneemelcher, W. (ed.), *New Testament Apocrypha* (2 vols.; Louisville, KY: Westminster/John Knox Press, 2nd edn, 1991–92).

Schneider, N., *Die Rhetorische Eigenart der paulinischen Antithese* (Tübingen: Mohr/Siebeck, 1970).

Schoenberg, M.W., '*Huiothesia*: The Adoptive Sonship of the Israelites', *The American Ecclesiastical Review* 143 (1960), pp. 261–73.

—— '*Huiothesia*, the Word and the Institution,' *Scripture* 15 (1963), pp. 115–23.

Schottroff, L., *Befreiungserfahrungen: Studien zur Sozialgeschichte des Neuen Testaments* (Munich: Chr. Kaiser Verlag, 1990).

—— 'Dienerinnen der Heiligen: Der Diakonat der Frauen im Neuen Testament', in G.K. Schäfer and T. Strohm (eds), *Diakonie—biblische Grundlagen und Orientierungen* (Heidelberg: Heidelberger Verlagsanstalt, 1994), pp. 222–42.

—— *Let the Oppressed Go Free: Feminist Perspectives on the New Testament* (Louisville, KY: Westminster/John Knox Press, 1993).

—— *Lydia's Impatient Sisters: A Feminist Social History of Early Christianity* (Louisville, KY: Westminster/John Knox Press, 1995).

Schottroff, L., and M.-T. Wacker (eds), *Kompendium Feministische Bibelauslegung* (Gütersloh: Gütersloher Verlagshaus, 1998).

—— (ed.), *Von der Wurzel Getragen: Christlich-feministische Exegese in Auseinandersetzung mit Antijudaismus* (BIS, 17; Leiden: E.J. Brill, 1996).

Schubart, W., *Die Papyri der Universitätsbibliothek Erlangen* (Leipzig: Otto Harrassowitz, 1942).

Schubert, P., *Form and Function of the Pauline Thanksgiving* (BZNW, 20; Berlin: Töpelmann, 1939).

Schüssler Fiorenza, E. (ed.), *Searching the Scriptures: A Feminist Introduction and Commentary* (2 vols.; New York: Crossroad, 1993, 1994).

—— *In Memory of Her: A Feminist Theological Reconstruction of Christian Origins* (New York: Crossroad, 1983).

Schütz, J.H., *Paul and the Anatomy of Apostolic Authority* (Cambridge: Cambridge University Press, 1975).

Scott, J.M., *Adoption as Sons of God: An Exegetical Investigation into the Background of YIOTHESIA in the Pauline Corpus* (Tübingen: J.C.B. Mohr [Paul Siebeck], 1992).

Scroggs, R., 'Paul and the Eschatological Woman', *JAAR* 40 (1972), pp. 295–96.

Seckel, E., W. Schubart, and W. Uxkull-Gyllenband (eds), *Der Gnomon des Idios Logos* (2 vols.; Ägyptische Urkunden aus den Staatlichen Museen Berlin; Griechische Urkunden, 5; Berlin: Weidmannsche Buchhandlung, 1919).

Sharples, R.W., *Stoics, Epicureans and Skeptics: An Introduction to Hellenistic Philosophy* (London: Routledge, 1996).

Shilo, S., 'Succession', in *Enc Jud*, XV, p. 479.

Siegele-Wenschkewitz, L., *Christlicher Antijudaismus und Antisemitismus: theologische und kirchliche Programme deutscher Christen* (Arnoldshainer Texte, 85; Frankfurt am Main: Haag & Herchen, 1994).

——— *Verdrängte Vergangenheit, die Uns Bedrängt: feministische Theologie in der Verantwortung für die Geschichte* (Kaiser Tashenbücher, 29; Munich: Kaiser, 1988).

Sly, D., *Philo's Perception of Women* (BJS, 209; Atlanta: Scholars Press, 1990).

Smith, D. Moody, Jr., '*Ho de dikaios ek pisteos zesetai*', in B.L. Daniels and M.J. Suggs (eds), *Studies in the History and Text of the New Testament in Honor of Kenneth Willis Clark* (Studies and Documents, 29; Salt Lake City: University of Utah, 1967), pp. 13–25.

Stählin, G., 'νυνὶ δέ', in *TDNT*, IV, p. 1109.

Stemberger, G., *Geschichte der jüdischen Literatur: eine Einführung* (Munich: Beck, 1977).

Stepien, J., 'Syneidesis: la conscience dans l'anthropologie de Saint-Paul', *Revue d'histoire et de philosophie religieuses* 60.1 (1980), pp. 1–20.

Stier, F., *Das Neue Testament* (Düsseldorf: Patmos, 1989).

Stowers, S., *Letter Writing in Greco-Roman Antiquity* (Philadelphia: Westminster Press, 1986).

——— 'Paul on the Use and Abuse of Reason', in Balch, Ferguson, and Meeks (eds), *Greeks, Romans, and Christians*, pp. 253–86.

——— *A Rereading of Romans: Justice, Jews, and Gentiles* (New Haven, CT: Yale University Press, 1994.)

Strahm, D., and R. Strobel (eds), *Vom Verlangen nach Heilwerden: Christologie in feministischer Sicht* (Fribourg/Lucerne: Exodus Verlag, 1991).

Sturm, R.E., 'Defining the Word "Apocalyptic"', in J. Marcus and M. Soards (eds), *Apocalyptic and the New Testament: Essays in Honor of J.L. Martyn* (Sheffield: JSOT Press, 1989), pp. 17–48.

Suggs, M.J., ' "The Word Is Near You": Romans 10.6–10 within the Purpose of the Letter', in Farmer, Moule, and Niebuhr (eds), *Christian History and Interpretation*, pp. 289–312.

Sutter Rehmann, L., 'Die Offenbarung des Johannes: Inspirationen aus Patmos', in Schottroff and Wacker (eds), *Kompendium Feministische Bibelauslegung*, pp. 725–41.

——— *Geh, frage die Gebärerin! Feministisch-befreiungstheologische Untersuchungen des Gebärmotivs in der Apokalyptik* (Gütersloh: Gütersloher Verlagshaus, 1995).

——— *Vom Mut, genau hinzusehen: Feministisch-befreiungstheologische Interpretationen zur Apokalyptik* (Lucerne: Exodus Verlag, 1998).

Swancutt, D.M., ' "The Disease of Effemination": The Charge of Effiminacy and the

Verdict of God', in S. Moore and J.C. Anderson (eds), *Semeia Studies* (forth-coming).

—— *Pax Christi: Romans as Portrepsis to Live as 'Kings'* (forthcoming).

—— *Sage Instruction: The Wisdom of God and the Salvation of the Nations: Romans as a Logos Protreptikos* (forthcoming).

Tamez, E., 'Der Brief an die Gemeinde in Rom.: Eine feministische Lektüre', in Schottroff and Wacker (eds), *Kompendium Feministische Bibelauslegung*, pp. 550–68.

Theissen, G., *The Social Setting of Pauline Christianity* (Philadelphia: Fortress Press, 1982).

Thurston, B.B., *The Widows: A Women's Ministry in the Early Church* (Minneapolis: Fortress Press, 1989).

Tobin, T.H., SJ, *The Creation of Man: Philo and the History of Interpretation* (CBQMS, 14; Washington: Catholic Biblical Association of America, 1983).

Tomson, P.J., *Paul and the Jewish Law: Halakha in the Letters of the Apostle to the Gentiles* (Compendia Rerum Iudaicarum ad Novum Testamentum, 3.1; Assen: Van Gorcum: Minneapolis: Fortress Press, 1990).

Turner, M., *Death Is the Mother of Beauty: Mind, Metaphor, Criticism* (Chicago: University of Chicago Press, 1987).

Van Seters, J., 'The Problem of Childlessness in Near Eastern Law and the Patriarchs of Israel', *JBL* 77 (1968), pp. 401–408.

Vellanickal, M., 'The Pauline Doctrine of Christian Sonship', *Biblebhashyam* 5 (1979), pp. 187–207.

Vermes, G., *The Dead Sea Scrolls in English* (London: Penguin Books, 3rd edn, 1987).

Via, D.O., *Self-Deception and Wholeness in Paul and Matthew* (Minneapolis: Fortress Press, 1990).

Vine, W.E., *An Expository Dictionary of New Testament Words* (Old Tappan, NJ: Fleming H. Revell Co., 1966).

Vööbus, A., *Celibacy: A Requirement for Admission to Baptism in the Early Church* (Stockholm: Estonian Theological Society in Exile, 1951).

Vouga, F., *Une théologie du Nouveau Testament* (Le monde de la Bible, 43; Geneva: Labor et Fides, 2001).

Wacker, M.-T., 'Historical, Hermeneutical, and Methodological Foundations', in L. Schottroff, S. Schroer, and M.-T. Wacker (eds), *Feminist Interpretation: The Bible in Women's Perspective* (Minneapolis: Fortress Press, 1998), pp. 55–62.

Walker, D.D., 'Paul's Offer of Leniency (2 Cor 10.1): Populist Ideology and Rhetoric in a Pauline Letter Fragment (2 Cor 10.1–13.10)' (Dissertation, University of Chicago, 1998).

Walzer, R., *Galen on Jews and Christians* (London: Oxford University Press, 1949).

Wanamaker, C.A., *Commentary on 1 and 2 Thessalonians* (NIGTC; Grand Rapids, MI: Eerdmans; Exteter: Paternoster, 1990).

Wander, B., *Trennungsprozesse zwischen frühen Christentum und Judentum im 1. Jh. n. Chr.* (Texte und Arbeiten zum Neutestamentlichen Zeitalter, 16; Tübingen: Francke Verlag, 1994).

Ward, B., *The Prayers and Meditations of Saint Anselm* (London: Penguin Books, 1973).

Ward, R.B., 'Musonius and Paul on Marriage', *NTS* 36 (1990), pp. 281–89.

Weber, M., *The Protestant Ethic and the Spirit of Capitalism* (New York: Charles Scribner's Sons, 1958).

Wedderburn, A.J.M., *Baptism and Resurrection: Studies in Pauline Theology against its Graeco-Roman Background* (WUNT, 44; Tübingen: J.C.B. Mohr [P. Siebeck], 1987).

Wegner, J.R., 'Philo's Portrayal of Women—Hebraic or Hellenic?', in Levine (ed.), *'Women Like This'*, pp. 41–66.

Welles, C.B. (ed.), *The Excavations at Dura-Europos: Final Report: The Parchment and Papyri* (New Haven, CT: Yale University Press, 1959).

Wengst, K., *Bedrängte Gemeinde und verherrlichter Christus: Der historische Ort des Johannesevangeliums als Schlüssel zu seiner Interpretation* (Biblisch-Theologische Studien, 5;Neukirchen–Vluyn: Neukirchener Verlag, 1981).

—— *Bedrängte Gemeinde und verherrlichter Christus: Ein Versuch über das Johannesevangelium* (Munich: Chr. Kaiser Verlag, 1990).

Wenschkewitz, L.S. (ed.), *Verdrängte Vergangenheit, die uns bedrängt: Feministische Theologie in der Verantwortung für die Geschichte* (Munich: Chr. Kaiser Verlag, 1988).

Whiston, W. (trans.), *The Works of Josephus* (Peabody, MA: Hendrickson, 1988).

White, J.L. *The Form and Structure of the Official Petition: A Study in Greek Epistolography* (Atlanta: Scholars Press, 1972).

—— 'God's Paternity as Root Metaphor in Paul's Conception of Community', *Foundations and Facets Forum* 8 (1992), pp. 271–95.

Wilckens, U., *Der Brief an die Römer* (3 vols.; Neukirchen–Vluyn: Neukirchener Verlag, 1980).

Williams, S.K., and S. Stowers, *Jesus' Death as Saving Event: The Background and Origin of a Concept* (HDR, 2; Missoula, MT: Scholars Press, 1975).

Wilson, B., 'An Analysis of Sect Development', in *idem* (ed.), *Patterns of Sectarianism* (London: Morrison & Gibb, 1967), pp. 22–45.

Wilson, W., *Love without Pretense: Romans 12.9–21 and Hellenistic-Jewish Wisdom Literature* (WUNT, 46; Tübingen: J.C.B. Mohr, 1991).

Wimbush, V.L., *Paul the Worldly Ascetic: Response to the World and Self-Understanding according to 1 Corinthians 7* (Macon, GA: Mercer University Press, 1987).

Winkler, J.J., *The Constraints of Desire: The Anthropology of Sex and Gender in Ancient Greece* (New York: Routledge, 1990).

Winston, D. (trans.), *Philo of Alexandria: The Contemplative Life, the Giants, and Selections* (New York: Paulist Press, 1981).

—— 'Philo and the Contemplative Life', in A. Green (ed.), *Jewish Spirituality from the Bible through the Religious Ages* (World Spirituality: An Encyclopedic History of the Religious Quest, 13; New York: Crossroad, 1988), pp. 198–231.

Winter, S.C., 'Paul's Letter to Philemon', *NTS* 33 (1987), pp. 1–15.

Wire, A., *The Corinthian Women Prophets: A Reconstruction through Paul's Rhetoric* (Minneapolis: Fortress Press, 1990).

Witherington, B., III, *Conflict and Community in Corinth: A Socio-Rhetorical Commentary on 1 and 2 Corinthians* (Grand Rapids, MI: Eerdmans, 1995).

—— *Women in the Earliest Churches* (SNTSMS, 59; Cambridge: Cambridge University Press, 1980).

Yarbrough, O.L., *Not Like the Gentiles: Marriage Rules in the Letters of Paul* (Atlanta: Scholars Press, 1985).

—— 'Parents and Children in the Letters of Paul', in L.M. White and O.L. Yarbrough (eds), *The Social World of the First Christians: Essays in Honor of Wayne A. Meeks* (Minneapolis: Fortress Press, 1995), pp. 126–41.

Yonge, C.D. (trans.), *The Works of Philo* (Peabody, MA: Hendrickson, 1995).

Young, I.M., *Justice and the Politics of Difference* (Princeton, NJ: Princeton University Press, 1990).

Zager, W., *Begriff und Wertung der Apokalypse in der neutestamentlichen Forschung* (Frankfurt: Peter Lang, 1989).

Zahn, T., *Einleitung in das Neue Testament*, I (2 vols.; Leipzig: Erlangen, 3rd edn, 1924).

Zeller, D., *Juden und Heiden in der Mission bei Paulus* (Stuttgart: Katholisches Bibelwerk, 1976).

INDEX OF REFERENCES

INDEX OF AUTHORS